Month-By-Month™

WHAT TO DO EACH MONTH TO HAVE A BEAUTIFUL GARDEN ALL YEAR

GARDENING IN KANSAS

Cataloging in Publication Data is available.
ISBN-10: 1-59186-289-9
ISBN-13: 978-1-59186-389-2

Published by Cool Springs Press, 101 Forrest Crossing Boulevard, Suite 100,
Franklin, Tennessee 37064

First printing 2007

Printed in Canada
10 9 8 7 6 5 4 3 2 1

Managing Editor: Ramona D. Wilkes and Mary Buckner
Horticulture Editor: Dee Maranhao
Copyeditor: Dee Maranhao
Production Artist: S.E. Anderson
Illustrator: Bill Kersey, Kersey Graphics
Cover Design: Marc Pewitt

On the Cover: Sunflower

Month-By-Month™

WHAT TO DO EACH MONTH TO HAVE A BEAUTIFUL GARDEN ALL YEAR

GARDENING IN KANSAS

MIKE MILLER

Cool Springs Press

Franklin, Tennessee
www.coolspringspress.net

DEDICATION

Tracy Ann, my love, whose magical laugh, wonderful smile, true heart, soul and mind offer suggestions and alternative pathways allowing us both to appreciate every aspect of life. Her patience and keen sense of surroundings expand my sensory perceptions, making for more drama and dynamics.

The endurance, involvement, and roles played by my younger sister Teri, and brothers Tom and Kevin make ours a funny, wild, crazy, music and garden loving family.

In memory of my parents D. Rex and E. Jane, and my grandmothers Maggie and Dorothy. Each shared their special way, knowledge, individual viewpoints and guidance which encouraged me to pursue the world's splendor. Each of you is an essential part of my being and I have tried to do just that.

ACKNOWLEDGEMENTS

Thanks and appreciation go to: Every person who stops to marvel, observe, wonder, or learn about any aspect of nature or plant life, from algae or moss, to the newest hybrids, cultivars, hummingbirds, cardinals, monarch butterflies, or dragon flies. These momentary stops create an appreciation that triggers a personal challenge, resulting in a single pot on a window sill, a solitary majestic oak standing in a lawn, or a fully developed landscape plan. I have witnessed these and many more such phenomenon everywhere I have lived and traveled.

Kansas botanical gardens are extremely important places for displays and educational programs. The University of Kansas and Extension Services extend beyond physical boundaries into surrounding communities throughout Kansas. This provides us a better place to live, work, play and garden.

Master gardeners, local plant societies, garden clubs, professional growers, horticultural groups, landscape contractors, and wholesale/retail nurseries are invaluable, each providing either plants or the wisdom allowing anyone a chance to "grow."

The St. Louis Community College at Meramec for giving me a chance to teach plant identification and landscape design. Today some of my students have become great horticulturalists and designers. KMOX Garden Hotline listeners who take a timeout from their busy life to call and provide personal experiences and know-how.

The Epilepsy Foundation of the St. Louis Region whose "Seeds of Understanding" program (yearly distribution seed packets) allows me an opportunity to share two very important aspects of life: my epilepsy, and a passion for the outdoors and watching plants grow.

Holiday Vacations whose gatherings encouraged stories and laughter while encountering the world.

Cool Springs Press: Ramona Wilkes, Mary Buckner, Roger Waynick, and Cindy Games—each person and many others were essential in either getting started, or keeping things on track, which will make sure your reading, learning, and enjoyment are one and the same.

CONTENTS

INTRODUCTION

In the Sioux language, the word "Kansas" means "people of the south wind," and the state motto, "*Ad astra per aspera*," means "To the stars through difficulties." Wind and stars are ideal adjectives that go straight to the heart of Kansas gardening. Though Kansas is part of the Great Plains, a close look reveals numerous environments.

Elevation is one environmental factor. The lowest point, 679 feet, is found along the Verdigris River near Oklahoma, and then there is a steady rise westward to 4,039 feet at Mt. Sunflower's summit. During this horticultural and physical climb, rainfall amounts decrease as elevations rise due to the rain-shadow impact from the Rocky Mountains. The statewide rainfall average is 27 inches. This is misleading, as eastern alluvial plains can receive 40 inches of rain on average, while out west, parched semi-arid ground gets by with 17 inches annually. The Kansas and Arkansas Rivers form the main watersheds, with headwaters in the Rocky Mountains and movement east and/or southeastward. Numerous lakes offer flood-control and recreation to all comers.

Weather could be called "continental," a term used with describing extremes. Cold, drying arctic blasts dehydrate all plants and soil, followed by hot summers with tornado winds and rainfall that can cause flooding. Kansas gardeners have weathered extremes. In 1989, April brought 107 degrees to Hayes, while Atwood fell to -34 degrees in December.

Significant changes in native vegetation types result from a direct relationship to elevation and rainfall amounts. These components set many parameters for landscapes and gardening. Many plant listings can have designations such as "SE-Southeast," "E-East", "C-Central", "SC-South Central" and so on, meaning particular plants will be better adapted to this specific region, but this does not mean these very same plants can't enjoy a robust and aesthetically fulfilling life in other places.

Equally important is soil type, depth, chemical content, particle size and relative density (ease of making a mud ball). Many times, plants that are easy to grow are considered weeds or invasive. Remember, beauty is in the beholder's eye, but think about your neighbor when formulating and implementing ideas. Diversity of Kansas outdoors was recognized by early politicians who chose a sunflower as the state flower, a cottonwood as the state tree, the brown meadowlark as the state bird, and the buffalo to represent the state wildlife, with "Home on the Range" sung proudly as the state's song.

THIS IS KANSAS

Kansas has 24 state parks, each an excellent outdoor classroom. A visit to any or all would make it possible to find forbs (woody plants), open glades, rills, streams, and vast expanses of land tracts like the Tallgrass Prairie Preserve, which is one of the largest virgin prairies remaining in the United States. Botanical gardens, the Kansas State University Extension Service, junior and four-year college programs, 4H clubs and national and local plant societies all offer a tremendous wealth of knowledge for sharing.

INTRODUCTION

On average, Kansas's herbaceous garden season begins in late March to early April with the installation of asparagus. It continues into early December with the final watering and lawn cutting at the end of the year. A lot of tree work, from pruning to cabling to deep root feeding, is winter work.

The best aspect of writing this book is the chance to share gardening successes, disappointments and observations from 30 wonderful years. I have looked out windows, down side yards, through fields, under high canopies. I've watched birds soar, deer leap, and moles tunnel. I've strolled in small public parks, botanical gardens, forested arboretums, and wholesale and retail nurseries. I've pored over catalogs, met interesting people, and experienced the magic of plants.

Kansas gardens are home to annuals (tropical), bulbs (mild coastal), edibles (worldwide), ground cover and vines (worldwide), houseplants (tropical), lawn (worldwide), perennials (worldwide), roses (worldwide), shrubs (worldwide), trees (worldwide), and water garden plants (worldwide).

Mixtures of trees, shrubs, perennials, and ground covers are often selected for aesthetic reasons, including texture, form, and color, without much consideration given to cultural requirements. Though this approach brings immediate visual success, it ultimately lead to horticultural disappointment. Think before doing, with the future in mind.

Yes, realistically there will be ups and downs, dreams and nightmares, but remember, each and every happening is an opportunity to learn and make projections for the future. Mother Nature sets limitations, and gardeners (inside and outside) continue to push, pull, tug, and shovel. Plants become a part of our lives, providing pleasure from many different angles. All partakers, from grower to viewer, will delight in accomplishments. Memories begin when you share a division of great grandmother's brilliant red peony with an awe-struck visitor. The same holds true when garden center professionals take time to explain the use of a hose-end attachment, offer insight on fertilizing or corrective pruning, or suggest a new hybrid which is more weather-tolerant or disease-resistant.

Change is a constant player outdoors from sky-high to down under the subsoil. Remember, change is part of gardening and growing plants.

SO MANY POSSIBILITIES

Do you dream of sitting under a 50 foot bur oak tree that is circled by a bed of variegated 'Beacon Silver' lamium and dark green liriope? Nothing could be better. Can you imagine a grove of hawthorns, each tree containing a bird's nest, while nearby sit topiary pyramids of morning glory vines centered in pots edged by rosemary swirls? Either place could vibrate with a breeze ever so slight, causing nearby prairie dropseed grass to sway.

Picture a gradually sloping back yard anchored with liatris spears accentuating mounds of shrub roses. Beyond, visualize a reflective water garden ringed with cardinal flowers and Japanese iris. Red begonias blaze like fire, and cannas appear to be lifting off from the launch pad skyward. Lilac's spent flowers trigger a virtual fragrance. A rainstorm enhances the lawn's magic carpet as it sweeps around trees, under hanging baskets of ferns and orchids. These are just a few images from Kansas landscapes, decks, patios, and well-planned commercial developments. It just takes time, patience and work, but boy, is it worth it!

This exhilarating excitement continues through all four seasons—from the basement grow light table and bottom heat mat triggering germination of wing-like cotyledons, to the ground covers where lightning bugs hide in the summer daytime,

QUICKIE PLANT TERMS

PLANT TYPES

- **Herbaceous** (annuals, biennials, perennials)
- **Lawn** (cool, warm season)
- **Woody** (trees/shrubs/vines/groundcovers—deciduous, evergreen—conifer, broadleaf)

PLANT PARTS

- **Buds** (primary, secondary, adventitious, dormant)
- **Flowers** (monoecious—both sex same flower; dioecious—flower/plant separate sex)
- **Leaves** (needles, blades, broad, variegated/non variegated)
- **Roots** (underground storage, hairs)
- **Stems/Twigs/Branches/Trunk** (herbaceous, woody)
- **Veins** (transportation system)

PLANT PHYSIOLOGY

- **Breathing** (leaf, root)
- **Nutrient/Water** (absorption and movement)
- **Photosynthesis** (food manufacturing)
- **Propagation** (cutting, seed)

PLANT GROWING

- **Amendments** (additives)
- **Hormones** (stimulators)
- **Installation/Transplanting** (planting, relocating)
- **Mulch** (organic, inorganic)
- **Potting Mix and Soil** (for container, pots)
- **Soil Testing** (indicates good/bad qualities)
- **Soil Profile Type** (qualities—thin rocky, heavy clay, etc.)
- **Top Soil** (top 2 inches of ground)

PLANT PURCHASE

- **Balled and Burlap** (field grown root/soil wrapped and tied)
- **Bare-Root** (dormant plant all parts exposed—no growing medium)
- **Container/Pot** (greenhouse grown or outdoors under supervision)

CARE AND MAINTENANCE

- **Aeration** (maximizing air penetration)
- **Animals** (pets)
- **Chemical Types** (granular, liquid, ready to use, etc.)
- **Dethatching** (removing dead lawn debris)
- **Diseases** (bacteria, fungus, virus)
- **Fertilizing** (adding nutrition)
- **Pests/Insects** (bugs, mites, snails, etc.)
- **Pruning** (removing plant parts)
- **Watering** (rainfall, hose, irrigation system)
- **Weeds** (unwanted plants)
- **Wildlife** (birds, deer, chipmunks, moles, voles, mice, etc.)

to harvesting fall's colorful fruits, to watching songbirds enjoying your feeders.

No matter which of Kansas's 105 counties is home, you can anticipate delight with each month of the year. This book will guide you through the planting and care of annuals, bulbs, edibles, ground cover, vines, lawn, perennials, ornamental grasses, roses, shrubs, trees, and water garden plants. Just like people, most plants have a history that started long ago in distant lands. Plants that our ancestors found growing in many landscapes have been gathered, hybridized, evaluated and then made available to all seekers. Plants, gardening, and their enjoyment continue from sunrise to sundown, and even later if you add Landscape Lighting.

NEW GARDEN OR MAINTAINING AN EXISTING GARDEN

Whether you are planning new gardens or maintaining existing ones, always take time to stop and enjoy. Plant growth (above and below ground) goes in all directions—up, down, sideways, bent, leaning, sagging—so each gardening day should begin with a stroll through the yard just to see what has happened. Front, back and side yards each have peculiar qualities, including exposure (north, south, east, west), topography, power poles, underground utility lines, septic tanks or fields, hanging roof eaves, downspout discharge, driveway surfaces, pathways, and so on.

Before rushing into action, think and observe where your time is best spent. Some tasks are easier if addressed early, such as weed control. This said, make an unplanned stop to marvel at a neighbor's informal woodland, sunny cutting flower garden, or the formal neatness of a brick-edged herb garden. While the ebb and flow of indoor plants is not quite as dramatic as their outdoor counterparts, still these tropical wonders provide a year-round tranquility.

As you learn from these pages, I hope you'll take pleasure from hearing the soft autumn melody of cottonwood leaves as you prepare soil for early spring daffodil flowers. As you pull weeds, you may detect an unknown fragrance, then seek and find sweet autumn clematis. Perhaps you'll savor home grown tomatoes while an orchid sits as your table centerpiece. You may see maroon-leafed begonia sparkling in the morning dew while a black-eyed Susans bloom near the patio or deck. One day, you may find yourself mesmerized by the reflection of a red Japanese maple on a new water garden.

Each chapter details a specific plant group with a calendar format, January through December. This concept offers a chance to delve completely into points of interest for an entire year, with a progressive understanding of what comes next.

Final note to everyone, long-time gardener or first-timer: What could be better than thinking, designing, planting, caring for and enjoying a creation that's uniquely yours? Mother Nature does have final say, but what FUN!

NOTES

USDA COLD HARDINESS ZONES

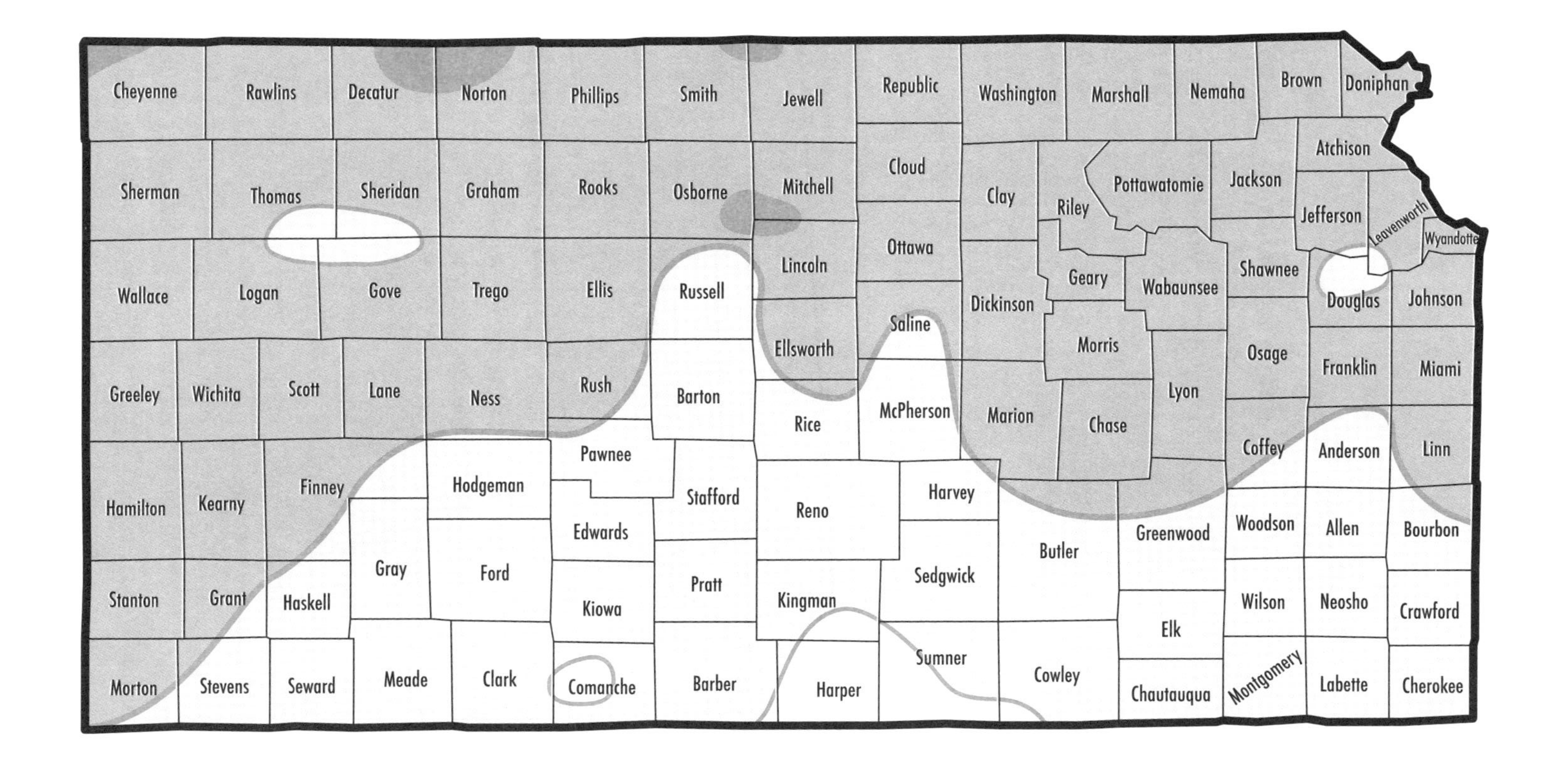

ZONE	Avg. Min. Temp. Degrees Fahrenheit
5a	-15 to -20
5b	-10 to -15
6a	-5 to -10
6b	0 to -5

CHAPTER ONE

ANNUALS

Annuals can turn heads, stimulate conversations and can make any landscape, patio, porch, deck, or window sill appear to be a picture taken in the tropics—like an exotic vacation experienced without leaving home.

Annuals provide electrifying colors, phenomenal single season growth, and the excitement of new textures and forms happens every year. The flowers we grow today can be traced to very specific and diverse regions of the world. This offers insight into the fact that all annuals are not created equal. The best way to start is with a dash of common sense. Thought and planning need to be done first.

Kansas' setting in mid-continent, our soil (or lack of), and our pets and wildlife, make learning to read nature's clock for annuals a fun and exciting challenge. Winds and weather sweep out of the north or southwest, river valley fertile soil gives way to rocky glades. The birds, deer, moles, and voles, along with the dog, cat, and maybe a pot bellied pig, all make up the workings of the annual's clock.

Over time we have learned that each year will bring a new chance to work with annuals and reap tremendous rewards, like watching people slow for a look at the variegated leaf color of the euphorbia or coleus. You yourself stop while bringing in the groceries to check the pansy, viola or toadflax for new leaves or buds. Enjoy sitting on the deck and watching the shadows and silhouettes of pots filled with fragrant flowering tobacco and hanging baskets of nasturtiums stretching out. How about the perilla filling the kitchen window—has it been 5 years? These and many more things are possible.

Bright white clouds of impatiens acting as landscape lighting under a tree, using single or multi-colored pansies as a harbinger of spring, zinnias providing nectar for the moths and butterflies, a morning glory vine screening a view within a few weeks of planting. Several annuals like alyssum and globe amaranth produce and drop seed outdoors that will germinate and grow the following year, self seeding. Using your imagination is the best way to take advantage of annuals. Each year or season can offer new opportunities for combining texture, shapes, and colors. An added bonus can be the stems and foliage, which are just as unique as the flowers. A close relative of annuals are biennials, which have two years of growing before flowering. The well known hollyhock is a great case in point, with huge roundish leaves followed the second year by a giant stalk of flowers.

DESIGNING

Whether your tastes lean towards the simple or complex, formal to informal annuals with their multitude of options can and will fulfill any desire. Many yards will feature various aspects of all design elements. The single/double row of red crested cockscomb running adjacent to the fence, or the strategically placed and measured bed spaces that mimic the size and shape of a house's window filled with petunias. A random collection of cardinal vine, morning glory, and moon vines grown from seed during the winter, now cover a trellis. How about planting only red flowering plants, those picked out by children, grandchildren, or yourself during a visit to the garden center? An informal plan may be placing taller growing cosmos among marigolds and red fountain grass, creating a roller coaster of heights front to back and side to side. Ideas can extend into containers, pots, planting pouches, and window boxes; a hanging basket filled with just one color trailing ivy geranium. Using a 30-inch pot as an experimental garden, jam in all the new types of plants that caught your eye this year. The possibilities are endless.

GENERAL REQUIREMENTS AND TIPS

Remember each annual is new to your landscape (whether home grown or purchased). Prior to being brought home they were nursed and pampered to attain present size and shape. Moving plants into the ground or pot is a completely different situation and their acclimation process will need help. Good performance results from taking time in choosing the right plant for the location, then providing correct growing conditions in the ground or pot and providing for care after planting. Without all of these factors occurring in unison success is unlikely. Be smart and enjoy.

HELPFUL HINTS

Learning Botanical Names of Annuals

A common name for a similar plant may be entirely different, not only from town to town, but also from family to family. So that everyone knows what plant you are talking about, try to learn the botanical Latin name. The second part of the botanical name is the species name, and many times this word is descriptive (see Introduction for a more complete explanation). If you know what species the Latin name is referring to, it can help you memorize the plant. The following chart provides you with some quick insight into the mystery of plant names. It may help you with the plant identification signage as you thumb through catalogs, visit garden centers, attend classes, and stroll through parks and botanical gardens.

Common Name	*Botanical Name*	General Meaning of Species
Alyssum	*Lobularia maritima*	of sea or shore
Begonia	*Begonia* x *semperflorens-cultorum*	cultivated to be ever flowering
Blue sage	*Salvia farinacea*	starch like, mealy
Cockscomb	*Celosia argentea* ssp. Cristata	comblike, crested
Coleus	*Solenostemon scutellarioides*	shield shape
Cosmos	*Cosmos sulphureus*	yellow
Euphorbia	*Euphorbia marginata*	margined with different color
Flowering tobacco	*Nicotiana alata*	winged
French marigold	*Tagetes patula*	spreading
Geranium	*Pelargonium* x *hortorum*	of the garden
Globe amaranth	*Gomphrena globosa*	globe shaped
Moonflower	*Ipomoea alba*	white
Morning glory	*Ipomoea purpurea*	purple
Perilla	*Perilla frutescens*	shrubby, bushy
Periwinkle	*Catharanthus roseus*	rosy, rose colored
Petunia	*Petunia* x *hybrida*	very mixed background
Portulaca	*Portulaca grandiflora*	large flowered
Red fountain grass	*Pennisetum setaceum*	bristlelike
Snapdragon	*Antirrhinum majus*	greater, larger
Viola	*Viola odorata*	fragrant
Zinnia	*Zinnia elegans*	beautiful

HELPFUL HINTS

Planning Your Annual Garden with B.A.S.I.C.S.

B. Big Picture = Nuances
Look at the big picture carefully, and consider the degree of aesthetic influences that any removal or addition of annuals brings. With additional annuals in the garden, will the new cultural (aesthetic) and maintenance requirements be reasonable? Considerations to achieve gardening success are plant related (health, population, compatibility), manmade (surfaces, access, utilities), and nature's influence (topography, wildlife, or pets).

A. Aim = Clarity of Goals
Have a clearly defined goal to your gardening plans. Develop a plan and a time frame to help with quantities, sizes, budget, and completion. Set landscape parameters to establish an outline for action to carry through with your "theme," from foundational to sensual. Extra planning minimizes back-pedaling in the installation process. Keep in mind that you may expand or reduce your plans, and that deviations from the plan will occur.

S. Silhouette = Form
Think of the individual parts of your garden, as well as the relationships they have to each other and to the whole. Make use of the existing frameworks while considering these three broad monikers: horizontal (spreading), mounded (gradual), and vertical (upright). Each plays a distinctive role. Nature really does it best, so simply mimic what you see. Select one framework to dominate, and two remaining frames to accentuate and support. The dominant feature is approximately fifty percent of the total area. Secondary plantings and design components make up thirty percent of the total, with the balance of plants and accents filling the remaining twenty percent of the design.

I. Implications = Coloration
Though weightless, color is a powerful tool and implies emotion, mood, and a message. The how, when, where, and how much make the difference. The energy color puts forth can concentrate and focus, or disperse and dilute. Red, blue, and yellow are primary colors. Any other colors are a combination of these three. Ultimate action applies equally to everything, with size, shape, and texture playing secondary and modifying roles, accelerating or slow-ing down the visual impact.

C. Coactive = Texture
The general terms fine, medium, and coarse have relevance to a setting, though not in a pure sense. Texture can be seen and felt. This liaison is very important to maximize the impact of individual parts and views. The stimulation of texture is two-fold.

S. Survey = Results
Review your plans and plantings frequently, and review with an open mind. Allow these results to guide you and to govern you in the future.

SOILS AND POTTING MIXTURES

The purpose of working the soil is to create a growing environment that makes it easy for air and moisture to go in and out. The ground needs to breathe. This will enable the plant to grow and establish a "roadway" that moves moisture and nutrients between tiny root hairs up to the leaves.

Preparation or correct potting mixtures is essential for annuals to make a great showing and withstand Kansas's changing weather, insect attacks, and/or disease potential. Elevate and enrich the planting bed. Add 1.75 cubic feet of organic material (compost, peat moss, leaf mold, etc.) per 100 square feet of planting area. Then shovel, rototill, or blend with existing soil until all obvious lumps are gone. Rake smooth, and spread 1 inch of mulch on top to give a finished look. Established beds benefit from 2 inches of new compost spread and worked in every 2 to 3 years. This recharges microorganisms in the soil. For container growing, potting mix formulated for growing in pots, pouches, or window boxes provides correct water and air exchange. Look at what the plants for sale are growing in—light, well drained potting mix.

PLANTS

Seeds or cuttings can be started at home and grown either under grow lights or directly planted in the garden bed space. The majority of annual plants used in the landscape are grown professionally in a greenhouse complex. It is possible to obtain a single plant, flats, or a pre-designed garden with plant collections and sold with layout for installation. This is available at garden centers, via email/internet, or mail order. Trade plants or seeds with friends, or gather seed (at appropriate sites only). Look for the plant tag to provide very basic plant needs.

SCHEDULING TIME FOR PLANTING AND INSTALLATION

Staging and orchestrating your garden is dependent upon several factors, such as starting seeds or taking cuttings for home growing, then knowing where and when to plant outdoors. The season to be grown—summer, spring, or fall—or planning a winter window garden all play in timing. Annuals can and do happen year round or efforts can be focused on one particular season. It is a personal choice. Preparation and installation are done later in one season to achieve results in the following season. Mid to late springtime is the launch time for the summer annuals, with variations according to the weather. Cooler temperatures and rainfall will keep the ground colder and this inhibits root and plant growth, so be patient and wait. Summer's planting of the fall season bloomers can be timed according to availability at local garden centers, or if growing from seed, start the seeds as the existing ones outdoors begin declining due to warm temperatures. If starting seeds under grow lights in the winter, wait until mid February, or call a local production greenhouse and ask their schedule, or even better: take a class.

SELF-SEED ANNUALS

Each year it is being discovered that seed produced during the previous growing season are germinating and growing great plants.

Allow this to occur by keeping mulch depths 1 to 2 inches at maximum.

AFTER-PLANTING CARE AND MAINTENANCE

Care and maintenance will vary according to several things: plant age (seedling vs. mature), specific variety (dry soil preference vs. damp moist), exposure (sun vs. shade), the setting (mid yard vs. street side, under trees vs. fully open) and actual growing situation. A hanging basket full of salvia or snapdragon vs. a full bed will require a different routine and quantities. Annuals will need basic care, watering and fertilizing, while the maintenance can vary regarding pinching, deadheading, and checking for insect-disease problems. Applications of fertilizers thru the growing season are needed to compensate for nutrients used or leached from the soil. This is essential for all container plants to stay vibrant.

BENEFITS AND REWARDS

There is a simple pleasure in seeing success, having flowers to cut, experiencing unmatched fragrances, seeing unexpected colors, and of course traveling to the tropics without leaving home.

ANNUALS

PLANNING

In the cold month of January, stay warm and dry, and use the time wisely. Use the time to reminisce about last year's gardening. Refresh your memory and your spirits, and review photographs of previous years' gardens. Make a list of the pluses and minuses of past gardens to help you plan for spring. Start working through the seed catalogs that are much more than just a place to order seeds. They are encyclopedias of statistics, facts, and methods—a wealth of information. There is still time to place an order, and January is a good month to do it.

Whether you are starting **portulaca** seeds under grow lights or direct sowing **hyacinth bean vine** at the base of the new trellis, make those determinations as soon as possible to avoid time conflict and late delivery. If your order arrives early, clearly label the outside of packet, using a waterproof pen, then keep the seeds cool and dry.

Make a journal page on each seed or bulb purchased, and do more research, if necessary, for propagation methods indoors under lights, or for sowing seed directly into the garden.

If you venture forth outdoors, check out a favorite garden center, especially if a greenhouse is attached. Thirty minutes in the tropics among those early arrivals, the colorful leaf **coleus**, or the fragrant **violas**, can do wonders to lift you out of the January doldrums. While you are there, explore the seed racks for **euphorbia** (**snow-on-the-mountain**), a cousin to the **poinsettia**, or **impatiens** seed packets to give away during the Super Bowl Party. Ask the garden center staff about that head-turning flower you missed last season. When will it be in stock this year?

Visit horticultural supply companies, in person, via email, or look at catalogs to update tools, acquire new "toys," or to modify your workbench. Check out the new products available—a grow light cart on wheels, a motion detector with water spray for those overly friendly pets.

PLANTING

Any previously used bedding plant cell packs, flats, containers, and pots (clay or plastic) should be cleaned prior to new use. A thorough cleaning eliminates last year's residues from pesticides, fungicides, and water and fertilizer deposits. Start the year clean, and soak everything in a water and bleach solution (10 parts water to 1 part bleach) overnight. Then rinse, scrub to remove anything not dissolved by soaking, and check for cracks and splits. Toss anything that may be possible trouble later on.

It is probably too early, but why not play around with a little early propagation. Sacrifice a few seeds, take a few cuttings, and see how it goes. For starting seeds, use only very lightweight, soilless potting mixes (shredded peat moss and vermiculite or perlite). For rooting **geranium** or other cuttings, use a soilless potting mix that contains a controlled, slow-release fertilizer.

Seed germination time for **alyssum** may be up to four weeks. **Petunias**, **snapdragons**, **marigolds**, **zinnias**, **periwinkles**, and **impatiens** take up to three weeks before you see signs of life sprouting out of the soil. Most annuals are dicots. When germinating, the seed first appears rising in the stem, the seed "hull" and stem stop elongating, the first set of true leaves opens, and the cotyledon hull drops or dries up.

Consider the amount of light needed by seedlings, cuttings, or transplants. The lights you use should be specifically for plant growing. There are both incandescent and fluorescent bulbs. Depending on the seeds and plants you are planning to grow, the fixtures should be adjustable to approximately 2 to 3 inches above the soil surface or cutting tops, and the lights raised or lowered to accommodate growth.

HELPFUL HINTS

Consider using growing containers made with molded compressed peat moss. When planting in the garden, the containers go directly in the soil and gradually decompose. These containers reduce transplant shock, because the plant roots are never disturbed.

CARE

Warm days mean a trip into the yard to check for cool season weeds popping up in the bed spaces. Hand dig them before they grow to their full potential. Did you forget about the windowboxes on the garage when you closed down for winter? Now is a good time to take them down, dump the soil into the compost pile, and clean up the container for a new season.

WATERING

Reduce potential problems during this preparation month. Research possible sites that can perform a water quality test of your tap water to determine pH and the presence of trace elements. Recently germinate seeds are very prone to water chemistry problems (pH above 7 is alkaline, below 7 is acidic). It might be necessary to let the seedling water sit out overnight before using, or consider buying de-ionized water.

FERTILIZING

This is one chore you don't have to worry about in January.

PRUNING

No pruning or pinching is needed. If seedlings or cuttings appear elongated, plant recovery is unlikely, so the struggling plant should be thrown away.

PESTS

Insects should not be a concern if everything has been cleaned and soaked. Do not forget to wipe down all the tools that may be used. Any residual fungus and bacteria are killed by the water and bleach solution soak, but keep an eye out for anything showing trouble—especially your seedlings or cuttings. Isolate the problem, change the cultivation routine, or toss out any infected plants.

Have you seen bark being stripped from trees, evergreens being munched on, or animal foot tracks? These are signs of wildlife, and once in the habit of moving through an area, they are difficult to discourage. Deer, rabbits, squirrels, and their friends are probably looking in the window, in great anticipation of those annuals to be planted. Try diverting the buggers by placing corn, salt licks, or other enticements away from the bed spaces.

NOTES

FEBRUARY

ANNUALS

PLANNING

This is a good time of year to check with local garden centers, city parks departments, and botanical gardens for classes, information sheets, and technical advice. They are already thinking ahead to the spring season. Utilize the local garden clubs. Members are a wealth of information, and eager to share successes and disappointments concerning all plant types.

Fight those winter blues. If any space remains open on a windowsill or under the grow lights, go to the garden center for a pick-me-up of some fragrant **violas** to add pizzazz to your indoor garden.

Peer out the windows, and consider your view looking out. Could this view be more exciting with a mass planting of **balsam**? Walk about on warm days to decide whether to increase the size or number of areas planted with annuals.

Make some quick sketches of those ideas you had earlier in the winter. They may need revision because the neighbor just built a fence. There is still plenty of time to make changes. Consider splitting the **morning glory** between the trellis and that new fence. Finalize your original concepts, and you may even think of some new ones.

PLANTING

Before creating new bedding areas, and in reviewing last year's plant performance for possible disappointments, take a soil sample to the local extension service, or check for soil testing labs in the phone book. The earlier this is accomplished, the better. When results are returned, make sure they are completely understood. If you don't understand the results or the recommendations, place a phone call to the testing agent to clarify. Then, follow the recommendations, and secure the supplies necessary to bring your soil up to speed.

Pansy or **toadflax** will start showing up at garden centers. These can be purchased, planted, and enjoyed early in the season. Have you seen any **blue sage** or **marigolds** already in the garden centers? Although these are two of the tougher and earlier annuals, this is a bit too early to plant them.

For seeding flats, examine seed packets, or do additional research on the specific depth the seeds must be placed to increase the chances of a successful crop. When filling open flats, cell packs, and pots with soilless potting mix, pack the soil down firmly to minimize sinking due to air pockets. Use waterproof labels and pens, and label the seed containers as soon as the seeds hit the soil. A label should include both the common and botanical name of plant, days to germination, and date of planting.

CARE

Stroll about the garden and tag the general area where that self-seeding **moon flower vine** was dropping seeds or any other areas you want to preserve and keep safe from spring cultivation.

Check on seedling growth a couple of times a day, particularly if multiple types are growing under lights. Adjust grow light height above the plants as needed (to 2 or 3 inches). Increase the length of time the grow lights are on to mimic longer days. Maintain a steady upright growth. Avoid letting the plants lean or bend, a result of low or fluctuating light intensity. Thin and remove any seedling, cutting, or plant showing signs of trouble.

WATERING

Monitor the soil moisture on any indoor plants, and seedling or cutting flats. The soil should be damp to the touch, but there should be no water sitting in any collection trays.

Outdoors, it is probably too early to start working up the beds. If nature has dropped a lot of snow, rain, or sleet, do a soil test by probing the area with a shovel, spade, or trowel. If the ground sticks to the tool, it is still too early to work the soil.

FERTILIZING

A very light formulation of a water-soluble fertilizer, applied bimonthly to healthy plants, is beneficial at this time.

PRUNING

Do not pinch seedlings if they appear thin and leaning. Pinching will not help at this stage. Also, don't prune cuttings yet either. Wait until they have strong root growth and new foliage.

HELPFUL HINTS

Insects are generally small and flying types this time of year. Use yellow sticky traps placed in the area to monitor the insect numbers. If you find any attached to the foliage or stem of the plants, treat with a cotton swab dipped in a solution of 1 part alcohol to 10 parts water, or use insecticidal soap per label directions. Consider discarding any very young, fragile seedlings. It may be easier to just start over.

To neutralize any de-icers or salt sprays along the streets or sidewalks, sprinkle some **gypsum** on the area. Sprinkle enough to appear as if a fall frost is on the ground.

Cut back the **geraniums**. Allow a few leaf scars (last year's attachment sites) to remain above the soil surface.

PESTS

Check indoor seedlings' soil surface for any gray mold. Stir very lightly and add a fan for air circulation.

NOTES

MARCH

ANNUALS

PLANNING

Days are warming up now and there are longer intervals between rains. Do a soil test to see how wet the ground is below the surface. Dig into the soil with a shovel or trowel. If a considerable amount of soil sticks to the tool, do not work the soil. If the soil has had a chance to dry out, prepare the beds. After spading, work in a light application of granular, all-purpose fertilizer, and rake the soil surface smooth. Work backwards out of the bed to minimize soil compaction from footprints. Apply a 1-inch layer of mulch to the surface of the soil. This shallow layer reduces visible mud, and protects the soil from drying completely out.

Insects start rearing their heads as the days warm up. Fill up the birdfeeders and hang them in the garden to encourage friendly birds to enter, looking for the tasty insect tidbits.

Visit the garden centers where early spring annuals **ageratum**, **snapdragon**, **begonia**, **hyacinth bean**, **geranium**, **marigold**, **blue sage**, **perilla**, and **viola** arrive daily. Ask questions about unfamiliar varieties, new tools, fertilizers, and soil amendments. Have your name added to the mailing list to receive the garden center newsletter.

PLANTING

It is not necessary to transplant seedlings you have grown indoors into larger containers. You may just wait to transplant them directly outdoors. However, rooted cuttings, healthy mature plants grown under grow lights, and packs or containerized annuals may be transplanted into larger containers. Pot up the rooted cuttings into 1- or 2-inch pots. Transplant the mature plants into a container that is just one size larger than the container it is currently growing in. If too large of a container is used, you run the risk of transplant stress.

Plant the next wave of seeds and place under the growing lights. This additional sowing maintains a continuous progression of annuals and also covers any unexpected problem or losses that occur.

CARE

1. It is best to leave your newly purchased annuals in their containers (or transplanted into larger containers, see Planting). This allows for better and easier care until the weather stabilizes. At this time of year, it is not unusual for a cold front to move in, bringing with it the possibility of hard frost. Containerized plants can be moved into the garage or under other protection until it is time to plant them outdoors.

2. Check seedling flats and cuttings growing under lights on a daily basis. If you sowed seed in early February, you should be seeing multiple sets of leaves. Thin seedlings to package specifications. Remove any seedling that looks distressed. Increase the grow light duration time to mimic longer days.

3. Clean debris off of unrooted cutting flats, eliminate any cuttings or seedlings that show signs of trouble. Cuttings should show signs of rooting. If they are rooted in peat pots, white fibrous roots show on the outside or on the bottom of the pot. If the cuttings are rooted in plastic pots, and the roots are not visible coming out of the bottom of the container, give a slight tug on the cutting. If there is resistance, there are roots forming. Maintain care regime until the cutting sends out new leaves.

4. Consider moving seedlings and plants outdoors during warmer days to give them a fresh breath of reality. Place them in the shade or partial shade (no direct sun), and bring them all back indoors before the nighttime temperatures drop. Keep a close eye out for those early season pests.

WATERING

Check annuals coming up from seed in the landscape for drought stress. Even the cool season fountain grass should not be allowed to water stress. When plants are regularly watered during the cold months, the water fills the air pockets around the roots and prevents cold damage to the roots.

Depending upon the container, be sure to water accordingly. Terra cotta can dry unevenly and also tends to have a salt buildup. Plastic pots allow for even moisture evaporation and hold moisture in the soil longer. The soil should look and feel damp, but not be soggy. The soil is too soggy if you push a finger into the soil, and moisture arises around it. If the soil is dry one-half inch into the soil, water deeply and slowly.

Wire window boxes or hanging baskets with liners made from woven coconut fibers are great for **cardinal vines**, **nasturtiums**, or **portulaca** to cascade from. However, there is almost no isolation from drying out. Plants that require a constant level of moisture need to be monitored carefully.

HELPFUL HINTS

Do not use any tools, outdoors and indoors, that might make trouble for new seedlings or cuttings. Bacteria, fungus, and mildews are invisible to the eye, but the spores and pathogens might be along for the ride. Keep tools cleaned and disinfected if you are using them on young plants.

FERTILIZING

Use a very light formulation of a water-soluble fertilizer on seedlings and rooted cuttings. Apply weekly. Weak, yellow, or spindly seedlings will not respond to any amount of fertilizer and are best discarded.

PRUNING

It is time to cut back and shape the plants that have been wintered over. Cut back no more than one-quarter of the total size of the plant.

Disbud any flower buds popping out of the **coleus** or any other annuals you are growing for their foliage only.

PESTS

With the warmer weather, windows and doors are opened more frequently. This provides increased opportunities for insects coming indoors. Watch and control these early intruders by either physical removal or by a direct application of insecticidal soap.

The area wildlife is producing their young, so that means more trouble, simply because of the increased numbers. Consider some means of control, whether chicken wire or other physical barrier, hot pepper spray, a wildlife predator, or a repellent such as urine drops.

NOTES

APRIL

ANNUALS

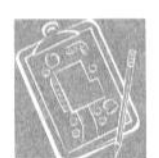

PLANNING

When designing the annual bed, a balanced or formal layout is not always needed. The ease of designing with annuals allows a yearly change and a different display from the previous year. **Begonias**, **spider flower**, and **petunias** work well in drifts, but can also be used in dots and dashes, interplanted with each other to highlight a birdbath. Using the taller **cosmos** in the back, with **globe amaranth** in the midground, accented in front with **alyssum**, certainly works. But you can take those same annuals and mix up the heights to create more visual animation. Consider that **perilla** naturalizes, and only stays where it is planted if it is physically forced to do so, with diligent digging and removal. Every year **ageratum**, **snapdragon**, and **cockscomb** are used in the garden, but create a completely new look, fulfilling the seemingly endless list of design possibilities.

Do not overlook the up-close and personal gardens we have in decorative pots and containers, hanging baskets, and window boxes. Clustering different plants in single pots creates a living bud vase. Use a pot of mounded periwinkle with its shiny leaves, matched with a bowl of stiffer **French marigolds;** add a big pot of whirling **cleome**, with combination pots of **alyssum** and **blue sage** in the mix for accents.

With newly generated ideas in hand, move into the outdoors and check the previously established bedding spaces. Measure areas currently used for perennials or bulbs where you will overplant with annuals, and any new areas to plant. Determine the total square footage you want to plant with annuals. Don't forget the containers in the square footage total. The number of plants you purchase is related to your patience level. If instant gratification is desired, then space plants closer together. Deciding this ahead of time will help you calculate the number of plants to buy.

PLANTING

This is a scary month for planting, as the weather is totally unpredictable. Use restraint when moving anything into the garden during this month. Cool season annuals should be fine to plant now.

1. There is still time to prepare the soil, but don't work the soil if it is wet. This creates compacted soil.

2. Make sure beds, planting spaces, and recycled potting soil are all weed free. Either pull weeds or treat with a herbicide, then rake area smooth.

3. If you didn't already do so, add some amendments to the soil. Blend in peat moss, leaf mold, or compost.

4. Check your flats and cell packs growing under lights for roots protruding from drainage holes or out of the flats. Make sure plant labels are in place to make transplanting outdoors less hassled.

5. For a succession of annuals, plant seeds in flats under grow lights. A bottom-heating mat is invaluable to stimulate germination.

CARE

Keep raising the height of the grow lights, and make notes related to any areas under the lights that have been troublesome. Use this information next year.

Move seedling flats outdoors (set in shade and partial shade, no full sun yet) during warmer days, but bring in after a few hours. Check for pests catching a ride.

Have old sheets, burlap, or fabric ready to cover those annuals that were installed in the ground. Cover the young plants when predicted temperatures are in the mid-30s or lower.

WATERING

Active growth of seedlings or cuttings requires watering adjustments accordingly. Do not allow either to dry out. The soil should be constantly damp to the touch.

FERTILIZING

All plants are still fragile. Continue using a seed starter type fertilizer, ratio 1-2-1. Apply weekly at the full label rate.

PRUNING

Pinch back no more than one quarter of any plant. The more healthy foliage a plant has, the easier transition it makes into the outdoors. Remove all flowers at time of planting to encourage strong root formation and a longer bloom period.

PESTS

Due to accelerated growth on seedlings and cuttings, routine inspection is needed to monitor for mold or fungus on the soil surface. Apply a soil drench, using a fungicide (at one-half the label rate), gently pouring it on the soil surface. As the mixture drains through and collects in trays below, discard the runoff.

Monitor hatching insects; sucking insects transmit plant diseases, so take action at the first signs of infestation. Physically remove the pests, or treat with insecticidal soap.

Wildlife, adults and newborn, seem to be everywhere. Consider diversions with a motion detector light or irrigation devices, or use physical barriers. You might try setting up a sacrificial buffet planting—away from your prized plantings.

HELPFUL HINTS

Seedlings available at nurseries and garden centers that are stocky, and have very little space between the leaves along the stem is the result of using a growth retardant, applied to the soil during the growing process at the production greenhouses.

NOTES

ANNUALS

PLANNING

1. Flexibility in your garden planning and design is essential. Check the area for any environmental changes, such as the loss of a shade tree that will thrust plants beneath it into full sun. They may have lived in shady comfort for many seasons and will need to be moved with the exposure change. Adjust your landscape plan accordingly.

2. If you can take the time, arrange **flowering tobacco**, **zinnias**, and other annuals, while still in containers or cell packs, into projected sites. Give yourself some time to evaluate your plan for impact before you plant. By moving the packs around into different positions, you can maximize the impact and your design intent.

3. Consider mixing seedlings grown under lights with some purchased to take the pressure off the homegrown crop.

4. Do not over-project on the amount of work that you can do at one time. Plants purchased in small containers decline quickly if extra care isn't given to them. Water them well, until it's their turn to join others in the garden.

Have you seen flats of annuals for sale at an unbelievable low price? These require the same care as seedlings that are homegrown. You may need to provide extra care for up to three weeks until the seedlings are ready to plant outside.

PLANTING

Mark designated locations of annuals with ribbons, flags, or marking paints. If possible, plant on a cloudy day. Plant annuals in prepared beds. Remove plant from container, or if it is a peat pot, tear off the sides, place plant into hole, make depth adjustments (plant slightly high or at the same exact level it was previously growing), replace soil, and firm around plant. Take care to not step on any previous installations.

Plant annuals into large pots, the larger the better if planting a mass of color. The smaller the pot, the more care it needs, as the soil dries out faster. Scatter biennial seeds of **hollyhock**, **foxglove**, **mulleins**, **Queen Anne's lace**, and even **pansies**. Scatter packets of self-seeding annuals, such as **gomphrena** and **impatiens**, in areas where the mulch is 1 inch thick or less. Rake the spot lightly to insure seed is in direct contact with the soil.

CARE

Moisten prepared beds and potting mixes prior to installation. This is essential to minimize root damage.

While installing plants in the ground, or transplanting to larger containers and baskets, stop at regular intervals to water in transplants and to water annuals still in packs or flats. Water thoroughly and look back to see if the soil has settled and if the roots are exposed. If this is the case, add soil and firm it around the exposed root mass. If the day is bright, sunny, and windy, several light waterings may be required throughout the day.

Add super absorbent polymers to the potting mix for those hanging baskets of **alyssum** and **coleus**, containers with **red fountain grass**, and window boxes of **violas** and **ageratums**. Even if you buy your containers already designed and potted, you can add the polymer to the surface of the soil and work it in.

Sprinkle a small amount of granular fertilizer on the surface of the soil after planting is completed. Top with 1 inch of mulch.

FERTILIZING

Begin a regular routine of feeding to insure a steady supply of nutrients. Determine the type of fertilizer to buy based upon your soil test results. An all-purpose type has both micro and macro nutrients, and is generally good for growing annuals.

Use a slow release, season-long, pelleted fertilizer in window boxes and hanging baskets. Sprinkle on the surface and blend in.

PRUNING

During installation, remove any flowers. Flower formation stresses a plant, regardless of its size. Until the root system is established, self-denial of the flowers now, pays off with a stronger, well-established plant.

Pinch back the stems of **coleus**, **geraniums**, and **zinnias** by one quarter to encourage bushy compact growth.

PESTS

Warm weather triggers signals for overwintering adult insects to emerge, for insect egg hatching, and for many of the bacteria, mold, and fungus spores to erupt. The softer stemmed plants such as **impatiens** and **snapdragons** are usually the first to be hit. Watch them and all of your new transplants closely. An explosive, damaging scenario can literally happen overnight.

Once plantings have acclimated for two to three weeks, continue to be observant, but if the plants are healthy, some leeway does exist at this growing stage.

Keep an identification book to make correct diagnosis of animals, pests, or diseases. Many chemicals applied to young plantings have an impact on the plant. Many insecticides are contact oriented (they only work if the spray is directed on the insect), and leave very little residual chemical on the plant. This is not the case with fungicides. They can be applied as a preventative.

Building a physical barrier is the best control for squirrels, rabbits, skunks, deer, and neighboring cats and dogs that look at freshly worked soil as an invitation to "help."

HELPFUL HINTS

In bed spaces, inexpensive, old-time sprinkler hoses turned upside down, and positioned throughout the plantings before mulch is added, keeps the ground damp, reduces surface evaporation, and eliminates potential problems from moisture on the foliage.

NOTES

ANNUALS

PLANNING

Gold and purple finches, along with other feathered friends, enjoy visiting the garden this time of year. Entice them with seed, and fill the birdbath once or twice a day. Not only do the birds bring wonderful color and activity into the garden, they also eat some of those pesky insects.

Start a photo journal of the garden showing growth on all plantings, and to view this year's garden layout and concepts. Next year's ideas start here.

Larger plants are available at garden centers to fill voids or gaps for a single loss of a seedling or for complete annual bed change outs.

Pull out spent **pansies** and **toadflax**. Consider **cardinal climber** creeping over some **balsam**, or lower growing **ageratums** mingled with **petunias**.

Plan ahead for the end of season cleanup. Plant annuals into black plastic nursery pots, and set these pots down into ornamental containers (with drainage holes). You can still fill any visible gaps with a fibrous moss filler or plant a tumbling **nasturtium**. This practice makes cleanup at season's end much easier.

PLANTING

If you are filling voids and gaps in beds, use caution not to disturb the surrounding roots or break the tender stems of other annuals. Be careful of particularly sensitive **impatiens** and **begonias**. They may be going strong, but a surprise pruning or severed roots could slow the maturing and flowering process.

Remember every footstep compacts the soil; rework your tread with a digging fork as the last task as you complete the bed.

Garden centers are still full of plants, so the planting urge is still there. Check out the naturalizing **perilla** and **dwarf snapdragons**. Bring home instant accent with a **moon flower vine** growing in a pot on a small trellis, or a **hyacinth bean**, already in flower, sweeping out of a hanging basket.

CARE

Depending on the type of mulch spread earlier (leaf mold or compost minimizes potential harm to the stems and leaves, but coarse wood or bark lasts longer), it may need refreshing. As scorching summer heat approaches, the mulch acts as a buffer to the fluctuations in temperature.

Check to determine that all of the plant name labels are still in place.

WATERING

Nature provides much of the watering this month. But if it is dry, make up the difference. Plants need a minimum of 1 inch of water every week. You may need to supplement with an automatic irrigation system, sprinkler hose, leaky pipe, hose and nozzle, or a watering can.

Water as early in the day as possible. This practice reduces bacteria and fungus problems.

Hanging baskets, pots, and containers may need watering twice daily if the weather is hot and windy, and if superabsorbent polymer was not added to the potting soil at planting time.

FERTILIZING

Feed bedding plants biweekly using a hose end attachment that mixes water soluble fertilizer and water in a prescribed proportion.

Feed hanging baskets, pots, containers, and window boxes weekly. Use a hose end attachment or watering can. This may seem like frequent fertilization, but nutrients are flushed out with each watering.

PRUNING

Determine the usual growth characteristics of the plant before you pinch. If an annual is typically tall, thin, and willowy, or if it is the basal leaf variety, pinching or cutting back does more harm than good. All others benefit if they are cut back, to about one-quarter of the total height of the plant.

Deadheading is a must for **marigolds**, **blue sage**, **snapdragon**, and **flowering tobacco** to keep the plants clean, and to encourage more blooms.

PESTS

Check for damaging insects in early morning and evening hours. Insect activity is highest during those times. Examine the stems, the leaf surfaces—top and bottom, and check on the ground for trails (slugs and snails). Only use a pesticide if it can be directly applied to the pest. If this seems overwhelming, consider physical controls like squeezing between the fingers, or a high pressure spray from the hose.

The more lush the leaf, the greater the appeal, particularly if the weather is dry. Animal pests will go to great lengths for survival. Use motion detectors with lighting or an irrigation component as a deterrent. Fence the garden, or use the same controls for neighboring pets.

Mole tunnels are showing up everywhere, since the babies are large enough to tunnel in the soft, prepared beds that have a generally higher earth worm population (the mole's favorite food). Set traps and move them daily.

HELPFUL HINTS

1. Monitor weed growth regularly. A great competition for moisture and nutrients occurs between the dandelions and clovers, and the **violets**, **cosmos**, **spider flowers**, and **zinnias**. If you are unsure of the identification of a particular plant or what controls to use, take a sample of the weed or a close-up photo to the garden center, extension office, or to a botanical garden. It is best to call ahead first to make sure a staff member is available to help.

2. Have you seen an odd looking growth on the top of the mulch? This is a sign that the mulch is breaking down. It is a fungus, which only grows on dead material. It will not harm healthy plants even if it grows up a plant stem.

NOTES

JULY
ANNUALS

PLANNING

1. If there have been no signs of any growth since installation, re-evaluate the situation. Consider plant selection, location, soil preparation, and planting technique. Attach notes to the page, add photos, and use this information for your planning for next year's garden.

2. Garden and home tours occur this month. Take some photographs and notes on whatever tweaks your interest. That **balsam** growing in the cracks in the patio (a little cheaper than pouring a new slab), or **alyssum** used between areas cleared among herbs just might work in your garden next year.

3. Check over the hanging baskets and decide if any should be revamped. Make a shopping list to prepare for the transplants in late August.

4. Gardening means enjoying this season, but planning for the next means fun and excitement. It's a good time to think about where to add cool season **pansies** and **toadflax**.

5. If you are making summer vacation plans, and will be away for more than two or three days, have someone check on the garden for water, or several months of work could be lost.

6. Take down hanging baskets to minimize drying while you are away.

7. Observe sun loving plants of the same type, but planted in different locations. A plant situated adjacent to any hardscapes (walk, drive, patio) may look completely different as the same plant located at the back of the border. Plan a 1-foot buffer away from the hardscape. The plants sited back a bit will grow, and fill in the space.

PLANTING

Plant or transplant only under emergency situations. Any gardening should not be done between the hours of 10 a.m. and 3:00 p.m. The plants are heat stressed (even though they don't show symptoms). Disruption can shorten their glory days.

If necessary, for those painfully -behind-schedule or slow-to-grow plants, dig as much root system as possible, and add some liquid root stimulator to the soil.

Need a little night fragrance? Check seed racks now as many seeds are arriving that are focused on fall planting. If you want fast vine action, the **moonflower** soaked overnight in a wet paper towel, and planted the next morning in a soilless potting mix, will be up and flowering within two to three weeks.

Have you seen a planting with a tropical flavor comprised of **begonias**, **periwinkles**, **globe amaranth**, and **impatiens?** All four respond to the warm weather and come to the forefront of the garden this month. They will remain so for the next eight weeks.

Start **pansy** and **toadflax** seed in flats, indoors, under lights.

CARE

Taller varieties of annuals may need staking. Place the stake within 1 inch of the stem and tie very loosely, to avoid damaging the tender stems and leaves.

WATERING

Annuals, even established plants, need 1 inch of water each week. But use common sense. If it is very humid and the ground appears damp, trowel down and check the soil at a deeper level for moisture. If it is moist quite deeply into the soil, then monitor the next irrigation for the length of the watering cycle. The same process applies to any containerized plantings. Check the soil before you water.

Buy a rain gauge, or maybe a couple of them, for each microclimate (under trees, full sun, on the side of the house). The weather person's rainfall predictions won't be as accurate as the gauge readings from your own backyard.

HELPFUL HINTS

For cutting and pressing flowers, cut early in the day, place blooms between a couple sheets of folded newsprint, lay a book on top for about a month, and the end result is flowers that are preserved for making gifts. To make a bookmark, simply use a warm iron and small piece of waxed paper folded to desired size. Insert the pressed bloom, gently move iron over waxed paper until it is sealed, then mount on a piece of light colored cardboard or construction paper.

FERTILIZING

Keep things roaring, fertilize to your own personal style—weekly, biweekly, or monthly. Just stay consistent and the plants will push growth.

If season long or slow release fertilizer pellets were added to soil at the time of planting, then additional feeding can be done now with no harm to the plants.

PRUNING

Cut flowers from the garden before you deadhead the plants. Cut the flowers in full bloom, and use the leaves too, for centerpieces to float in bowls of water.

Deadheading should occur daily. Neglecting this for a few days could set back the flowering cycle for a period of time.

Cutting back of one-quarter of the plant leaf and stem (never during the heat of day) could rejuvenate the plant, and amaze you with a comeback.

PESTS

Although it is probably the worst month for insects, strong and healthy plants recover from almost any attack. The time needed for recovery is the factor. Take this course of action:

1. Check for pests during various times of the day. Check all surfaces of the leaf. Identify the pests. If you are not sure what it is, take a sample and have it identified.

2. Determine if the pest population warrants action, and at what level controls are necessary to insure plant health.

3. Physically remove the pests by running fingers along stem or applying a strong stream of water.

4. Release predatory insects. Read and follow label directions for successful release.

5. Apply an insecticide. Make sure the chemical is labeled for use on this particular plant.

Only take action on plants that have a pest problem. Preventive measures are a waste of time when dealing with annuals.

If one particular plant or area seems to be inundated, consider removal of the infected plants. Often times, overpopulation causes migration to other plants.

NOTES

AUGUST

ANNUALS

PLANNING

1. Evaluate large planted areas, all pots, containers, hanging baskets, and window boxes. Any planting that is no longer fulfilling its aesthetic niche should go. Some early departures are **cosmos**, **spider flowers**, and **flowering tobacco**. This lightening up on the workload leaves you with less responsibility, and more time to enjoy the fantastic remains of **red fountain grass, begonias, impatiens,** and **globe amaranth.**

2. Make notes related to the current weather and the plants that did not survive the summer heat. Note particular plant characteristics that pop up in response to heat. The **coleus** continually sets flowers, and the **nasturtium** may resemble a single string loaded with flowers.

Though hot and humid weather is still here, nighttime temperatures begin dropping, and the rate of growth decreases. In gardening words—this is as big as everything gets. Early morning, or later in the day, is the best time to work—less stress for you and for the plants.

PLANTING

Prepared beds, where plants have just been removed or where there are newly created spaces, welcome cool season plants, available in cell packs, flats, or 6-inch plastic pots. Dig a hole in the prepared soil. Remove the plant just prior to planting so that roots will not dry out. Place the plant into the hole, adjusting the planting depth so that it is approximately the same as it was in the pot, replace soil, and firm around plant.

Hold back on any ambitious ideas for moving existing plants. They are established, and they would not survive the change, nor look nearly as good. If plants are elongating, take cuttings of the top leaf cluster, and root for a late season showing.

Annual **asters** are making a showing at the garden centers, usually in 4-inch pots. These have a built-in obsolescence at this point. Usually, the more open the flowers, the shorter bloom time. Pop some into the bare spots for a last minute color burst.

CARE

If spring mulch has disappeared, apply another 1-inch layer to give a crisp look to the planting. Use the mulch to fill in the gaps that have begun to crop up from annuals expiring.

When moving in and out of bed spaces remember the soil is compressing with each step. Lightly turn the compressed surface, taking care not to damage remaining plants.

WATERING

Established good performers still need 1 inch of water each week. Use common sense if it is very humid and the ground appears damp. It probably did not rain overnight, the moisture is simply fog that does very little to supply the plant with necessary water. Push a trowel in the ground and pull up a soil sample. Use your hand to do a moisture test. Take a handful and squeeze. Does the ball stay formed or does it break down as soon as the hand is opened? If it doesn't hold its shape, the soil is too dry. Change the watering for that day, but do not get into a watering routine for days at a time. Depending on the sun intensity, wind, temperature, and soil exposure, soil moisture needs change also.

Check plants in the morning for wilting. If they are up and perky, then soil moisture is good. If they wilt with the heat of the day, check the soil for moisture, and water if soil is dry. They should bounce back in a few hours. Wilting is also a signal for stem or root rot. If soil is soggy, work it up just a bit to allow it to dry. Allow it to dry well before installing any new plants or before adding mulch.

FERTILIZING

Fertilize all plantings on a regular basis to keep them blooming and growing.

Season-long or slow-release fertilizers have probably fizzled out. If you have been relying solely upon that initial application, start a new fertilizing regime. It could result in three more months of great production

Slow-release fertilizer, mixed into the soil at this time of year, is not readily available to new installations. Use water-soluble fertilizers at full label rate. This system allows for ease of cutting off the fertilizer when the weather cools.

HELPFUL HINTS

Bee activity increases, triggered by cooler nights and diminished food sources, to prepare for the winter. They need to keep "busy as bees" to maintain their current colony through the winter, and to ready the hive for the split-off of a queen that will start another hive next spring.

PRUNING

No need to deadhead. Cut back everything left growing such as **cardinal climber**, **coleus**, **blue sage**, and **ageratum**. Cut back one-quarter of the entire plant (never during the heat of day). You may be sacrificing a little color now, but you will have a stronger plant show in two to three weeks,

While newly planted **pansies** or **toadflax** are acclimating (takes approximately two weeks), cut off flowers to reduce stress.

PESTS

Insect activity on **cockscomb**, **petunias**, **zinnias**, and **periwinkle** should be on the decline. Remain attentive, and keep an eye out. Use early detection, identification, and evaluation. If the problem is obvious, get rid of the infested plants. Allowing the plant to remain could turn that harmless looking, **balsam** weakling into a henhouse of insect egg storage activity.

In the sunny areas, aphids, lace bugs, and spider mites are dominant. In the shaded space, slugs and snails could be munching holes in the leaves.

NOTES

ANNUALS

PLANNING

1. As plastic containers used for liners in the ornamental pots are pulled from service and the plants are dumped, check the phone book for a recycling center to take the excess. Another option is to locate a local plastic wood manufacturing company. They use a process that creates plastic wood from many different types, gauges, and colors of unusable products. Ask about a collection day, bin, or pick up service if the quantity is large enough. Get together with garden clubs, garden writers, or garden centers, and see what can happen when you pool your resources.

2. Gather all information from the past season, find those labels, and take measurements. Note what plants outperformed the expected, list others that may have been a disappointment. Try to determine the reasons for the disappointments—the area, the soil, the exposure.

3. Review the indoor growing facilities. Check the plant cart for placement, the light fixtures for any repairs, heating mat operation, and rooting and growing supplies on hand.

4. Consider relocating a planting area, creating a new one entirely, or abandoning one that no longer provides an adequate return for the time spent. If you have beds that are going to be used next year, now is the perfect time to work the soil, clear areas, and add compost and organic matter.

5. Every other trek into the landscape, go without tools, pencils, or paper. Take this time of year to remember why you do all this work and how much fun it is. Take the time to experience one of the most beautiful times of the year in the garden.

PLANTING

Purchase plant starter, soilless potting mixes to fill flats and containers, in anticipation of what is coming. Soon cuttings will be taken or whole plants (**geraniums**) are coming indoors. Do not bring any soil from outdoors inside. This is a disaster waiting to happen. Plants should be gently pulled from their location, and washed in a bath of mild, dishwashing solution. First, dunk the entire plant. This action removes any soil from the roots that may be harboring bacteria and fungus, and washes any insects from the leaves and stems. Follow the soapy bath with a double-dip into a completely separate bucket of clear water. Pot plants in clean pots, with fresh, soilless potting soil. After plant removal from beds and planting spaces, turn over soil, rake smooth, and add 1 inch of mulch.

As containers are emptied, and if you are going to use them again, a quick brushing with the same soapy solution described above would be smart. You can do a more thorough cleaning later on when there are not quite so many things on the "To Do List."

Prior to taking cuttings or to gathering seeds, label separate envelopes for each species and note the date collected.

Take stem cuttings for indoor rooting. Cut the stem at an angle (exposes more veins). Cut sections 4 to 6 inches long, remove the bottom third of leaves. Keep cuttings in a wet paper towel or in a jar of water until they are brought indoors. Make a second angle clean cut, just prior to sticking it into soil. Dip the cutting into rooting hormone and position into soilless mix immediately. Water the cutting flat thoroughly before placing on heat. Take about twice the amount of cuttings than you anticipate needing. Disposal of extra cuttings is easier than coming up short.

CARE

Continue care and maintenance of existing plants. Rewards can be reaped up until December. Some of the warm weather types of annuals may still be hanging on, a planting of **French marigolds** near the house, **begonias** canopied by an evergreen tree, maybe the **alyssum** dribbling out of the window box. They still need deadheading, fertilizing, and water.

WATERING

Continue providing 1 inch of water, every seven days, on bedding areas. Continue to water spaces that have had all plants removed, to maintain the soil structure and microbe activity.

Continue to water all containers that still have plantings, those at the back door, up by the mailbox, or the groupings on the deck or patio.

FERTILIZING

Large surges of growth are not going to happen as the day length becomes shorter, but good leaf and flower production continues by continuing with monthly feeding. The containerized plants especially benefit, as the nutrients are constantly leaching through the bottom drainage holes.

PRUNING

Annuals for sale at reduced prices will be in the garden centers. If you are in need of new color, or simply on a whim, and the plants are healthy, go on ahead and buy. Skip pinching off the flowers at the time of planting.

PESTS

Check for weeds, control (apply herbicide or pull) as the beds are cleared, and before updating with cool season plants.

Damage from insects is basically nonexistent, but keep all plant debris picked up to eliminate overwintering sites for pests.

Problems from bacteria, fungus, and molds for this year are over, but it helps to understand nature. Take photos and make notes. An early season soil drenching may be to the advantage.

Annual weed seeds, such as henbit and chickweed, will be germinating soon. If you apply a pre-emergent to bedding areas before seedlings are observed, the pre-emergent will stop germination. If the weeds are up and growing, application will still stop some seeds from germinating and reduce the problem; however, it will not kill the already germinated seedling. Apply a herbicide, in the heat of the day, directly to the weed foliage (crush it first to open wounds) to kill.

NOTES

OCTOBER

ANNUALS

PLANNING

Keep in mind, during these wonderful days for getting out and working in your yard, the energy and enticement is maximized to accomplish several tasks, but do not overdo it. Plan ahead to take extra days to spread the entire load of mulch just dumped on the driveway.

1. Make a new parking plan until the job is done. Allow some extra time for large projects, if the weather turns and it rains. Running a wheelbarrow over muddy soil contributes to compaction.

2. This is Halloween month. Plan for some fall color to add to the beds near the doors, fill some pots and containers, and even plant a larger window box. A great choice for this time of year is **ornamental cabbage** or **kale**. No plants exude more of the scary factor, and the leaf configuration and colors (there are several) only bring added magic to the landscape. Another plus for this choice is that these characters show no signs of actually being affected by early frosts.

3. Plan ahead for inevitable frost. Hanging baskets with **cardinal climbers** or **alyssums**, or containers of **euphorbia** and **periwinkle** would last longer if relocated near house or structure for protection.

Covering plants with fabric during the night and removing it in early morning helps to prolong life. It is not recommended that you use plastic. Plant flowers and leaves can stick to the plastic, due to the high humidity factor under this umbrella. If parts adhere, then removal of plastic makes for an ugly mess.

4. Take time to look up, flocks of blue jays are flying low to the ground. Step out at night and listen, maybe a chance to hear the katydid's song.

PLANTING

Toadflax and **pansies** are primed to be installed as mass plantings in concentrated areas. Plant in well prepared beds or in prepared containers.

This is the last call for any bedded out plants to be brought inside for the winter. The plants should be pulled up, the soil removed, and the plant washed entirely with a weak solution of dishwashing soap and water. Pot plants into clean containers with new plant starter, soilless potting mix. Be daring, and try bringing in some **snapdragons** and **petunias**.

Add a couple of inches of organic matter to vacated bed spaces. Work organic matter in until a good blend is made between the old and new.

Check for mature seedpods on plants. Select and gather for next year.

CARE

Depending on the location and exposure of plantings, frost or freeze-kill will most likely occur first to plants with softer fleshier stems. **Impatiens**, **petunias**, **cosmos**, **portulaca**, and **balsam** show signs of damage, with the tops having a strange, almost clear, appearance. **Perilla**, **French marigolds**, **morning glory vines**, and **blue sage** are much more resilient.

Frost killed plants are heaps of mush and not very fun to see or clean up. This can be avoided by removing the doomed-to-frost-damage plants before nightfall. Do so, without sacrificing too many of the end of the season flowers.

1. Take care of the vacated bed spaces. Cover with 1 to 2 inches of mulch to dress up the

area for the long winter, and to help the soil profile for next year's gardening.

2. Remove stakes, labels, and debris from the planting beds.

3. Do not leave any valued containers out in the weather. Mother Nature will try to break up anything exposed. Small hairline fractures this year are major cracks next year.

WATERING

Do not allow any planting to become drought stressed. The cool season **pansies**, **toadflax**, **ornamental cabbage**, **kale**, the cold-resistant **French marigolds**, and the **hyacinth bean** protected by the arbor all need 1 inch of water every seven to ten days.

FERTILIZING

Apply a seed starter type fertilizer to build up the roots of the cool season annuals. This increases the chances of survival through the winter.

PRUNING

Continue to deadhead any spent flowers on the cool season annuals. This will prolong the bloom cycle.

HELPFUL HINTS

If you are depositing annual plant material in compost areas, be sure to layer it with other materials to insure proper "cooking." A giant wad of one component will not cook down properly. The result is a heap of unusable, smelly stuff. On cooler days, you should notice steam rising from the pile. This indicates that the blending and resultant cooking are just right.

PESTS

Remove all plant debris. It harbors insect eggs and diseases during winter.

Have you seen weeds popping up? At this time of year, the herbicides are basically ineffective. So hand weeding, with a tool to pull out the entire root system, is the best control. Hand pulling simply gets the top, and makes the root system more aggressive. Check bed areas and containers that are still filled with soil.

Wildlife is sensing the impending cold. Chipmunks and voles are looking for nooks and crannies under the patio or front stoop. Squirrels are everywhere, busily planting, digging, and gnawing (essential, for the squirrel to keep lower teeth from getting to long). Deer are more than likely deep in the woods, where there is plenty to eat—be grateful.

NOTES

NOVEMBER

ANNUALS

PLANNING

1. Horticultural supply company catalogs are arriving daily. Dream away. How about a grow light cart for starting **cosmos, zinnia,** or **cockscomb** seeds, or those cuttings of **perilla** and **portulaca** brought in earlier? Or maybe just a new spade, or smaller grip pruners. . .

2. Take black-and-white photos of garden views and spaces in the garden, from inside and out. Off-season black-and-white shots are a great indication of design specifics, such as hidden views, bends and turns, and focal points. Then get out the color prints and do an informal overlay. This is very revealing and is a tremendous help in making garden decisions.

3. Garden centers, botanical gardens, city or county parks, and extension services, may be offering classes. Maybe you could take a class on the construction of trellises or arbors.

4. Garden club meetings generally have a slide presentation each month, and provide great company, fun, and discussions.

5. Keep an eye on the birdbath. If it is frozen, change the water, or consider purchasing a warmer. The benefits reaped will far exceed any work or cost that is involved.

PLANTING

All salvageable annuals are safely nestled indoors, though the urge to get dirty may still be there. Experiment, if room is available under the lights, and fill a few cell packs sowing some leftover seeds from this past season. Use this for a learning experience; watch as they germinate, and continue growing until succumbing to the rites of winter.

Clean up the digging, soil preparation, and transplanting tools, and sharpen blades. Give all a light oiling to minimize rust. Do an inventory for future projects.

CARE

Find a very bright spot in the basement, in front of a sliding glass door, or a greenhouse window. Daylight hours are shortening, so expect all the freshly repotted **geraniums**, **coleus**, **alyssums**, and other transplants to lose some foliage and bend towards the brightest light. Have the homemade grow light table set and ready, because these plants will decline as the daylight length shortens.

Check for any changes in bed surface drainage patterns, paying particular attention to any newly created beds. Settling, shifting, or maybe even the family dog has taken a new path to the back fence directly across the area, making a nice trail. Do any re-grading necessary.

Work backward out of beds, to prevent soil from being compacted. This, plus the depressions created where the water accumulates, may cause trouble. A few extra minutes, here and there, could mean a big difference during the busier months.

Get all of your containers cleaned, stored, or at least brought into protection, to reduce weather impact with snow, ice storm rains, and temperature fluctuations caused by warm days and frigid nights. A small hairline crack now could be fatal after the freeze-thaw cycle.

WATERING

Disconnect and store hoses. Elevate one end while coiling, to force the water to drain, and then tie it up for easy storage. Place indoors out of the weather. Plastic and rubber breaks down readily by nature.

Keep a hose available, just in case the **pansies** need a drink midwinter.

FERTILIZING

Inventory the types and amounts of any remaining fertilizer. Make sure fertilizers are kept dry, and that moisture will not come in contact with the bag. Consider the plant performance when a specific product was applied. Consult your records to decide if a change needs to be made for next year. Garden centers may have stock reduction sales as tax time is nearing.

If a hose end attachment was used for fertilizer application during the growing season, clean it thoroughly. Fertilizers have a salt base that clogs orifices. This makes the correct calibration impossible. Soak the spray head, and use a piece of wire to clear openings. Flush with clear water

HELPFUL HINTS

Pansies that are lying flat on the ground in the early morning hours, as if dead, are simply responding to a mechanism to reduce moisture loss. This enables the plant to recover as the temperatures warm above the lower 30s. Plants in pots or containers have little insulation and may die, rather than making a rebound.

PRUNING

Deadhead **pansies** and **toadflax** to keep them flowering. Pinch back or prune cuttings under grow lights. Do not allow the upper leaves to overshadow the lower foliage. It may be necessary to reduce the actual leaf size by cutting a portion off. This puts less strain on the developing root system.

PESTS

Hand weed, but be sure to get the entire root system. Cooler weather makes herbicides ineffective. Although you may have checked earlier when you brought cuttings indoors, go over each cutting closely, and if any problems are observed, determine what should be done. Unless minimal action is necessary, discard the cutting.

NOTES

DECEMBER

ANNUALS

PLANNING

December is a good month to research, to learn, and to dream.

1. The new seed catalogs are in the mail. Some are advertising the new plants for next year. If you are interested, better order now, as quantities may be limited. If you can, delay delivery to minimize the time you have to store seeds. Upon arrival, inspect products for quantity and appearance. If you have any questions, call the seed company.

2. Maybe a multi-tiered mobile flora cart would be worth checking into. The ultimate dream is a small, attached greenhouse offering a respite, a learning facility, and for just plain fun. Imagine **ageratums**, **periwinkles**, and **euphorbia** plants within reach. Contact a local franchised dealer or contractor, with experience in construction of greenhouses, and have an evaluation for plumbing, electrical, and other greenhouse essentials.

3. Take stock of anything plant related to make sure all is prepared for winter. Is the compost pile steaming? Does the rototiller need the oil changed and the motor winterized? Was the irrigation system winterized?

4. Make one more sweep through the garden. Remove anything that looks out of place, such as debris, stakes, ties, and supports.

5. Check all birdfeeders and baths. Keep them full and available for winter visitors.

The national catalogs offer entire annual gardens, delivered to your door next spring. A universal garden that works for everyone is hard to find, so consider carefully before you buy. The pre-packaged garden could be the springboard to greater heights. Consider and decide carefully where it fits in with your plan, what the delivery date is, and in what form the plants are delivered (bareroot or cell pack). Call the vendor and ask questions before you buy.

PLANTING

Take time out for the holidays this month. Nothing should need potting or transplanting. Allow anything growing to become rootbound (strong roots make healthy plants).

CARE

Potted **red fountain grass** and **geranium** plants should start to show a little growth. Rotate any plants sitting in front of windows or on the windowsills. This keeps the growth even and gives equal light to the plant. Do not allow foliage to press against the window, as it could freeze.

WATERING

Only plants growing indoors need attention. Potting soil should be damp and moist to the touch, but not dripping.

If the tip of the foliage dries out, the cause may be the alkalinity of the water. Short of filtration, your best defense is to have buckets of water sitting out, allowing some of the chlorine gas to dissipate. Use that water for your plants.

FERTILIZING

Consider starting a vermicompost bin, a self-contained, plastic bin with red wiggler worms. You can use the bin for many types of kitchen waste and garbage. The worms will turn the scraps into some of the best compost around. All of your annuals will benefit from this odor-free composting factory. Keep it right in the kitchen pantry or in the basement.

PRUNING

Do not allow any plant to stretch or elongate. Pinch back as much as one-half of the entire length. The next day, if the seedling has not recovered, get rid of it.

PESTS

Gnats and tiny whiteflies are likely to appear. Install yellow sticky tape nearby. You may see tiny spider webs between the stem and leaf. This is mite webbing. Wash plants with soap and water or a safer soap product.

Regardless of the type of pest or disease, each related chemical has a shelf life. Keep track of expiration dates, and do not apply anything past its shelf life. Additionally, proper storage is crucial, as the chemistry of the product may be altered during the course of cold and freezing weather. If a chemical is frozen, settling occurs.

If any fertilizers, pesticides, or fungicides require disposal, contact the State Department of Natural Resources, or the County Extension office for disposal procedures and locations of hazardous waste facilities. Do not throw bottles, bags, or cans into the trashcan or dumpster.

HELPFUL HINTS

Houses are very dry this time of year because the furnaces and heat sources dry the air. Keeping the humidity up, by having plants indoors, is clearly to everyone's benefit.

NOTES

CHAPTER TWO

BULBS

Colorful, versatile, fragrant, and flavorful, bulbs are a hugely diverse palette from which to plant and grow ideas. Dramatic and dynamic distinctions are everyday qualities that make having bulbs easy and fun.

Bulb success is easily achieved and enjoyed by everyone. If you are interested in a formal or informal pattern (like clustered or scattered), having a garden indoors or out, bulbs can fill just about any idea, situation, and location. Maturing to heights of a few inches to several feet, bulbs can be thin to almost invisible, to huge and unforgettable. Words can't describe the impact.

Some bulbs for all seasons: earliest spring white flowering snowdrops; spectrum wide fringe tulips with grape hyacinth; summertime pink magic with surprise lilies; colorful cutting gladiolas; fall miniature and pink hardy cyclamen edging; 6-foot-high multi-color dahlia displays; autumn (saffron) crocus; wintertime radiant red amaryllis (indoors); or blue hyacinth sitting atop forcing glass (special goblet-narrowed middle). Bulbs can carry family history, such as an iris (flag) from great grandmother's yard. On the opposite end of this, new varieties are quite a process from testing fields to your retail garden center—up to 15 years. Some unusual ways used for development are exposure to X-rays, nitrous oxide, or using aphids to inject a gene altering virus.

TYPES OF BULBS

"Bulb" is an all encompassing term which stretches and includes plants from A-*Allium* (onions) to Z-*Zante deschia* (calla lily) and includes Kansas's native Turk cap lily, and Jack in the pulpit. Take full advantage of your bulb interest. There are 5 major categories each with unique characteristics and varying cultural requirements. Obvious physical differences will mean unique growth processes, leaves, stems, and flower impact.

BULB CATEGORIES

- True bulb: amaryllis, daffodils, tulips and lilies—miniature plant enclosed by modified leaves
- Corms: crocus, gladiolas, and freesias—storage stems, growth points (eyes) on top, tunic (paper thin covering) and basal plate
- Tubers: winter aconite, cyclamen, caladiums, ranunculus—swollen stems with growth eyes or points all over, no tunic or basal plate
- Tuberous roots: dahlia, tuberous begonia—swollen root, new growth at base of last year's stem
- Rhizomes: canna, lily of the valley, agapanthus, flags (iris)—thickened branching roots growing at or on the surface

DESIGNING, USAGE AND TIPS

- Siting: sun/shade exposure—spring bulbs need 4 to 6 weeks of strong sunlight to restore energy for next year, sunlight length and time of day can impact both hardy and tropicals; afternoon shade could extend bloom period but may cause stems to flop.
- Check immediate backdrop (display qualities) and surroundings (tree root competition). Delineate bed (landscape paint), or determine individual locations (flag).

• Smaller garden/beds/containers cluster bulbs, limiting quantity and colors.

• Underplant spring bulbs with summer annuals reducing impact of browning foliage.

• Mix varieties (with pots or close proximity)—only if compatible care/maintenance.

• Bulb selecting—hand pick, selecting the largest and firmest. Avoid bruises, extreme fungus, and sprouting. Over the phone or internet ask size, shipment time, and planting instructions.

BULBS WITH GOOD BLOOMS OR GREAT FOLIAGE

• Late Winter—winter aconite, snowdrops, harmony iris, lily of the field, dwarf iris

• Early Spring—crocus, glory of snow, Peeping Tom daffodil, Red Riding Hood and Emperor tulip

• Mid Spring—snowflake, fritillaria, grape hyacinth, oxblood tulip, lily leek

• Early Summer—giant purple onion, king's spear, caladium*, chives, summer snowflake

• Mid Summer—canna*, elephant ear*, gladiola*, lily, surprise lily

• Early Fall—autumn crocus, dahlia, fire of Eden, hardy cyclamen, wandflower*

• Winter indoor forcing—ice follies daffodil, apricot beauty triumph tulip, delft blue hyacinth

*Not Hardy

STORAGE

• Never wash

• Lay out on newspaper for 7 to 10 days to determine health, smell (for damp moldiness), look for black spots—anything suspicious get rid of it—contamination occurs quickly.

• Place in paper bag or cardboard box, with newspaper or styrofoam peanuts between. Set in dark, cool, dry spot. Do not use a plastic bag which facilitates moisture development.

PLANTING POINTS

Water growing area (soil or potting mix) before planting and after installation to get rid of air pockets. Prevent contact if multiple bulbs are placed in close proximity, preventing rot.

Direct contact with granular fertilizer can burn/damage bulbs. Use water mixture and drench soil. An option: spread fertilizer over the area prior to installation. Use 2 1/2 pounds of balanced, complete fertilizer per 100 square feet. After planting, apply 1 to 2 inches of mulch.

CONTAINERS FOR WINTER AND SUMMER

For winter-forcing (hardy or tropical) use at least a 6-inch container, fill with well-drained potting mix, place bulb mid point, backfill, firm soil and water, keep cool (approx. 40 degrees Fahrenheit) 8 to 10 weeks, remove, water, place pot in sunny window.

Use pot a minimum size of 15 inches with drainage holes for summer containers. Use potting mix (light, well drained), and an optional addition of water absorbing polymer gel and slow release fertilizer.

Plant at same depth it was in the ground. Water when gap appears between potting mix and side of pot.

PLANTING IN THE GROUND

• Blend amendments (see glossary) with existing soil creating a well drained raised bed.

• Do not use manure as an amendment; this causes bacteria and disease.

• Keep soil pH 6.0 and 7.0, slightly acidic to neutral for best results.

• Do not routinely add bonemeal; use soil test results as a guideline.

HELPFUL HINTS

Maximizing Bloom Sequence with Hardy Spring Bulbs

To create a blooming sequence, plant the same variety in varied exposures—north, south, east and west. Soil temperatures trigger the growth, and each direction offers different amounts of sunlight.

- Be aware of the background and viewing distance when making planting decisions.
- A white-sided house overwhelms pink and pale yellow.
- Blue, purple, and lavender are lost if too far away.
- Test the area with smaller pots of annuals (the annual colors matching the prospective bulbs) and make adjustments. A little time, thought, and effort are well worth it.

Common Name	Botanical Name	Color
Late Winter		
Winter aconite	*Eranthis hyemalis*	yellow
Snowdrops	*Galanthus nivalis*	white
Harmony iris	*Iris reticulata*	violet
Lily of the field	*Anemone blanda*	mixed
Dwarf iris	*Iris* Danfordiae	yellow
Early Spring		
Crocus	*Crocus*	mixed colors
Glory of the snow	*Chionodoxa lucilae*	blue
Peeping Tom daffodil	*Narcissus cyclamineus*	yellow
Red Riding Hood tulip	*Tulipa* Greggii	red
White emperor tulip	*Tulipa* Fosteriana	white
Mid-Spring		
Snowflake	*Leucojum aestivum*	white
Crown imperial	*Frittilaria imperalis*	red/oranges
Grape hyacinth	*Muscari armaniacum*	blue
Oxblood tulip	*Tulipa* Darwin	red
Lily leek	*Allium* Molly	yellow
Late Spring		
Giant thunder ball	*Allium giganteum*	purple
Kings spear-fox tail lily	*Eremurus spectablis*	yellow
Chives	*Allium oreophilum*	lavender
Summer snowflake	*Ornithogalum umbellatum*	white

• Installation time for fall planting is when soil temperature (use soil thermometer) is below 60 degrees Fahrenheit, usually after a hard frost. Warmer soil causes premature sprouting reducing flower potential.

• Planting depth for true bulbs, corms, and tubers is three times the bulb diameter. Place tuberous roots with previous year's stem at surface, dangling roots lowered into hole, and rhizomes at or just below the surface.

CARE AND MAINTENANCE

• 1 inch of water per week.

• Fertilize year round with balanced fertilizer (ratio 1-1-1, i.e. 10-10-10).

• Poor blooming can be due to improper siting, aging bulbs, or incorrect or inadequate nutrient level.

• Cut all spent (wilting) flowers as soon as possible to reduce stress and keep bulb vigorous.

• Hardy bulb foliage should be left on bulb until at least 1/2 brown, but is better left until completely dead.

• DO NOT bend, rubber band, or braid leaves, as this reduces strength.

• Remove dying flowers.

• Mulching 1 to 2 inches only prevents problematic moisture retention.

PESTS AND DISEASES

• Recently planted bulbs are prime targets for squirrels. Lay chicken wire over area and cover with mulch.

• Daffodils are poisonous, so wildlife will not disturb them.

• Aphids are the most problematic on dahlias, gladiolas, iris, and lilies (causing mosaic, blotchy foliage).

• Botrytis Disease (causing spotting, slimy leaf or flower, gray fuzzy mold, or black spots on bulb) effects dahlias, hyacinths, tulips, daffodils.

BEYOND SPRINGTIME

There are a wide array of possibilities for summer and fall.

• Gladiolas: planting depth and spacing is 3 to 5 inches; extend bloom sequence by planting new bulbs every two weeks. For cut flowers, time new plantings as the first flower opens. Flowers can be damaged by insecticides. The largest bulb, with two flower stalks, is the hardy *Gladiola byzantinus*.

• Lilies: pollen can stain; allow them to dry and brush them off. Try species *Lillium aurelian*, *L. auratum* and *L. candidum* for fragrance, 'Rubrum' has the largest flowers, tiger reflex petals with black dots. The earliest bloomers are 'Chinook', 'Enchantment', and 'Connecticut King'. When planting, tilt bulb at a 45 degree angle—reducing water collecting potential. Remove stem bulb-ette (small dark ball stem/leaf intersection), leave 2/3 stem when cutting back. Several varieties are eaten in Japan. Candidum pollen is an essential oil in perfume. These bulbs are appealing to voles and chipmunks. Roll in sulfur prior to planting.

• Dahlias: there are more than ten varieties, categorized by size and flower petals. They grow best in a vegetable garden with soil 1 inch deep. When planting, lay dangling roots on their side in a hole 7 inches deep. Backfill hole as plant grows; leave a 1-inch depression around the stem to collect water.

JANUARY
BULBS

PLANNING

Prepare for the spring bloom and for summer purchases. Review your journal notes and garden photographs, and create a list of bulb plusses and minuses.

Plan your continuous bulb blooms depending on the varying flowering times. Smaller bulbs, such as **crocus** and **snowflakes**, come into bloom sooner than **tulips** or **daffodils**.

Explore newly arrived seed at the garden centers for **toadflax**, **lettuce**, or other cool season annuals or vegetables to plant over the bulbs. This gives a bed of **snowdrops** a completely new look. Or how about combining autumn **crocus** and **thyme** into one planting?

Read seed catalogs. They are encyclopedias of statistics, facts, and figures. Investigate recommendations for the upcoming potting of **canna** bulbs. Information should tell you how to get a head start indoors, under grow lights, for the May planting season.

Visit horticultural supply companies to update your tools, and to acquire new "toys." If you are tired of the homemade workbench converted to a light table, consider a manufactured flora grow light cart on wheels. Check out a motion detector/water spray for those overly friendly pets doing their own cultivation during the summer in the **caladium** and **gladiola** beds.

Formal design is based upon straight lines or specific patterns of bulbs, such as linear **tulips** that mimic architectural features. Use larger numbers of fewer varieties, with the same or sequential bloom periods. Minimize the spacing to accent the difference in colors, heights, and the varied frilliness of flowers.

Informal design allows greater freedom for the use of smaller growing bulbs, such as **grape hyacinth**, and has fewer limitations. Some guidelines are helpful. Plant no less than five of the same type in close proximity. Select bulbs to extend the bloom sequence. Plant some new varieties each year.

Mixing heights, from front-to-back and from side-to-side, gives a roller-coaster of visual activity. It allows for riots of colors and types. Scatter clusters of **lily** bulbs among annuals, perennials, and ground covers for backing. Plant **winter aconite** near shrubs or trees to provide a setting. Minimize colors and varieties in smaller planting spaces to prevent overstimulation and chaos.

PLANTING

Bulbs you have dug from the garden to overwinter or bulbs planted for forcing are new plants. Use only clean, new, potting soil. Clean up the bulb thoroughly after digging. Make sure pots are clean. Monitor the soil surface on a regular basis for fungus gnats.

You may find some good, firm **Gregii tulips**. This gem has great red striped leaves in addition to a flower. Bulbs may be available that could be potted up for forcing or on a warm day, planted in the garden. Look for **bearded iris** and **amaryllis**.

Do not transplant **amaryllis** or **cyclamen** (when they have finished blooming) in larger pots, regardless of how potbound they appear. The tighter the pot, the better the performance. If the bulb begins to push itself out of the pot, then transplant up a size, but the pot should be no more than 1 inch larger than the one previously used.

CARE

Continue to bring out pots of bulbs you are forcing, and place in bright windows. Don't place pots in the direct path of the furnace heat.

Warmer days during the winter may stimulate the foliage growth of many different hardy bulbs, in particular ones planted in more protected locations. There is no need to take any action. This early growth usually results in the tips of the leaves being winter burnt as the cold weather returns. This burn will not impact the flowering cycle.

WATERING

Keep all bulbs indoors damp, but do not allow water to sit in the saucer.

FERTILIZING

Apply fertilizer at one-half the recommended rate. Use a water-soluble (ratio 1-1-1) fertilizer every two weeks while actively growing.

PRUNING

Cut off any browning foliage, as close to the bulb as possible, to reduce potential disease problems. Do not remove any healthy leaves.

HELPFUL HINTS

Paper-white **narcissus** flopping over just before the flowers open is a natural habit, and it will be more pronounced if the pot is sitting in lower light. The only recourse is to plant the bulbs in a taller pot, with sides that brace the foliage. When **narcissus** are finished flowering, discard the bulbs. They will not perform again.

Prune and remove flowers as the bloom cycle is finished on forced bulbs.

PESTS

Check all plants indoors for any fungus gnats flying around the pots or in the potting soil. Use a combination of insecticidal soap and yellow sticky traps to monitor and to control.

Outdoors, the **magic lilies** and many other bulbs are very attractive meals for hungry squirrels. They find the plantings by simply looking for the most recently cultivated areas. Remember that it was only five or six weeks ago when the bulb planting was finished. Consider laying chicken wire on the top of the ground and then covering it with mulch (only 1 to 2 inches) to deter digging animals.

Check on all bulbs that are being stored for the wintertime. Make sure there is no foul odor (damp moldiness), and look for black spots. If anything looks suspicious, get rid of the bulb. Lay out any others to dry that may have been in contact with the discarded one.

Use caution when selecting **dahlias**, **hyacinths**, **tulips**, and **daffodil** bulbs. Make sure there are no black spots. This could be botrytis (disease). It causes spotted foliage or flowers, slimy or fuzzy (moldy) leaves and petals. Once infected, there is no cure. If bulbs are planted and show these signs, dig them up and discard. Do not plant a similar variety in that location.

If you have wildlife troubles, try hanging deodorant bath soap from the trees. Or completely surround the bed with fishing line, placed 3 to 4 feet high, to deter deer. (Also see Helpful Hints in September and November for more information.)

FEBRUARY

BULBS

PLANNING

If you missed the bulb forcing in December and January, garden centers have a full array of hardy and tropical bulbs sitting and ready to go.

Ask the garden center staff when the **dahlias** and the **elephant ear** bulbs are expected in. They probably have a listing available to see what new cultivars will be available.

Begin to finalize the planting design for summer. Make use of the new varieties of **cannas** to soften and embrace the area around the patio. Or consider that eye-catching white with green veined **caladium** to act as natural landscape lighting in the densely shaded front yard. **Elephant ears** work well making the transition from the front to side yard. Mix in some **dahlias** in the vegetable garden for a real kick.

Pansies and **toadflax** are great companion plants for any bulb grouping, check with the garden center for availability.

Take photographs and notes on the earliest bulbs, **winter aconite** and **snowdrops**.

PLANTING

Get an early start on bed renovation or on the new planting area. The early start allows for the soil to settle before the tropical and nonhardy bulbs are installed.

The sequence: Ready a garden space, purchase the bulbs, and install the bulbs. See Helpful Hints for the S.O.I.L.S. Method of readying your space.

Do not transplant **amaryllis** or **cyclamen** into larger pots, even if they are potbound. They seem to flower more if they are potbound. If the bulb is trying to push its way out of the pot, then transplant, but move the plant into a pot that is just 1 inch larger in diameter and depth than the pot it is currently in.

Install any **autumn crocus**, **crocus**, **daffodils**, or other overlooked hardy bulbs (if firm and healthy). You may not see any flowering this year, but the longer it is in the ground, the better the chance it has to build strength with foliage growth for next year.

If you notice the bulb foliage growing and healthy, but there are no flowers, as foliage begins to brown, dig up the bulbs. If they appear undersized, then discard them. If they are full size and healthy, it is time to divide them. Carefully pull the bulbs apart, replant in prepared sites or beds, water in, and apply a balanced fertilizer at one-half the label recommendation.

CARE

Warmer days during the winter may stimulate the foliage growth of many different hardy bulbs, in particular ones that are planted in more protected locations. The tips of the leaves may burn from the cold evening temperatures. There is no need to clean the plant, and this burn will not affect the flowering cycle.

Spring bulb flowers and buds are not affected by cold temperatures, so there is no need to cover them with landscape fabric, plastic, or mulch. This action could do more harm than good, as added moisture or false warm pockets may stimulate more growth that cannot be supported due to lack of sunlight.

When adding a thin protective layer of mulch (less than 1 inch), do not pitch it randomly over the tops of the growing bulbs. The mulch could collect in the foliage, hold on to moisture, thereby increasing the potential for rot. Place the mulch carefully around the plants.

WATERING

Prevent drought stress. Monitor the amount of rainfall during the emergence of foliage. Supply the plants with a minimum of 1 inch of water every ten days.

Do not allow potting soil of the indoor bulbs to dry out. This can shorten the bloom period.

FERTILIZING

Hardy bulbs benefit from a monthly fertilizing with a balanced food.

PRUNING

To reduce potential disease problems, clean off any browning foliage as close to the bulb as possible, but do not remove any healthy leaves.

Prune and remove the flowers as the bloom cycle is finished on all bulbs forced indoors.

PESTS

Tulips, along with many other bulbs, are very attractive to wildlife and are dug up or the leaves eaten. Controlling the critters is difficult. For deer, try hanging deodorant bath soap from the trees. Surround the area with fishing line at 3 to 4 feet high. (See Helpful Hints in September and November for more information.)

HELPFUL HINTS

The S.O.I.L.S. Method

S – Scope of the area. Perform a site evaluation.
- Check all aspects of the site, both natural and manmade. Project the impact the bed has on the entire area.

O – Order in which to tackle the job.
- The sequence of events is: delineate area, take a soil sample, control existing plantings, prepare the site, purchase, install, and stabilize the plants.

I – Intermingle and blend amendments to build the earth.
- Methods and tools are rototilling or spading at four separate times.
- Amendments are organic (leaf mold, compost, peat moss, topsoil) and inorganic (sand, gravel).
- Amount of amendments to use is approximately 2 cubic yards per 100 sq. ft.
- Grade change after amending will elevate the area by 6 inches, creating positive drainage.

L – Liveliness is determined by the health of the bulbs.
- Check bulbs carefully for consistency in shape, the color of the bulb, and the smell of the bulb.
- Installation time warrants another check. Dig the hole. Shake the bulb to remove any loose parts. Check the condition of the bulb if it was stored, place it in hole, and backfill.

S – Safeguard your planting to get it through the planting and establishment transition.
- Water the bed immediately, and check water needs on a daily basis.
- Fertilize lightly with a water-soluble fertilizer.
- Apply mulch at 1 to 2 inches deep.

NOTES

MARCH

BULBS

PLANNING

Spend some time visiting government buildings, botanical gardens, and parks with notepad in hand. This is the beginning of the sixty-day peak bloom season. There are new varieties, combinations, and planted sites that offer great possibilities for next year's fall planting.

Take photographs and notes as the earliest bulbs, **winter aconite** and **snowdrops**, are finishing. Get ready to record the next sequence of **hyacinths**, **tulips**, and other midseason bloomers.

New arrivals of summer bulbs are at the garden centers or coming through the mail. Compile your planning list to prepare and include pots (large ones for the **elephant ears**), potting soil, amendments for the **canna**, stakes for dinner plate **dahlias**, growing lights, bottom heat, and space in a sunny window. This preparation applies regardless of the final location. You will want to get a head start on summer and pot them up early to break bulb dormancy.

PLANTING

After bulbs forced indoors complete their bloom cycle (**crocus**, **daffodil**, **hyacinths**, **grape hyacinth**, and **tulips**), move them outdoors.

Soil preparation is essential for bed renovation or new bed creation. Not only do the bulbs put on a great show, but also healthy soils reduce the likelihood of environmental problems such as effects from weather patterns, insect infestation, and soilborne diseases. Create a raised bed space by adding almost 2 cubic feet of organic material (compost, peat moss, leaf mold). Shovel or rototill in amendments to blend with existing soil.

CARE

Continue to bring pots of forced bulbs out and place in bright windows, but not in a direct path of furnace heat. Flowering time varies according to the bulb type. Continually monitor the soil surface for any signs of insects, mold, and mildew.

Place mulch carefully in beds of bulbs, being careful not to cover the leaves.

Check bulbs in storage at least every two weeks for any dampness, mold, or black spots. Toss any suspect bulbs, take the others out of storage, and lay them out to dry, then repack.

WATERING

Prevent drought stress. Monitor the amount of rainfall. As soon as you see the emergence of foliage, supplement rainfall to give the bulbs a minimum of 1 inch of water, every ten days. Continue with regular watering throughout the growing season.

Do not allow indoor bulb potting soil to dry out. This shortens the bloom period.

FERTILIZING

Hardy bulbs benefit from monthly fertilizing with a balanced food.

PRUNING

Remove flowers as soon as you see the first signs of the petals browning. You want to avoid seed formation; the seeds are not viable and the process drains the nutrients from the bulb.

When cutting the browning foliage on tropical and non-hardy bulbs, cut the foliage down as close to the bulb as possible. This reduces potential disease problems. Do not remove any healthy leaves.

Unless absolutely necessary, allow all the brown foliage on hardy bulbs to remain until completely brown. Hardy bulbs benefit from holding onto their leaves while they store energy for next year. If you don't like all that brown foliage, plant the bed with annuals to mask the fading leaves.

PESTS

Tulips, along with many other bulbs, are very attractive to wildlife that dig them up or eat the leaves. Use controls and barriers as listed in Helpful Hints in the September and November calendar.

Check the surface of potted plants for gray mold and fungus gnats. Control both with repeated applications of insecticidal soap, and soil drenches of Neem (organic pesticide).

HELPFUL HINTS

Make the most of your **caladium**. Purchase the largest bulbs possible. A few days before the scheduled planting, remove the growing tip gently (it looks just like a potato eye). Simply snap it off or carefully cut it out. Allow the bulb to sit (unplanted) for a few days so the open wound heals and calluses over. Then plant the bulb. This increases the number of leaves and stems that grow from each bulb.

NOTES

BULBS

PLANNING

It is mid-season and time to survey the landscape and evaluate the plantings. Pull out last year's photographs and notes of specific areas and bulb varieties. Evaluate the performance level this year as it compares to last year. Consider that new hybrids (fringed **tulips**, super-sized **crocus**, new shades of pink **daffodils**) with new characteristics sometimes have shortened lifespans.

The best way to gather wisdom and minimize gardening pitfalls is to look out the window or to take a walk in the garden. The information and understanding gained through personal observations are your best indicators of what and when things should be done. Add a dash of common sense and you net the best use of your time, while still obtaining the most results.

A conundrum exists if **crocus** were planted in lawn areas. The lawn may need mowing but the **crocus** foliage needs several more weeks of exposure to the sun. Next year, plan to move all bulbs out of the lawn.

Check out bed spaces where **snowflakes**, **grape hyacinths**, **glory of the snow**, **magic lilies**, and **autumn crocus** are growing. Plan on trying some new varieties, moving some of the old ones around, and mingling them in different combinations with other perennials, annuals, and groundcovers.

PLANTING

Tulips, **daffodils**, **hyacinths**, and other hardy bulbs that have been purchased already potted are fine in the soil they come with. However, when planting outdoors in the garden, shake all the potting soil off completely, and then plant the bulb into regular garden soil. Potting mixes do not hold their soil structure in the outdoors.

When dividing clumps of hardy bulbs, it's best to wait until after the leaves have turned brown, but are still attached to bulb. The brown leaves help you determine the perimeter of the bulb colony. Dig deeply, completely around entire colony. Lift the bulbs, root mass and all, with a prying action. This is best done with a digging fork, as there is less chance of slicing multiple bulbs. Lay the clump on ground and shake it until the bulbs are exposed. Remove and discard any damaged bulbs. Select the largest for planting in visually high impact locations, place the smaller ones in other areas (see Planning for tips).

For a jump on summer planting and growth, pot up tropical and non-hardy bulbs indoors. Consider **giant purple onion**, **gladiolus**, **caladium**, **king's spear**, **chives**, and **summer snowflake**. Use bottom heat to speed up the dormancy breaking process. Do not set outdoors until the air temperatures remain in the upper 70s.

CARE

If adding mulch (less than 1 inch), do not pitch it randomly over growing bulbs. The mulch could collect in the foliage and increase the moisture on leaves, creating a potential rot situation.

Warmer days stimulate the foliage growth of many hardy bulbs, particularly those planted in protected locations. Just ignore the growth. At this stage of the season, the foliage will burn with the return of frosty nights. This doesn't affect the bloom period.

WATERING

Water all areas involved with planting, transplanting, and dividing activities a day ahead of time. Working with a moist soil (not soggy) minimizes root damage to established plants and reduces air pockets for new plantings.

Water all hardy bulbs if they are dry, through the entire growing season, until the leaves are brown.

FERTILIZING

Although they may be totally disappearing, **winter aconite**, **snowflakes**, **snowdrops**, **glory of the snow**, **crocus**, **tulips**, and **daffodils** all benefit from an application of a balanced food (use a granular type and water it in), and of course, watering during dry spells.

PRUNING

Remove all flowers at the first signs of the petals browning. This reduces strain on the bulb and encourages bloom season after season.

HELPFUL HINTS

Always read the label on any chemical weed control product. Many bulbs are monocots, and close relatives to lawns and grassy weeds. If the label says the formulation kills grass, your bulbs may be susceptible as well.

Foliage on hardy bulbs should remain, unfolded or twisted, until at least until fifty percent are brown. The leaves add energy for next year.

PESTS

Watch your bulbs you are forcing for signs of botrytis (spotting on the leaf or slime on the leaf surface). Susceptible bulbs are **dahlias**, **hyacinths**, **tulips**, and **daffodils**.

If you notice that the foliage in the background of the bulb planting looks as if someone took a pruning shear and made a perfect 45-degree angle cut, these cuts are a rabbit's winter gnawing.

Expect your bulb foliage to disappear quickly as rabbit young are born. Protect the susceptible bulbs by surrounding them with chicken wire, and keep your fingers crossed for good luck.

NOTES

BULBS

 PLANNING

Plans are made as spring blooming bulbs give way to the summer varieties. The key word here is flexibility. Be realistic and understand that the grandest plans envisioned are not etched in concrete. Our weather is very unpredictable from hour to hour, day to day, let alone month to month. Additionally, in the same yard, a northern exposure could be entirely different from a southern one. This impacts the temperature, moisture, and wind speed, that in turn relates to removal of mulch, application of fertilizer, and pesticide reaction. A miscalculation could harm various plant parts, ranging from stems, buds, leaves, or even the entire plant.

Purchase or order **autumn crocus** bulbs and other late summer, early fall bloomers in late spring for timely arrival.

Consider the **iris** hybrids that need so little care to fill in any bare sunny spots that pop up in the landscape. Newly purchased plants can be dumped out of the pot and tossed into the garden. Incredible colors arise.

Check out the emerging foliage of the **giant flowering onion**. It looks like a gray-green star in the garden with a spear shooting from the middle. Watch the **magic lily** foliage disappear into crispy brownness.

 PLANTING

Provide evenly moist, rich, organic, fertile soil to produce best results with bulbs.

Divide clumps of any hardy midseason **tulips**, **snowflakes**, or late season **daffodils** after leaves have turned brown but are still attached to bulb. Dig deeply and completely around the entire colony, and lift with prying action. Lay the clump on ground and shake it until bulbs are exposed. Discard any damaged bulbs. Select the largest bulbs for planting in high impact locations. Use the smaller in other areas.

For planting summer bulbs:

Water the area thoroughly a few days before installing bulbs.

For placement under trees, measure the trunk diameter and multiply by 5. Do not install bulbs any closer to tree than this distance.

Site **caladium** in afternoon shade to minimize leaf scorch.

To plant **canna** in a container, select a pot with no less than a 20-inch diameter. Use a well drained potting mix, place bulbs one-third of way into pot, back fill, firm soil and water thoroughly.

Dahlias require a rich organic soil to a minimum depth of 1 inch, and a nutrient level similar to a vegetable garden. However, an overly rich soil results in lots of leaves and no flowers. Lay the tuberous root on its side in the hole. Plant tuber 7 inches deep, cover partially with 2 inches of soil. As the bulb grows, continue to add 2 inches of soil at a time until the hole is filled in.

Elephant ear requires a rich, organic, fertile soil ranging from well drained to standing water of a few inches. Place bulb on its side in the bottom of a pot or hole, back fill, firm soil, water thoroughly, and add 1 to 2 inches of mulch.

All tropical bulbs should be planted in containers a minimum of 12 inches in diameter. Use well drained potting mix, place bulbs one-third of way into pot, back fill, firm soil, and water thoroughly.

Amaryllis and **cyclamen** can be grown for their foliage at this time. Move the pots outside if temperatures are in the 70s.

Cannas, **caladiums**, and **gladiolas** potted up a few months ago can be moved into pots for the deck and patio or into the garden to provide real impact. Do not move outdoors until daytime temperatures reach the 70s.

 CARE

Site **canna** in afternoon shade to extend the length of bloom, but if the area is too shady, taller varieties will lean or flop over.

Stagger plantings of **gladiolas** at intervals of fourteen days to have continuous blooms throughout the summer. Do not plant after mid-July. Siting where there is afternoon shade extends the length of bloom. **Glads** need staking unless they are a miniature variety.

Taller varieties of **lilies** may need staking if they are planted in an area with dense shade. Normally, if the bulbs have adequate light, staking is not a concern.

Use care when adding mulch (less than 1 inch). Mulch collecting on the foliage can lead to standing water, rot, and decay.

If **cyclamen** appear to be actively growing, with new leaves emerging from the top of the bulb, then new growth suddenly wilts and flowers droop, DO NOT water. This is the regular life cycle. A period of dormancy of three or more months is advised, then begin watering and fertilizing the **cyclamen**.

WATERING

Water all areas involved with planting, transplanting, and dividing a day ahead of working the soil. This minimizes root damage to established plants and reduces air pockets for the new plantings.

HELPFUL HINTS

When using **dahlias** as cut flowers, dip the end of stem in boiling water for a few seconds to increase longevity. To increase your enjoyment time, cut **gladiolas** when the first flower opens along the flower stalk.

FERTILIZING

Iris requires a lower analysis fertilizer than other crops, so adjust your type of fertilizer and application process to accommodate different plant needs.

PRUNING

To keep bulbs producing annually, remove all flowers as soon as you see the first signs of browning petals. Seedpod formation is draining to the bulbs and the seeds produced are not viable.

Much of the foliage to emerge from **cannas**, **caladiums**, **dahlias**, **gladiolas** and **elephant ears** will be undersized. Allow this foliage to remain until entirely brown and then remove with sharp pruners or garden scissors.

Cut spent flower stalks as near to foliage as possible on earlier blooming **iris**.

When cutting **gladiola** flowers, allow a minimum of five leaves to remain to increase the chances for a healthier repotted bulb for next year.

PESTS

Do not plant **gladiolas** in the same location the following year. Due to disease problems with this bulb, it is best to discard the bulb after flowering.

Watch for aphids on all bulbs.

Weeds could be trouble for up to five years in a new bulb garden. Use caution when applying herbicides or hand dig weeds.

Keep an eye out for insects. At very early signs, consider releasing predatory insects. If releases are done before the populations of pests are significant, the predators will not stay on site. An adequate and substantial food source is needed for releases to be effective. Lace wings and ladybugs are good for controlling aphids. If the population is out of hand, control immediately by spot spraying directly on insects with an insecticidal soap. Aphids weaken plants and are transmitters of many disease problems experienced by summer bulbs.

BULBS

PLANNING

While in the midst of the enjoyment of watching the maturing of all the tropical bulbs, this month marks the beginning of fall bulb season. Review your journal notes and photographs of previous years. Create a list of pluses and minuses in preparation for planning the next season's spring bloom and summer purchases.

Bulb catalogs are arriving. It's not too early to think about the pots you have available and what bulbs to plant for forcing for a new showing next winter. The smaller bulbs like **crocus** and **snowflakes** need smaller pots. In the proper container, they begin growing faster when brought out of dormancy, and they flower much quicker than the larger bulbs such as **tulips** or **daffodils**.

Check your notes to determine if there were problems with fungus gnat, roly-poly, or others. If these were issues last season, consider changing the placement of pots during cold treatment. Maybe buy an old working refrigerator at a garage sale and use it strictly for forcing bulbs.

Explore the new fall seed racks, for **toadflax**, **lettuce**, or other cool season annuals or vegetables to plant. This overplanting gives those **elephant ears**, **dahlias**, or **caladiums** a boost later this summer and into the fall, and also creates a completely new look.

Rethink the formal straight lines or triangular patterns of **tulips** that mimic architectural features. Use large numbers of fewer varieties, with the same or sequential bloom periods. Minimize spacing. Play up the difference in colors, heights, and the frilliness of flowers.

Informal design allows greater freedom for the use of **grape hyacinths** and other smaller growing bulbs. Though looser in structure, some guidelines are helpful. Plant no less than five of the same type in close proximity to each other. Select bulbs to extend the bloom sequence. Consider strong linear plantings of the larger growing **hyacinth**, with a serpentine island enclosure of **winter aconite**.

Plant some new varieties each year. Try a different flowering onion. Mixing heights, front to back and side-to-side, gives a roller-coaster of visual activity and allows riots of colors and types. Scatter clusters of the same variety of **lily** bulbs throughout the entire landscape, causing the eye to bounce from one grouping to another, unifying the entire garden.

PLANTING

If you missed out on the May planting, site **cannas** where there is afternoon shade to extend the length of bloom. Stagger **gladiolas** at fourteen-day intervals to have continuous blooms throughout the summer. Site where there is afternoon shade.

Magic lilies may be pushing up flower stalks, depending upon soil temperature. Watch for them and do not tread on the promise of blooms.

Multiple varieties of **lilies** are available, but with some differences: *L. candidum* flowers May to June and is very fragrant. **Dwarf pot lily** grows to 1 to 2 feet and can be forced during winter; give them ten weeks of cold (30 to 40 degrees) dormancy. **Tiger lily** has orange petals with black dots, and up to twenty blooms per stem. *L auratum* (oriental) have a spicy fragrance and prefer a cooler soil temperature (shade). *L. aurelia*n (trumpet) has the tallest stem, growing up to 5 feet, and over ten fragrant blooms. **Asiatic lilies** are the earliest blooming with more than ten flowers on a 3 to 4 foot stem.

Prepare the soil before planting bulbs. Bulbs prefer a rich, organic, fertile soil that is well drained but holds some moisture (add fifteen-percent sphagnum peat moss for water retention).

Water the planting or digging area thoroughly a few days before dividing and or installing bulbs.

Divide clumps of any hardy bulbs after leaves have turned brown, but are still attached to bulb for ease of locating.

Plant **autumn crocus** in mid to late summer. **Crocus** prefer well-drained, rich, organic, fertile soil. Site well away from any woody plants whose aggressive roots may compete for nutrients and moisture. Siting where there is afternoon shade could extend the bloom period.

Cannas can be planted in containers (20 inches in diameter or more). **Lilies** planted now add loud and vibrant color to the garden.

CARE

In the heat of the summer, make sure **caladium** receive no direct sun between 11 a.m. and 3 p.m. or leaf scorch can occur.

If adding mulch (only if less than 1 inch), do not simply pitch it randomly over growing bulbs. The mulch could collect in the foliage and increase moisture on leaves, creating a potential rot situation.

HELPFUL HINTS

Any saucers sitting under tropical bulbs should not have any standing water. This is a haven for mosquitoes. Either dump the water every other day, or place some mosquito dunk (natural bacteria) in the saucer to remedy the problem. Plants that benefit from this consistent moisture are **elephant ear**, aquatic **canna**, and a few other tropical bulbs.

Remove all seedpods that may form after flowering.

If the stems on bulbs begin to decrease in height, it is time to lift and divide.

WATERING

The bulb foliage might sag during the heat of the day. Check them at dusk and if they are still sagging, water thoroughly.

FERTILIZING

All tropical bulbs need monthly fertilizing with a balanced food.

Feed **iris** with a lower analysis fertilizer.

Feed **lilies** monthly with a balanced fertilizer. If you use a granular type, do not allow any to sit adjacent to stem. This may cause burn.

PRUNING

Remove all flower buds and side shoots from **dahlias;** leave one or two flower buds to ensure maximum bloom size.

PESTS

Watch for aphids and cutworms on **dahlias**. The pests gnaw at ground level. Experienced **dahlia** growers cut open a soup can horizontally, place it around the stem, and push it two inches into the ground to provide a barrier for the munchers.

Control all insects immediately (try insecticidal soap) as they are transmitters of many disease problems. Give spider mites and thrips (both make the leaves look blotchy) a good blast of water on the underside of the plant leaves. Repeat this routine every few days.

JULY

BULBS

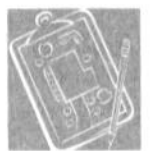

PLANNING

You may find pots of **cannas**, **caladiums**, **cyclamen**, **border dahlias**, **elephant ears** and even some **gladiolas** at the garden center. Take advantage of these "instant bulbs" to add to an existing planting, or to create a new container or window box combination. Consider placing a group of them in the center of the table for a dramatic setting during a summer get together.

Enjoy the midseason **lilies** that are reaching peak performance, as the later blooming varieties are showing strong bud presence. The early, mid-, and late blooming sequence really applies if bulbs are placed in similar scenarios. A late blooming variety planted in a more exposed setting (planted in full sun) suddenly becomes an early or midseason blooming type. The same thing happens if an early bloomer is planted on the shaded north side; now it becomes a mid- or late bloomer.

PLANTING

Tropical bulbs can be planted this month. Be aware that if tropical bulbs are purchased already growing, they are probably adapted to a shade cloth environment. Planting these bulbs directly into the full sun will result in leaf scorch. Take a few days to climatize the plant and move the pot back and forth out of the sun to minimize the leaf scorch.

Miniature **gladiolas** are perfect in a 12-inch container. To minimize the taller varieties from blowing over, place a pot of the taller **glads** inside a larger decorative pot.

Iris like full sun and to be planted in a soil that is well drained. Regardless of the size of the pot purchased, keep the plant watered until the planting. Place the bare-root section virtually right on top of the ground. Push it down slightly, firm the soil, water thoroughly, and place 1 inch of mulch around the plant, but not directly over the root.

If stems on the bulbs begin to decrease in height, lift and divide.

CARE

Maintain weed control, and read the label on any herbicides used. Many of the bulbs are monocots, a close relative to all lawn and grassy weeds. If the label says the chemical will kill grasses, exercise caution.

WATERING

Keep the ground moist during dry spells.

FERTILIZING

Feed **lilies** and **magic lily** monthly with a balanced fertilizer. If you are using a granular type, do not allow granules to sit on the stem or too closely to the stem. It will burn the plant.

PRUNING

Remove any browning or discolored foliage and spent flowers that can harbor insects and diseases. Cut flower stalks 2 to 3 inches above ground surface.

Remove all seedpods that may form after flowering.

PESTS

Aphids are usually visually obvious with small individuals clustering in large colonies. Look for spider mites by the small webbing spanning the leaf stem and the main stem. Thrips are difficult to see, but the damage is apparent in a flower bud that is distorted and will not open. Regular sprays of water, on both the top and the bottom of leaves, provide some control. Consider several insecticide options, ranging from organic to synthetic or manufactured.

Check the bottoms of any containers sitting out on the ground or on the patio for snails and slugs. They leave shiny streaks across the soil and pots and eat holes in the plant leaves.

If **dahlia** plants suddenly wilt and do not recover, they are probably infected with verticillium or another type of fungus. The best tactic is to dig up entire plant (and the whole root system) and discard. Composting is not advised unless the pile is reaching proper internal temperatures, which kills fungus and some pathogens. (See Helpful Hints in this month for composting information.)

HELPFUL HINTS

Composting Basics

The composting process begins with the decomposition of the ingredients whereby bacteria forms and aids the process. This is followed by the formation of actinomycetes, followed by other fungi and protozoa. The final wave of activity is the appearance of the centi- and millipedes, sowbugs (roly-pollies), and the earthworms—each with a particular job to do. This process, depending upon several factors, could occur as quickly as six weeks or take as long as nine months. Influences include the time of year, location of the pile or bin, the components, the amounts of each, and the layering technique.

Ingredients can be pieces of sod, grass clippings, leaves and needles from trees and shrubs, hay, straw, weeds, vegetable garden remnants, shredded newspaper, woody plant prunings, and kitchen wastes. Do not use grease, animal fat, meat scraps, or bones. These attract uninvited guests, create an unpleasant aroma, and don't break down properly. A proper layering technique is required to make all the processes work. Use a light sprinkling of compost starter, and 1 inch of soil for every 3 inches of fresh grass clippings, and 1 inch of soil for every 6 inches of fallen leaves or needles. As each layer is added, dampen the pile with a diluted water-soluble fertilizer. Do not wait until the pile is complete to try to wet. It is not necessary to turn piles or rotate, but this chore encourages break down and the availability of finished compost sooner. Do not add lime to the pile. During the initial reaction of elements, the pH will be very acidic. As the process continues, the pH rises and ultimately ends up near neutral. The internal temperature during the cooking (decomposition) should be from 110 to 140 degrees Fahrenheit. Any cooler, the decomposition is not happening, and much hotter may mean that everything is getting fried.

NOTES

BULBS

PLANNING

Purchase **winter aconite** bulbs at garden centers or by mail order. Select the largest and firmest bulbs. Although the bulb may appear as small as a piece of dirt, make sure it is not sprouting. If ordering by mail, ask about the size, time of shipment, and planting instructions.

Take some photographs of the flowering bulbs, particularly of the **magic lilies**, and their impact on surrounding plants.

Make note of the location of **gladiola** planting to insure a different location for next year to avoid disease problems.

Design a planting site where **tulips** will have afternoon shade. This site could extend the bloom period.

Use realism when deciding to create a new colorful bulb bed that may be the dominant focal point in a design, such as outside the breakfast room window, along the front walk, or flanking the porch. Perform an in-depth site analysis of the projected area for all natural occurrences, people-related activities, tree roots, standing water, pathways, adjoining areas, cable television lines just below the surface, and storm water drainage swales. Basically, you want to take into consideration anything obvious that may interfere with the success of your design.

PLANTING

Locate **daffodils**, **flowering onion**, **glory of the snow**, **snowdrops**, **snowflakes**, and **magic lilies** for dividing. Dig deeply and completely around the entire colony. Lift with a prying action (use a digging fork to lessen the chance of slicing multiple bulbs), lay the bulb clump on the ground, and shake until bulbs are exposed. Discard any damaged bulbs and select the largest for replanting in high impact locations.

Plant **iris** in full sun, with well-drained soil. Keep the plant watered until planting. Place the bare-root section virtually right on top of the ground. Push down slightly, firm soil, water thoroughly, and place 1 inch of mulch around the plant, but not directly over the root.

If stems begin to decrease in height, lift and divide bulbs.

Plant new **giant flowering onion** bulbs every three years. A **glory of the snow** colony should be replenished every three to four years.

Plant **tulips** (at the end of this month and on into September) in a container that is a minimum of 6 inches in diameter. For forcing indoors, use a well-drained potting mix, place bulbs two-thirds of the way into the pot, back fill, firm soil, and water. Store in a cold spot, but above freezing, for minimum of eight weeks, then set pots in a sunny location, and water regularly.

CARE

The **canna** stops flowering and round seedpods form. On a variegated leaf variety, they may lose most of their coloration and turn pale. These are indications that the plant is sensing shorter daylight hours and a slight dip in nighttime temperatures. The plants are going into a self-imposed dormancy cycle that can last for several months. Plants maintain their current height, but do not expect any new growth, even coming from the root system.

WATERING

Keep the ground moist to prolong the active growing season.

Always water all areas involved with planting, transplanting, and dividing a day ahead of working the soil. This minimizes root damage to established plants and reduces air pockets for new plantings.

FERTILIZING

This is the last month to fertilize **elephant ear**, **dahlia**, **canna**, and **caladium**. Use a balanced food and keep on top of the watering if any of these bulbs are to be dug up and stored over the winter for replanting next season.

PRUNING

Remove seedpods that may form after flowering on **lilies**.

Cut flower stalks 2 to 3 inches above the ground surface when foliage is browned.

Cut the **magic lily** flower stalk to keep the plants looking nice.

PESTS

Watch for aphids, spider mites, and thrips. Use regular hard sprays of water, on both the top and undersides of leaves for control. For heavy infestations, consider several options of insecticides, ranging from organic to synthetic or manufactured types.

Newly prepared bed spaces, not planted yet, are open invitations for squirrels to start planting walnut trees. Do not be alarmed when you come upon a nut with the taproot starting to emerge.

Check the bottoms and drainage holes on all containers outdoors for snails and slugs. They also leave shiny trails and holes in the leaves to tell you they are around. Treat accordingly.

Control weeds. Many of the bulbs are monocots, a close relative to lawn and grassy weeds, so if the label on a herbicide says it kills grass, it may kill the bulbs also. Use caution.

HELPFUL HINTS

Mulching Bulbs

The mulch over planted bulbs should be at a depth of 1 to 2 inches. Do not use a deeper layer or a product that compresses or mats. These materials hold in too much moisture. Too much moisture is the main cause of problems with rotting bulbs. Leaf mold, larger pieced compost, and many of the bark mulches work well and allow the prepared ground pore spaces to "breathe," and allow the soil to dry out between waterings.

- Try 'Widow', 'Flaming Parrot', and *T. clusiana* (**oxblood lily**).
- For late spring, plant 'West Point', 'Burgundy Lace', or 'Carnival de Nice'.

NOTES

SEPTEMBER

BULBS

PLANNING

A poorly drained planting area is the major reason for bulb problems.

PLANTING

Always plant into a rich, organic, fertile, well-drained, but evenly moist, soil.

Divide clumps of hardy bulbs after leaves have turned brown, but are still attached to bulb. Dig deeply and completely around the entire colony. Lift out the clump with a prying action, lay clump on the ground and shake until the bulbs are exposed. Discard any damaged bulbs, and select the largest for planting in the higher impact locations.

Water the new planting area thoroughly a few days before installing bulbs.

Do not plant hardy bulbs if soil temperature is above 60 degrees. Warm soils cause early underground sprouting. Use a soil thermometer for an accurate reading.

If you are planting bulbs under a tree, measure the trunk diameter and multiply by 5. Do not install bulbs any closer to tree than this distance.

HELPFUL HINTS

The following bulbs are either poisonous or repel wildlife and reduce bulb pilfering and consumption: **daffodils**, **jonquils**, **narcissus**, **winter aconite**, **grape hyacinth**, **hyacinth**, **squill**, **glory of the snow**, **snowdrops**, **fritillaria**, **wood hyacinth**, and many of the **flowering onions**.

CARE

Continue to control weeds in the bulb bed. Many of the bulbs are monocots, a close relative to lawn and grassy weeds. Read the label on herbicides carefully. If the label says the chemical kills grasses, it may harm the bulbs as well.

WATERING

Do not allow any bulbs to dry out. Check the soil and water as needed. Keep soil in pots with bulbs moist.

FERTILIZING

This is the last month to feed tropical bulbs.

Do not add bonemeal routinely. These nutrients remain in the ground for many years after one application.

PRUNING

Remove all seedpods that may form after flowering

Remove the bulbs after frost has killed the leaves. Allow the soil to dry on the bulbs and then shake it off. Discard any spotted, moldy, or undersized bulbs. Store the remaining bulbs in a dark, cool, dry location, in a box or paper bag with vermiculite.

PESTS

Do not use manure as an amendment if disease is a problem, or as a remedy to problems.

Check all containers sitting on the ground or on the patio for snails and slugs. They will hang out on the bottoms of pots and also around any drain holes. If you see shiny streaks on the pots or on the ground and holes in the leaves, treat for these pests.

Discourage the eating of **tulip**, **crocus**, and other palatable bulbs by dusting the bulbs with sulfur or copper oxide, just prior to installation.

OCTOBER

BULBS

PLANNING

Plant some new varieties each year. Mixing heights front to back and side-to-side gives a roller-coaster of visual activity and allows riots of colors and types each year. Scatter clusters of **lily** bulbs among annuals, perennials, and ground covers for backing. Site **winter aconite** near shrubs or trees to provide a setting. Minimize colors and varieties in smaller planting spaces to prevent overstimulation and chaos.

PLANTING

Carefully select **hyacinths**, **tulips**, and **daffodil** bulbs. Make sure there are no black spots. This could be botrytis disease that causes spotted foliage or flower, and slimy or fuzzy (moldy) leaf or petal. There is no cure for botrytis. If it is detected on existing plants, dig and discard, and do not plant a similar variety in that location.

Do not purchase sprouting bulbs. After purchasing, store in a dark, cool, dry spot, but not in a plastic bag, which results in moisture development, that in turn leads to rotting.

When ordering by mail, ask about bulb size, time of shipment, and planting instructions.

To calculate the quantity for formal plantings, divide the square footage of the bed space by 2; this equals the number of bulbs needed for the total space for a mass planting.

Bulbs forced indoors and then planted outdoors may take several years to begin flowering again.

The minimum planting depth should be three times the diameter of bulb. When planting multiple bulbs in a single hole, do not allow them to touch.

To plant **lilies**, place the bulb in the hole at a 45-degree angle to reduce the chance of moisture collecting in the bulb's scale-like outer covering.

CARE

Keep all bulbs in a dry, cool, dark place prior to installation.

Remove tropical bulbs after the frost has killed the leaves. Allow the soil to dry on the bulbs, then shake it off (do not use water due to rot potential). Discard any spotted, moldy, or undersized bulbs. Store in a dark, cool, dry location, in a box or paper bag with vermiculite.

Remove and cut the tops off of **gladiolas** prior to storage. If bulbs are the same size or larger than when you planted them, then store for use next year. If the bulbs are smaller or soft, then discard.

WATERING

Plant bulbs into ground that is moist, and water bed immediately after installation to remove air pockets.

FERTILIZING

It is not necessary to mix any product into planting hole. If the soil test indicated problems or a lack of nutrients, then it is essential to add nutrients to the entire planting area.

PRUNING

Prune browning or yellowing foliage on indoor or tropical bulbs.

PESTS

Check the pots used for indoor forcing for any fungus gnats flying around. Use a combination of insecticidal soap and yellow sticky traps (available at garden center) for control.

NOVEMBER

BULBS

PLANNING

Now is the time to plan for your summer bulbs—the winners and challenges. Consult the chart in Helpful Hints when planning your summer bulb lineup.

PLANTING

Always water the area thoroughly a few days before installing your bulbs.

Because of potential disease problems, do not use manure as an amendment.

Paper-white, 'Omri', 'Soleil d'Or' or 'Ziva' **narcissus**, **freesias**, **hyacinth**, **ranunculus** hybrids, and **anemone giants** are good bulbs ready for forcing. Other bulbs, such as botanical **tulips**, **crocus**, and shorter growing **daffodils** are listed as "suitable for forcing." "Forcing" is making a bulb react as if the weather, setting, and environment are correct for growth. Bulbs listed as ready for forcing have previously been given a dormant or cold treatment. This pretreatment allows the bulb to simply be placed in a medium (either water or soil), in a warm, well-lighted place, and the growth and flowering cycle begins. The "suitable for forcing" bulbs involve planting the bulbs in pots with potting mix, and placing the potted bulbs in a refrigerator or outdoors for at least eight weeks. The temperatures should be less than forty degrees. This dormant time period triggers growth when exposed to warmer temperatures and light.

For forcing bulbs such as **tulips** indoors, use containers a minimum of 6 inches in diameter. Use a well-drained potting mix. Place bulbs two-thirds of the way into the pot, back fill, firm potting mix, and water. Store in a cold location (but above freezing) for minimum of eight weeks, then remove from cold storage, set in a sunny location, and water.

Winter aconite must be in the ground at least two months or more prior to the anticipated bloom period.

CARE

To store nonhardy bulbs, dig carefully either just after or just before killing frost. Allow the soil to dry on the bulbs, then shake off loose soil. Discard any spotted, moldy, or undersized bulbs. Store in a dark, cool, dry location, in a box or paper bag with vermiculite.

If hot pepper sprays (animal repellents) are being used to protect bulb foliage, they should be reapplied after each rainfall or snow melt. The product is water soluble and is diluted and or washed completely off with water. Multiple home remedies for repelling wildlife have evolved over the years, each with its own supporters and detractors. If you have had luck with a particular method, continue using it as long as the impact on the environment is healthy.

WATERING

Water all areas where bulbs are growing during dry periods.

Allowing tropical or houseplant types to become completely dry triggers dormancy.

FERTILIZING

Do not add bonemeal routinely. The nutrients remain many years after one application.

No fertilizing is needed for bulbs unless they are seasonal bulbs such as **amaryllis** or **agapanthus**. Fertilize them when watering, using one-half the recommended label rate.

PRUNING

Remove any discolored foliage on potted bulbs.

HELPFUL HINTS

Recommended Bulbs

Common Name	Botanical Name	Location and Use
EARLIER-SUMMER		
Giant flowering onion	*Allium giganteum*	*+Sun Garden
King's spear/foxtail	*Eremurus spectabilis*	*++Sun Garden
Angelwings/caladiums	*Caladium bicolor*	+!Part Sun and Shade Garden
Chives	*Allium schoenoprasum*	*+Sun Garden
Star of Bethlehem	*Ornithogalum umbellatum*	*+Natural Garden
Dutch iris	*Iris xiphium*	*+Sun Garden
Wild hyacinth	*Triteleia hyacintha*	**!Containers
Clivia	*Clivia miniata*	**+Containers/Houseplant
MIDSUMMER		
Agapanthus	*Agapanthus africanus*	**+Containers/Houseplant
Canna	*Canna x generalis*	**+Sun Garden
Elephant ears	*Colocasia esculenta*	**+Sun to Shade Garden
Gladiola	*Gladiolus* grandiflora	**+Sun Garden
True lilies	*Lilium* sp.	*+Sun/Part Shade Garden
Surprise lily	*Lycoris squamigera*	*+Sun/Shade Garden
Eastern hyacinth	*Camassia scilloides*	*+Natural Garden
Red spider lily	*Lycoris radiata*	*+Sun Garden
Tuber begonia	*Begonia tuberhybrida*	**Containers/Houseplant
Hardy gladiola	*Incarvillea sinensis*	*Part Shade Garden
Pineapple lily	*Eucomis comosa*	**+Container/Houseplant
LATER-SUMMER		
Dahlia	*Dahlia* hybrids	**+Sun Garden
Fire of Eden	*Crocosmia masoniorum*	*Light/Part Shade Garden
Cyclamen	*Cyclamen hederifolium*	*Shade Garden
Harlequin flower	*Sparaxis tricolor*	**Shade/Containers
Peruvian daffodil	*Hymenocallis narcissiflora*	**+Shade/Containers
Saffron crocus	*Crocus sativus*	*Sun to Part Shade Garden
Autumn crocus	*Colchicum autumnale*	*+Sun to Part Shade Garden

*—hardy bulbs
**—nonhardy, tropical, or houseplant types. Most of these bulbs are found in garden centers.
+—proven winners that almost always pay off with a reasonable amount of preparation and care.
!—daring and challenging types need more care, are more soil and location specific, with end results possibly being less than hoped for, but fun and challenging anyway.

PESTS

Many bulbs are very attractive to wildlife. The animals are drawn to the area by the freshly worked soil, where the digging is easy, but the controlling is difficult. Discourage squirrels, voles, and field mice by dusting bulbs with sulfur or copper oxide just prior to installation.

Check on all bulbs that are being stored for the wintertime. Smell them for damp moldiness. Check for black spots. If anything looks suspicious, get rid of that bulb, and dry out any others that were in possible contact with the infected bulb.

DECEMBER

BULBS

PLANNING

Forcing bulbs in pots and indoors keeps the color rolling. Just before a pot full of bulbs begins to flower, head down to the basement or refrigerator (where pots are being held for six to eight weeks of cold storage), remove the pots, and place under grow lights or in a bright sunny warm window to trigger growth. This is such an easy way to have uninterrupted, indoor, hardy bulb color pizzazz throughout the winter season.

Try to learn the botanical names for plants. The common name for a plant may be an entirely different name from town to town and from family to family. The second part of the botanical name (official) is the species. Many times this word is descriptive (see Introduction for more complete explanation) or defines a particular plant characteristic. Learning the botanical names is easier if you can associate the word with the plant. Knowing the botanical name helps when paging through catalogs, strolling about in parks and botanical gardens, with signage in nurseries, and if you are attending classes.

Consider getting a bulb planter (a hand held tool with a footstep) if you are planning on making **tulip**, **daffodil**, and **gladiola** plantings an every year project. This really saves time and physical strain. Better yet would be the use of an auger (a large drill bit) that is used with an electric drill. Buy the largest diameter auger available. Neither of these tools is helpful when planting **canna** or **iris**, because of their physical shape.

PLANTING

There is still plenty of time to install recent bulb purchases or a bag of bulbs that may have been overlooked earlier in the fall.

To force bulbs indoors, use a container a minimum of 6 inches in diameter, fill with well-drained potting mix, place bulbs two-thirds of way into pot, back fill, firm soil, and water. Place in a cold or cool (above freezing) location such as an old refrigerator in the garage, a cold frame, or easily accessible garden space (if placed outside, the pot must be buried) for eight to ten weeks.

CARE

Continue to bring pots of bulbs planted for forcing out and place in bright windows, but not in the direct path of furnace heat.

Flowering time varies according to the type of bulb. Smaller bulbs such as **crocus** and **snowflakes** flower faster than **tulips** or **daffodils**.

These are new plants and the potting soil being introduced into the home environment may contain pests such as fungus gnat and roly-poly. Clean the outside and bottom of the pots thoroughly, and monitor the soil surface.

Any remaining tropical and nonhardy bulbs designated for reuse next year that are still in the ground should be removed as soon as possible. Never wash the bulbs before storage. Let the soil dry naturally, then shake the soil off the bulbs. Dust the bulbs with sulfur, and store in either vermiculite or a paper bag. Keep cool and dry.

Do not allow fallen leaves to build up over planted areas, moisture retention could be problematic.

WATERING

Make sure that 1 inch of water is falling on all bulb planted areas, whether a formal bed of **daffodils** near the front door, or **snowdrops** clustered in a woodland garden.

HELPFUL HINTS

More Recommended Bulbs

Common Name	Botanical Name	General Meaning of Species
Autumn crocus	*Colchicum autumnale*	fall blooming
Cyclamen	*Cyclamen persicum*	of Persia
Elephant ears	*Colocasia esculenta*	edible
Giant flowering onion	*Allium giganteum*	gigantic
Glory of the snow	*Chionodoxa luciliae*	bright, shiny
Hyacinth	*Hyacinthus orientalis*	oriental, eastern
Naked, surprise lily	*Lycoris squamigera*	scale-like leaves
Snowdrops	*Galanthus nivalis*	snowy, white
Snowflake	*Leucojum aestivum*	of summer
Winter aconite	*Eranthis hyemalis*	of winter

FERTILIZING

Fertilize only bulbs growing indoors at one-half the label rate.

Fertilizer labeled as "Bulb Food" generally has an analysis ratio of 1-4-1 (i.e. 4-12-4). This specific product, unless stated on the package, contains nothing more than a common fertilizer with a similar ratio. If the cost is similar, the choice makes no difference. However, be conscious that the series of three numbers represents the percentage of nitrogen, phosphorus, and potassium. None of the numbers should be any higher than 12, or the blooming cycle may be disrupted.

PRUNING

If **grape hyacinth** leaves are showing above the surface, DO NOT prune them. Allow the young leaves to remain, building strength for next spring.

PESTS

All bulbs recently planted could be prime targets for the squirrels. Consider laying chicken wire on top of the ground and masking it with 1 to 2 inches of mulch.

Check on all bulbs that are being stored for the wintertime. Smell them for damp moldiness. Examine them for black spots. If anything looks suspicious, get rid of that bulb. Lay out any others to dry that were in contact with the discarded one.

NOTES

CHAPTER THREE

EDIBLES

Edibles are an opportunity to enjoy pleasures and beauty with plants once thought of as one dimensional—simply foods or spices. Edibles are grown many times in out of the way places, a change of attitude will bring great enjoyment and unexpected satisfaction. The helping hand in the landscape could be an edging of tulips, or daffodil bed with lettuce. You can get great fall color from blueberries, use thyme to fill spaces in a patio, or shade a south facing window with a cherry tree. Being a "farmer" can mean simply growing a pot of hot peppers on the porch or deck, a window box herb garden, a vegetable patch, or a yard filled with fruit trees. Remember when planning to keep common sense in mind and know your yard is unique and, of course, Kansas's weather is very unpredictable. These factors impact soil temperature, moisture, and winds, each with a direct bearing on the care, the maintenance, and ultimately the success of your harvest. Understand that edible plants (more than ornamentals) require a consistent level of fertilizing, watering, and watching for insects and diseases during the growing season.

THE BASIC REQUIREMENTS FOR EDIBLES

1. A sunny location (garden plot or container)
2. Soil (prepared ground or potting mix)
3. Equipment (trowel to rototiller)
4. Seeds (gathered or purchased, germinated under lights or sown directly in ground)
5. Plants (home grown or greenhouse)
6. Pollination (wind, self, cross, hand, insect)
7. Fertilizer (compost to manufactured)
8. Watering (drip, overhead, sprinklers, hose)
9. Harvesting (time, storage)
10. Pest or disease control (finger tips, predators, chemical)
11. Time to work and enjoy them!

The "farming" phenomenon can be a year-round, seasonal, or monthly occurrence. The possibilities are endless. There's June bearing 'Surecrop' strawberries, 'Pik Red' tomatoes, and pineapple sage with miniature thyme potted and growing indoors; arbors or trellises covered with either 'Niagara' grapes or 'Blue Lake' beans; a row of 'Stardust' sweet corn screening a view; 'Duke' blueberries among other shrubs, or comfrey's huge leaves giving bold texture to the perennial garden. In flower, the 'Red Haven' peach tree is truly ornamental, and in a few months has delicious fruit.

A QUICK SEASONAL REFERENCE

When to grow, to eat fresh, to freeze, to can, to store, or to dry:

Late winter: onion sets, asparagus roots, seed potatoes, broccoli seeds (indoors)

Early spring: bare cherry trees, packaged grapes or raspberries, rhubarb in pots

Mid-spring: balled burlap or container-pear trees, blackberry canes, tomato seeds (indoors)

Late Spring: peppers, okra, peas, beans, pumpkins, spinach

Early Summer: containers or in-ground rosemary, oregano, sage, tarragon

Late summer: cauliflower, lettuce, winter squash, chard seeds

Fall: balled burlap, container grown apple trees and blueberry shrubs

HELPFUL HINTS

Sunflower Harvesting

In mid-September to early October, the center florets of **sunflowers** will brown and shrivel, exposing the sunflower seeds. Flower heads will droop with the back of the head turning yellow. To save the seeds from birds, secure a waterproof paper bag or plastic mesh bag over the flower head and tie it to the stalk. Check a few seeds for black and white stripes. When you see stripes, it's time to harvest!

USE YOUR IMAGINATION

Have a narrow space along the property line that needs screening during the summer? Train an apple tree with a vertical axis growing method or an espalier.

Tired of the mulched look and want to add pizzazz under the spring flowering bulbs? How about colorful red and green leaf lettuce as a ground covering?

Want an old fashioned look, without the typical picket fence? Consider a raspberry living fence.

Could your sedum ground cover on a slope use invigorating? Dot in some herbal catmint.

Need to help your compost pile? Adding fruit and vegetable peels will help beneficial bacterial growth.

Want to attract butterflies? Parsley, carrot foliage, dill, cherry, and plum trees attract black/tiger swallowtail.

Did you know? Juices can be used as dye for yarn and other materials.

GROWING AND MAINTENANCE TIPS

1. Choose a location with open areas that have a minimum of five hours of direct sun. Sun is most important. Most other factors can be altered in the landscape to grow edibles. Despite some opinions that leafy-type vegetables, beans, or berries can grow in part shade—forget it! Use full sun, for quality and quantity.

2. It's important to prepare the soil. In your garden space, turn an area at a minimum depth of eight inches.

3. For vegetables and fruits, create a raised bed, adding six inches of organic amendments, worked into the planting space. For herbs, create raised beds with three inches of inorganic amendments and a three inch mixture of pea gravel, and large grain traction sand (smaller grain doesn't help drainage).

4. If you're growing in containers, larger sizes (15 inches or more) will reduce routine care scheduling.

Before planting, water the potting mix and stir to eliminate air pockets. Remember, plastic, clay, hanging pots, pouches, window boxes, or herb jars must have drainage holes. Potting mix may contain larger perlite pieces, composted bark, or sphagnum peat moss. Heavier potting soil may not drain properly, so add traction sand, gravel, etc.

ESSENTIALS FOR GOOD GROWTH: SOME BASIC NEEDS

1. **Digging and Soil Preparation:** rototiller, spade, shovel, fork, hard tined rake

2. **Watering:** hose, sprinklers, drip system, or buckets

3. **Supports:** stakes, tie yarn, plastic tape

4. **Harvesting and controlling:** scissor cut pruners, lopers, saws

5. **Applicators:** hose end sprayer, pump sprayer, squeeze or trigger bottle

6. **Tagging and marking:** labels

7. **Notes and observations on your garden's activity:** a garden journal

8. **Dates for seeds gathered, saved, traded, or purchased:** note dates on the packet or envelope

9. **Moisture:** use clear plastic wrap (with holes for ventilation) over pots and flats until seeds sprout—then remove

10. **Various shapes:** with attention to plant shapes

11. **Significant quantity:** up to 30% lost during germinating/transplant process

12. **Good soil temperature:** upper 40s thru 60s. Use a soil thermometer, and do not plant if soil is colder.

GROWING

1. **When tansplanting:** choose plants with several sets of mature leaves and strong stem.

2. **Plants to buy:** field or container, in cell packs, flats, or pots.

3. **Plants available for direct installation:** perennials, annual herbs, vegetables, vines, shrubs, canes, trees, or rooted cuttings.

4. **Pollination:** Remember it's essential for production.

5. **Attracting bees:** Try attracting with smell of peppermint or spearmint.

6. **Fertilizer decisions:** have soil tested before additions. Fertilizers are offered in granular, powder, or liquid form. N, P, K are fertilizer's major ingredients represented by numbers on the bag. Secondary ingredients are Ca, Mg, S. Minor elements are B, Cu, Fe, Mn, Mo, Zn.

7. Do not routinely add bonemeal, lime, and wood ashes.

8. **Aerating soil:** Do this post-season by turning the soil in your garden. If growing in containers, dump mixes and blends either in a compost pile or in storage bins for next year.

9. **Pruning:** Prune fruit trees in winter (January is best).

PROBLEMS, WEEDS, INSECTS, AND DISEASES

1. Control competition for nutrients by hand weeding, mulching, pruning, and cutting back.

2. Weakened plants are prone to damage from diseases and insects, and harbor problems that move into other landscape areas. Remove any suspect plants immediately.

3. New garden space weeds can be a problem for up to five years. Control with hand digging.

4. When using fungicides, insecticides, or herbicides—use with care and be aware of drifting chemicals as a potential problem. Read the label.

5. Uncomposted (less than year) manure can cause possible bacteria and disease problems.

6. Don't worry, herbs are generally not eaten by wildlife.

7. Cherry, peach, and apple trees planted in lawn areas can have increased crown and root rot because of the quantity of water lawns need. Tree trunks get wet, and leaf rust and spotting is increased due to sprinklers wetting the foliage.

HELPFUL HINTS

Care of Strawberries

Near Thanksgiving time, covering plants with 3 inches of well composted organic matter will prevent winter crown damage and the heaving of roots from the ground.

CHAPTER THREE

Vegetables, Herbs, Fruiting Canes, Bushes, Vines, and Fruit Trees

The focus below will be on common names and specific varieties which are used when discussing or purchasing vegetables, fruiting canes, bushes, vines, fruit trees or seed, with the exception being herbs. Botanical names (genus and species) are seldom used and offer little insight in locating, using, or caring for a specific plant found in catalogs or garden centers. Three examples illustrate this point:

Common Name	Botanical Name (Genus/species)	Variety Name(s)
Pear tree (fruiting)	*Pyrus/communis*	'Kieffer' or 'Stark Delicious'
Lettuce (red leaf)	*Lactuca/sativa*	'New Red Fire'
Raspberry (red)	*Rubus/ideaus*	'Latham'

NOTE: full sun is required for best production

VEGETABLES

Common Name: Asparagus
Good Variety(s): Jersey Gem, Jersey Knight
What: 1year old healthy crowns (swollen and obvious) - bare root
When to Plant: March thru April
Planting Time to Harvest: 3 years
Specific Needs: Well drained, rich, 12 inches or more deep, alkaline soil, plant crowns 6 inches deep
Common Problems: Asparagus beetles, cutworms, aphids, grasshoppers
Tip-Plants Per Person: 10 to 15 roots

Common Name: Beans
Good Variety(s) Topcrop, Roma II (bush), Blue Lake, King of the Garden (pole)
What: Seed directly sown into ground
When to Plant: Mid April thru May
Specific Needs: 3 inches between each seed, plant seed 1 inch deep
Common Problems: Melon fly, pod borer, potato leafhopper, seed corn maggot, Mexican bean beetle
Planting Time to Harvest: 2 to 3 months
Tip-Plants Per Person: 10- to 15-feet or 3 hills, type dependent

Common Name: Broccoli
Good Variety(s): Arcadia, Brigadier
What: Transplants
When to Plant: Mid March or Late July
Specific Needs: Cool temperatures
Common Problems: Aphids
Planting Time to Harvest: 2 to 3 months
Tip-Plants Per Person: 5 to 7 plants

Common Name: Cabbage
Good Variety(s): Bronco, Gideon
What: Transplant professionally grown
When to Plant: Mid March or Mid July
Specific Needs: Cool temperatures
Common Problems: Cabbage maggot, cabbage root maggot
Planting Time to Harvest: 2 to 3 months
Tip-Plants Per Person: 3 to 4 plants

Common Name: Corn Sweet
Good Variety(s): Saturn (supersweet yellow), Candy Corner (supersweet bicolor)
What: Seed
When to Plant: Mid April or Early August
Specific Needs: 2 feet between plants and rows
Common Problems: Corn earworm
Planting Time to Harvest: 2 to 3 months
Tip-Plants Per Person: 10- to 15-foot row

Common Name: Lettuce
Good Variety(s): Crisp n' Green (leaf), Dark Land (romaine), Ermosa (Boston/head) New Red Fire (red)
What: Transplant professionally grown
When to Plant: Early March or Mid August
Specific Needs: Cool temperatures
Common Problem: Wildlife
Planting Time to Harvest: 1 to 3 months depending on type
Tip-Plants Per Person: 10- to 15-foot row

Vegetables, Herbs, Fruiting Canes, Bushes, Vines, and Fruit Trees (continued)

Common Name:	Onion
Good Variety(s):	Sweet Sandwich Hybrid & Red Hamburger
What:	Sets/plants
When to Plant:	Mid March
Specific Needs:	Row 2 feet linear, 3 inches between each set
Common Problem	Onion thrips, onion maggot
Planting Time to Harvest:	1 to 2 months
Tip-Plants Per Person:	10 to 15 feet for green

Common Name:	Peas
Good Variety(s):	Green Arrow (English), Super Sugar Snap (snap), Mississippi (field)
What:	Seeds Directly Sown
When to Plant:	Mid May
Specific Needs:	Seeds 1 inch deep, 2 inches between plants in row
Common Problems:	Pea aphid
Planting Time to Harvest:	2 to 3 months
Tip-Plants Per Person:	10- to 15-foot row for fresh, double if canning/ freezing

Common Name:	Peppers
Good Variety(s):	King Arthur (sweet), Hungarian Yellow (hot)
What:	Transplants, professionally grown
When to Plant:	Mid May
Specific Needs:	2 to 3 feet between plants, 2 feet between rows
Common Problems:	Aphids
Planting Time to Harvest:	2 to 3 months
Tip-Plants Per Person:	2 plants

Common Name:	Potato
Good Variety(s):	Irish Cobbler, Red Pontiac, Norgold Russet
What:	Seed potato
When to Plant:	Mid March
Specific Needs:	Elevated rows of well drained soil
Common Problems:	Colorado potato beetle, flea beetle, green peach aphid
Planting Time Harvest:	3 to 4 months
Tip-Plants Per Person:	3 to 4 pounds

Common Name:	Rhubarb
Good Variety(s):	Canada Red
What:	Bareroot divisions
When to Plant:	Mid March thru April
Specific Needs:	Spacing—9 square feet per plant
Common Problems:	root rot
Planting Time to Harvest:	2 years
Tip-Plants Per Person:	2 to 3 fresh, add 2 to 3 for canning

Common Name:	Squash
Good Variety(s):	Peter Pan, Zucchini (summer), Sweet Mama, Early Butternut (winter)
What:	Transplants or directly sown seeds
When to Plant:	Mid May
Specific Needs:	Plant on elevated mound, 2 plants per—remove 1 after month
Common Problems:	Cucumber beetle, squash bug, squash vine borer
Planting Time to Harvest:	2 to 3 months
Tip-Plants Per Person:	2 plants

Common Name:	Tomato
Good Variety(s):	Determinate fruiting: Pik Red, Red Rocket, Bush Early Girl; Indeterminate fruiting: Jet Star, Brandywine, Better Boy, Beefsteak
What:	Transplants—professionally grown
When to Plant:	Mid May
Specific Needs:	Side dress with fertilizer after major harvests, 1 to 2 inches water per week from June through August
Common Problems:	Cutworms, hornworms, spider mites, leafminer, stinkbug, flea beetles
Planting Time to Harvest:	2 months
Tip-Plants Per Person:	3 for fresh, add 3 for canning

HERBS

Common Name:	Anise
Highlight:	Leaves and seeds have sweet licorice taste
Type:	Annual
Where:	Full sun – garden or pots
What/When to Plant:	Transplants or seed/Mid May
Specific Requirements:	Alkaline soil
Possible Problems:	Aphids

CHAPTER THREE

Common Name: Basil
Highlight: Dried leaves for flavor, can be grown indoors
Type: Annual – multiple varieties available
Where: Full sun – garden or pots
What/When to Plant: Transplants or seed/ Mid May

Common Name: Chives
Highlight: Chopped leaves for flavoring, can be grown indoors
Type: Perennial
Where: Full sun to very light shade
What/When to Plant: Transplants/spring and fall

Common Name: Coriander
Highlight: Seed (whole or crushed) for spice mixes and curry powders
Type: Annual
Where: Full sun – garden or pots
What/When to Plant: Transplants in Mid May
Specific Requirements: Needs room for air circulation

Common Name: Dill
Highlight: Chopped leaves and seeds both for flavoring
Type: Annual
Where: Full sun – garden or pots
What/When to Plant: Transplant or seed
Specific Requirements: Rich soils, do not plant near fennel
Possible Problems: Aphids

Common Name: Lemon Balm
Highlight: Flavorful leaves added to jams, jellies and fruit salad
Type: Perennial
Where: Full sun to light shade – garden
What/When to Plant: Transplant/spring or fall
Possible Problems: Weedy appearance

Common Name: Marjoram (sweet)
Highlight: Spicy/sweet flavor for meats, can be grown indoors
Type: Perennial
Where: Full sun – garden or pots
What/When to Plant: Transplants/spring or fall
Specific Requirements: Rich soil
Possible Problems: Spring sown seeds will only live one year

Common Name: Mint
Highlight: Numerous flavors variety specific/uses limitless
Type: Perennial
Where: Full sun to part shade – garden or pots
What/When to Plant: Transplants/spring or fall
Possible Problems: Aggressive/invasive growing, rust on foliage

Common Name: Oregano
Highlight: Flavoring for vegetables and meats
Type: Perennial
Where: Full sun to light shade – garden
What/When to Plant: Transplants/spring or fall
Specific Requirements: Cut back in fall

Common Name: Parsley
Highlight: Decorative/breath freshener, self-seeding
Type: Biennial
Where: Full sun to light shade-garden or pots
What/When to Plant: Transplant
Specific Requirements: Rich soil
Possible Problems: Spider mites

Common Name: Sage
Highlight: Numerous varieties and foliage color/flavor for meats
Type: Perennial
Where: Full sun – garden or pots
What/When to Plant: Transplants/spring or fall
Specific Requirements: Extremely well-drained soil
Possible Problems: Spider mites

Common Name: Thyme
Highlight: Numerous varieties with differing foliage/universal flavoring
Type: Perennial/evergreen
Where: Full sun – garden or pots
What/When to Plant: Transplants/spring or fall
Specific Requirements: Extremely well drained soil, grow indoors
Possible Problems: Short lived plant

Vegetables, Herbs, Fruiting Canes, Bushes, Vines, and Fruit Trees (continued)

FRUITING CANES, BUSHES, and VINES

Common Name:	Blackberry
Good Variety(s):	Darrow (thorns), Arapaho (thornless)
Highlight:	Hybrids fruit in mid summer, one pint of fruit per each 1 foot of row length
Type:	Upright canes spread by underground root system
Planted Where:	Full sun with ample space for some colonizing
Size/When to Plant:	Canes/spring
Specific Requirements:	Do not plant in same space where non-producing black-berries previously were sited, organic well-drained soil
Years Until First Harvest:	2 (erect), 3 (trailing)
Possible Problems:	Non hybrid (from wild) contaminates soil for future blackberry

Common Name:	Blueberry
Good Variety(s):	Blueray and Bluecrop
Highlight:	Fruiting 4 to 8 quarts per bush and great fall foliage color
Type:	Deciduous shrub
Planted Where:	Full sun to light shade
Size/When to Plant:	1+ gallon shrubs/spring
Specific Requirements:	Well drained, acidic soil, 2 varieties for pollination, 25 square feet per shrub
Years Until First Harvest:	3 to 4 (highbush)
Possible Problems:	Birds love fruit, structure or netting needed

Common Name:	Grapes
Good Variety(s):	Concord (table-seeds), Reliance (table-seedless). Know your zone (either zone 5 or 6). Most will grow in either. Some varieties: Catawba (multipurpose), Steuben (red-blush wine), Ventura (white wine).
Highlight:	Table-eaten fresh, used for jellies and jams – 10 to 20 pounds/vine, multiple uses natural fencing, screening
Type:	Vine needing structure to grow on trellis, arbor
Planted Where:	Full sun, well-drained soil only
Size/When to Plant:	Vigorous No. 1's (year old) vines/spring
Specific Requirements:	Prepare soil fall prior to spring planting; allow 8 foot linear space for vine, 4 feet between rows
Possible Problems:	Minimize mulch (breakdown causes high nitrogen-uneven growth), several insects and diseases

Common Name:	Raspberry
Good Variety(s):	Latham, Redwing (both red)
Highlight:	Combination allows harvest during June and August, good for freezing, each 1 foot row produces 1 quart
Type:	Cane (off underground root system)
Planted Where:	Full sun
Size/When to Plant:	Potted canes/spring
Specific Requirements:	Adequate room for colonizing (remove 3-year-old canes reduced fruit production), dig relocate to original site
Years Until First Harvest:	2 (red), 2 (black and purple)
Possible Problems:	Disease potential, invasive-ness, and thorns

Common Name:	Strawberry
Good Variety(s):	Earliglow (early), Surecrop (midseason) and Lateglow (late)
Highlight:	Combination fruits June thru August, second fruiting weather dependent, each plant/shoots 1 quart of fruit yearly
Type:	Herbaceous ground cover
Planted Where:	Full sun, well-drained soil
Size/When to Plant:	Bare root plants/spring
Specific Requirements:	Rich organic soil, no fruit set first year, position runners and root keeps colony productive
Years Until First Harvest:	2 (June bearing), 1 (everbearing)
Possible Problems:	Several diseases in poorly drained soil, leaf roll/mal-formed fruit insect damage

FRUIT TREES

Common Name:	Apple
Good Variety(s):	Pristine or Golden Delicious (yellow), Redfree or Enterprise (red)
Highlight:	Combinations extend harvest season, ripening different month, 2 and 4 bushels per tree
Tips:	100-square-foot clearance, dwarf trees (fruit full size)
Years Until First Harvest:	3 to 4 (dwarf), 4 to 5 (semi-dwarf), 5 to 7 (standard)
Common Problems:	Fall webworms, eastern tent caterpillar, borers

Common Name:	Cherry
Good Variety(s):	Montmorency & Meteor (sour), Starkrimson & Hedelfingen (sweet)
Highlight:	Sour cherries self-pollinate, not sweet, 5 year old fruit production potential to 50 pounds.
Tips:	100-square foot-clearance, well-drained soils protected from colder winds-early season flower damage
Years to First Harvest:	5 to 7 (sweet cherry), 3 (dwarf tart cherry), 4 (standard tart cherry)
Common Problems:	Fall webworms, eastern tent caterpillar

Common Name:	Peach
Good Variety(s):	Belle of Georgia (white fruit) & Red Haven (yellow fruit)
Highlight:	Above combination produces fruit from mid July through August bearing 2 to 4 bushels per tree
Tips:	100-square-foot clearance, well-drained soils protected from colder winds-early season flower damage, use two varieties for cross-pollination, dwarf trees-fruit production is erratic
Years to First Harvest:	3 (dwarf), 4 (standard)
Common Problems:	Tree borers and cankers

Common Name:	Pear
Good Variety(s):	Starking Delicious & Kieffer
Highlight:	Combinations extend harvest season, ripening different month, 2 and 4 bushels per tree
Tips:	100-square-foot clearance, dwarf trees (fruit full size) produce in 3 or more years; semi-dwarf/standard 5 or more years; pick fruit green/firm (allow ripening off tree)
Years to First Harvest:	3 to 4 (dwarf), 5 to 7 (standard)
Common Problems:	Fire blights stems, twigs and fruits

HELPFUL HINTS

Using a Soil Thermometer

Using a soil thermometer will allow you to check the soil temperature before planting vegetable seeds. The proper seed germination temperatures for some common vegetables are: **Peas** at 40 degrees F; **lettuce, parsnips** and **spinach** at 35 degrees F; **tomatoes, corn,** and **beans** at 55 degrees F; **cucumbers, melons, sweet potatoes** at 60 degrees F.

JANUARY

EDIBLES

PLANNING

1. This is a good month to enter into the planning and design phase for the spring garden. Consider establishing a new garden plot, or adding to the existing vegetable or herb garden, and including new fruit trees, bushes, or vines.

2. Make a call to the local utility companies to locate any underground lines in the projected areas.

Check for easements and surrounding buildings that have an affect on the garden space.

Look at the existing trees, their size, height, and the shadows they cast in making the final design determination.

3. Pay special attention to the direction the ground slopes, access to water, ease of entry for bringing in equipment and tools, and access to a nearby composting space.

4. Note the existing vegetation, lawn, evergreen shrubs, flower beds, and trees.

5. Consider the condition of the soil chemistry by preparing a soil sample for testing.

6. Soil drainage is critical. Note existing drainage and water percolation.

7. When siting garden plots, determine if the forest or adjacent common areas are possible sources for wildlife.

8. Gather all the plant propagation necessities, such as sterile potting mixes, clean pots, cell-packs, peat pots, and seeds. Check the grow light rack or table for burnt out bulbs, and replace if necessary.

9. Review your garden notes for successes and disappointments experienced last year. Make adjustments and changes in your production plans. Were specific plants disappointing? Did the potting mix hold too much moisture? Were the bottom heating pads not warm enough to germinate some seeds?

Construction of a cold frame (an in-ground wooden framed structure with a glass or plastic covering) provides a good deal of protection for planting during the cold weather. Basic greenhouse seedlings, cuttings, and smaller plants are installed in the cold frame, allowing for sunlight penetration and protection from frost and cold. Site the cold frame in full sun. The cold frame can be temporary, removed in mid-April, and stored for next year.

Herbs need at least six hours of direct sun for maximum oil production. Consider this when placing pots in the indoor site. They prefer wetter soils, but not swampy soils. Only **mint**, **lovage**, and **angelica** survive in wetter conditions.

PLANTING

During dry spells, if the ground is not frozen, work or rototill the garden, then rake it level.

If you get some warmer days, add 1 inch of compost or organic matter to the designated vegetable garden soil surface. Add nothing to the herb planting area.

CARE

Longer days will mean growth to herbs wintered over indoors. Pinch growth to maintain plants at their current size. Pinching at this time preserves their strength. The new growth, triggered by longer days, cannot be sustained.

Increase the amount of time the grow lights are on from ten hours to twelve hours.

Check **asparagus**, **rhubarb**, **chives**, and perennial **sage** for surges of growth triggered by warm days. Insulate the plants with burlap or cloth when the temperatures return to normal.

WATERING

If the winter has been dry, pull out the hose and give **apple**, **pear**, and other fruit trees, **grapes** and **blueberry** bushes a soaking for an hour. Do not leave the hose out overnight as it may freeze and be damaged.

FERTILIZING

Provide a deep root feeding to **peach** and **cherry** trees.

Do not apply fertilizer to any other trees or plants at this time.

Check the supply of fertilizers; determine if any changes need to be made from last year; purchase fertilizer to prepare for the next season.

HELPFUL HINTS

• Propagate herbs quite easily by layering. Layering is simplest for **thyme**, **lemon balm**, **sage**, and **rosemary**. Bend a branch over until it is in contact with soil; pin the branch to the soil using a roofing staple or piece of wire; cover the staple with a small amount of dirt. In thirty days or so, the roots emerge on the bottom of the pegged stem. Cut the new plant away from mother plant, transplant in the garden, or pot up the new plant in a small container.

• Many herbs are "deer proof," including **wormwood**, **basil**, **catmint**, **chamomile**, **chives**, **comfrey**, **dill**, **lemon balm**, **mint**, **oregano**, **rosemary**, **sage**, **tansy**, and **thyme**. There is some comfort in knowing that not everything planted is a deer snack food.

PRUNING

Check all fruit trees for damage at the branch and trunk intersection for cracking from the weight of ice or very heavy wet snows. If you see cracking, secure the branch and trunk to prevent further damage. If cracking is severe and tearing the bark, cut off the branch.

Prune any stems missed during fall cleanup on **raspberry** canes, **blueberry** bushes, and **grapevines**. Discard any pruning debris; it may contain or harbor insects and eggs if allowed to pile on the ground.

PESTS

Check fruit trees, bushes, and vines for signs of bark or stem gnawing by wildlife. Place a physical barrier (screen) around the trunk and bury the screen to prevent animals from burrowing underneath.

Move **basil**, **dill**, and other herbs to different sites and from under the grow lights into windows. Rotation of plants offers the opportunity to check for insects and diseases, and increases the air and light exposure. You may see roly-poly bugs (gray in color, and they roll up into a ball when touched) and soil fungus gnats (small winged bugs that fly out of the pot when moved).

Check vegetable and herb seeds (new or held over) for viability. Place a few in a wet paper towel and fold over to enclose the seed. If seeds do not germinate in three to four days, discard the seed, and purchase fresh seed.

Have you seen a black or dark brown clump (looks like a lump of chewing gum) wrapped around a twig or branch of a **cherry** or fruiting tree? The tree may have been infected with tenting or webbing caterpillars. This is an egg case waiting for warmer weather to hatch. Prune off the branch with the egg and destroy.

NOTES

FEBRUARY

EDIBLES

PLANNING

Garden centers, the Extension Service, city parks, and botanical gardens may offer classes this month on using edible plants in the landscape.

Consider personal aspects and family traits when adding a single pot of thyme, anise, or herbs to the deck, designing an arbor for **grapes** over the patio, positioning an **apple** tree near the backyard gate, or adding a patch of **raspberries** along the fence. Give some thought to mold allergies rearing from the compost pile or by the compost spread around the fruit trees or new beds. Consider family member's fears of bees and wasps that pollinate the strawberries; the available time you have for the care and maintenance of added plants; the budget you have to work with for the purchase and preparation of new plantings, and specific diet and taste preferences of the family.

PLANTING

Start **onion** and **celery** seeds indoors this month.

For the daring and optimistic, direct sow some of the cool season vegetable seeds into the garden. Try some **peas**, **lettuce**, and **spinach**. The only loss is a few seeds, and you may be the first on the block to have veggies. Check out the seed racks for new and interesting vegetables and herbs to try.

Ask about the arrival of bareroot stock **pear** and other fruit trees, and **grape** vines.

Rhubarb and **asparagus** roots are at garden centers. It's time to purchase new plants or dig and divide existing plants.

Seed **potatoes** will start showing up at garden centers. Before planting, cut the **potato** into sections so each section has an "eye," then plant the section.

If you are growing herbs from seed, most take a long time to germinate, so be patient. Smaller seeds should just be dropped onto the potting soil surface and pressed lightly (not buried) into the soil. **Anise**, **coriander**, and **dill** will not germinate under most home grow light situations. Buy these as seedlings or in packs.

CARE

Check on vegetables being stored such as **potatoes**, **onions**, or **marjoram**, **dill**, and other herbs. If rotting, discard immediately. The rot can spread rapidly through a bin of produce.

Make some easy changes to tools that make care and maintenance chores of the edibles less stressful. Extend the handles on loppers with added sections of PVC pipe. Add PVC pipe to trowels and digging claws for better leverage. Slip a bicycle handlebar grip over the end of the trowel for extra padding.

WATERING

All perennial vegetables, bushes, and trees need 1 inch of water. Supply any deficit.

Allow the soil to shrink away from sides of pot on established indoor plants, then water thoroughly.

Keep the potting mix damp, but not wet, on germinating seed and young seedlings.

FERTILIZING

Provide a light application of a granular fertilizer to newly installed cool season **cabbage**, **perennial rhubarb**, and **asparagus** plants. Water in thoroughly after applying. Or use a water-soluble fertilizer per package directions. Apply one week after planting, and then apply again every four weeks until harvest.

PRUNING

Prune **grapes** back to main trunk leaving 1 foot of growth on each lateral branch.

HELPFUL HINTS

• Pests to watch out for include aphids, leafhoppers, maggots, thrips, beetles, moths, grubs and larva, mites, borers, and arachnids. Diseases could come in the form of bacteria, fungus, rot, blight, or wilts. Signs of damage are: leaf discoloration or yellowing, sagging or full collapse, unnatural or lack of growth, leaf drop, gray film, blackened spots, small depressions, distorted growth, unusual or diminished color, holes, jagged edges, and a sticky feel. Controls for edible crops include:

• Early detection. Check the upper and lower leaf surface, the stems, twigs, and branches.

• Physical removal. Remove before the population explodes.

• Limit chemical controls to specific sites where pests are observed. Consider using dormant oils, lime-sulfur mixes.

• Encourage or release natural predators.

• Avoid planting large numbers of the same plant varieties together.

• Use healthy transplants (professionally grown or grown under grow lights) when possible.

• Remove expired or stressed plants and invasive weeds immediately.

• Select plants that have been hybridized for genetic resistance to known problems.

• Rotate crops yearly.

• Control insects; many transmit disease.

• Allow adequate space between individual plants, clusters, and rows to increase air circulation and to reduce opportunities for disease spores to cause damage.

Cut back **raspberry** and **blackberries** to the soil surface.

Prune **apple** and **pear** trees by pruning any crossing branches. Shape the trees to create an upside-down umbrella appearance to improve air circulation and make fruit picking easier.

Remove any broken branches or sections of roots before planting.

PESTS

Aphids are probably the most commonly recognized plant pests. Cool season **broccoli**, **spinach**, **cauliflower**, and **brussels sprouts** are susceptible to aphids, with concentrations on the newest and most fragile growth of a plant. This insect comes in numerous colors, from almost clear to black, and reproduces by laying eggs or by live births. If a plant is overpopulated, some grow wings and fly to a nearby host. Their feeding habit causes ants to gather and collect the residue. Interestingly, ants will pick up and relocate the aphids if necessary. Additionally, the undigested sugar left from aphid feeding causes molds and fungus to develop. The green peach aphid is most problematic in the edible landscape. Control is most effective when several methods are used. Releasing predatory ladybugs, parasitic wasps (no harm to people), and lacewings only works if enough aphids are present. When you see sufficient populations, turn predators loose. They are available at many garden centers and by mail order. Follow the instructions carefully. Keep a close eye on new soft plant tissue for aphids, and at the first signs, apply a hard spray of water to knock them off the plant. Most won't find the way back to the plant. Lightly running fingers up and down stems and squeezing kills the aphids. Finally, as a last resort, use insecticidal soaps or horticultural oils for control.

MARCH

EDIBLES

PLANNING

There is still time to order seed or plants from regional sources. Vendors include: Boston Mountain Nurseries in Mountainburg, AR., Burgess Seed in Bloomington, IL., Shumway Seedsman in Rockford, IL., Stark Brothers in Louisiana, MO., and DeGiorgi Co. in Council Bluffs, IA. Check catalog listings for additional sources. Exact address and phone numbers are available via the internet or yellow pages.

PLANTING

Take a handful of garden soil and squeeze it. If moisture is obvious between the fingers, the soil is too wet to work at this time. Working wet soil is damaging to the soil structure. Rototilling and digging creates pockets where cold air and water accumulate and cause soil compaction—both mean troubles for plantings.

This is the latest you want to install new **rhubarb** and **asparagus** roots. Plant as soon as the ground can be worked. Also plant **broccoli**, **cabbage**, **cauliflower**, **brussels sprouts**, seed **potatoes**, and **onion** sets.

If you have limited space and enjoy **tomatoes**, consider hanging baskets or containers. Good varieties to grow are 'Balconi Red' and 'Balconi Yellow'. Both seeds and plants may be available.

Plastic hanging pocket pouches offer a chance to grow herbs just outside the kitchen window for easy picking.

Start seeds of **tomato**, **pepper**, and **eggplant** indoors under grow lights for planting out in May. Sow seeds of **beets**, **carrots**, and **parsley** this month.

Take stem cuttings from **grapevines** by cutting a 6 inch section from where the old (brown) twig transitions to new (green) growth. Remove the foliage from the bottom 3 inches of stem. Dip the cut end into rooting hormone, and place into a growing mix formulated for starting seeds or cuttings. Place pot under grow lights, or sink into the ground in a cold frame or a protected location. Water to maintain soil dampness (not wet), and allow minimum of four to six weeks for rooting. If half the container is filled with developed roots, then transplant to a larger container or plant outdoors. It is very difficult, (and rarely done), to propagate fruit trees from hardwood or softwood cuttings. **Grapes,** on the other hand, are propagated by cuttings.

Many times the landscape space available restricts the number of trees that can be grown in an area. Often times, fruit trees are asked to fulfill multiple tasks in the landscape by providing shade and by producing fruits. The **cherry**, **peach** and **apple** are able to do this, but do not plant them in lawn areas because lawns require more water than the fruit trees. Crown and root rot can occur if the trunk is continually wet; also fungus on wet foliage is dramatically increased in lawn plantings.

Do root divisions of fruiting cane plants. Push the trowel or shovel deeply down into the soil over the root zone of the plant, cut out a pie-wedge piece that includes the entire root crown (stem and root are present). Either plant the section into a container, or move it to new locale in the garden.

A blue dot painted on the trunk of a fruit tree is for planting orientation. Turn the dot towards the north (the direction the tree faced in the growing field). Positioning the tree with the same orientation lessens the chance of sunscald. Sunscald can lead to bark cracking that offers entry for disease, insect invasion, and other problems.

CARE

Remove any browning leaves from perennial herbs and vegetables, and inspect for overall health. Decide if the plant is worth saving or if replacement is needed.

Keep up with removing weeds, the smaller they are the easier they are to remove. Either dig the weed out, root and all, or apply a light layer of mulch or black plastic laid between the rows.

Always read label rates when considering the use of any chemical in the garden or container space. Many times the rate of application is noted as "per acre" or for a large space, making it difficult to determine the correct mixture rate for smaller areas. The table in Helpful Hints may prove helpful, but always read the label before applying any substance to the garden.

WATERING

Indoor plants and plants under grow lights need careful monitoring to prevent soil dryness. New growth needs consistent moisture, but not soggy or wet soil.

FERTILIZING

When applying fertilizers, allow at least 6-inch spacing away from the base of the tree trunk, where there are twigs or canes emerging from ground. It is very easy to burn new growth or bark if you are not careful.

HELPFUL HINTS

Figuring Chemical Application Rates

Liquids Label Rate	Equivalent Tablespoons per 1000 sq. ft	Equivalent Teaspoons per 100 sq. ft.
1 pint per acre	3/4	1/4
1 quart per acre	1 1/2	1/2
1 gallon per acre	6	2
DRY MATERIALS		
1 pound per acre	3/4	1/4
3 pounds per acre	2 1/4	3/4
4 pounds per acre	3	1

Provide a light fertilizer application (one-half the label rate) to all indoor plants.

PRUNING

Unlike **apples**, **peaches** fruit on last year's growth, so keep pruners away from the peach trees.

Pinch back weak or excessive growth on **tomatoes**, **peppers**, **and squash** growing indoors.

Cut back herbs that are growing indoors by about one-third to prepare the plants for next season's growth. This applies to herbs that are to remain indoors or to those that will be moved outside.

Remove any winter-killed stems that are sagging, wilted, black, or brown from perennial herbs and vegetables.

PESTS

The Kansas Department of Agriculture has a website on pesticides and application perimeters.

If the stems of a young herbaceous plant are cut or nicked, and they fall over, cutworms (larva of several moths) may be the culprits. Cutworms are tunnel makers and spend the day below the surface, curled up into a letter "C" shape. For early detection, gently stir the dirt to 1 inch deep. If you see any, squash them.

EDIBLES

PLANNING

Spend some time checking for hummingbirds. Their migration north could occur during this month.

PLANTING

Start **cucumber**, **melon**, **pumpkin**, and **squash** seeds under grow lights for planting in the garden in May. Use peat pots (formed from compressed peat moss) to reduce root damage later when they are planted outdoors.

Direct sow all types of **beans**, **corn**, and **parsley** seeds in the garden. It's also time to divide perennial herbs.

Plant bare-root trees and/or shrubs as soon as the ground is dry enough to work the soil. Plant bare-root **apple** trees in full sun and in well-drained soil. Soak the roots overnight in a bucket of water with liquid root stimulator added. Dig a hole at least twice the diameter of the extended roots, building a small mound of soil in the bottom of the hole. Place the tree into the hole with the graft sitting a few inches above the soil line. Spread the roots over the mound, back fill the hole (no fertilizer added), tamp and firm soil to eliminate air pockets. Continue to back fill and tamp, but do not compact the final 4 inches of backfill. Water well, and apply a 2-inch layer of mulch (none against trunk). Check the tree the next day for any soil settling; add backfill to bring soil level up to the surrounding grade.

Plant **grapes** in a hole that is three times the diameter of the pot it is growing in, or in a hole that is twice the width of extended roots. Spread the roots in the bottom of hole, positioning the vine so that it is at the same exact depth as it was in the container. (Find the soil mark on the stem from the prior planting.) Begin covering the root mass with soil, a few inches at a time, firming the soil with each shovelfull. Build a shallow basin around the stem to initially fill with water. As the soil sinks and settles, over the course of a few days, fill in the depression so that it meets the current soil level. The rootball can sit a few inches higher than the surrounding grade.

Prepare a soil for container vegetables and herbs. Combine a mix made of two-thirds soilless potting mix and one-third standard potting soil. Add water absorbent polymer (lengthens time between waterings) and a slow-release fertilizer for vegetables. Follow package directions for proper rates.

CARE

On warmer days (above 40), start hardening off seedlings. Set them outdoors during the day (not in full sun), and bring them back in at night.

Begin harvesting **rhubarb** and **asparagus** this month. Control the colony growth by digging, dividing, and transplanting.

Do not apply any kind of pesticide to any blooming plant. It may cause flowers to drop, thereby preventing fruit and vegetable formation.

Thin any root (**carrots**, **beets**, **turnips**) vegetable crops to allow ample room for maturing. Provide a minimum of 4 inches between plants.

As new **grape** stems emerge, wind the flexible stems onto a growing structure. The tendrils will make the connection (grasping, holding, and twisting modified stem growth), and continue to spread.

WATERING

Apply 1 inch of water weekly. Check the soil regularly. If rain fell in large amounts over a short period of time, rainfall was over a week ago, and it has been clear and windy, the soil has already dried out. You may need to water containers daily.

FERTILIZING

Apply a high phosphorus fertilizer, such as 10-20-10, to help newly transplanted vegetables. Herbs require no fertilizer application or rich organic mulch. **Grapes** should be fertilized at time of installation.

PRUNING

Prune all unwanted shoots and branches to maintain an open habit on fruit trees and shrubs

Prune the **peach** tree at installation. Cut any elongated stems to 12 to 18 inches to stimulate growth. Maintain a height of 8 feet or less on **peach** trees for a more manageable picking and maintenance size. Reduce the twig mass by 10 to 20 percent each year.

PESTS

Rabbits, squirrels, moles, and deer are giving birth so prepare for the onslaught of hungry animals. Control rabbits with fencing barriers made of small grid hardware cloth or a double layer of chicken wire. Bury 20 percent of the fence to prevent digging. Squirrels will not be much damage at this time, but place dry corncobs away from the future summer vegetable planting space to detract them from the area. Change this location to avoid establishing a pattern. Moles cause damage by uprooting new transplants by burrowing below, and then voles and mice eat root systems. Try to change deer habits by placing salt blocks and corncobs away from garden. Think about getting a motion detector water gun that shoots water when a deer is close by.

Watch for stink and tarnish bugs that cause leaf damage.

Keep weeds away from **raspberry**, **strawberry**, **blackberry**, and any other plantings.

Spray light horticultural oils on fruit trees within two weeks of petal drop. Dormant oil sprays kill red spider mites and scale, while reducing the impact on beneficial insects that may not have emerged yet.

Have you seen orange, mushy, jelly-looking growths on the native **cedars** (upright evergreen **junipers**)? This is the eruption of the galls formed by cedar apple rust. These spores are airborne and if they land on the leaves of **apple** trees, the disease causes spotting, and premature fruit drop, as well as a host of other difficulties that reduce the overall health of the tree. Only plant varieties of **apples** that are hybridized to resist these spores.

HELPFUL HINTS

• Keep the garden surroundings clear of dead, declining, diseased, insect infested, and seasonal debris.

• The season determines the types and times to plant vegetables. Plant canes, bushes, vines, and trees in early spring or fall. Plant herbs in spring or summer.

• Provide physical supports, if needed, such as tomato cages, support stakes for dwarf fruit trees, and arbors and trellises for **grapes** and **berries.**

• Sometimes **tomato** plants sit for weeks without putting on a single new leaf. Garden centers may offer plants for sale a bit premature for actually planting out in the garden. Pot them up, and place under the grow lights or in the bright window until early to mid-May. Then start to harden the plants off by moving them outdoors on warmer days, and bringing them back in during cooler nights.

• Some notable varieties of vegetables and fruits not detailed in the plant listing are: **bush beans** 'Hialeah', 'Benchmark', **cantaloupe** 'Superstar', 'Eclipse', **pumpkin** 'Gold Rush', 'Jack-Of-All-Trades', **watermelons** (seedless) 'Ace of Hearts', and 'Stars N' Stripes' (seeded).

EDIBLES

PLANNING

Step back and take a close look at how the edible landscape is performing, aesthetically as well as functionally. Do the garden areas have invitational qualities, other than work oriented? A bench or birdbath offers a mental respite. Where is the focal point (dominant feature) of the upright **sweet corn** or **pole beans**? Do the textures (leaf and stem) of **oregano** and **mint** play against the colors, silhouettes, and shapes of companion plants? Are the evening and nighttime aspects of these plants just as exciting as those in the day? These are just a few considerations that may enhance the taste of a **bell pepper**, a **rhubarb** pie, **mint** flavoring in a glass of ice tea, or perhaps a fruit salad made with homegrown **blueberries** and **strawberries**.

The best way to gain wisdom and to minimize gardening pitfalls is to observe the garden looking out the window and by or walking the garden path. The information and understanding gained through these personal observations are the best indicators of what and when things should be done. Add a dash of common sense and you have the best usage of your time to gain the most results.

Mark the exact location where any vining plant seed was put into ground. Use a strong label, stake, or decorative flag to indicate the exact site to determine where the hose-end sprayer will go for watering and fertilizing when the **squash** vine starts sprawling.

PLANTING

Plant **tomato** transplants 1 inch or deeper (up to the first set of leaves is fine) into the ground. Put stakes or cages out now to eliminate hassles later trying to squeeze or bend the plants into their cages.

Plant **sweet potatoes** this month. As the cool season vegetables are harvested and removed, work up the space, add some organic matter, and plant warm season varieties such as **pepper**, **eggplant**, and **beans**. Maintain proper spacing for sweet or pop **corn** to encourage cross-pollination and room for mature growth.

CARE

Shading from the direct sun allows for a longer harvest time. Use fabric (density of window screen) or shadecloth over **lettuce**, **spinach**, and other cool season green leafy vegetables.

Cut and enjoy **asparagus** spears until the stalks are pencil size. Then allow the plant to grow and fern out (opening of leaves). Thin out and remove plant seedlings of **peas**, **anise**, and **beans** from any situation to avoid overcrowding. If possible, select the weakest plants to get rid of. Tie up new growth on vines as they need it to avoid breaking stems and damage.

WATERING

Minimize overhead watering. Keep as much moisture off the plant leaves as possible to reduce the chance of disease. If you must water overhead, do it in early morning to allow the leaves to dry during the day.

FERTILIZING

Feed **grapes** a balanced (12-12-12 or similar) fertilizer. Apply 1/4 cup around each vine installed earlier this year. For older vines, apply fertilizer as the buds swell. Use 1 cup for two-year-old vines; 1 to 1 1/2 cups for three-year-old vines; and use 1 to 2 cups of fertilizer each year of growth on older vines.

Fertilize **tomatoes** with a fertilizer formulated for **tomatoes** (analysis 6-24-24) or a similar product. Minimize adding nitrogen (first number is low). Nitrogen encourages foliage growth and minimizes fruit formation.

Fertilize **apple** trees that have been in place one year or longer. Apply 1 pound of 12-12-12 each year.

PRUNING

Cut off flower and seed stalks on the **rhubarb** to save the energy of the plant. Pinch off any **squash** flowers and certainly any fruits at the time of installation. The plant energy will be spent trying to keep the fruit growing, leaving little energy for acclimation and establishment in the garden.

PESTS

Watch for **asparagus** beetles and striped and spotted **cucumber** beetles. Both pests chew and transmit diseases in specific host plants. Watch **apple** trees for signs of codling moths; the caterpillars are leaf eaters.

Caterpillars start showing up on many vegetables this month, **broccoli** and **cabbages** in particular. Check the leaves for chewing, hand pick or apply a safe chemical control directly on the caterpillar, or use *Bacillus* (Bt) biological spray per package directions.

HELPFUL HINTS

• Purchase an insect identification guide with color pictures to help identify unknown insects.

• Use **grapes**, **strawberry**, **raspberry**, **blackberry**, **gooseberry** and **currants** that are self-pollinating. It is not necessary to plant multiple varieties for good fruit production.

• **Apples**, **apricots**, **cherry** (sour), **nectarines**, **peaches**, **pears**, **plums** need a different variety for cross-pollination. In other words, at least two different types of **apples** are needed for good fruiting. This is good information to know when you are laying out the design for the fruit trees.

Grapes are visited by several insects that disrupt fruiting; control them with insecticidal soap to lessen the impact.

If you see a blackened or gray film on the **grape** foliage, thin out the leaves, increasing air movement through the plants. Check the base of **grapevines** after a severe winter for unusual looking growth. Cut the vines down to the ground and retrain the new growth onto the arbor or trellis. If foliage appears pale or stunted, the nutrient level may be inadequate. Take a sample to your garden center if you are unsure of the problem.

Yellowing discoloration of the leaves on **blueberry** bushes is a sign of iron deficiency or unavailable nutrients. Use iron sulfate, at the label rate, to begin the recovery process. It may take a few seasons.

NOTES

JUNE

EDIBLES

PLANNING

Growing fruits and vegetables successfully requires extra time for care and for monitoring insect and disease problems. Allow time to look at the plants daily, and assess the damage. It will always be less if the plant is healthy.

PLANTING

If **broccoli**, **cauliflower**, and **cabbages** are planned for the fall garden, start seeds now in a place where you can keep a watchful eye. Young seedlings need a lot of attention; another option is to wait until transplants (professionally grown) and seedlings are available at the garden center.

Extend the harvest season and plant **pea** and **bean** seeds.

CARE

Consistency is critical to reap anticipated harvests; this applies to watering, fertilization, pruning, harvesting, and seasonal clean up. There is much care needed this month.

• A 1-inch layer of mulch applied to vegetables insulates the root systems from quick and severe drying out.

• Use black plastic as a weed barrier between the rows in the vegetable garden. Use care to dispose of plastic at the end of the growing season. Recycle if possible.

• When production is finished on June bearing **strawberries**, cut the plants back, thin the patch, weed as needed, and add 1 inch of mulch to prevent weed seed germination.

• Harvest new **potatoes** before the vines begin to die back.

• Prevent undersized fruit by removing at least one fruit from each spur that fruit is attached to, allowing it to achieve a juicy, normal size.

WATERING

Regular watering is critical. If plants show wilting in the morning hours, water immediately. Allow herbs to stay a bit on the dry side; this enhances their richness.

FERTILIZING

Vegetable crops such as **corn**, **onions**, and **potatoes** benefit from a side dressing (sprinkled near) of 12-12-12 seasonal fertilizer. Water fertilizer in well, specifically on **strawberries** and **asparagus**.

Apply 1/4 cup of balanced (12-12-12) fertilizer around each **grape** vine and **strawberry** plant.

PRUNING

Prune **cherries** and other fruit trees after their first year. Begin to shape and form the tree, opening up the center and establishing strong center leader.

Regularly pinch the side shoots off the **tomatoes** to encourage continued fruiting. Remove any suckering growth on **pear**, **peach**, and from all fruit trees. This summer pruning will not initiate new twig growth. Employ this practice throughout the summer, remembering that the main structural pruning will be done during winter dormancy.

PESTS

As pests start appearing in the garden, the predatory or beneficial insects will be close behind. Regardless of how safe or natural a control may be, it can potentially cause harm to any beneficial insects that are hit with spray.

Before **squash** and **cucumbers** start to sprawl and vine, watch closely for **cucumber** beetles and **squash** vine borers; hand pick or apply chemical controls, or lay a light weight netting fabric directly on plants to keep insects out. Watch the **corn** for boring earworms. Use a few drops of mineral oil as a preventive. Apply when tassel (silk) appears by putting a drip onto the top of the ear. *Bacillus* (Bt) is a natural bacteria that also works.

If you suspect spider mites, take out a white piece of paper; hold it under the leaf while shaking, and look for scampering red dots (spider mites). Spray off the top and bottom of leaves to physically wash them off, or apply a miticide (general insecticides will not work). Additionally, minimize the dust buildup on the leaves with an occasional overhead watering. Dust is a breeding area for the mites. **Apple** maggots lay eggs on the fruits. You can lure them away from the actual fruit with styrofoam balls or other round balls painted red and covered with any sticky substance (petroleum jelly works). Hang them in the tree to attract the females.

Weeds are trouble as they compete for water, nutrients, and sun. Although they may be difficult to keep up with, do not allow the weeds to mature and form seed heads. Next year the problem will be worse.

HELPFUL HINTS

• Plants need 1 inch of water every seven to ten days, either by natural rainfall or by irrigation.

• Maintain nutrient levels to promote steady and productive growth. Use low levels of nitrogen (first number on the bag), at 12 percent or less. Higher levels reduce flower and fruiting. Do not routinely add soil nutrients without testing the soil first, or unless plants indicate a deficiency. Feed germinating seeds and seedlings with a seed-starter fertilizer, such as 4-10-4 or a similar product.

• Build a scarecrow or two for the garden. Make them mobile so they can be moved as the garden focal area changes. Add an antique box or milk can with a lid near the garden and fill it with ties, markers, pens, labels, jars for catching bugs, and other small items for quick access.

• Pruning is the manual removal of plant parts for overall health and to enhance fruit and vegetable production. Remove all crossing branches and sucker growth (fast growing single stem) on fruit trees, bushes, and vines to insure an open habit for air circulation. Pinch off flowers and fruits, and all excessive top or side growth on vegetable plants at the time of planting. Cut or pinch stems on herbs to control the height and spread.

Look at the entire pest scenario, and then decide whether to use of a spray of water, your fingertips for squashing, predatory insects, or a natural or chemical control. Most contact pesticides have little residual effect, so it must come into direct contact with the insect, or control will not happen. Use safe, organic pesticides, like *Pyrethrin*, an insecticide derived from **chrysanthemum** flowers, or *Bacillus thuringiensis* (Bt), a naturally occurring bacteria.

Remember the pest of today (caterpillar) may be a pollinator of tomorrow (moth).

NOTES

JULY

EDIBLES

PLANNING

Invest in a soil thermometer and record the temperatures at specific locations when plants are installed or seeds are sown. Too high or too low soil temperatures explain the necessity to waiting before direct sowing of seeds into the garden, and the need for bottom heat cables or pads for germinating seeds indoors during the late winter.

PLANTING

Remove any remnants of cool season vegetables. Add 1 inch of organic matter and work it into the soil to ready the space for planting the fall crops later this summer.

Plant seed **potato** for fall harvest.

Mushroom kits are available, either locally or through mail order.

Shiitake **mushrooms** are harvested in ten days. Soak the kit in water and cover with provided plastic. Portabella **mushrooms** are pre-inoculated and are packaged in a medium for mushrooms. Harvest in less than two months. Button **mushrooms** (either white or tan) require watering upon arrival, then they want to be left alone until harvesting—about five weeks.

Take divisions of June bearing **strawberry** plants.

CARE

Set time aside to harvest **peaches** and **blackberries**. Harvest sweet **corn** when tassels turn brown. **Garlic** and **onions** are ready for digging if the leaves are brown. **Potato** vines are dying, so it is time to harvest **potatoes**.

Apply 2 to 3 inches of mulch around **peppers** and **tomato** plants to minimize the soil drying out.

WATERING

Do not allow drought stress. Monitor the rain gauges. Vegetables and fruits require either 1 inch of rainfall or 1 inch of irrigated water each week.

Water all seed or transplants for the fall garden immediately after planting. Do not delay, and maintain a consistent watering schedule to reduce any chance of drought stress.

FERTILIZING

Use a light application (one-half the label rate) of fertilizer for all plants currently setting fruits or vegetables. Use caution when applying; keep fertilizers off fruits and foliage, and away from stem to avoid fertilizer burn.

PRUNING

Cut the **raspberry** and **blackberry** canes back after the picking is finished.

Cut the tops of **sage**, **thyme**, and **basil** for harvesting and drying earlier in the day, when no moisture is on the leaves, preferably after two successive bright sunny days. Cut segments 5 to 10 inches long. Do not put into any plastic bag or container for more than a few minutes; this causes immediate decline. Take indoors, wash with cold water, lay out to dry, then bundle and hang to complete harvest.

PESTS

Blossom end rot (blackening on bottom) of **tomatoes** and **pepper** is the result of calcium deficiency and inconsistent water. The garden center has a soil additive. Maintain an application program and a consistent watering program.

If **tomato** leaves look unnatural, are curled under, shriveled, or the edges appear shredded, it could be the result of a herbicide applied close by that has drifted onto the **tomato**. These are very sensitive plants. Use care when using any herbicide or chemical.

Hotter, drier weather means spider mites (small red spiders) feeding on plants and sapping their energy. Speckled or blotchy yellow leaves are an indication of their presence.

Porous netting (allows sun and water in) stretched over semicircular hoops, positioned over **cabbage**, **broccoli**, and **cauliflower** transplants keeps all troublesome moths at bay (eliminating the need for any insecticide).

Once the vining and flowering starts on **squash** and **cucumbers**, then the netting fabric insect barrier can be removed. The insects are out of their munching cycle.

HELPFUL HINTS

Optimum Soil Temperature Ranges

For germinating seeds indoors or out:

- 65 to 85 degrees Fahrenheit: **beans**, **tomatoes**, **peas**, **sweet corn**
- 50 to 65 degrees Fahrenheit: **lettuce** (all types), **rhubarb**
- 50 to 85 degrees Fahrenheit: **broccoli**, **cabbage**, **chives**, seed **potatoes**, **spinach**

Attracting Lightning Bugs

Fireflies come out this month. They are wonderful to watch on these warm evenings. They remain active until around midnight, when they find a resting spot on the trunk or branch of a tree. The best environment to lure them to is one with lower vegetation (ground covers, **strawberries**) and a source of moisture nearby. The juvenile lightning bugs are beneficial insects, consuming snails, slugs, and aphids. The prey is paralyzed when the firefly injects them with a fluid, which also partially dissolves the insides of the pest. The larvae then use their hollow mouthparts to slurp up the mushy innards. The actual glow is a combination of oxygen and two chemicals found in the lightning bugs abdomen. Frogs love to eat lightning bugs, and if they eat a lot, the frog will begin to glow—and that is a lot of bugs.

NOTES

AUGUST

EDIBLES

PLANNING

Spend time wandering in the vegetable garden, sitting on the deck, patio, or in the yard.

See Helpful Hints for Avoiding yellowjacket and ground hornet stings.

PLANTING

Seeds of many fall vegetables. such as **lettuce**, **radishes**, and **spinach**, can be direct sown in the garden. Refrigerate seed for a week prior to planting. Garden centers may have transplants available in cell-packs. Planting from packs allows for harvest two to three months sooner than growing from seed.

Dig up tender herbs such as **chives**, **sage**, and **thyme** growing in ground. Pot them in a well-drained potting mix (cactus mix) for overwintering inside.

If **strawberries** are growing out of control, check your favorite garden center or mail order house for a prefab **strawberry** bed that includes materials to construct a circular, terraced, pyramidal bed with space for up to fifty plants. The system has a flexible metal framework and includes all the necessary parts to put it together. Additional options include an irrigation system, bird netting with supporting frame, and a covering to buffer harsh unexpected cold snaps.

Check **blackberry** and **raspberry** patches for invasive growth. If the plants are pliable, bend and pin the stems, root them, then dig and replant in the garden. Or simply prune off out-of-bound runners if the colony size is adequate.

Divide herbs for potting and moving indoors.

CARE

Remove plants as they cease production. Compost or work the expired plants deeply into the soil. If branches are sagging from the weight of the fruit on **peach** and **cherry** trees, either remove some of the fruit and discard, or construct bracing timbers to prevent any cracking of limbs. Pinch back new growth on **pumpkins** and **gourds** to concentrate the energy into existing fruits.

Blueberry, **grapes**, and other fruits are ripening. Protect from birds with netting, bags (paper only), or screened cages. The harvest time for **grapes** is when the stems holding the bunches begin to turn brown, or check inside an individual **grape** (seeded); if the seed is brown, it's time to gather the fruit.

Set **onions** in a warm dry spot for curing for at least two weeks before long-term storage.

Start cleaning out the cold frames and preparing them for fall use.

WATERING

Monitor watering closely. The cooler longer nights provide the perfect situation for root rots, fungus, and bacteria. Water new transplants gently to avoid knocking over tender seedlings and damaging stems and roots.

FERTILIZING

Make the last applications on container vegetables. However, do not apply fertilizer to any containers scheduled to be brought indoors.

PRUNING

Pinch and harvest herbs; air temperatures cause greater concentration of flavors and oils in the leaves.

Colorless or whitish spots on red **raspberries** at peak harvest season is likely the result of too much direct sunlight on fruits. As soon as the **raspberries** begin to color, drape a light shade cloth over the canes.

 PESTS

Carefully check any plants currently growing outside for insects. Spider mites continue to be a dilemma. Regularly wash off the foliage tops and bottoms. Check the ends of branches for fall webworms on fruit trees. Prune off affected branches and destroy or apply *Bacillus* (Bt).

Moles are in maximum mode and will undermine garden areas. Use spear or choker loop traps. Look for the most active areas (new mounds of dirt on surface), and place the trap over or in the tunnel. Smash down a few feet of soil on either side of the traps. Check traps each morning, if you have no luck, move trap to a new location. There are generally no more than a few moles in an entire landscape; they are territorial and it is the strongest that survive, so keep at it. As these tunnels are abandoned, they fill with cold air and water, causing plant root systems to stress.

Birds realize that many fruits are ripening; protect with netting.

HELPFUL HINTS

Don't Get Stung

This is yellow jacket and ground hornet season, some can be far more dangerous than most bees. There are several types of yellow jackets, and one type is obvious in late summer through mid-fall. Its diet shifts from protein gathered from plants (pollination), to caterpillars (predatory), and to sweet drinks or food. Additionally in dry weather, the yellow jacket will sit on the side or top of a can or bottle, to satisfy its need of moisture. This time of year they are gathering nutrition, as the nest is being prepared to populate the colonies for next year. The nests are located in the ground or in structures. Vibrations can cause a swarming that is their defense mechanism. Stinging (poison gland) and biting occur, and can happen multiple times. If you are stung, apply ice and meat tenderizer. If swelling continues past several hours, seek medical help.

Avoid problems with yellow jackets. Swish them away with slow deliberate movements; fast swings causes panic and defensive attack. A squashed or dead yellow jacket releases a scent that can result in additional attacks from others. Fragrances and brightly colored clothes are attractants—not resulting in attack, but they will hover around.

Check your soda can before taking a drink. Yellow jackets are attracted to pet food; dogs may bite them unknowingly and get stung in the mouth. Place traps with pheromones and attractive scents to control. Seek a professional pest control service for eradication of nests. It is not advisable that you personally attempt to kill the nest with an insecticide. If you do spray, do so at night, spray the insecticide into the hole and plug immediately. Watch for secondary exits, and wear protective clothing.

SEPTEMBER

EDIBLES

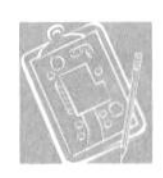

PLANNING

The weather is fantastic and it is time for butterfly watching. There are approximately 198 species of butterfly found in Kansas. The three most common are tiger swallowtail (*Papilio glaucus*), cabbage white *(Pieris rapae)*, and painted lady (*Vanessa cardui*).

The main identification ingredient is the diverse color among the species. This diversity is carried over to the outward appearance of the egg, its size, shape, and arrangement. Ultimately, a caterpillar emerges with its own extremely unique markings; the colors and diet requirements give no hint of who the parents are. See Helpful Hints for more on butterflies.

If you are trying to attract more butterflies into the landscape, use some of the extra fruit from the harvest. Cut open **peaches**, **apples**, **apricots**, and lay out **blueberries** and **raspberries**. The butterflies enjoy fruits; remove and replenish every other day or when fruits blacken.

Hummingbirds are visiting tubular shaped herb flowers for the nectar on their continuing migration south for the winter; some come from as far away as Central America.

PLANTING

This month is your last chance to sow **lettuce**, **radish**, and **spinach** seed into the open garden with any hopes of getting a harvest. Consider sowing seed in the cold frame for extended harvest period.

Divide herbs in the garden for potting and moving indoors.

CARE

Place herbs brought in from the garden in a window or under grow lights. Harvest **broccoli** regularly to encourage new growth. Pinch off any new **tomatoes** forming. Pinching allows existing fruit to grow and mature to full size. As **cauliflower** heads form, tie or pin the leaves over the head to prevent sunburn.

Regardless of the time of year, use caution when cutting back severely or removing plantings that are food for the caterpillar. This can lead to a wilder look to the garden, and although it is essential to cut back some foliage to encourage lush growth (the caterpillar preference), prune with a light hand. Eating continues twenty-four hours a day, with occasional stops for molting or maybe sightseeing. Caterpillars crawl to move themselves around; the amount of travel is dependent upon finding another leaf to munch.

WATERING

Provide 1 inch of water on any **bean**, **lettuce**, or **pea** plant that continues to produce, and water **asparagus**, **blackberry**, or **apple** trees to prepare for winter.

FERTILIZING

As spaces are vacated with harvest, consider planting a cover crop (**annual rye**, **winter wheat**), a winter legume (**pea**), **alfalfa**, and **black medic**. Turn the crops under in late winter to enrich the soil. **Pea** family members also add nitrogen. Scatter the seed, rake in lightly, and water. Keep damp until the plants are 6 inches tall, and then allow rainfall to water, unless there is a severe drought.

PRUNING

Harvest sections of **rosemary**, **lavender**, **mint**, and **parsley** for use during the winter, then either dry or freeze. Remove any suckering growth from **apple**, **peach**, **apricot**, and **plum** trees to maintain the open vase (upside down umbrella) shape.

PESTS

Check herbs being brought indoors. Examine the leaves, stems, root systems (pull out of pots), and bottoms of containers for any insects or signs of fungus. Provide controls for the pests; remove the section affected by fungus. Isolate the plant and check for several days, determining that the problem is gone before moving near other plants.

HELPFUL HINTS

More on Butterflies

The butterfly life cycle is basically four stages: egg, caterpillar (larvae), chrysalis (pupa resting), and final emergence as butterfly. The female lays eggs near the food source. Upon hatching, the small caterpillar begins feeding immediately. If a food source is not available, the caterpillars starve. With each bit of the leaf consumed, growth occurs equally as fast. Small black dots on the remaining portion of the leaf signify digestion. The time spent as an eating machine caterpillar is seven days or less. This constant buffet means rapid body growth, which in turn leads to a repetitious shedding of the exoskeleton until the caterpillar reaches mature size. A resting period (chrysalis) follows. The pupa resembles a small wad of brown paper. Some butterflies can have two or more broods each year, illustrating the importance of maintaining caterpillar food sources.

Adults prefer flowers that have relatively flat surfaces, created with either larger clusters of small flowers or single ones with lower lips that have substantial size. In either situation, it is a two-fold scenario. The nectar is the attraction, and the structure offers a resting place. Avoid over hybridized varieties that are visually more glamorous, but sometimes the nectar production is reduced. Additionally, **peonies** and **gladiolas**, which have the physical characteristics, are passed by.

NOTES

EDIBLES

PLANNING

Planning and growing an edible landscape allows for the use of the emptied garden space for very different plant groupings. The well-prepared and properly draining garden soil for the vegetables is a perfect environment for spring flowering bulbs. Consider that October is the bulb-planting month. This month is also the time when the vegetable garden spaces are emptied. Fall vegetables have limited space needs. The bulbs start blooming in February, and with planning, they will probably be finished by May—just in time for the main flow of readied summer vegetable seedlings to be installed into the garden.

Since this month ends the harvest cycle for summer crops, plan to compost all the expired plants being pulled from the garden.

The composting methods in Helpful Hints all produce compost when all the other conditions are met. The end product has many uses in the garden; but we use it mainly to blend with the existing soil to allow for better air and water penetration. This leads to healthier roots and more productive harvests. Besides its physical presence, compost also encourages building of essential bacterium and microbial substances.

PLANTING

Add organic matter to the garden space. Layer the materials and work them into the soil.

Take stem cuttings on the pruning branches you cut off the **grapevines**. Cut a 6 inch section from where the old (brown) twig transitions to new (green) growth. Remove foliage from the bottom 3 inches; dip the cut end into rooting hormone, and place in a growing mix formulated for starting seeds or cuttings. Place pot under grow lights or in the cold frame. Water to keep the soil damp, but not wet. Allow up to four to six weeks before transplanting.

CARE

If the soil test indicated the need for lime, this is best time of year to apply the material. Work it into the soil. Direct fruit tree and **grapevine** growth with velcro straps or similar material that are easy to use and remove.

WATERING

All trees, bushes and vines cannot go through any type of drought stress, most specifically the spring flowering varieties; the buds are set and a low moisture period could impact next year's production.

Regardless of rainfall amounts, do not irrigate **peach** trees anymore this year; watering now reduces their hardiness.

FERTILIZING

Cover all previously planted areas with 1 to 2 inches of compost. The compost serves as winter mulch and a source for lower analysis fertilizer when fully decomposed.

PRUNING

Cut back the **grapes** to two obvious buds just off the main trunk. Continue to remove branching (for openness) on all deciduous trees and bushes as the leaves drop. This pruning gives you a clearer look into the twig structure. Before a hard frost or freeze (temperature below 30 degrees), harvest **sweet potatoes**, **gourds**, **winter squash**, and **pumpkins**. Pick the last of the **tomatoes**, **peppers**, **peas**, and **beans**.

PESTS

Garden cleanup is important for control of overwintering insects and diseases.

- Stir the top few inches of soil and check for beetle or grub larva; remove and destroy if discovered.
- Check the fruit trees for egg capsules of tent and webworms.

If you see odd scratching or marks in the bark of young trees, this is the result of male deer rubbing off the "velvet" from their antlers. Very little can be done to prevent this, short of erecting a strong temporary fence surrounding the individual trees.

When picking **pumpkins** or **gourds**, keep a few inches of the stems attached for easier and longer storage.

HELPFUL HINTS

Composting Methods

There are a few composting structures to select from:

1. The top-of-the-line three stall system allows for turning the compost from one stall to the next, accelerating and maximizing the end results.
2. A single space or stall allows for turning the pile in place. A freestanding heap, with no sides or back, is the simplest method, and it still works fine.
3. A roll around plastic ball or a mounted barrel is made of heavy gauge plastic, and has ventilation. These systems provide smaller amounts of compost.
4. Construction of stalls or a single space composter consists of cinder blocks stacked to form a rectangle (5 feet x 5 feet x 3 feet), or use heavy duty wire fencing shaped in a square or circle. The pile compost system should encompass an area that is 3 feet x 3 feet x 5 feet for easy turning. It is best to have something under the stalls, spaces, or heaps to enable air circulation at the bottom. The preformed plastic type has ventilation holes, but still needs to be rolled or turned.

NOTES

EDIBLES

PLANNING

Get the kids involved. Pull out the catalogs or go to the garden center, and allow them to pick out some seeds; it only brings out the best in everyone when the planting begins.

Take soil samples and send to a lab for testing. If you do it now, it allows for plenty of time, after the results and recommendations are back, to plan your soil "strategy" for next season.

When considering next year's vegetable garden, crop rotation should be used to prevent the buildup of disease organisms in a certain location. Troubles can result even when resistant varieties are planted in the same spots year after year. Keep this in mind when planning the garden for next year.

PLANTING

Run the rototiller or spade the garden after the expired plants and debris are removed. This stirs up any bugs or eggs trying to overwinter below the surface. The local birds will appreciate this buffet.

If the herbs sitting on the windowsills have direct contact with the glass, pull them back from the panes to lessen the amount of leaves that might freeze, dampen, or rot from condensation. If herbs are elongated and leaning cut them back by about 25 percent.

After several night temperatures of mid- to low 20s, apply a layer of straw to the **strawberries**. Loosely shake the straw to disperse it, and to prevent large clumps of straw from piling up (breeding ground for diseases). Provide a thin layer of straw over the entire plants. If the **rhubarb** is overcrowded or unproductive, dig and divide into two to four sections and replant. Remove any remaining fruit and bury it deeply in the garden, or add it to the compost pile. Be sure to layer the pile with other materials.

Sage, **mint**, **chives**, and other hardy variety herbs benefit from winter protection from the freeze/thaw cycle that pushes root systems out of the ground. Apply a 1- to 2-inch layer of mulch after the ground is frozen for one full day. Select mulch that will not compact down or hold in wetness (consider a bark type); do not remove mulch until new growth is consistently strong in the spring.

WATERING

Continue to supply fruit trees and bushes, and perennial vegetables and herbs with at least 1 inch of water each week. A regular supply of water minimizes the possibility of root damage during the winter, as water fills any air pockets around roots, preventing cold air from sinking and damaging fragile root hairs.

FERTILIZING

Fertilize fruit trees every three years, with the first deep root fertilization occurring during the tree's second winter. Use compost or a very low analysis type fertilizer. Do not fertilize any other plants at this time. Cold temperatures kill forced, tender growth. Do not fertilize any plants under grow lights. They need a dormant rest cycle to store energy for later.

Bone meal, dried blood, kelp, cottonseed meal, and fish emulsion are available at garden centers or in catalogs. These products are considered organic fertilizers and can be used in garden spaces.

PESTS

Inspect foliage and stems of herbs for bugs and disease. If discovered, isolate and control, or discard.

Run the rototiller or spade the vegetable and herb garden spaces to bring soil dwelling insects and eggs to the surface. The exposure reduces populations, either due to temperatures or the feasting birds.

NOTES

HELPFUL HINTS

The Science of Composting

Composting ingredients include pieces of sod, grass clippings, leaves and needles from trees and shrubs, hay, straw, weeds, vegetable garden remnants, shredded newspapers, woody plant prunings, and kitchen wastes. It is best if you do not use grease, animal fat, meat scraps, or bones. These attract uninvited guests, produce a foul smell, and do not contribute to the compost. Also, use only slight amounts of fireplace ash, and do so infrequently. Use a layering technique to build your compost pile. Layer with different materials using a light sprinkling of compost starter, 1 inch of garden soil, 3 inches of fresh grass clippings, 6 inches of leaves or needles, and 2 inches of kitchen scraps, vegetables, or fruit.

The science of composting involves the formation of primitive bacteria that assist in the decomposition of the ingredients. The bacteria are followed by actinomycetes (a filamentous bacteria), then come fungus and protozoa. The final degradation is the result of higher life forms such as centipedes, millipedes, sowbugs (roly-polies), and earthworms that go about the business of breaking portions of the materials into more usable parts. This process occurs as quickly as six weeks, or takes as long as nine months. The rate of breakdown is influenced by the time of year, the location of the compost and surrounding environment, the specific components and quantities, layering techniques, and care of the pile.

Alternate the layers of the different material, adding soil or compost starter every two or three layers. As each layer is added, dampen it (can be a diluted water-soluble fertilizer, rather than just water). Do not wait until the pile is complete to wet the pile. Water with each layer. It is not necessary to turn the piles or rotate between the spaces; but this process does encourage a quicker break down and availability of compost. Do not add lime to the pile. The initial reaction of the elements causes a pH that is very acidic; as the process continues, the pH rises and ultimately ends up near neutral. The temperature during the cooking should be from 110 to 140 degrees. Use a soil thermometer to determine internal temperature. If the temperature is cooler, there will be minimal reaction or decomposition; too hot of temperature literally fries the material.

DECEMBER

EDIBLES

PLANNING

Put together all plant labels, notes, and information gathered on production and performance of the vegetable garden plants. Determine if any changes need to be made for the next year.

How did your knees hold up? Consider purchasing cushions or guards. Maybe you are due for a new pair of gloves for cutting back **blackberries** and **raspberries**.

Colder weather brings an array of nuts to the grocery stores. If space is available in the landscape, why not grow some? Varieties that grow well in Kansas are 'Thomas Black' **walnut,** 'Lake English' and 'Champion English' **walnut,** and 'Colby', 'Major' and 'Peruque' **pecan.** Depending on the garden situation, harvest may come as soon as eight years.

PLANTING

Check at your favorite garden center for discounted prices on healthy **peach**, **pear**, and other fruit trees and bushes. Make sure that there are no scrapes on the trunk, broken branches, and that the plant has good overall structural shape (balanced branching). This time of year, the ground is still relatively warm to encourage root growth, so it is fine to plant.

If you really like to get a jump-start on the spring garden by setting vegetable or herb transplants into the garden in late winter, provide protection from a severe cold snap. Place plastic water filled tubes around the plants for insulation from the low temperatures.

Have you seen lighted grow tables available in catalogs? The grow table is an all-in-one manufactured kit that allows for organized seed growing that is also set up for ease of maintenance and plant care.

CARE

Clean up frost or freeze killed damaged stems and leaves lying on the ground.

Bring in all the **tomato** cages, check for strength, replace broken or damaged cages, and clean salvageable ones.

Clean and sharpen gardening tools (pruners, lopers, saws) as needed. Winterize gas powered equipment (drain gas tank, remove and replace spark plugs, service).

WATERING

Keep the hoses and irrigation system available to insure that trees receive 1 inch of water each week.

Check catalogs to determine if a new type of irrigation system (drip or soaker type are excellent) would be beneficial and time saving in the long run.

Bring in the rain gauges before a hard freeze occurs to prevent damage.

PRUNING

This is an excellent time to observe the limb and branching structure on deciduous trees (the leaves have fallen). Prune deciduous trees and shrubs to insure openness. This maximizes the amount of sunlight to all limbs during the growing season and increases the chance for more blooms and a good harvest. Make all cuts at a 45-degree angle to expose more of the healing layer of the branch, making for quicker and stronger mending.

PESTS

Continue to clear any dead plant materials lying on the ground to reduce locations for overwintering insects, eggs, or diseases.

Watch the mulched areas for sign of tunnels; set traps to catch voles or field mice.

HELPFUL HINTS

Soil Analysis

A completed soil analysis indicates either an abundance or deficit of the following nutrients:

Chemical Symbols/Nutrient	Function
B: Boron	Micro nutrient works in combination for overall health
Cu: Copper	Micro nutrient affects plant resistance to disease
Fe: Iron	Micro nutrient affects foliage health
K: Potassium	Macro nutrient promotes thick, strong, cell walls
Mg: Magnesium	Micro nutrient aids in uptake of other nutrients
Mn: Manganese	Micro nutrient speeds seed germination
Mo: Molybdenum	Micro nutrient is important to nitrogen fixation
N: Nitrogen	Macro nutrient assists in stem and leaf growth
P: Phosphorus	Macro nutrient aids root system and plant establishment
S: Sulfur	Changes soil chemistry to free nutrients for uptake

Any number below 7.0 is considered acidic. Most plants in the edible landscape perform best in a neutral soil. The addition of lime raises the pH, making it more alkaline. Do not add lime unless the soil test indicates a need.

Range for Optimal Growth

Plant	Ph
Apples	5.5–7.5
Asparagus	6.0–7.5
Blueberry	5.0–6.0
Cabbage	6.0–7.5
Corn	6.0–7.0
Garlic	5.5–8.0
Grapes	5.5–8.0
Lettuce	6.0–7.0

Range for Optimal Growth

Plant	Ph
Onions	6.0–7.0
Peas	5.5–6.5
Potatoes	5.0–7.0
Raspberry	5.5–6.5
Sage	5.5–8.0
Spinach	5.7–6.5
Strawberry	5.3–6.5
Tomatoes	5.5–7.0

NOTES

CHAPTER FOUR

GROUND COVERS & VINES

Texture, form, and color sweeping across an open vista, climbing up and over, calling a halt to a view, creating peace where once chaos reigned—this sums up our tremendously diverse collection of plants.

SO MANY CHOICES

Ground covers and vines are valued for their aesthetic qualities and are most often looked to as a key component to solving potential or existing problems. Many of these plants can be planned and used as both ground cover and vines within the same yard or landscape. Add pizzazz to pots, containers or window boxes by adding ground covers or vines.

English ivy will add foliage that is dark green with whitish veins. It can grow in an area under large mature trees in the front yard, and around the back it can climb a wooden fence to create a softer, more natural look and feel. Dropmore scarlet honeysuckle (scarlet trumpet honeysuckle vine) moves up and through an arbor while sending out shoots at its base that generate a stabilizing carpet-like scene. Herbaceous bishop's weed's (snow on the mountain) variegated leaf can be dotted throughout evergreen ground covers providing a highlight from May through October, then disappearing underground to return next year.

Planting a bed or edger of lilyturf allows its deep green blades to reduce the glare of a concrete walkway or drive. An added bonus is short stalks of blue flowers in summer or fall. Silver vine, while rambling through a chain link fence, gives upright clusters of white flowers for several weeks as stone crop's (dragon's blood sedum) uniformity calms and amplifies rolling topography. Yellow or green leaf creeping jenny creates cascades over a stone wall or water fall during the summer, as Jackman clematis twine up a mailbox or light post.

Whether the front, back, or side yard, very few situations will not be improved by a planting of a ground cover or vine. Almost forgotten is the fruit, seed, and/or protection they offer to a wide variety of birds. Boston ivy is a prime example of this with black/blue fruits for feeding and large dense foliage perfect for nesting. Causing wonder and excitement but aggressive and invasive—these growing habits are hallmarks of variegated leaf chameleon plant ground cover and wisteria vine. Give ample thought before incorporating either into a landscape. It's nice to know there are several choices of ground covers and vines that will work well—giving way to your personal preferences.

INSIGHTS, REQUIREMENTS, AND TIPS

Planting

What Size to Plant: Garden centers and mail order nurseries offer climbing hydrangeas in 4-inch or larger containers, or bare root (no soil) plants. Winter creeper or bugleweed are offered in cell packs, flats or gallon pots. Regardless of point of purchase, always inspect plants for the amount of roots (turn container upside down allowing plant to slide out), foliage consistent in size and color, and establishment time. Routine care and maintenance is reduced by installing larger plants or pots of dead nettle or myrtle due to increased root mass. Annual cardinal climber, hyacinth bean, moon flower, morning glory, and scarlet runner bean are planted from seed gathered and stored from the previous year, or from new packets.

When to Plant: There are multiple chances through the year. The best is spring (after the ground thaws) through June (summer requires more vigilant care during establishment due to heat related stress); or in early September through October (later planting causes greater winter kill potential). Plants in gallon or larger pots can have a delayed installation period to due their heavier root mass.

Where to Plant: Site analysis involves looking closely at all aspects of the proposed planting location, and the amount of sun. For example, stone crop requires full sun, lilyturf can transition from sun into shade, myrtle grows best in part shade to shade, and clematis likes sun with shaded roots (such as the backside of a trellis). Boston ivy is adaptable, while climbing hydrangea wants no direct sun from 10 a.m. to 3:00 p.m.

Check for hardscapes (walks/drives), water runoff, and possible heat transference into soil. Your planting's root system can leave very little soil near a trunk. Leaving a distance of 5X the diameter of the trunk provides a buffer zone. Consider the placement of vines according to fundamental vine categories: clinging and non-clinging. Clinging stems in the form of small suction cups or rootlets adhere to almost any rough surfaces. Non-clinging vines grow upward by twining stems or tendrils, and need an open support system for weaving. Mature plants have weight, and can cause damage. Container growing allows for mobility on a deck or patio.

Planting Preparation and Installation

Outline the planting space, and remove undesirable plants by using an herbicide, rototilling or digging with a spade to a depth of 6 to 8 inches. Use extreme caution planning new gardens under existing trees for two reasons: changing soil elevation against the trunk could rot bark, or working soil may result in possible root damage. Blend 6 inches of organic matter (compost, leaf mold, etc.) into the existing soil and rake smooth.

Dig a hole 3 times the width of the root system, and remove and shake off any potting soil (loses structure and disappears outdoors). Loosen the roots if pot bound, and place in a hole slightly higher than the surrounding ground. Back fill firm soil, water thoroughly, and place 1 inch of mulch around plant. Do not cover the plant even if it is dormant. This could cause moisture and fungus problems as new growth breaks ground. In a sloped site consider using biodegradable erosion netting. If growing in a container, fill 2/3 of pot with soilless potting mix, and combine with 1/3 potting soil to help with water retention. Remove flowers, brown leaves, and damaged stems at installation. This conserves energy for root growth.

After Planting Care and Troubleshooting

If fallen leaf debris is collecting on the ground cover plants, stiff and rigid oak leaves are fine. Thin and flexible leaves such as maple or ash can be problematic, compressing and maintaining too much moisture over the plant crown.

Weeds could be trouble for up to 5 years in new plantings. Control with pre- and post-emergent herbicides according to label instructions. A safe alternative is hand digging to get the entire root.

Fertilizing: Needed monthly during the growing season with balanced food (1-1-1 ratio) at the rate on the label.

Mulching: Never exceed a depth of 1 to 2 inches at any time and never place mulch over the crown of any plant.

Pruning: Vines will benefit from an annual cutting back to 1 foot for the first three years after installation, then pruning to control growth. Large stands of ground cover can be mowed (at the highest blade setting) every year to keep plants vigorous, and prevent stem build-up (which make plants more prone to winter damage). Or mow as needed in fall to eliminate leaf raking. Chopped leaves will act as low grade fertilizer.

Propagation: Allow seed heads to form and

mature (they will darken and begin to split open). Gather and store, or relocate. Divide only healthy plants. Others carry problems to a new location and/or die. Section and lift with essential root attached. Back fill hole with compatible dirt.

Take 6-inch stem cuttings in early spring. Dip in rooting hormone and place in containers filled with seed starter potting mix. Routinely check both seeds and cuttings for soil/potting mix moisture. Do not allow to plants to wilt.

Practice Integrated Pest Management

Apply an application of pesticide directly onto insect pest(s) rather than generally spraying the entire plant). Predatory insects are most effective in sunny locations where plantings are attractive to pests (as potential food). The presence of disease such as mildew, mold, or fungus growth may occur on the mulch surface. The impact on healthy plants is minimal. Gently stir the area and realize the problem may return or pop up elsewhere.

BASIC GUIDELINES FOR GROUND COVERS AND VINES

Planning

Use caution when planning new gardens under existing trees. The change in soil elevation around the trunk could rot the bark and working the soil may result in possible root damage.

Trees have extensive root systems. If ground covers are planted closely to the trunk, that area may be heavily inundated with roots, preventing establishment of new plants. To determine where the starting point for planting should be, measure the trunk diameter and multiply this number by 3 or 5. Use the resulting figure as the distance from the trunk to begin the planting. Selecting the best plant, with the appropriate maximum size, for the individual site makes a difference.

Garden centers have ground covers available as bare-root cuttings and as plants in containers ranging from 2 1/4-inch cell-packs to 5-gallon pots. The larger size plants provide an instant landscape impact, and have better established root systems that provide effective erosion control and require less daily monitoring during the establishment period. Mail order plants are shipped bare root, wrapped in moss, or in smaller pots. This reduces weight and saves on shipping costs, but smaller sizes will have smaller root masses and less root hairs (nutrient absorbers), thereby requiring more after-care.

Planting

• Spring is the best time for planting, after the ground thaws through early June. Planting later in the summer has the potential for high losses. Planting in the fall and into mid-October increases the chances of winterkill.

• The soil requires preparation before planting ground covers. Outline the planting space. Remove undesirable plants by digging or by applying a herbicide. Rototill or spade to depth of 6 to 8 inches. Blend in a total of 6 inches of organic matter with the existing soil and rake smooth, creating a raised bed. Use biodegradable (paper weave) erosion netting, if needed, during establishment on slopes or large areas. Dig a hole twice the width of root system, remove the plant carefully from the container, loosen the roots if plant is potbound, place in the hole slightly higher than the surrounding ground, back fill and firm the soil. Water the plant thoroughly, remove existing flowers, and apply a 1-inch layer of mulch.

• **Before purchasing,** inspect the plants for consistent leaf color and size. If the plant is dormant, or bare-root, check the amount of roots, number of buds, and stem flexibility.

The coverage rate for ground covers is related to the container size and the square footage of the planting area. For example, a 1-quart plant:

• spaced 6 inches apart provides area coverage in one full growing season.

• spaced 9 inches apart provides area coverage in two full growing seasons.

• spaced 12 inches apart provides area coverage in three or more growing seasons.

Have patience with growing vines in the garden. Do not expect a quick impact regardless of the noted growth rate. Some varieties may take three or more years for roots to establish and for subsequent top growth rate.

• **To propagate plants from seed,** allow the seed to darken and begin to split. Gather pods and store for future germination, or scatter them in a prepared soil area. Plant in containers using a flat with seed-starter potting mix, place under grow lights or in a protected (out of direct sun and wind) locale, and keep the soil damp.

• **For divisions and cuttings,** use only healthy plants. Take cuttings or divisions on new growth or at end of growing season just before dormancy occurs. For divisions, cut a pie-wedge piece out of the ground cover and lift out, making sure that the entire growing crown (intersection of leaf, stem, and root) is present. Transfer to new locale, plant, back fill, and water. For cuttings, cut sections off of new green growth and move to other locations or plant in containers until rooted.

Care

• If leaf debris collecting over plants is thin and flexible, such as the leaves from maple and ash, it can be problematic for the ground cover or vine. Fine textured debris can compress down and trap too much moisture over the plant crown. If the tree happens to be an oak, the stiff and rigid leaves collecting on the planting allow for air spaces, and so work well as natural mulch.

• Building foundations, posts, and support structures made of concrete have the ability to leech lime into the soil. Check the pH level often in these areas and correct if necessary.

• Maintain a 2-inch layer or less of mulch. Apply at anytime.

• Do not dump and spread mulch to cover the plants. The plant may not have the ability to push healthy growth through the mulch.

Watering

• Prior to installation, watering is a necessity. Also, keep the potted plants out of the direct sun and wind before planting.

• New installations that have been acclimating less than one growing season should be monitored closely for water stress. Water if the plants wilt in the morning hours.

• Established plants, in a location for a minimum of one growing season, should receive 1 inch of water every seven to ten days.

Fertilizing

• During the establishment period (the first growing season), feed ground covers and vines monthly with a balanced analysis (same numbers) fertilizer.

• After the establishment period, add fertilizer or amendments according to the soil test results.

• Follow the label directions or use less than recommended rate of granular or liquid fertilizers. Using less is best, as using more could cause unnatural floppy growth or foliage or flower burn.

Pruning

• Cut off flowers or browned leaves at the time of installation and throughout the growing season to reduce chances of disease or insect outbreaks.

• Remove buds or blooming flowers at the time of planting on new installations to conserve the plant's energy. Do not cut back the foliage.

• Set the mower to the highest level and mow ground covers in midsummer if the foliage has browned. New growth will emerge and be fuller.

• Trim or cut back ground covers and vines to control growth.

Pest Control

• FOLLOW LABEL RATES whenever applying any fungicide, insecticide, or herbicide.

• Many insecticides are contact killers only.

Apply chemicals directly on the insects for the best results.

• If you are applying pre-emergent herbicides, they could also impact any seed germination of wanted plants. Post-emergent herbicides have the ability to drift while being sprayed and can impact surrounding plants.

• The use of a fungicide is most effective if treatment is made prior to detection. Use if a history of need dictates. Do not be alarmed if mildew, mold, or fungus growth occurs on the mulch surface. The impact on healthy plants is minimal. Gently stir the area.

• Slugs and snails can be present in all shaded areas. Check for shiny and squiggly trails. Use baits or traps for control.

• Weeds could be trouble for up to five years in a new garden. Post-emergent herbicides are labeled for a broad plant group, such as the grasses or for broadleaf plants. Always exercise caution and be on the safe side. The safe alternative is hand digging. Pre-emergent herbicides may have an impact on garden soil and on new plant installations. READ THE LABEL prior to making a purchase or applying any product.

• Geotextile weed barriers could slow plant establishment by preventing the roots growing along stems from having contact with the soil.

Ground Covers & Vines

AESTHETIC ATTRIBUTES:

For bloom with abandon:	Try scarlet trumpet honeysuckle, silver vine, bugleweed, hyacinth bean
Color:	snow on the mountain, dead neetle, chameleon plant, Jackman clematis, morning glory, scarlet runner bean, trumpet honeysuckle
For texture and forms:	Try climbing hydrangea, Boston ivy, winter creeper, stone crop, cardinal climber
Want versatility?	English ivy, lilyturf, yellow creeping jenny, myrtle, moon flower, wisteria

KEY:

Common Name:	Frequently used, sometimes location (city, town, county) specific
Botanical Name:	Scientific name—assures correct plant when making purchase
Good Variety(s):	Recommendation—among numerous possibilities
Height/Flower Color:	Average/Dominant
Bloom Period/Type:	Season/Distinguishing characteristic
Light Requirements:	Sun = minimum six hours; part shade = no direct sun 10 a.m.-3:00 p.m.

Common Name: Boston ivy
Botanical Name: *Parthenocissus tricuspidata*
Good Variety(s): 'Green Showers' or 'Purpurea'
Height/Flower Color: 30 feet or more/Pale green
Bloom Period/Type: Early summer/Deciduous clinging vine
Light Requirements: Full sun-full shade

Common Name: Bugle weed
Botanical Name: *Ajuga reptans*
Good Variety(s): 'Metallica Crispa' or 'Burgundy Glow'
Height/Flower Color: 1 to 2 inches/Blue
Bloom Period/Type: Spring/Semi-evergreen
Light Requirements: Full sun-shade

Common Name: Cardinal climber
Botanical Name: *Quamoclit sloteri/ Ipomoea quamoclit*
Height/Flower Color: 20 feet/Red
Bloom Period/Type: Summer until frost/Annual vine
Light Requirements: Full sun

Common Name: Chameleon plant
Botanical Name: *Houttuynia cordata*
Height/Flower Color: 1 foot or more/White
Bloom Period/Type: Summer/Herbaceous ground cover
Light Requirements: Full Sun-Light Shade

Common Name: Climbing hydrangea
Botanical Name: *Hydrangea anomala* ssp. *Petiolaris*
Height/Flower Color: 20 feet or more/White
Bloom Period/Type: Summer/Deciduous clinging vine
Light Requirements: Part sun-shade

Common Name: Dead nettle
Botanical Name: *Lamium maculatum*
Good Variety(s): 'White Nancy' and 'Beacon Silver'

Height/Flower Color: up to 1 foot/Pinkish purple
Bloom Period/Type: Summer/Herbaceous ground cover
Light Requirements: Part shade-shade

Common Name: English ivy
Botanical Name: *Hedera helix*
Good Variety(s): 'Bulgaria' and 'Thorndale'
Height/Flower Color: up to 1 foot/Greenish
Bloom Period/Type: Summer/Evergreen ground cover
Light Requirements: Part shade-shade

Common Name: Hyacinth bean
Botanical Name: *Dolichos lablab*
Height/Flower Color: 20 feet/Purple
Bloom Period/Type: Summer until frost/Annual vne
Light Requirements: Full sun

Common Name: Jackman clematis
Botanical Name: *Clematis* x *Jackmanii*
Good Variety(s): *Candida, maximowicziana,* hundreds of varieties
Height/Flower Color: 10 feet or more/Dark purple
Bloom Period/Type: Summer/Deciduous non-clinging vine
Light Requirements: Full sun

Common Name: Lilyturf
Botanical Name: *Liriope spicata*
Good Variety(s): species *muscari* and 'Variegata'
Height/Flower Color: up to 1 foot/Pale blue
Bloom Period/Type: Late summer/Herbaceous ground cover
Light Requirements: Full sun-shade

Common Name: Moon Flower
Botanical Name: *Ipomoea alba*
Height/Flower Color: 20 feet/White
Bloom Period/Type: Summer until frost/Annual vine
Light Requirements: Full sun

Common Name: Morning glory
Botanical Name: *Ipomoea tricolor*
Height/Flower Color: 20 feet/Pale red or blue
Bloom Period/Type: Summer until frost/Annual vine
Light Requirements: Full sun

Common Name: Myrtle
Botanical Name: *Vinca minor*
Good Variety(s): 'Alba' and 'Bowlesii'
Height/Flower Color: 3 to 4 inches/Blue
Bloom Period/Type: Spring/Evergreen ground cover
Light Requirements: Full sun-shade

Common Name: Scarlet runner bean
Botanical Name: *Phaseolus coccineus*
Height/Flower Color: 20 feet/Scarlet
Bloom Period/Type: Summer until frost/Annual vine
Light Requirements: Full sun

Common Name: Scarlet trumpet honeysuckle
Botanical Name: *Lonicera pericyclymenum*
Good Variety(s): Multiple closely related vines
Height/Flower Color: 20 feet or more/Reddish with yellow
Bloom Period/Type: Summer/Semi-evergreen non-clinging vine
Light Requirements: Full sun-part shade

Common Name: Silver Vine
Botanical Name: *Polygonum Aubertii*
Height/Flower Color: 30 feet or more/Off white
Bloom Period/Type: Mid summer to early fall/ Deciduous non-clinging vine
Light Requirements: Full sun

Common Name: Snow on the mountain
Botanical Name: *Aegopodium podagraria* 'Picta'
Height/Flower Color: up to 1 foot/White
Bloom Period/Type: Late spring/Herbaceous ground cover
Light Requirements: Full sun-shade

Common Name: Stone crop
Botanical Name: *Sedum spurium* 'Dragons Blood'
Good Variety(s): 'Tricolor' and 'Weihenstephaner Gold'
Height/Flower Color: 6 inches/Dark red
Bloom Period/Type: Summer/Evergreen ground cover
Light Requirements: Full sun

Common Name: Trumpet honeysuckle
Botanical Name: *Lonicera sempervirens*
Height/Flower Color: 20 feet or more/Reddish with yellow
Bloom Period/Type: Summer/Semi-evergreen perennial vine
Light Requirements: Full sun-part shade

Common Name: Winter creeper
Botanical Name: *Euonymus fortunei* 'Colorata'
Good Variety(s): 'Minima' and 'Kewensis'
Height/Flower Color: up to 6 inches/Pinkish
Bloom Period/Type: Summer/Evergreen ground cover
Light Requirements: Full Sun-Full Shade

Common Name: Wisteria
Botanical Name: *Wisteria floribunda*
Height/Flower Color: 40 feet or more/Whitish lavender
Bloom Period/Type: Late spring/Deciduous perennial vine
Light Requirements: Full sun

Common Name: Yellow creeping jenny
Botanical Name: *Lysimmachia nummularia* 'Aurea'
Height/Flower Color: 1 inch/Yellow
Bloom Period/Type: Summer/Herbaceous
Light Requirements Full sun-part sun

JANUARY
GROUND COVERS & VINES

PLANNING

For a new addition for part sun, part shade, or a full shade garden, choose **bishop's weed**, *Aegopodium podagraria*. From mid-spring until the nighttime temperatures have gotten quite cold, this plant adds substance to any location. Diversity is the best description for this multipurpose plant, from glowing in the moonlight to accentuating the shade during the day. The ability of **bishop's weed** to transition through so many different types of landscape environments is unbelievable. Repetition and visual rhythm in the landscape is a notably important quality for any design. White and green variegated leaves blanket the ground with a coarseness that contrasts nicely with other plants and landscape features. Sprays of white flowers, though not eye popping, flutter above the foliage, adding an element of mysticism.

Review and evaluate the notes and photos of previous years' plantings of ground covers and vines. Did the **dead nettle** highlight the tree trunk as anticipated? Are **climbing hydrangea** stems growing on the trellis providing a nice contrast? Move through all the prior plantings and review your notes.

Plan ahead if you are considering adding to an existing planting. Will the **clematis**, with its lower bare stems, benefit from a **lilyturf** planting at its base to mask the deficit?

Step back and look at the entire landscape. Remember how the domino effect works. Successes and disappointments will probably require additional changes down the road. Has the idea of using annual **morning glory** vines in pots to provide privacy to the patio come to an end? Are the trees overhead creating more dense shade or less? Is the **winter creeper** being over run by the **chameleon plant**? Decide if any action is needed to maintain design quality.

Look at the year-round colors and textures each planting provides. The variegated, silver-white foliage of **dead nettle** creates a fine texture. The winter look of the dark evergreen **myrtle** provides a large, course textured blanket in the landscape, highlighting other plantings. All year-round the herbaceous and deciduous plants come and go, while the evergreen plants stabilize and unify.

Good planning includes a series of steps. Purchasing the size and type of plants to be installed is pre-empted by the determination of how much time will pass after the purchase and before the planting. This time frame is the period when plants may suffer stress from exposure to the environment. The amount of time you have to devote to after-care and the subsequent routine care and maintenance until the plant reaches mature size should also be considered in the planning phase.

Ideas and concepts can be roughed out if you take classes, read catalogs, and attend garden club meetings for additional information. The local slant on the performance of vines and ground covers, blended with personal site analysis, will insure the best results.

PLANTING

If you are starting or growing cuttings under lights, use only clean containers (clay or plastic) or new ones. Make sure the used containers are washed thoroughly to eliminate any residues or potting soil residuals. Soak in a water and bleach (ten parts water to one part bleach) solution overnight. Scrub with a stiff bristled brush and rinse. Discard any cracked (open site for bacteria spores) pots.

To root cuttings taken directly from the home landscape or cuttings received early via mail order, plant in a soilless potting mix that contains slow-release starter fertilizer.

The amount of light needed by cuttings or transplants cannot be overemphasized. The lights should be specifically for plant growing. There are both incandescent and fluorescent bulbs. Depending upon the type of seeds or plants, adjust the fixtures to approximately 2 to 3 inches above the cutting tops. Adjust the height as needed as the plants mature.

CARE

Evergreen **dragon's blood sedum** shrinks during the winter and appears as a reddish moss-like growth on the ground. This is a natural occurrence and the plant will recover to its full 6 inches later in the spring.

Keep leaf debris from collecting over the tops of evergreen plants. The moisture retention of the soil increases, as does the possibility of rotting or fungus problems.

Migration of mulch, specifically on plantings of **lily turf** on a slope, can occur. Replenish the mulch, but never exceed a 2-inch layer. Never broadcast mulch over shorter growing, finer textured ground cover plantings, and don't apply over 1 inch of mulch. The maximum depth of mulch over root systems of **silver vine** or **dropmore scarlet honeysuckle** vine is 2 inches.

HELPFUL HINTS

Evergreen vines or ground covers can be wind burnt when the wind chill factor is below zero. Healthy plants will recover with the spring growth surge. An application of an anti-desiccant on a monthly basis during the winter reduces the problem.

WATERING

Keep soil moist on cuttings under grow lights. If rainfall during the month is less than normal, pull the hoses out and water **creeping jenny**, **English ivy**, and other ground cover and vine plantings.

FERTILIZING

Cuttings should be fed a formulated seed-starter fertilizer, unless you used a potting soil with a fertilizer mixed in. Fertilize unmulched, outdoor plantings in mild winter areas with one-half inch of compost topdressing.

PRUNING

If cuttings or transplants appear elongated, plant recovery is unlikely, so discard them and start over.

PESTS

Look closely at all cutting flats for any unnatural brownish or discolored growth on the soil surface or around the cutting stem. Treat with a soil drench mixture of fungicide and water. If the problem is not eradicated within five days, discard the cuttings.

Many weeds are evergreen or they will begin germinating after a few unseasonably warm days. Keep a close watch.

Newer plantings of **bugle weed** ground cover have more space between the plants and so they have a greater potential for weeds. Additionally, **Boston ivy** vine plantings that are less than three years old will establish quicker and be healthier if weed competition is eliminated. Use a digging tool to remove the entire weed root system.

FEBRUARY

GROUND COVERS & VINES

PLANNING

Plan a new addition for sun, part sun, part shade, and shade—for anywhere in the garden. Plan for a **winter creeper**, *Euonymus fortunei*. **Winter creeper** trails across the ground with 2-inch elliptical, dark green leaves that spread so thick and dense that the supporting stems below are invisible. Take full advantage of the superior qualities of this ground cover and plant it in larger spaces where it can naturalize. Markings on the foliage highlight the plant. Expect no flowers or fruit for as long as five years until the plant reaches maturity. When the flowers are pollinated, red fruits embraced by capsules are enjoyed by the birds. Winter cold brings about a change in foliage color. Multiple season appeal and the ability to grow just about anywhere make **winter creeper** a good candidate for any landscape.

What was the performance level in each ground cover locale? Successes and disappointments is often plant specific. For example, **lily turf** culturally transitions from full sun into deep shade. If this has happened where you don't want it to, investigate the possible reasons beyond the obvious—has the water flow pattern changed? Are there effects from nearby work that increases or redirects foot traffic? Has there been any use of herbicides, fungicides, or fertilizers?

Has the **climbing hydrangea** begun to pull away from the structure and reattached itself somewhere else? Note these occurrences to plan for the next season.

Re-evaluate the vines in the garden. If the percentage of the **dropmore scarlet honeysuckle** leaf mass is more than anticipated, consider an entirely different variety of plant for the area.

Make decisions, based upon previous year's growth, in considering an increase to the number of **clematis** being grown for thicker coverage. Keep that graph paper nearby to make some quick drawings so you don't forget.

Add a touch of the landscape to seasonal floral arrangements. Bare twigs of **Boston ivy** or **silver vine** may be just perfect.

PLANTING

Begin new bed preparation for **bishop's weed** if the ground is not overly wet. Working an overly wet soil creates air pockets that serve as collection sites for harmful cold air and rains. Do a probing test using a shovel, spade or trowel. Push the tool into the ground and if you hear a sucking sound or you extract mud on the tool, then the ground is still too wet to work.

If the temperature is above forty degrees, dig up healthy sections of ground cover and relocate them to fill in gaps. Use a root stimulator for faster acclimation. Be careful if spring flowering bulbs are sited in the bed space. Use a waterproof pen and large plastic labels that can be seen above the ground cover to mark the date of the cutting movement for future reference.

If large areas of **dead nettle** or **bugle weed** lack vigor or are in a state of decline, a soil test done early in the season will provide information for any required changes. Take a clean quart of soil (no mulch, stem, or leaf) to the local Extension Service or soil testing lab. You may have to mail the sample if there are no labs in your area. The earlier you send the samples, the quicker you will have the results. If the results are confusing, ask for clarification from the Kansas State University Extension Office or the lab you use.

Keep adjusting the grow light to 2 to 3 inches above the plants. Thin and remove plants showing any signs of rot or fungus. Increase the "ON" cycle to maintain upright growth

HELPFUL HINTS

Insects will be small and flying. Control with yellow sticky traps placed among plants.

Watch for well-beaten pathways into **English ivy** beds. They could be voles (mammals that burrow and consume bulbs and plant roots).

Set larger mousetraps baited with peanut butter and or soft cheese.

Use gypsum in bed spaces adjacent to walk or roadways that may have been overspread with de-icers. Gypsum minimizes damage by neutralizing the chemical reaction potential.

and to acclimate to longer daytime hours.

To air layer sections of **silver vine**, select a stem laying on the ground, scrape the underside lightly, and move any mulch away to allow direct contact with soil surface. Place a rock, large enough to anchor the stem to the ground, on top of the stem. In a few months, a substantial amount of roots will have grown. Cut the stem off of the main plant and move the plant to new location, or give as a gift.

CARE

If leaf debris accumulates (see January) and exceeds the recommended depth, set the lawn mower blade as high as possible and run it over the top of the planted area, mulching the leaves.

Spread one-half inch of compost on deciduous ground covers to protect early emerging growth.

WATERING

Maintain the soil moisture on potted cuttings. Keep soil damp to the look and touch, but not wet.

Place several rain gauges throughout the landscape and keep a few spares to replace any broken gauges. Keep an eye on the rain gauges and note amounts of snow melt. Move the gauge into a warm location, allow the snow to melt, and note quantity. During rainfall, monitor the amounts. If you have a dry spell, compensate for any below normal amounts as soon as possible. Make sure ground covers and vines receive at least 1 inch of water every seven to ten days.

FERTILIZING

Use a very light application of water-soluble fertilizer at one-quarter of the label rate on healthy seedlings and plants.

PESTS

Inspect the soil surface of cutting flats and containers for any gray mold. Stir the soil surface very lightly and add a fan for air circulation.

NOTES

GROUND COVERS & VINES

PLANNING

Plan for a new **silver vine** (*Polygonum aubertii*) in the full sun or part sun garden.

The bare, nonclinging stems of the **silver vine** persist through the winter, softening a structure. The warmer days of mid-spring set off the alarm, and the leaves emerge amazingly fast, so that winter is forgotten. The **silver vine** is great for a tough location that you want pumped up during the most brutal time of the growing season. When many plants are melting down in midsummer, the fine textured fragrant flowers provide impact because of the huge quantity of blooms on the vine at one time. This big show by the **silver vine** makes it a candidate for many circumstances.

Plan for a new ground cover addition in the full sun, part sun, or part shade. Plan a spot for the **chameleon plant**, *Houttuynia cordata*. **Chameleon plant** demands a second look at the alternating leaves in three different colors. Green is highlighted by milky white, and then pale red adds a visual charge to individual leaves, growing to 3 inches across during the growing season. The height of the plant reaches to 15 inches, and is very useful in the distance where some uplift is needed for background plantings. A lower area where water puddles for a period of time becomes an asset when planted with **chameleon plant**. This ground cover is best used in a larger area where no other herbaceous plants are located.

Have you observed a visually mangled mess spreading across the landscape? This is the result of not understanding the function of ground covers and planning accordingly. Ground covers are treated differently than other types of plants in the landscape. Do not mix too many varieties in close proximity to each other. It creates visual chaos and is not beneficial to the plants. However, selecting one evergreen **myrtle** and interplanting it with **dead nettle** is an excellent way to prevent boredom, yet avoid the chaos. Stands of the same type of ground cover can be equally rewarding. Important to the planning process is how much plant interaction occurs when combining species.

PLANTING

Soak bare-root plants in a solution of rooting hormone and water for one hour or until any dry roots have begun to swell and show signs of absorption. If there are any roots with questionable viability after soaking, notify the source. You can still pot up the questionable root. Start it in seed-starter potting mix and transplant into the garden when healthy.

If there have been recent rains, it is best to stay out of the wet beds. When working in the garden, always work backward out of bed to loosen any compacted soil in areas you have just finished.

Cuttings should be showing signs of being well rooted. If they are rooted in peat pots, you will see white fibers showing through the sides and bottom of the pots. If they are rooted in plastic pots, give a slight tug on the cutting and resistance should occur. To insure continued growth, maintain current cultivation schedule.

CARE

When making plant purchases this time of year, ask the garden center about any acclimation of the plants that you might do to insure that the damage from a cold snap would not be fatal. Plants that are greenhouse grown and not allowed to sit in a cool house prior to purchase are a liability. Have some burlap or similar material ready for cold protection.

New plantings (arrived via mail order and installed) of **climbing hydrangea** and **winter creeper** benefit from 1 to 2 inches of mulch placed around the stems, but not over the foliage.

WATERING

Water containerized plants before installation.

FERTILIZING

Add a light application of granular all-purpose (5-5-5) fertilizer to spring planting areas. Work it into the soil to benefit new **sedum** plants.

PRUNING

Prune only diseased, damaged, or winterkilled sections.

PESTS

Track and note nights of a hard freeze. This will help in the diagnosis of **bugle weed** or **clematis** that may look dead at this same time of season next year. The appearance of frost damage is similar to fungus or root rot. By noting the recent cold, it may save you from applying fungicides unnecessarily.

Wildlife is having their young so there could be potentially more soil compaction. The earliest plant growth on ground covers and vines may be eaten, causing **Boston ivy** or **creeping jenny** difficulty in getting off to a good spring start. Plants are tough, but repeated nibbling from increased animal population is not good for the plants. Use a variety of deterrents such as wire on the ground as a physical barrier, applications of hot pepper sprays, or spotting wildlife predator urine drops.

Watch for all types of weeds that are from germinating seeds or warmer season perennial types. Check new purchases for any weeds growing in pots. Keep up the weed battle early by using herbicides (follow label rate) as needed. Make sure application is directly onto the exact plant or specific area of the garden where weeds need eradica-ting. Hand dig the weed, but be sure to get the entire root system. If you just snap off the top growth, root growth is accelerated and new top growth will emerge.

HELPFUL HINTS

Nonclinging **silver** or **honeysuckle** vines grow upward by twining stems or tendrils. This group needs an open support system to twine and weave in and out of, such as an arbor, lattice, trellis, or chain link fence. The best climbing structure has cross members or openings that are spaced 1 to 2 inches apart.

NOTES

APRIL

GROUND COVERS & VINES

PLANNING

For a full sun vine, plan for a **Jackman clematis**, *Clematis* x *jackmanii.*

Clematis vines deserve royal status for their diversity of color, size, shape, and length of bloom season. The **clematis** is divided into several different categories based on proper pruning practices that maximize the results. The **clematis** are slow to establish, have a rather stiff demeanor, and some specific growing criteria, but they are worth it. Stems hold onto the facade by leaflets reaching around and locking, as if shaking hands. The heavily veined, deep green leaves provide a background to the living bouquet of huge, up to 7 inches across, flowers exploding in June from the oval-shaped, single or clustered buds. Depending upon the climate of the year, flowering can continue until early fall. Take full advantage of this wonderful vine by using it as a ground cover or by weaving it through evergreen shrubs in sunny locations.

It is time to make a decision for the garden's overall theme. If the theme is formal, then make use of plants that have similar color, texture, and growth habit. **English ivy** and **climbing hydrangea** bring a sense of formality to a garden. An informal theme may mean mixing together **bugle weed** and **dropmore scarlet honeysuckle**. Each has an element of looseness. Certainly, different areas of the garden can have qualities of both themes, but it is best if one idea sends the dominant message.

Give new ideas and directions a place by moving outdoors to check on previously established bed spaces or locations of new undisturbed spaces. Take measurements of the boundaries to plan on what and how many things can occur in the spaces. Does the area occupied by the **myrtle** require more space to accomplish your design goal? Would another section of lattice with a **Jackman clematis** vine provide the intended view?

Use journal information to review past happenings in the garden. Make new notes in your garden journal of anything atypical. Note planting dates and track progression of weekly growth of **dead nettle** or **chameleon plant**. Keep a close eye on plants surrounding any recent installations for rate of growth, and note the changes in the journal.

Vines have different growth habits. They may be clinging (**climbing hydrangea**) and nonclinging (**clematis**). Clinging vines use an adaptation of the stems in the form of small suction cups or rootlets. They adhere to almost any rough surface such as walls, foundations, tree trunks, trellises, arbors, posts, and anything within reach. Consider this when you plan for vines in the landscape.

PLANTING

Plenty of time remains to ready a new bed or to reorganize an established one. Be sure to do a soil wetness test before any major undertaking.

Garden centers could have best selection of the year, but be sensible on the amount of time and work that you can do. Ask some questions before you purchase. Can the nursery center hold the purchased plants for a period of time before you pick them up? Do they deliver, and if so, what is the added cost? Do they have an installation service?

Check the soil temperature. If it is less than fifty degrees, there will be limited seed germination.

CARE

Rewrite the plant labels as they fade for the most accurate record keeping.

Mail order **winter creeper** and **Boston ivy** benefit from being installed as soon as possible, but not if the ground is overly wet. If plants cannot be installed right away, remove them from the package and inspect. Make notes as to the amount of roots (size and density). Hold over the bare roots or small plants in wet sphagnum peat moss. Store them out of cold temperatures.

Eliminate any observed problems such as standing water, digging animals, etc.

Scatter a light application of all-purpose (10-10-10 or similar) fertilizer and water the area lightly just prior to spreading any wood or bark mulch products. These types of mulch may wick moisture and bind nutrients while decomposing.

Hot and steaming mulch may physically burn plants.

WATERING

Check the rain gauges. Have the hose and irrigation system ready to compensate for less than 1 inch of rainfall every ten days.

FERTILIZING

New growth on well-established **creeping jenny** or on newly installed **silver vine** is fragile. If weather is warm, use only one-half the package rate of a fertilizer with a ratio of 1-2-1.

HELPFUL HINTS

Put the date of purchase on the package or bottle of any chemicals, fertilizer, pesticides, herbicides, or amendments. Do not write over the application instructions. Store any liquids to prevent freezing. If any are suspect, safely discard. Purchase quantities that can be used during one season.

PRUNING

Any flowers present on seedlings or purchased plants should be removed for the first year after installation to conserve energy for root growth.

PESTS

Insect hatching is rampant; therefore disease transmittal is as well. Double and triple check for pests and take action at the first signs. Either remove physically or apply insecticidal soap or a similar product.

Wildlife (adults and newborn) is everywhere. Consider diversions with motion detector/light or irrigation devices, with physical barriers, or by changing habits. Set up a sacrificial buffet away from prized plantings.

Read the label before using a pre-emergent herbicide. Determine if the chemical will impact new plant installations and how long the chemical is effective. The ground temperature must be above fifty degrees for pre-emergent effectiveness.

Make a final sweep to rid the area of any weeds. Hand dig or apply herbicides prior to any soil preparation or plant installation, especially in a bed or planted area that is less than three years old.

NOTES

May

GROUND COVERS & VINES

PLANNING

Add a new vine to the sun or part sun landscape. Plan an area using **dropmore scarlet honeysuckle** vine, *Lonicera* x *brownii*. Striving to reach its pinnacle, regardless of the circumstances, is how best to describe the **trumpet honeysuckle**. The twining, nonclinging stems will not stop reaching, and even twist among themselves as they stretch across open space. Though a lot of top growth activity will always occur, the bottom one-third of the plant carries only a few leaves on the stem. If you are using **trumpet honeysuckle** for screening, plant a filler plant at the base to get a complete blockade. In mid-spring, purple tinted leaves appear, maturing to a shiny, clear, bluish green. During milder winters, the foliage persists until spring when it is pushed off by new growth. The clusters of tubular shaped flowers, red with yellow throats, occur on and off from May until August. In a naturalistic or rustic landscape, turn it free, but keep on eye out for your neighbors, as it may want to colonize their yard.

Plan a new ground cover to highlight the shade garden. **Dead nettle**, *Lamium maculatum*, fills the shade garden gaps among perennials, shrubs, and trees. The foliage and growth habit is a sea of very consistent texture that allows the eye to move through the landscape without interruption. This offering is truly a very pleasant attribute in the shaded gardens of the summertime. A close-up inspection of the heart shaped foliage exposes the pleasing nature of the versatile planting. Add to the scene a spiky cluster of flowers that call for a more thorough view, as the color almost disappears in the shade. Midsummer accents of color via the inflorescence makes **dead nettle** a champion of the shade garden, whether planted in a small colony or installed over a large area.

Remember to check out the site just prior to planting for any environmental changes such as downspout discharge (the area is super wet now), shaded areas now in the sun (seasonal movement), or surface tree roots that are more prominent this spring. Prior to installation, use flags, marking ribbon, or landscape friendly paint to delineate or designate a bed or new planting space in the landscape. Take time to look at the area and position from all angles to make sure of your design lines.

Spend time enjoying the outdoors when you can. So many times, so many things come all at once.

PLANTING

Save some steps by having all the necessary tools and goods readily available for the planting process.

While installing larger quantities of ground cover or vines, stop regularly and water. Watch for settling around new installations, and adjust the soil level as you plant.

Keep plants in pots or bare-rooted plants well watered prior to and during planting. The best days to plant are cloudy days with minimal wind to reduce root and leaf moisture loss. If you are installing multiples of **bishop's weed** or **dragon's blood sedum**, stop regularly and water the plants in.

All plants growing indoors under lights should have ample rooting systems before planting outdoors. Discard any unrooted plants. On a rainy day, clean the entire lighting and propagation area.

Have you seen flats of ground cover for sale at prices that seem cheaper than normal? This could simply be a good bargain possibly because of over production at the grower's greenhouse. Check several of the individual plants by giving a gentle tug, and if there is resistance, they are well rooted. If the cutting pulls out easily, pass on this bargain. The plants will need extra care to root before establishing in the garden.

CARE

Before replenishing mulch (1 to 2 inch maximum depth) around plants, sprinkle some lower-analysis, granular fertilizer to compensate for the mulch breaking down and binding up certain nutrients.

WATERING

Moisten prepared beds and potting mixes prior to installation. The added moisture is essential to minimize root damage. Water again as each plant is put into the ground, or after every few plants. Water thoroughly and look back to see if soil has sunk and if the roots are exposed. If the day is bright, sunny, and windy, several light waterings may be required.

FERTILIZING

Steady growth occurs with a regular routine of using fertilizer formulated for either shade or sun plants.

Each plant group will need different formulas.

HELPFUL HINTS

Check all the watering tools (hoses, sprinklers, nozzles, etc.) and replace any worn or damaged pieces with similar products or consider other alternatives. Ask at the garden center for new equipment on the market that may save you time, water, and money.

PRUNING

Remove any damaged or dead leaves, as well as all flowers, during the first growing season, allowing the new plant to build root strength.

PESTS

Release lacewings, predatory ladybugs, and/or praying mantis. Follow the instructions for effective release.

Insect adult emergence and egg hatching is triggered by warm weather. Keep an eye out. The aphids are the most problematic. Use a stream of water or simply smash the pests between your fingers. If insecticidal soap or other contact insecticide is used, apply spray directly on pests.

Keep a pest identification book on hand to make correct diagnosis of pests and whether it is a damaging pest or a beneficial bug. Many chemicals applied to young plantings may have an adverse impact. Some insecticides are contact and are only effective if directly sprayed onto the insect. They have very little residual that remains on the plant. This is not true of fungicides that are applied in anticipation of problems.

Review photos of weeds that have been problems in the past before digging out anything. You may be digging in your test patch of ground cover planted last year.

NOTES

JUNE

GROUND COVERS & VINES

PLANNING

Plan for a vine that can take part shade or full shade. Plan for a **climbing hydrangea**, *Decumaria barbara*. **Climbing hydrangea** is a focal point plant that is surely a conversation piece. The clinging habit (do not plant in areas of strong wind that can blow the vine off the structure) can be used to mask and decorate a textured, deciduous tree trunk (**maple**, **oak**, **ash**), to soften and change the side of a building, or to twine in a section of fencing. The lace-cap, hydrangea-like flowers stand out perpendicular from the glossy, dark-green foliage. The added plus is the hint of fragrance embracing the area. In early spring, the leaves unfurl from the stems on into summer's shininess, and finish in the fall with a golden, harvest-yellow foliage. The three-season qualities of the climbing hydrangea are not to be underestimated. Plant it at the base of a climbing edifice and attach it initially with glue backed hold-fasts or twine. Within two years the rewards will be forthcoming.

Gold and purple finches, hummingbirds, and chickadees will be making a visit. Have thistle feeders and plenty of annual sunflowers (many varieties are great in pots) dotted in the garden. Hummingbird feeders allow the ruby-throated types to stay a bit longer during their migration north, and possibly they will stop by for a return visit on their way south in later August.

Update the photo journal with spring blooming vines that are showing leaf and flower at the same time. Use these photos for comparisons in relationship to the ground cover and vine current locations. Note if the growth habit is heaviest in the fall or the spring.

PLANTING

This is the final month of the spring planting season (summer planting means a lot more care). The garden centers could have larger potted **clematis** for the mailbox or **sedum** to fill along the sidewalk. **Lily turf** can act as a bed edger, unifying the space under the **oak** tree. Larger 2-gallon pots could be available making the impact time much shorter.

Planning for a garden get-together allows time to fill in color voids and gaps. Do not forget a flat of **myrtle** to circle around the **gingko** tree. Make use of the **bugle weed** to amplify the changes of topography.

CARE

Check to make sure that the plant labels are still in position. If the writing is fading, replace the label.

Working and walking into the garden or bed, while the soil is wet or damp, compacts the soil. Rework the soil surface to loosen it before moving onto the next project.

Scorching summer heat will dry the ground and could influence root health on any plants in the ground less than one full year. Mulch may need refreshing. Changing mulch types is a consideration as each will leave behind (when finished decomposing) a slightly different nutrient base.

WATERING

Nature provides much of the watering this month. If you do hit a dry spell, make up the difference and supply a minimum of 1 inch of water every week. Adjust the automatic irrigation system, or use a sprinkler and hose, leaky pipe, hose and nozzle, or watering can.

Watering early in the day is advantageous as it reduces bacteria and fungus problems, and there is less evaporation.

FERTILIZING

Consider using a liquid root stimulator on newly installed or slower growing plants.

PRUNING

New installations may need to be pinched or cut back (never more than one-half of the stem length). Allow multiple leaves to remain after cutting, but pinch off any flowers for the first year.

PESTS

Check for damaging insects during early morning and evening hours. Insect activity is highest during those times. Examine the stems, the leaves (top and bottom), and on the ground for trails (slugs and snails). Contact pesticides must be applied directly on pest or use physical controls.

HELPFUL HINTS

Any new plant that was installed, bare root or containerized, that has shown no signs of new growth since installation is probably not establishing itself. Make some notes as to the location, plant, planting period, and neighboring plants to determine the possible problem. Make adjustments as needed to fill the space.

Mole tunnels are showing up everywhere and the babies are large enough to tunnel in beds that are easy for them to dig. They prefer freshly cultivated soil that is generally higher in earthworm population—moles favorite food. Set traps and move them daily.

The heat of this month is stress time for many ground covers that have shallow roots. Any vine in the ground less than two years is not able to fight with weeds, so keep an eye out and spend time on this chore, unpleasant as it is. Dig out the weed or carefully use a herbicide.

NOTES

JULY

GROUND COVERS & VINES

PLANNING

Plan a new ground cover addition that grows in sun, part sun, or part shade.

Bugle weed, *Ajuga reptans*, is one of the few plants that appear to be leaping over the edge of the flat or container to get out into your garden. This growth indicates what can happen in the garden, as this living mulch, full of color and texture, is planted. Heavily textured individual leaves multiply quickly, lending full impact to the garden in a short amount of time. Iridescent blue flowers shoot straight up from the base of the foliage and are spectacular, lasting long into cooler weather. Whether used as a stand-alone planting or an understory for perennials, trees, or shrubs, **bugle weed** fills all requests magnificently.

Public parks, botanical gardens, and home and garden tours all lend great insight and allow comparisons between the similar or dissimilar plants in vastly different settings. Check out **bishop's weed** and **tickseed** in combination. Look for all those different **clematis** varieties. Some varieties have just finished flowering, others are showing full color, and some are still in bud form. Each is at the peak level of aesthetics, but in a differing manner. The information and photos gathered make changes considered for the fall seem much more reachable. Always, take time out of the gardening chores for enjoyment and appreciation of your outdoor environment.

The vacation was planned long before the new planting of **myrtle** under the trees was installed last May. If you are going to be gone for longer than fourteen days, make sure the watering will be done, either with a programmed irrigation system or by a gardening friend.

Ground cover or vines planted a year ago may suffer from extreme humidity and high temperatures, but effects should not be long term.

It's best not to do any garden chores between the hours of 10 a.m. to 3 p.m. The plants will be heat stressed, possibly shortening their glory days period. Do not cut flowers during this time.

PLANTING

Planting should be done on an emergency basis only—the great deal at the garden center, divisions or cuttings that must go in the ground. The stress of planting, combined with our typical weather, causes a quick downturn. Use a root stimulator to help with acclimation process of the **climbing hydrangea**.

Watch for seedpods forming on plants and make a note to gather them when they ripen (turn brown).

CARE

Keep up a regular routine of walking through the yard, looking for anything out of the ordinary. Watch for voles.

River birch, tulip trees and others begin dropping leaves. Either remove or scatter any piles that collect on top of the ground cover or at base of a vine planting. An accumulation of leaves and debris could cause leaf or stem problems related to moisture retention.

Replenish mulch if it is less than one-half inch thick. Use caution with hot mulches. They build up heat if they are piled or are in a bag. During the hot summer months, the increased temperature of the mulch could cause damage to **dead nettle** or **silver vine** stems. Wash mulch from the tops of foliage.

WATERING

When watering a pot of **ivy**, if you hear a bubbling sound, the water is trying to fill the air pockets in a soil that has gone dry. Fill the pot to the top, let it drain, then water again.

Supply 1 inch of water each week to ground covers and vines. If the weather is very humid and the ground appears damp, take a trowel and dig down 6 inches to check for soil moisture under the surface. If the soil is damp 6 inches deep, then hold off on watering.

Set the automatic irrigation timers for longer running periods, but run them less often, allowing the moisture to penetrate deeper into the ground for a stronger plant root structure.

FERTILIZING

Do not apply fertilizers to any stressed or unhealthy plants. If the ground is dry, water the area around healthy plants before fertilizer application. Fertilize early in the day using a water-soluble fertilizer mixture. Use a hose-end sprayer for large areas and a watering can or bucket for individual plants.

PRUNING

Remove browning foliage and spent flowers that are either natural or storm related.

If the leaves of **bishop's weed** appear to be sun scorched or burnt, mowing or hand pruning of the foliage (maintain 2 to 3 inches of plant) stimulates new growth that is more heat and sun tolerant. The new growth occurs within fourteen days of cutting.

HELPFUL HINTS

Watch for an unusual amount of bee (ground hornet, yellow jacket) activity in the **English ivy** or other ground cover plantings. If you notice many flights in and out of the same location throughout the daytime, it's a sure sign of increased activity. These insects can sting and bite. I recommend using a professional exterminating service to eradicate the problem.

PESTS

Although this may be the worst month for insects, strong and healthy plants can recover from almost any attack. You need to decide what level of damage a planting can sustain without being severely harmed.

This will help you determine what course of action (if any) to take.

Examine your plants a couple of times day to determine pest populations. Either physically remove the pest, apply an insecticide, or release predatory insects. The most problematic insects to watch for are spider mites and aphids in the sun garden and slugs and snails in the shade.

Is your garden being invaded by an unknown plant? Take a sample and have it identified. If herbicides are used for weed control, be sure the type selected is labeled for use on this particular plant. Read and follow label directions.

NOTES

AUGUST

GROUND COVERS & VINES

PLANNING

Plan a new ground cover addition for the full sun garden. **Stonecrop** 'Dragon's Blood', *Sedum spurium*, provides bronze or deep reddish green carpeting that thrives on a dry, hot and sunny slope, and in gaps between boulders in a rock garden. This foliage color gives the impression that it is not real. If you are looking for a texture that is both medium and coarse, or if you want a plant a little out of the ordinary, **stone crop** meets both of these expectations. Unexpectedly, at summer's hottest period, a sea of red stars appears, as though sitting on top of the ground. Afterward, the finishing foliage returns with its unique tone. The approach of winter causes shrinkage in height, giving the appearance of a red moss covering the ground.

Flats of ground covers and containers of vines begin to arrive at the garden centers this month in anticipation of fall planting. Selection is the best now as generally only one major shipment from growers occurs this time of year.

PLANTING

Existing garden areas that are scheduled for expansion, newly created spaces, or bedding spaces that are to return to a lawn area, would benefit from working the soil prior to planting. This allows for any amendments to blend together and for soil settling to take place. Do this chore now to remove a considerable amount of work pressure in the fall.

Install new plants in the morning or in the late afternoon and evening. This is the best time to work in the landscape. There will be less stress for plants.

There are multiple types of rooting hormone available. Use a specially formulated hormone for woody plant cuttings.

CARE

Soil compacts with each trip in and out of a bed space. At the end of the workday, churn up any soil that is compressed. This action prevents water pooling and allows for proper air circulation.

Prior to installation, place all plants out of the direct sun. Do not allow plants to sit more than two to three days before planting.

Remember less is best with mulch. Maintain a depth of between 1 to 2 inches.

During the first two years of a ground cover or vine's life, do not expect a tremendous amount of growth. The **dropmore honeysuckle** or **silver vines** are the most aggressive vines. The **chameleon** and **bugle weed** are the fastest to establish among the ground covers.

WATERING

Check the soil moisture prior to irrigating. Do not rely on automatic timers. Overwatering could result, which leads to root rot or fungus problems for **dead nettle**, **bugle weed**, and **Jackman clematis**. Dig down 6 inches with a shovel. If the soil is moist, do not water. If you squeeze a handful of dirt into a ball, and the ball does not retain its shape or crumbles apart, then it is time to water.

Water any new purchases daily until they are installed.

Stay flexible and change your watering habits. Watering is dependent upon sun intensity, wind, and exposure. If plants show afternoon wilting, check the plants again on the following morning. If they are still wilted, then water. Sometimes the larger foliage will fold during the heat of the day to reduce the amount of evaporation.

FERTILIZING

This month marks the final fertilizer application to **lily turf** or **dropmore scarlet honeysuckle**. If you are using a granular fertilizer, be sure to wash off the plant foliage after application to prevent fertilizer burn to the leaves.

Remember to have a soil test done every three years. Should the analysis indicate a nutrient problem, amend the soil as needed and water the area thoroughly.

PRUNING

For the first five years after installation, vines should be deadheaded (spent flowers removed) to prevent seed formation and to reduce energy loss.

When large flowered **clematis** are in full bloom, take cuttings early in the day. Place a flower between a couple of sheets of folded newsprint; lay a book on top for about a month. Then place the dried flower between two sheets of clear glass, solder the edge, and you have made a perfect wall hanging.

PESTS

You may be working the soil and find white grubs. There are five major varieties commonly found in this region. The true white grub has several types within the group that are distinguished by life spans of either two, three, or four years. We also see the annual grub, May, Green June, and Japanese grub.

In the larval stage, the grub has a whitish body curled into a "U" shape. The head is brown; it has three pairs of legs; the tip of the abdomen is shiny and transparent. The annual grub is most often found in lawn areas (prefers bluegrass). The other grubs are found anywhere—in the lawn, flower, or vegetable garden spaces.

Growth activity of summer weeds is at a peak level. Herbicides are extremely effective at this time. Use caution and do not allow any herbicide to come in contact with wanted foliage. If you are hand digging weeds, be sure to get the entire root system.

NOTES

SEPTEMBER

GROUND COVERS & VINES

PLANNING

Plan to add **myrtle**, *Vinca minor*, to a part sun, part shade, or full shade bed.

The smooth, glossy, dark green leaves of **myrtle** track thickly across the ground. This habit provides a look of both fine and coarse texture in the very same view. Allow **myrtle** to cover spaces and naturalize year-round. Warmer early spring days bring about a harbinger with the flowering. Pastel blue blooms pop out unconcerned if the day is cloudy or in the heat of the full sun. The cooler temperatures will allow the flowers to persist for a considerable amount of time. Lustrous foliage, accentuated in spring with unmatched flower color, gives **myrtle** a place in any landscape.

Do you have a stockpile of plastic flats, pots, and containers stacked or hidden away that is ever increasing with each purchase of a **chameleon plant**, **winter creeper**, or **silver vine**? Check the phone book for a recycling center or a local manufacturer that utilizes recycled plastic. Get together with garden clubs, the newspaper, and garden centers to see about making it a recycling group effort.

Determine the amount of growth and the growth habits of plants. Locate the original plant labels of the **lily turf** and determine how far a single clump has spread or how much the entire bed has grown. Check the length of the **climbing hydrangea** and how well it is adhering to the growing surface. This time of the year is a good time to strategize for next year. Would a full sun ground cover be more exciting with a few **obedient plants** breaking up the expanse, or do you prefer the monostand? Maybe adding hosta to the base of the tree where **English ivy** is growing would lend some pizzazz. Take notes regarding your over- and underachiever ground covers and vines and decide if you want to make any changes.

PLANTING

This is the best month for planting. The ground is warmed by the summer sun, and that encourages root growth. The rains are less torrential, and the time period before the onset of winter allows for acclimation and a gradual slide into dormancy.

Stone crop dragon's blood or **winter creeper** are quite tough plants and could be considered for growing in containers.

Soften the ground and water the plants before taking divisions. Use a spade or shovel and cut a ring around each plant. Push the digging tool deeply into the ground to root prune the main plant and to get sections that have roots. Before taking root divisions from vines, cut them back to 1 foot and carefully remove branches from structures if they are attached or intertwined. Dig a 6-inch circle around the individual stems that are to be transplanted. Then pry the root divisions out, plant in containers or relocate immediately. Place containers out of the sun and wind, and keep plants watered.

Add fall color to the edge of the ground covers or at the base of the vines by planting cool season vegetables, **lettuce**, **ornamental cabbage** and **kale**. This will pay unexpected rewards for several months as nature prepares for a less colorful season.

CARE

Begin the process of fall cleanup by cutting back the stems and foliage on ground covers and vines as the shorter and cooler days signal the end of the growing season. This practice simply reduces the hibernation spots for insects and disease problems.

Gently cultivate open areas in ground cover beds and those at the base of vines. This reduces soil compaction. Fall rains penetrate the ground easier and fill below-surface air pockets, reducing root system damage from cold air.

Do not reapply mulch this month, allowing the depth to diminish. The soil surface benefits from the additional air circulation and the direct sunlight discourages the spread of disease spores.

HELPFUL HINTS

Daffodils, **grape hyacinth**, and **surprise lilies** are available to carry color themes into the next spring. Take advantage and add clumps of bulbs in beds of ground covers to bring a welcome relief from winter, as the **myrtle** is blooming.

WATERING

Check the rain gauges and compensate for lack of rainfall to gain 1 inch of water every fourteen days. Cooler, cloudy days mean longer periods between waterings. Do not allow water stress to the plants or to the soil, as the microbes (living elements in soil) and soil structure could suffer.

FERTILIZING

If plantings are less than two years old, apply root stimulator.

PRUNING

Either hand prune or mow over (with mower blade set at highest level) ground covers to keep all declining (going dormant) plant debris removed. Prevent accumulations (mow over) of fallen leaves from sitting on top of any ground cover plantings. This reduces air circulation and may breed bacteria and disease problems.

PESTS

Insect damage season is over, but keep all plant debris picked up to eliminate overwintering egg or adult sites. Watch for fall webworms in overhanging tree branches. Remove the webbing to control the worms.

Henbit, chickweed seeds, and other annual winter weeds will be germinating. Apply a pre-emergent herbicide. A pre-emergent will kill all seeds at time of germination. Post-emergent herbicide application to actively growing weeds will be partially effective this time of year, as the weed metabolism is slowing in preparation for winter. Hand digging with a weeding tool always works if the entire root system is removed.

NOTES

OCTOBER

GROUND COVERS & VINES

PLANNING

Plan for a versatile, tough, new ground cover for full sun. **Creeping juniper**, *Juniperus horizontalis*, works on steep hillsides and those large flat areas between driveways. It is happy along sidewalks and the house where it is exposed to direct hot sun. The spreading coarse texture mimics and follows the contours in the planting space, and it requires very little care. The silhouette or form is noncompetitive with nearby structures, seating, or plantings. The form of **creeping juniper** enhances hardscape features making them more dynamic. The deep green coloration is not duplicated very often by other evergreens, but it will change tones and hues with the coming and going of winter. If you need a single plant to highlight a boulder or section of a rock garden, or you are faced with a challenging incline that is impossible to maintain, **creeping juniper** is the answer.

Plan for a new addition for the part shade or full shade bed. Consider **sweet woodruff**, *Galium odoratum*. A sea of perfectly tailored foliage moves out and through the shaded space, in large expanses, under individual shrubs, or along the foundation of a building. The whirled, darker-green single leaf overlaps the neighboring foliage creating a fine textured, dense carpet. This magnifies the aesthetic qualities of any plant that grows adjacent to or around **sweet woodruff**. Companion plants pop out and the colors and contrast are astounding. Midsummer, when the garden is evolving from the explosion of late spring, a cluster of small, fragrant, star-shaped flowers float above the leaves.

Take late season color photos and take notes as ground cover plantings show-off their fall tints and hues. Capture the brilliant red foliage of **Boston ivy**, and the sea of blue **lily turf** flowers. If color changes are occurring, make notes as to the exact locations. A critical look should be taken from the inside of the house, as well as from the other angle while walking in the yard.

Stay flexible as flats or pots are purchased for installation. The weather at this time of year may not cooperate. Place plants in a protected location, and water to keep them moist until installation.

PLANTING

Adding spring flowering bulbs to an area of ground cover pays huge dividends next year. Choose a bulb that will grow high enough to be seen above the foliage if the ground cover planting is evergreen.

CARE

Depending on the location and exposure of plantings, frost or freeze kill will most likely occur on plants with softer fleshier stems, such as **dead nettle**. As the **silver vine** or **climbing hydrangea** foliage dies, examine the support structure, arbor, pergola, or trellis for repairs or replacement. Action may require that the vines be cut back to 1 foot or removed from the structure and laid on the ground during restoration or substitution.

Check for plant name labels and reset or replace as needed.

Prevent falling leaves from collecting in large amounts over the tops of ground covers. Too thick of a leaf layer results in moisture retention and the possibility of disease sites. Mow over the ground cover with the catch bag to collect the debris. Raking pulls and weakens **English ivy** or **myrtle**.

Do not apply any mulch. Hold off until the ground temperature becomes cold. Application of mulches over warm soil maintains warmth and could stimulate bud break or new foliage growth, subjecting both to winter damage.

It is birding time, so resume feeding the birds. As more

leaves fall from trees, a completely forgotten environment is exposed hanging above the **Dropmore scarlet honeysuckle** vine or in the space vacated by the herbaceous **bishop's weed**. Check out the bird nests and resting locations of the cardinals and chickadees and other tree mysteries now exposed.

WATERING

Continue watering all plants in the landscape. Water will enclose the root, providing insulation from frost and freeze.

FERTILIZING

If you have taken cuttings this time of the year, they need to be grown indoors under lights. Apply fertilizers at one-quarter of the label rate.

PRUNING

Remove all dead or dying debris from ground covers and vines. These sites harbor insect eggs and diseases during winter.

PESTS

Wildlife is sensing the impending cold. Chipmunks and voles are looking for nooks and crannies, under the patio or under the front stoop. Squirrels are everywhere planting, digging, and gnawing (an essential function keep their lower teeth from getting too long). Deer are more than likely deep in the woods where there is plenty to eat—be grateful.

Control with herbicides is becoming ineffective with weed plant dormancy a seasonal occurrence and with the slowed translocation from leaf to root. Hand weeding is the most effective. Remove the entire root system. Breaking off the top foliage encourages stronger growth next year.

HELPFUL HINTS

In building your compost pile, remember to layer plant debris with other materials. Add a layer of topsoil every few layers to insure proper blending. Do not add big clumps of any one material. A good compost pile will have noticeable steam rising during cooler temperatures.

NOTES

NOVEMBER

GROUND COVERS & VINES

PLANNING

Plan for a new vine addition that thrives in the full sun or part sun landscape. **Sweet autumn clematis**, *Clematis terniflora*, is a vine of unmistakable qualities. As much of the landscape begins to slow and head for dormancy, this potentially large, self-seeding, fragrant vine fills many niches in the sunny or lightly shaded garden. Growth begins mid-spring, and for the unknowing, the rate is astonishing. A trellis or fence is soon covered. Buds form in mid- to late July, adding another texture quality to this unclematis-like appearing vine. Aromatic flowers are sure to make day or evening strolls more exciting. Fast growing **clematis** planned for now, will have plenty of time from late winter through early to mid-May to reach the desired size and shape for the upcoming season. Almost yearly, new varieties of **clematis** are described in the plant catalogs. Place your order early, as plants may be available in limited quantities.

To provide more design information for your gardening journal, take black-and-white photos. This type of photo eliminates possible distractions and creates clearer design lines. The function and purpose of a bed are outlined clearly and the photos illustrate the planting relationship to buildings, and show whether a vine is softening, but not blocking, a view from a window.

Birds add to the outdoor garden, so make sure feeders and birdbaths are kept full.

Clean and sharpen all tools, and add a light application of oil to reduce rusting during winter.

CARE

Walk around the bedding areas as the rain is falling or after a good soaking rain to check for any changes in drainage patterns or water movement. Raise the soil level to prevent puddles; clean out gutters if they are full of leaves. In particular, check any new beds or plantings for settling, shifting, or erosion. Soil compaction is a serious problem as it prevents water absorption and root development. Always work backwards out of beds. Footprint depressions could collect water causing root damage

Evergreen vines or ground covers show signs of windburn when the wind chill factor is below zero. Healthy plants recover with spring growth surge. Use an application of an anti-desiccant on some of your more tender plants. Apply it monthly during the winter to reduce any problems.

Measure the depth of mulches before adding for the winter. Cover planted area with up to 2 inches of mulch.

WATERING

Now is the time to winterize the in-ground irrigation system. If the outside faucets aren't frost proof, turn off indoors.

Drain and store sprinkler hoses and watering cans out of the weather to prevent freeze damage. Keep one hose available to use if a winter drought occurs.

Place several rain gauges throughout the landscape and buy a few spares to replace any that are damaged.

FERTILIZING

Inventory the types and amounts of fertilizers being stored. Seal the bags and containers to prevent moisture related problems; liquids can freeze. Consider the plant performance where a specific fertilizer was applied. Determine if changes need to be made for next year.

Clean the hose-end attachments to insure correct calibration and application next year.

PRUNING

Remove extra long sections of **silver vine** to increase compact growth next year.

PESTS

Proper storage of dry and liquid products minimizes losses due to carelessness. Take note of the shelf life (effective period), and properly discard any expired products. Contact the Kansas Department of Health and Environment for proper disposal information.

Hand digging is the only defense against weeds at this time of year. Herbicides will not work during cold (below 50 degrees) temperatures. Plant systems are functioning at a very slow pace or the plant is completely dormant, which prevents the absorption of any chemical applications to the foliage.

Newer plantings of **bugle weed** (more space between plants) have a greater potential for weeds. **Boston ivy** vine plantings that are less than three years old establish quicker and are healthier if weed competition is eliminated.

HELPFUL HINTS

Using Vines in the Garden

Vines are problem solvers and add a very unique feel to any situation. The use of vines in the garden is only limited to the imagination. Use them to block a view from a deck, cover an arbor, cover free standing walls to create an outdoor room for coffee in the morning, soften blank walls, weave and anchor a fence section, or to let them sprawl across the front yard as a ground cover. For an accent or focal point, use **clematis**. To add color or fragrance, try **chocolate vine** and **wisteria**. For champion vines in containers, pot up **morning glory** or **mandevilla**. Plant **sweet autumn clematis** or **trumpet creeper** to invite the birds and insects. **Passion vine** and **Dutchman's pipe** have exotic flowers.

Add **bittersweet** and **hyacinth bean** to your flower arrangements. For early morning or nighttime flowering use **morning glory** or **moon vine**. **Sweet potato vine** and **hops** have unique foliage.

Multiple types of **clematis** are available each year. Some worth planning for are:

- 'Contessa de Bouchard' has rose pink blooms in June through September. Prune it hard in spring.
- 'Earnest Markham' has magenta red blooms in August through October. Prune it hard in spring.
- 'Candida' has white blooms in June through September. Prune it hard in spring.
- 'Blue Bird' has blue blooms in April through May. There is no pruning required.
- 'Ramona' has lavender blooms in July through September. There is no pruning required.

The local garden centers or mail order catalogs offer topiary animals (wire sculptures with moss lining and centers filled with potting soil) that are covered with **ivy**. Sometimes this is a variegated form of **English ivy** and it should be treated as a houseplant. Do not leave it outdoors during the winter. Though the **ivy** may be hardy, the lack of insulation from cold winter winds can kill or damage the plant.

DECEMBER

GROUND COVERS & VINES

PLANNING

Plan a new ground cover that is adaptable to any exposure in the garden—sun, part sun, part shade, or full shade. Readily available only during the past twenty years, **lily turf**, *Liriope spicata* has moved to the top of the ground cover list. Waving fields of green shine and glisten, even if the wind is not blowing. This remarkable plant offers a great deal to any setting. Use **lily turf** throughout the landscape, in any sort of terrain, whether relatively level, slightly inclined, or an exceptionally steep hillside. Its astonishing animation, dark green foliage, bluish flowers, and black fruits add diversity and texture to the landscape, while stabilizing and minimizing soil erosion. It has the ability to grow right up to the base of trees, and to serve as a stage for larger growing perennials, shrubs, bulbs and ornamental trees. Even more amazing is the consistent healthy growth and vigor, regardless of the environment or setting.

Creeping Jenny, *Lysimachia nummularia* is a living moss without truly being one. The mature height of this plant reaches only 1 inch; therefore it is an outdoor carpeting. Hugging and embracing tree trunks, shrub branches, or perennial stems only enhances those plants more. Spreading out on its own, the **creeping jenny** is multipurpose, as it also has the ability to grow in all sun/shade exposures. **Creeping jenny** works as a living mortar between stepping stones or as an excellent transition from the deck or patio into the landscape. Tiny, solitary, bright yellow flowers sit above the circular foliage during the summer months. **Creeping jenny** requires minimal care, while supplying a tasteful boost to any landscape, large or small.

Consider arbors, trellises, lattice panels, and pergolas that are manufactured from pots, containers and flats that have been recycled. These structures continue to improve and are worth consideration to reduce the amount of maintenance required on similar wood products.

CARE

1. Find last season's plant labels and take inventory of your notes. Add any plant information you may have missed earlier.

2. Keep the leaf debris from collecting over the top of any evergreen plant. The moisture retention of the soil is increased, and possible rotting or fungus problems can occur.

3. Make a final sweep through the garden. Remove anything that looks out of place such as debris, stakes, ties, and supports.

4. After a hard frost, cover the area at the base of vines with mulch.

5. During milder temperatures and in areas with little mulch (less than 1 inch), top dress with one-half inch of compost.

The **wintercreeper**, **English ivy**, **Boston ivy** or **climbing hydrangea** climbing the trunks of trees presents no problems, unless the growth moves out onto branches. The weight and shadowing of leaf and flower buds reduces the overall strength of the tree. Intertwining growth of vines certainly adds texture and an unexpected visual quality to trees

WATERING

Monitor rainfall amounts and maintain moisture in all of the beds. This is especially crucial for fall plantings.

FERTILIZING

If you have cuttings growing indoors, use a regular, light application of fertilizer to replenish nutrients leached by watering.

HELPFUL HINTS

Learning Botanical Names

During the long winter months, accept a new challenge to learn the botanical Latin names for ground covers and vines. Common names for plants may be entirely different from town to town, but botanical names are the same worldwide. The second part of the botanical name is the species. Many times, this Latin word is descriptive and this can help you remember its name. Learning the botanical names of plants provides you with quick insight while paging through catalogs, attending classes, shopping at the garden center, and while strolling about in parks and botanical gardens.

Common Name	Botanical Name	General Meaning of Species
Boston ivy	*Parthenocissus tricuspidata*	having three points
Bugle weed	*Ajuga reptans*	creeping
Chameleon plant	*Houttuynia cordata*	heart shaped
Dead nettle	*Lamium maculatum*	spotted
Lily turf	*Liriope spicata*	with spikes
Myrtle	*Vinca minor*	smaller
Stone crop	*Sedum spurium*	false

PRUNING

Pruning is minimal this time of year. Prune only to remove storm damaged branches.

During cold, snowy, and icy weather, the birds flock in and remain in vines that are either evergreen or a tangled mass of deciduous stems. This is a good reason to hold off pruning until the weather begins to break, some time in mid-February.

PESTS

The mole activity is slowing, but still keep a watchful eye for new tunnels and place traps as needed.

Hand digging is your only defense against weeds at this time of year.

Storage of chemicals is crucial, as the chemistry may be altered during the course of cold and freezing weather. Settling and hardening can occur if the package is open to humidity.

NOTES

NOTES

CHAPTER FIVE

PERENNIALS & ORNAMENTAL GRASSES

Plants of color, with a tradition and texture that invites a touch, and produces shapes and forms that are straight up or flat—perennials and ornamental grasses are constantly growing bigger, brighter, and better each year.

Successful growing means a chance to share in a tradition. Everyone can benefit from starting a new garden, adding to a collection, filling a pot, or highlighting a front door, patio edge or evergreen hedge. There is not a group of plants that is more versatile, remarkable, or satisfying.

KANSAS SEASONS

Kansas's four seasons swing incredibly wild with winter's wind chills of -50 degrees Fahrenheit, or summer's humi-temps of 120+ degrees Fahrenheit occuring within a few months. In the gaps can be pounding rains or extended dry periods. Changing weather over years will test any plant's durability.

Proven to withstand countless fluctuations are columbine, Shasta daisy and bleeding heart, whose stems and foliage are February's harbingers of early spring. October features fall windflowers and blades of feather reed grasses as highlights for the nearing gardening season's end. Linking together these days, weeks, and months are peonies, balloon flowers and blue lyme grass for cutting, or speedwell, blanket flower, mums and obedient plant simply for enjoying. Unexpected is the tickseed, blooming all summer is barrenwort, lady's mantle and hosta—providing terrific looking foliage. Fountain grass, yarrow, daylilies, iris and hardy sage are fantastic show-offs and require minimal care. Tall phlox fill the air with fragrance in drier bed spaces. Rose mallow, maiden grass, and astilbe will grow strong in wetter areas.

Yes, all the proven winners can be the backbone of the landscape, but never stop looking for new electrifying cultivars or varieties. Maybe beard tongue (*Penstemon digitalis* 'Husker Red'), lady bell (*Adenophora confusa*), or sweet flag (*Acorus calamus* 'Variegatus') will work into the landscape. Do remember when planning and planting that perennials and ornamental grasses are colonizers, spreading with underground roots and/or self seeding.

Careful consideration is recommended to minimize frustration for any reason, but never stop the desire to be experimental. Sometimes the greatest feeling is achieved by successfully growing plants that are "labeled" but that cannot survive in Kansas's four seasons. The following are guidelines to increase fun, and to elevate anticipation and enthusiasm.

SELECTING, PURCHASING AND CARE

Start with a dream list compiled from catalogs, parks, Kansas botanical gardens, favorite garden centers, or talking with gardeners. Narrowing the list is a step-by-step process to determine the best plant, combination, or garden location.

Basic Guidelines

1. Perennials are herbaceous plants with soft and fleshy stems. Even if some stems remain standing through winter, the top growth of perennials dies back in the winter, so these standing stems will not leaf out the following spring. Essential plant parts

of perennials include stems, buds, flowers, leaves (variegated and nonvariegated), roots (underground storage roots and root hairs), and veins (the plant transportation system). As with other plants, perennials breathe (gas exchange through the leaf and root), and require nutrients and water that combine in photosynthesis (food manufacturing) to stay alive. Perennials are propagated by divisions, cuttings, and by seed.

2. A perennial grouping or garden offers a plant metropolis, just like a city or town. Perennials greet insects, asking for pollination in exchange for pollen. They give reason for a pause. Spans of perennials wave a greeting from a distance. Perennials reflect personal qualities, much like home decorations, and make a constantly changing aesthetic statement.

The perennial plant combinations are endless, but not without consideration for a few main factors.

There are vastly different seasonal changes in temperature, precipitation, sunlight, humidity, and winds. Weather directly impacts plants. The fluctuations between hot and cold, freeze and thaw, and rain or drought all affect plant growth. Extremes can weaken plants, reducing the ability to aesthetically or functionally perform as anticipated. Additions and modifications with mulch, supplemental watering, soil preparation, routine care, and maintenance really makes a difference in performance. Water should total 1 inch every seven to ten days. How long to wait between waterings is related to temperature, humidity, wind, and other weather variables.

The soil profile and how it relates to water percolation and soil drainage also impacts plants. Productive soil is more than just dirt. There is structure (varied particle size), nutritional level (fundamental building blocks), organics (beneficial bacteria and fungi), chemistry (pH, soil component interaction), and animal activity (insects, moles, spiders, and voles). Soil is a temporary reservoir that takes in water and air, "sweats," and exhales. Influences on the soil include plant root growth, seasonal loss of leaves, needles, flowers, and animal, insect, and human activity (above and below the surface). A soil sample indicates the relative levels and relationship of the soil components. Use this information to make modifications as needed. Provide soil preparation to furnish the best possible environment for a new plant, garden, and landscape.

3. To design exciting perennial gardens, consider these three major factors:

Silhouette and Form

Structure carries, holds, and presents the more obvious and showier components of plants such as the plant texture and color. Silhouettes and forms add the subliminal message. Start with a projected outcome for the view; do you want to convey smooth serenity, undulating anticipation, or surprising interruptions? Make use of the three broad monikers of structural forms, horizontal (spreading habit), mounded (intermediate), and vertical (upright), with each making their presence known.

Engage in Color

Color is truly weightless. It is a fascinating and powerful tool. Color brings three broad reactions that are controlled by lighting. Receding is blues and violets. They have short wave lengths, requiring fore- or midground placement. Plant three times the projected quantity to create great impact. Stability and unification hallmark pinks and yellows. Give them freedom of placement. The capacity of these colors is enhanced, as these colors appear slightly larger than they actually are. Activity is spelled out by reds and oranges. They move forward with longer wavelengths. Use these colors in the midground or background. Use one-half of the quantity needed—these colors go far.

Texture Is Touched and Seen

Tactile and visual sensations unfold with patterns, animation (lighting, shadows, wind, rain), and are a presence that move and change. The labeling and emotions can change from an almost non-existent, wispy fineness, to a dominating, rough coarseness. All of this can occur when viewing a single plant or if viewing an entire panorama. Generally, smaller, lighter textures mean foreground or midground use, with an increase in physical and emotional size. Coarser (larger sized) plants placed further away allows for surprises to be maximized.

Soil preparation will most likely be part of any perennial planting. It makes for successful plant growth, and also serves as an invitation to insects, which spend a portion of their life underground. This insect activity, in combination with a well worked soil, is easy digging for moles. Moles are territorial and tunnel towards distinctive sounds when looking for food. Basically, the healthier the soil, the greater concentration of subterranean insects (centipedes, roly-pollies, spiders, grubs, and earthworms). These make up the majority of the mole's diet. Plant roots are consumed in small amounts by other mammals, such as voles, field mice, and chipmunks, which use the abandoned tunnels to forage for plant roots. Moles live in and use a two-tunnel system. The upper is to search for food. The lower tunnel, sometimes just 1 foot deeper, acts as a "highway" for returning to the nest (moles generally have four young), or for moving relatively quickly from one place to another. If the feeding tunnel has been flattened, the mole will repair it within twenty-four hours. This is where a trap (spear or choker) should be positioned. There is a hit and miss circumstance with traps, but multiple studies have been conducted, and traps are proven to be the most effective means of control. Some gardeners have had success with mothballs, poison peanuts, Juicy Fruit chewing gum, and gas bombs.

It is recommended that you use edging in the perennial beds. This is a physical barrier, installed or dug, to keep the lawn, groundcovers, and the perennials confined to a designated space. There are many types and methods. A **spade cut** is made by digging a 4- to 6-inch deep trench. The trench can be lined with black plastic, bricks, cobblestones, stamped concrete, faux brick, or rocks. **Steel edging** is another option. Steel edging materials vary in length from 8- to 16-foot sections. To install:

- Cut a continuous trench 4 inches deep (or 6 inches deep, if using wider sections), lay the edging in the trench and set it upright. Make adjustments in depth to insure the top one-half inch of the edging is above the finished grade.
- Starting at beginning of first section of edging, drive stakes halfway into the double loop pockets along the length. Stake approximately every 2 to 3 feet.
- Splice sections together as needed, overlap sections so the brackets on the end of each piece line up and interlock.
- Drive splicing stake down from the top, through all loops.
- Repeat steps as needed until entire bed area is surrounded with edging.

CONSIDER THE BASICS

Site evaluation determines the possibilities:

- Full sun (6 hours minimum), part sun (more direct sun), part shade (no direct sun 10:00 a.m.–3:00 p.m.), shade (no direct sunlight). All can change seasonally.
- Manmade influences such as buildings, patios, walkways, downspout discharge, underground utility wires, irrigation system.
- Topography that's flat, sloped (use biodegradable erosion netting), or a lower depressed hollow.
- Soil that is wet, dry, rocky, improved, or new.
- Existing vegetation types and health of trees, shrubs, ground covers, lawns, and mossy plants.

Prepare bed or planting space before acquiring plants:

• Outline space; remove undesirable plants by digging or using herbicide; rototill or spade to a depth of 6 to 8 inches, add 6 inches (1.75 cubic yards per 100 square feet of garden area) of compost leaf mold or other amendments to raise planting area and improve plant growth. Rake to insure positive drainage away from structures.

Planting seasons for seed, containerized plants or divisions:

• Springtime (after ground thaws) through early June (in later summer the kill potential is greater), or fall before mid-October (afterwards winterkill potential is greater).

Getting plants from garden centers, catalogs:

• Double check pot tag, catalog information, or ask for complete plant name or any additional helpful tips such as light, moisture, and nutrient requirements.

• If purchasing, never only use cost as a factor.

• Purchase container sizes from 4 inches and up—larger sizes have shorter garden impact time, and established root systems need less monitoring care (fertilizing, watering). Perform routine inspections (for bugs and diseases) and maintenance (pinching, pruning) while plants are acclimating.

• Ask about care and maintenance, particularly fertilizers, insecticides, and fungicides needed.

• Plant health is vital. There should be no wilting, with minimal damage to stem and foliage (such as bugs and bruises).

• The container/pot should not be overly misshaped. Such symptoms are root damage related. Check drainage holes on bottom for bugs, slugs, and snails.

• For catalog orders ask about the potting/packing, and shipping date. Upon arrival, immediately unpack and inspect.

• Remember to share among gardening friends.

Planting:

• Look at the color and size of any new growth; check for anything flying, hovering, crawling, or stuck to the plant; look for unexpected leaf browning, leaf drop or bruising.

• Removing plant from pot or moss, look for white root hairs (true nutrient absorbers).

• Dig hole three times the width of the root system; remove and shake off any potting soil (it loses structure and disappears outdoors); loosen roots and check for white root hairs that are pot bound. Place in a hole slightly higher than surrounding ground. Backfill and pat soil firm, water, and place 1 inch of mulch around the plant. Don't put mulch over crown to avoid fungus problems.

After installation, allow a 30 day transition into garden:

• Weeds are competition for nutrients and water. Monitor and remove ASAP by hand digging or using an herbicide.

• Do not overwater. If plant is wilting in the heat of day, this is a natural response. Check later, and water if plant is drooping.

• After fourteen days, fertilize at 1/2 the label rate. Use a powder water mixture for flowering plants, none on grasses.

• Prune to remove flowers, browning, bent blades, or foliage.

• Examine routinely for insects chewing or diseases leaving a sticky leaf surface and unnatural surface coating. Blackened spots or bruises (at top or bottom leaf and stem) or persistent drooping are symptoms. Determine the cause and take action accordingly. This may involve plant removal for isolation or the compost pile to benefit unaffected plants.

• Uprooted plants lying above ground partially or totally after hard rains are a sign of squirrel and pet activity. Replant immediately and water.

CHAPTER FIVE

Perennials & Ornamental Grasses

AESTHETIC ATTRIBUTES:

For reliable bloom:	balloon flower, bleeding heart, Shasta daisy, speedwell, live-forever, tickseed
For color:	astilbe, hardy sage, maiden grass, mums, peony, rose mallow
For texture and forms:	barrenwort, fall windflower, feather reed grass, hosta, tall phlox
For versatility:	blue lyme grass, daylily, fountain grass, lady's mantle, yarrow

Best growth is obtained using amended, well-drained soil that is kept evenly moist.
Numerous flower colors are a possibility within same genus.
Full sun = minimum of six hours
Part shade or Part sun = no direct sun from 10 a.m. to 3 p.m.
Shade = no direct sun

KEY:

Common Name:	Local name
Botanical Name:	Assure correct information—for care or purchase
Flower Color:	Color of species or variety listed, botanical name
Tip:	Insight into growing, uses, and or highlight
Light Requirement:	Exposure for Best Growth:
Silhouette/Growth Habit:	Aids in designing
Companion Plant:	Similar care/complimentary/not included on plant list

Common Name: Astilbe
Botanical Name: *Astilbe* x *arendsii* 'Snowdrift'
Flower Color: White
Tip: Multiple plants clustered, consistently damp areas
Light Requirements: Part shade to shade
Silhouette/Growth Habit: Spreading foliage, upright flowers
Companion Plant: Cardinal flower

Common Name: Balloon flower
Botanical Name: *Platycodon grandiflorus* 'Sentimental Blue'
Flower Color: Blue
Tip: Unusual flowering—place in foreground
Light Requirement: Sun
Silhouette/Growth Habit: Upright stems growing in clump
Companion Plant: Autumn phlox

Common Name: Barrenwort
Botanical Name: *Epimedium versicolor* 'Sulphureum'
Flower Color: Yellow
Tip: Semievergreen, no mulch over foliage, great edger
Light Requirements: Part shade to shade
Silhouette/Growth Habit: Low spreading foliage, flowering above
Companion Plant: Larger hosta

Common Name: Blanket flower
Botanical Name: *Gaillardia* x *grandiflora* 'Kobold'
Flower Color: Yellow & Red
Tip: Dry soil, deadhead for reblooming
Light Requirements: Sun
Silhouette/Growth Habit: Slow dense spreading
Companion Plant: Statice

Common Name: Bleeding heart
Botanical Name: *Dicentra spectabilis* 'Luxuriant'
Flower Color: Pink
Tip: Evenly moist, sporadic blooming through summer
Light Requirements: Part shade to shade
Silhouette/Growth Habit: Low open mounding
Companion Plant: Hardy geranium

Common Name: Blue lyme grass
Botanical Name: *Leymus arenarius*
Flower Color: Tan
Tip: Dry soil, low care, good erosion control
Light Requirements: Sun
Silhouette/Growth Habit: Spreading
Companion Plant: Prickly pear cactus

Perennials & Ornamental Grasses (continued)

Common Name: Daylily
Botanical Name: *Hemerocallis* x 'Pardon Me'
Flower Color: Red
Tip: Deadhead, encourages rebloom, average soil
Light Requirements: Sun
Silhouette/Growth Habit: Mounded
Companion Plant: Bee balm

Common Name: Fall windflower
Botanical Name: *Anemone* x *hybrida* 'Whirlwind'
Flower Color: White
Tip: Prevent drought
Light Requirements: Sun to part shade
Silhouette/Growth Habit: Upright
Companion Plant: Turtlehead

Common Name: Feather reed grass
Botanical Name: *Calamagrostis* x *acutiflora* 'Karl Foerster'
Flower Color: Reddish
Tip: Keep ground moist, good winter appearance
Light Requirements: Sun
Silhouette/Growth Habit Very straight upright
Companion Plant: Spiderwort

Common Name: Fountain grass
Botanical Name: *Pennisetum alopecuriodes* 'Hameln'
Flower Color: Tan
Tip: Average dry soil, equal height and width
Light Requirements: Sun
Silhouette/Growth Habit: Mounded
Companion Plant: Thermopsis

Common Name: Hardy sage
Botanical Name: *Salvia* x *superba* 'May Night'
Flower Color: Dark purple
Tip: Great performer with minimal care
Light Requirements: Sun
Silhouette/Growth Habit: Mounded
Companion Plant: Pincushion flower

Common Name: Hosta
Botanical Name: *Hosta sieboldiana elegans*
Flower Color: White
Tip: Slow growing—worth the wait, striking round blue leaf
Light Requirements: Part shade to shade
Silhouette/Growth Habit: Mound
Companion Plant: Painter's palette

Common Name: Lady's Mantle
Botanical Name: *Alchemilla mollis*
Flower Color: Greenish yellow
Tip: Semievergreen, do not mulch over top
Light Requirements: Sun to part shade
Silhouette/Growth Habit: Low spreading
Companion Plant: Maltese cross

Common Name: Live-Forever
Botanical Name: *Hylotelephium telephium*
Flower Color: Pink
Tip: Stem cluster separates midsummer, tough, durable
Light Requirements: Sun to part shade
Silhouette/Growth Habit: Upright
Companion Plant: Painted daisy

Common Name: Maiden grass
Botanical Name: *Miscanthus sinensis* 'Gracillimus'
Flower Color: Tan
Tip: Best growth, use damp soil, divide, replant every 3+ years
Light Requirements: Sun
Silhouette/Growth Habit: Upright, vase
Companion Plant: Gooseneck loosestrife

Common Name: Mum
Botanical Name: *Chrysanthemum* x *hybrida*
Flower Color: Numerous—variety dependent
Tip: Cut back growth monthly 1/4 - 1/2 May-late August,
Light Requirements: Sun
Silhouette/Growth Habit: Mounded
Companion Plant: Catmint

Common Name: Obedient plant
Botanical Name: *Physostegia virginiana* 'Vivid'
Flower Color: Pink
Tip: Allow plenty of room for spreading, cut flower
Light Requirements: Sun to part shade
Silhouette/Growth Habit: Low carpeting
Companion Plant: Culver's root

Common Name: Peony
Botanical Name: *Paeonia lactiflora* 'Sarah Bernhardt'
Flower Color: Pink
Tip: Slow growth, cut and remove foliage each fall
Light Requirements: Sun
Silhouette/Growth Habit: Mounded
Companion Plant: Oriental poppy

Common Name: Rose mallow
Botanical Name: *Hibiscus moscheutos* 'Lord Baltimore'
Flower Color: Red
Tip: Keep soil damp, foliage declines at flowering
Light Requirements: Sun
Silhouette/Growth Habit: Large mound
Companion Plant: Meadowsweet

Common Name: Shasta daisy
Botanical Name: *Leucanthemum superbum* 'Becky'
Flower Color: White
Tip: Self-seeds and colonizes, cut flower
Light Requirements: Sun
Silhouette/Growth Habit: Upright/basal foliage
Companion Plant: Dianthus

Common Name: Speedwell
Botanical Name: *Veronica longifolia* 'Icicle'
Flower Color: White
Tip: Dry areas similar to herbs
Light Requirements: Sun
Silhouette/Growth Habit: Spreading, upright
Companion Plant: Oriental lily

Common Name: Tall phlox
Botanical Name: *Phlox paniculata* 'Fujiyama'
Flower Color: White
Tip: Site near seating or walking—great fragrance
Light Requirements: Sun
Silhouette/Growth Habit: Upright,wide top
Companion Plant: Baby's breath

Common Name: Tickseed
Botanical Name: *Coreopsis verticillata* 'Moonbeam'
Flower Color: Pale yellow
Tip: Cut 1/3 plant after flower flush to speed reblooming
Light Requirements: Sun
Silhouette/Growth Habit: Low mounding
Companion Plant: Comfrey

Common Name: Yarrow
Botanical Name: *Achillea millefolium* 'Paprika'
Flower Color: Reddish-orange
Tip: Dry average soil, fern-like foliage
Light Requirements: Sun
Silhouette/Growth Habit: Upright
Companion Plant: Gaura

HELPFUL HINTS

• **Iris/Flags:** Cut foliage in late August to reduce chance of fungus leaf spot and to remove iris borer eggs laid previously. Iris borer eggs overwinter on foliage, hatch in spring and burrow into the tuber (root system) causing major damage.

• **Daylilies:** Flowering happens best if plants are divided every three to five years.

• **Mums:** Cut mums to a height of 2 to 3 inches after flowering. Mums love water (not swampy environments), so minimize or prevent any drought stress through the entire growing season.

JANUARY

PERENNIALS & ORNAMENTAL GRASSES

PLANNING

Review and analyze all previous years' notes and photographs. Look at the big picture. Consider all the influences that come from beyond property line, the neighboring topography, trees in your landscape and your neighbor's garden, an annual migration of mulch or mud, or background plantings of evergreen shrubs that might set the stage for perennials.

Look closely at the projected location, and consider the past history of the location. Ask these questions: Does the sun or shade influence the area, or is there is a blending of the two? How have previous plants fared in the area? What is growing there now? Are downspouts or runoff areas prone to hold standing water for a day or more? Do dogs impact the area? Is there anything that would make the **peonies** take seven or more years to get to full size, rather than the usual five?

Get personal with your garden using your favorite colors, textures, and growing habits. It is not necessary to make combinations and compromises according to a "correct way." Just think of nature and the inspiring woods, meadows, and hillsides. Herbaceous plants growing in close proximity to each other can have many similar visual traits and similar cultural needs. As crucial as flower color may seem, most perennials have a bloom period of only about fourteen days.

Consider the mature size of the chosen clump-forming **mums** and spreading **speedwell**. A dash of excitement to this mixture holds less impact with mass planting of the finer textured **balloon flowers** than adding a single, coarse textured **peony**.

Explore new seed racks at your favorite garden center for **tickseed** or other **sunflower** family members. Look for seeds to add to the **yarrow** planting. Check to see if any new varieties of **rose mallow** or **live-forever** are for sale.

Increase your gardening knowledge by taking classes offered, reading catalogs, or attending garden club meetings.

PLANTING

Prepare to grow seeds under lights. Clean containers and pots by washing thoroughly to eliminate all of last year's residues. Soak in a water (ten parts water to one part bleach) and bleach solution overnight. Scrub with a stiff bristled brush and rinse. Discard any cracked pots.

The amount of light needed by seedlings, cuttings, or transplants cannot be overemphasized. Use lights specifically for plant growing. There are both incandescent and fluorescent bulbs. Depending on the seeds or plants, adjust the fixtures to 2 to 3 inches above the soil surface or above the cutting tops. Raise as needed.

For starting **hardy sage** or any seeds, use only very lightweight, soilless potting mixes.

Use the same soilless potting mix for rooting divisions, but select one that contains a slow-release starter fertilizer.

CARE

If the leaf debris collecting over plants is stiff or rigid (**oak**), it creates a good mulch. If the leaf debris is fine, thin, and flexible (**maple, ash**), this can be problematic as it compresses down and maintains too much moisture over the plant crown.

Check the mulch level, as heavy rains or snowmelt may have washed it away from the plants. Replenish as needed.

WATERING

Keep potted seedlings moist and damp to the look and touch, but not wet or soggy.

Reduce potential problem for recently germinated seeds that are prone to water chemistry problems. Ask a technician at your water company for recent readings and about the presence of trace elements. It might be necessary to set the water out overnight before using, or consider buying de-ionized water. Plant divisions are much stronger and the impact of the water chemistry is less than for seedlings.

FERTILIZING

No fertilizer is needed for plants under grow lights.

Outdoors, apply a half-inch topdressing of compost around the stem of the plants.

PRUNING

No pruning or pinching is needed. If seedlings, cuttings, or transplants appear elongated, plant recovery is unlikely, so discard.

Outdoors in the garden, remove any remaining stalks or stems from perennials and grasses. Do not remove stems or stalks from the fall bloomers (they benefit from the added structural protection), or any plant showing winter's basal leaf rosette (a live miniature-appearing plant on the surface).

HELPFUL HINTS

If growing small clumps of **maiden grass** or **hosta** under grow lights, minimize transplant shock by placing the original divisions into peat moss containers.

PESTS

Insects should not be a concern outdoors, but monitor any seedlings or divisions indoors. Wipe foliage gently with cloth dabbed in insecticidal soap to control pests. If stem or soil fungus is observed, isolate the plant and treat with a fungicide. If control is not reached within seven days, discard the plant.

Look for bark being stripped from tree trunks or at the base of the trunk. This damage indicates the presence of wildlife. Also check for signs of animals feeding on winterizing mum foliage. Use a section of hardware cloth and lay it over the plants as a deterrent.

Use a weed-digging tool to remove, root and all, any broadleaf weeds. Mulch will not kill weed seeds unless it is very thick. If it is used for this purpose, many perennials can be harmed, especially those self-seeding types.

Some natives, plants naturalized in Kansas, and imported plants that have been extremely successful, are considered weeds. There are three major categories:

1. **Broadleaf plants** with fat multi-branched veins are annual or perennial. They colonize by underground offshoots of the mother plant and disperse seeds to colonize other areas. Examples include dandelions, violets, chickweed, and spurge.

2. **Grass plants** have skinny narrow leaves with veins running parallel to the leaf margin. Grasses are annual or perennial, colonize by underground-modified roots (tillers) or seeds. Examples include crabgrass, wild onions and garlic, and goosegrass.

3. **Sedges** are narrow blade grass plants with a triangular stem that emerges from the ground with the same qualities of broadleaf and grass plants. Sedges are a perennial that spread seeds both under and above ground. They have a root system that will tiller to colonize spaces as well. Nutgrass (nutsedge) is the most common example.

PERENNIALS & ORNAMENTAL GRASSES

PLANNING

Daylily, *Hemerocallis* sp.—Probably no plant is more widely known or has the interest or dedication that this group of **lilies** has. They are found growing almost anywhere, from along abandoned fencerows and roadways, to the rural and suburban landscape, and into the urban yards. The allure is due to many factors; the medium green, grass-like leaves transition very smoothly from one designated landscape area to another. The colors, size, and star shaped qualities of the flowers give the summertime a bit of pizzazz, as they hover above the foliage on stick-like stems. A combination of early, mid, and late season bloomers basically can carry the dog days on its aesthetic shoulders. Several varieties will offer an added plus by filling the air with a welcomed fragrance when in flower.

Fall windflower, *Anemone* x *hybrida* is virtually an unknown perennial, and mysteriously undiscovered in many gardens. The darker green dissected or segmented leaves form a mound, from the time they emerge in the spring through the entire growing season. The shear color and bulkiness of the habit make it a great backdrop for early blooming, fine textured plants. As the heat of the summer has passed and the nights have the enjoyable coolness that signals fall is on its way, **fall windflower** comes forth to give the late season pollinators a source of food. The stem rises above the foliage, and even from a close look, it appears to be unattached to anything, merely suspended in midair. The timing adds a true flash of color to the late season garden. **Fall windflower** is a winner, whether planted singly or in larger quantities.

Monitor the weather in the landscape. Have several rain gauges, the first one for the wooded area (overhanging trees influence the amount of rainfall reaching ground), one for open spaces, and a backup for each. If collected water becomes frozen, it is easy to switch to another.

Review notes on specific plant successes and disappointments, in particular if the plants were located in multiple sites. For example, the **tall phlox** is very upright in the east end of the garden, yet it was leaning severely at the opposite end. Determine the cause. Is soil compaction preventing root penetration? Are there overhanging branches casting more shade?

Consider increasing the colony size of **tickseed** and adding more **speedwell** to reduce the amount of lawn.

On colder days, look at the view out the window. Maybe the dogwood grove needs more **big blue leaf hosta** to break up the stand of **ivy**. Keep graph paper nearby to make some quick drawings, so as not to forget.

Look for bare-root **daylilies** and **peonies** at the local garden center.

PLANTING

Make sure beds planned for **live-forever** and **blue lyme grass** are not overly wet. Do a probing test. Use a shovel, spade or trowel; push the tool into the ground. If you hear a sucking sound, or when the tool is lifted out of the soil and the soil sticks to the base, it is too wet.

Read **lady's mantle, balloon flower**, and **blanket flower** seed packets, and do research on the specific depth the seeds are placed to maximize the percentage of germination.

Pack potting mix firmly in pots or flats to reduce seeds sinking into air pockets.

Label pots or flats with name of seed planted, on the front side, list the common name (**bleeding heart**), and the botanical name (*Dicentra*) and cultivar or variety

('Luxuriant'). Note the day planted, projected germination time, growth rate, etc.

Have a soil test done if performance of any section of the perennial border was not up to par last season. Collect a quart of soil (with no mulch, dead stem or leaf matter), take it to the local Extension Service, or check for soil testing in the phone book. The earlier the sample is sent, the quicker the results return. Then if changes are needed, you have plenty of time to prepare. If the results are confusing, ask for help at Kansas State University.

CARE

Top dressing is a process of spreading a thin layer (approximately 1 inch) of compost or other organic matter around perennials. There are microorganisms present in the compost that aid in decomposition and improve the soil's physical and chemical structure. After application, lightly rake or water to move materials into the ground. For better results, use fully composted materials of any sort (manure).

HELPFUL HINTS

If you spread gypsum on the bed spaces adjacent to walk ways, it reduces any type of potential burn to the perennials from de-icer products.

Keep adjusting the height of the light on the growing bench to insure 2 to 3 inches above plants.

Increase the "ON" cycle to maintain upright growth on seedlings and to acclimate to longer daytime hours.

Thin and remove any seedling or division showing any signs of rot or fungus.

Look closely around the areas where various perennials are currently growing, for seeds that may have been dispensed last year. Collect for relocation, or simply watch and see what happens.

WATERING

Keep soil moisture damp to the look and touch on potted seedlings.

Keep a rainfall log and prepare to compensate for a dry winter by providing supplemental watering.

FERTILIZING

Apply a very light application of water-soluble fertilizer, and apply only to healthy seedlings and plants.

PRUNING

No pruning or pinching is needed this month on plants or seedlings being grown indoors.

Outdoors, leave any stems or stalks remaining on the fall bloomers (they benefit from the added structural protection), or any plant showing winter's basal leaf rosette (a live miniature, appearing plant on the surface).

PESTS

Inspect the soil surface of seedling flats and packs for any gray mold on the soil surface. Stir the soil very lightly, and add a fan for air circulation.

Insects will be small and flying. Control with yellow sticky traps placed among plants.

MARCH

PERENNIALS & ORNAMENTAL GRASSES

PLANNING

Plan for a new addition to the perennial shade garden—try **hosta**.

Mass plantings or single clumps of **hosta** (*Hosta sieboldiana*) dotted in the shade garden give wonderful textural changes and a smooth domed silhouette. Additionally, the **hosta** serves to transition between woody plants and lower growing perennials. Cool green foliage color, which is heavily veined, is a welcome relief during the heat of the summer, as earlier blooming plants are headed for underground dormancy. Introduced only twenty-five years ago to the American landscape, this plant has taken over in the popularity polls. The instant impact, regardless of size planted, and little care means there are never too many **hostas** in the garden.

Plant for a new addition to the perennial sun border. Try **feather reed grass**.

If a sunny location needs framing, or you need a symbolic gatepost to mark an entrance, or you want a transition from one part of the landscape to the next, **feather reed grass** (*Calamagrostis* x *acutiflora*) can do it all. Mingled among perennials, an annual planting, or standing alone in the distance are some of the better ways to employ this grass. The straight up and almost unnaturally rigid form is the initial impression that the **feather reed grass** gives. This strong linear feature makes it very useful as a living structural component in the landscape. Additional pluses are the dazzling fall coloration of the foliage, wet or dry soil happy, and it works well to screen roads or views. The intended function is achievable either as a monostand or intermixed with other plantings. Also, nothing is more eye-catching than a clump growing and reflecting in a pond or water feature. The flower rises above the leaves in the summer, and can be cut for seasonal arrangements.

Parcel delivery at home is arriving, containing multiple clumps of different types of **barrenwort**, and large divisions of **bleeding heart** for the area under the tree. Keep an eye out at garden centers for plant materials arriving daily. Look for a new dwarf variety of **Shasta daisy**, or **mum** cuttings in 2¼ inch-pots for growing in the yard.

PLANTING

Bare root plants need to be prepared before planting. Soak them in a solution of rooting hormone and water for one hour or until any dry-appearing roots have begun to swell and show signs of absorption. If the root is questionable in terms of viability after soaking, notify the source. Pot up healthy rooted plants in a seed starting potting mix and transplant into the garden when healthy.

Water containerized plants well before installation.

Avoid working in bed spaces if there have been recent rains. Work backwards out of a bed, and loosen soil in the areas just finished to prevent compaction.

Divide plants as needed.

With seed dispersal, either by plants self-seeding or by scattering seed that you have collected or purchased, remember that pre-emergent weed controls kill any seed. If the mulch is applied heavily, more moisture is retained, and this may lead to damping-off for the tender seedlings.

CARE

Cold temperatures are still possible this month. When you purchase plants from the garden center, ask where the plants were grown, if they were greenhouse grown, and how long they have been at the garden center. The longer they have been at the center, the longer time they have had to acclimate to your growing area. Have some burlap or similar material ready to offer some buffering from the cold. Perennials are tough, but blackened frozen leaves are not very appealing, particularly when you have just installed them.

Begin to slowly acclimate your homegrown plants that are undersized and under the lights. Begin acclimating during warmer days (no direct sun as it causes leaf stem scorch), return indoors as temperatures drop during day or night.

Mulch new plantings of **yarrow** and **feather reed grass**, and the established **daylily** planting. Do not exceed a mulch layer of 1 to 2 inches.

WATERING

Do not allow seedlings in containers or just planted in beds to dry out. Water newly planted perennials to supplement periods of no rainfall.

HELPFUL HINTS

Make friends with the local birds (maybe not the starlings and grackles). Keep the suet, thistle, or any feeder full as recent hatchlings are on the look out for some food and will stay in the vicinity. The payback could be insect control, which is not needed by most perennials, but other plants in the landscape could benefit.

FERTILIZING

Make a final application of fertilizer on indoor growing plants. Use a seed-starter type (if there were no nutrients included in the potting mix) in preparation for the **fall windflower** seedlings to be moved outdoors. Discard any weak or diseased seedlings.

Cuttings should be showing signs of being well rooted. If they are in peat pots, you should see white fibrous roots showing. If the cuttings are in plastic containers or flats, give a slight tug on the cutting. If there is resistance, the cutting is rooted. Continue current maintenance schedule.

In anticipation of the planting season, apply a granular, all-purpose fertilizer (at a light rate) to the bed spaces, and then work it into the soil.

PRUNING

There are no pruning chores this month.

PESTS

When removing any diseased part of a plant with pruners, the possibility exists for the pruners to transmit disease from plant to plant. Carry along soap or alcohol solution (ten parts water to one part alcohol), and dip pruners after each cut.

The wildlife are giving birth to their young, so there will be more trouble, simply because of the increase in numbers. Consider chicken wire or another physical barrier, hot pepper sprays, or wildlife predator urine drops as repellents.

Many weeds are actively growing from seed. Keep up with them early using herbicides. Follow label directions.

PERENNIALS & ORNAMENTAL GRASSES

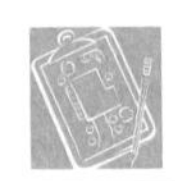

PLANNING

Add to your full sun, ornamental grass collection.

Fountain grass, *Pennisetum alopecuriodes*—The name "fountain" relates to the lower mounding growth habit of this variety of ornamental grass. This allows for numerous uses, ranging from a single specimen softening a shrub planting, to adding dimension to a bed of annuals or perennials. The impact is greater when plants are grouped closely together. When the wind blows, the view is unmatched. The inflorescence has a pinkish purple cast, and shoots past the foliage to bounce and weave above. This affect is enhanced due to the shear number of flower clusters. This accentuates the rounded silhouette even more when viewing the plant up close. In the distance, the inflorescence creates the illusion of a fog or mist. Toughness, durability, heat, and dry soil tolerance allows for planting **fountain grass** adjacent to roads, driveways, side and front walks, and patios.

Plan a new perennial for the full sun border.

Mums, *Chrysanthemum* x *hybrida*—No fall picture is complete without **mums**. If **mums** are allowed to grow, unpinched, they flower in the summer, so they take a little work, but it's well worth it. **Mums** have deeply cut foliage of medium to dark green coloration. They are a perfect, stout, fine textured plant in the sun garden. As the garden is moving towards the dormancy of winter, **mums** are the last plants to provide a mixture of rich harvest-like colors. The inflorescence sits on top of the leaves, totally obscuring them from view. If you pinch the **mums**, they bloom during the cooler part of the year. This means an extended bloom period for the perennial garden. Also, several varieties color as they age, and flowers will change hues or sometimes change to a completely different color.

Repeating forms and textures does not necessarily mean repeating the exact plant at opposing ends of the plantings. Use plants of similar color, texture, and growth habit to achieve a sense of formality in a garden. Planting a hedge-like plant in the background, such as **feather reed grass** or **peonies** enhances the repetitive elements.

Perennials are flexible from season to season, as well as from year to year. A formal garden becomes informal with the addition of spring blooming **pansy** or **toadflax** (see Annuals Chapter). Randomly siting summer annuals adds a completely new look to the perennial bed. Consider adding **begonias**, **spider flowers**, or **petunias**.

Keep informal garden settings organized. In the full sun, plant clumps of **maiden grass** as bookends. In the shade, surround two benches with large leaf **hosta.**

Balcony, patios, terraces, and decks come alive this month with containers, hanging baskets, and window boxes planted with perennials. Combine a cascading variety of **mum** with annual **periwinkle**, and add **Boston ferns** and **hosta** to existing shade bowls for a completely new look.

Take measurements of established and new bedding spaces. Take inventory of what you have going into these spaces, make sure you have room, and determine if you need to fill in spots with more perennials.

Take photographs and start a photo journal of your favorite perennials in the glory of spring activity.

PLANTING

Plenty of time remains to ready new beds or to reorganize established beds. Do a test for soil wetness before any major undertaking.

Check all plants remaining inside under grow lights for root development. Lift pots, and check for roots protruding through drainage holes or roots piercing the sides of peat pots. If plants are rooted, plant outdoors as soon as ground (wetness) allows. Discard any seedlings or divisions not showing healthy root growth.

After spending summer in a container, if they are healthy, **hardy sage**, **blanket flower**, and **barrenwort** can be moved right into the garden.

It is a good time to divide mature stands of perennials and grasses and to relocate plants to other areas of the garden.

CARE

Make notes in your garden journal logging the date of planting for home grown plants, dates purchased or gifted of divisions of **fall windflower**, **tickseed** and **astilbe**.

Keep a close eye on any newly installed plant for two weeks. Watch for early signs of problems such as standing water (poor drainage), pets or animals digging, and soil drying out. Take necessary measures to eliminate any observed problems early on.

HELPFUL HINTS

When you purchase any chemical fertilizer, pesticides, herbicides, or amendments, put the date of purchase on the package or bottle (do not write over the application instructions). Store any liquids to prevent freezing. If you suspect an expired shelf life, discard old chemicals. Purchase quantities that can be consumed during one season.

WATERING

Adjust the irrigation or supplemental watering for seedlings, divisions, and established plants to accommodate a lack of rainfall. All perennials need a minimum of 1 inch of water per week. Check the rain gauges, both in the shade garden and in the sunny border.

FERTILIZING

Apply seed starter (ratio 1-2-1) at one-half the package rate to well-settled **speedwell**, **yarrow**, **hardy sage**, and other seedlings. They are fragile at this early stage, but need a light boost of nutrients.

Do not feed ornamental grasses. Fertilizer causes floppy growth.

PRUNING

Pinch back or cut no more than one-quarter of any multi-stem plants such as **mums**, **hardy sage**, **obedient plant**, or **speedwell**. Plants with a single leaf on a single stem will not benefit from pinching and may be harmed.

Any flowers present on seedlings or purchased plants should be removed the first year after installation to conserve energy for root growth.

PESTS

Insect hatching is rampant this month. Sucking, eating, and disease transmittal is on the rise. Check for pests routinely and take action at the first signs. Use physical removal or insecticidal soap or a similar product for control.

Wildlife (adults and newborn) seems to be everywhere. Consider diversions with or irrigation devices, motion detector/light physical barriers, or set up a sacrificial buffet away from prized plantings.

PERENNIALS & ORNAMENTAL GRASSES

PLANNING

Plan a new addition for the full sun perennial bed.

Shasta daisy, *Leucanthemum* x *superbum*—Imagine a valley filled with white, as if the light snow had just fallen. This is the impact a mass planting of **Shasta daisies** provide to garden settings. The dark green basal rosette of leaves is formed during the preceding growing season and offers some color in the winter garden. Shooting up out of the thicket of foliage is the flower stalk, with the classic, white petal, yellow center, daisy flower. The bees and insects know when the first flower opens, and arrive to gather pollen. **Shasta daisy** is a garden classic that has gone through a complete name change from *Chrysanthemum* to *Leucanthemum*, and has experienced an explosion of new varieties. This newly evolved plant is a conversation piece and a true asset to any garden situation.

Plan a new addition for a full sun or part sun garden.

Obedient plant, *Physostegia virginiana*—Native **obedient plant** is easy to grow and fulfills many different roles in a multitude of garden settings. It has a vigorous growing habit that spreads from an underground spreading root system that allows for quick coverage and almost an instant impact. The denseness of the foliage is more pronounced near the ground. Further up on the stem, the leaf size and shape changes. This variation sets the scenario for the flower stalks to emerge and sit above the plant. The individual flowers are up to 1½ inches long, tubular shaped, with a lower portion that looks as if it is pouting. Place it in the front of a garden space, or plant it along a walk or near a patio.

Check out the site just prior to planting for any environmental changes such as downspout discharge (the area is super wet now), shaded areas that are now in the sun (seasonal movement of the sun), or surface tree roots that are more prominent (accelerated spring growth).

Before you plant, use marking ribbon or paint to delineate or designate the bed for **balloon flower**, **peony**, or **astilbe.**

Don't overproject on the amount of work that you can do at one time. Plants purchased and left in limbo decline quickly. Have you seen **peony**, **hosta**, and **maiden grass** available in pot sizes from 4 inches up to a 2-gallon size? A combination of sizes creates a garden with character and presence, rather than appearing as an assembly line of new plants.

PLANTING

Save some steps by having all necessary tools and goods readily available when it's time to plant.

When installing multiples of **barrenwort** or **rose mallow**, stop regularly and water plants just planted in the ground.

Keep bare-root plants and plants in pots well watered prior to and during planting. The best days to plant are cloudy days with minimal wind. These conditions reduce root and leaf moisture loss.

Allow a 20-inch minimum diameter for pots used for perennials. For cost savings, fill the bottom half of the large container with plastic peanuts and add potting mix to fill. Use a slow-release fertilizer, and a water retentive polymer to reduce maintenance.

Scatter seeds of **blanket flower** and **fall windflower** and keep notes on their progress.

Divide, give away, relocate, or discard the invasive **yarrow**, **blue lyme grass**, or **daylilies**.

CARE

Before replenishing the mulch (1 to 2 inches maximum) around plants, sprinkle some low analysis (5-5-5 or less) granular fertilizer on the soil surface to compensate for the mulch breaking down and binding up certain nutrients.

WATERING

Moisten prepared beds and potting mixes prior to installation and planting. A moist soil is essential to minimize root damage. Thoroughly water again as each plant is put into the ground, or after every few plants. Check to be sure the soil has not sunk and roots are exposed. Add soil if necessary. If the day is bright, sunny, and windy, several light waterings may be required.

FERTILIZING

Establish a regular routine of using fertilizer formulated for either shade or sun plants. Each plant group has different requirements. Ask to see if a balanced, all-purpose fertilizer will fit your needs.

HELPFUL HINTS

Check all the watering tools (hoses, sprinklers, nozzles, etc.), and replace any worn or damaged pieces. Ask the garden center staff about new irrigation supplies available this season. They may save you time and contribute to more efficient water discharge, which in turn is more cost effective.

PRUNING

Remove any damaged or dead leaves, as well as all of the flowers during the first season the perennial is in the ground. This allows the plant to build root strength.

Cut flowers before they are fully open and hang upside down for drying. For fresh arrangements, cut the stem at a 45-degree angle, and immediately place in water.

PESTS

This is the time to release predatory ladybugs, praying mantis, and lacewings.

Insect emergence and eggs hatching are triggered by warm weather. Keep an eye out for early sightings. The most problematic are the aphids. Use a strong stream of water, or simply smash them between your fingers. If insecticidal soap or other contact insecticides are used, apply the chemical directly on the pests for control.

Keep a pest identification book on hand to make a correct diagnosis. Many chemicals applied to young plantings can have an impact on the plant. Most contact sprays leave very little residual. This is not the case with fungicides. Fungicides should be applied as a preventative measure.

The seeds of warm season weeds are germinating. Simply raking can uproot the weed and end the problem before the roots get established.

NOTES

JUNE

PERENNIALS & ORNAMENTAL GRASSES

PLANNING

Plan a new addition for the shade garden.

The first impression one has of the **bleeding heart** (*Dicentra spectabilis*) is that it is a mutated fern, producing some very unusual shaped dangling and bouncing flowers. The extremely fine-textured leaf has an airy surreal look and a pale, blue-green coloration that is unmatched in the woodland garden. The stem has an arching habit, and emerges from the center to rise above the foliage. Very small buds open revealing the inflorescence. The two-toned flowers, accented white, are heart shaped and hang from the stem like a pendant on a necklace. This improved variety is more heat and sun tolerant the species. Under ideal conditions, **bleeding heart** continue to bloom in the early fall.

Have you seen a large stand of pink flowers blooming in September, in the middle of a grove of trees? This is the **hardy begonia**, *Begonia grandis*. It acclimates and spreads quite readily in the shade. The real plus is that most fall blooming perennials truly peak around July 4. Another plant to add pizzazz to the fall shade garden is the **toad lily**, *Tricyrtis hirta*. It is subtler than the **hardy begonia**.

Plan something new for a full sun bed.

Speedwell, *Veronica longifolia*—It is hard to believe that a plant with such elegant qualities and appearance could be one of the easier ones to grow. Dark green, pointed, glossy foliage alternates and whirls around the upright, spear-like stems. This eruption occurs in spring and makes a great backdrop for earlier spring flowering bulbs, annuals, and perennials. The crowning touch is the elongated, deep blue spike. Flowers bloom from the bottom up, with the spent blossoms turning brownish red. An added plus is the length of the bloom time—up to six weeks for a single variety. After flowering, the foliage remains as the fall season approaches.

Gold and purple finches, hummingbirds, and chickadees will be making a visit. Have thistle feeders and plenty of annual **sunflowers** (many varieties are great in pots) dotted in the garden. Hummingbird feeders allow the ruby-throated type to stay a bit longer during their migration north.

Update your photo journal with the spring blooming **peonies** that are showing leaf and the other perennials starting to peak. Use these current shots for comparison to your expectations for the garden. Use this information for making changes in the fall or the following spring.

PLANTING

This is the final month of the spring planting season. Although planting can still occur in the summer, it does mean more care for the plants.

The garden centers could have larger potted **blanket flowers**, **tickseed**, and **mums** to fill in along the sidewalk. **Barrenwort** acts as a bed edger, unifying the space under an **oak** tree. Larger two-gallon pots are available, making the impact time much shorter.

Fill in the color voids and gaps. Do not forget a flat of new sun tolerant **impatiens**, circling around the **fountain grass**. Dark-red leaf **coleus** has a dramatic effect on the **tall phlox**, or blend the **hardy sage** and **annual sage** for the summer garden.

You may want to allow some of your perennial favorites to form seeds for collection and dispersal. The seeds formed by hybrid perennials might revert back to the previous generation when sprouting.

CARE

Depending upon the type of mulch spread at planting time, it may need refreshing. The scorching summer heat will dry out the ground and could influence the root health of young or newly planted perennials.

Consider changing mulch types. Upon decomposition, different materials leave a slightly different nutrient base. Spread some granular (5-5-5 or similar) fertilizer on the surface of the soil before applying mulch.

WATERING

Nature provides much of the watering this month, but if it's dry, make up the difference by supplying 1 inch of water weekly.

Water early in the day. You lose less water due to evaporation, and watering early reduces bacteria and fungus problems.

FERTILIZING

Mums are heavy feeders, so feed regularly for the best fall showing.

HELPFUL HINTS

Many of the plants used for shade gardens have larger leaves that lend a coarse texture to the bed. Consider adding ferns. The following ferns are either native, naturalized, or are quite easy to grow: **hay-scented fern** (*Dennstaedtia*) for drier areas, **ostrich fern** (*Matteuccia*) for moist locations, **Japanese painted fern** (*Athyrium*) for moist locations has a silver tinted frond, and **Christmas fern** (*Polystichum)*, for dry and well drained sites, has evergreen fronds.

Ornamental grasses fall over if they are fed. Keep annuals or other plants requiring summer fertilizing 1 to 2 feet beyond the grass plants.

PESTS

Check for damaging insects during the early morning and evening hours. Insect activity is the highest during those times. Examine the stems, the tops and bottoms of leaves, and on the ground for trails (slugs and snails). Contact pesticides are the safest to use, or consider physical controls.

Mole tunnels are showing up everywhere and the babies are large enough to tunnel. In beds that are prepared and planted, it is easy to dig the soil, and generally those areas are higher in earthworm population—the moles' favorite food. Set traps and move them daily.

This is a critical time for the **fall windflower** and **bleeding heart**, and at the same time, weed populations are ready to explode. Keep an eye out, and spend time pulling the weeds as they sprout.

PRUNING

Pinch back **mums** by one-third. This is the final pruning for fall blooming.

Cut back all brown and dead leaves on **daylilies**. Generally, as **daylilies** flower, the foliage begins to decline.

Pinch or cut back new installations (never more than one-half of the stem length). Multiple leaves must remain after cutting. This means that there will be no flowering the first year the perennial is planted in the garden.

Deadheading and removal of all seedheads benefit the overall strength of any plant.

JULY

PERENNIALS & ORNAMENTAL GRASSES

PLANNING

Plan a new addition to the full sun border.

Peony, *Paeonia lactiflora*—**Peony** remains one of the most popular perennials that spans many generations of gardeners. It does take a little patience. It takes several years for **peony** to reach its full size and true flower color. In early spring, the red foliage thrusts upward, as if it is a hand reaching for the sky. The red tint changes to dark green, as the alternating compound flowers spread and cover the entire center. As the unfurling flower buds gain in size, they eventually push even higher, stopping when their heads are just beyond the leaves. The buds continue to swell and grow into almost a perfect sphere shape. Overlapping protective guards uncurl and the flower pops out, looking like an artificial paper inflorescence. Individual varieties finish flowering within a week, so mix early, mid, and late season bloomers in a planting.

Blue lyme grass, *Leymus arenarius*—Fine textured, spreading habit, semievergreen to evergreen, and weather tough are the backbones of this plant. Add to these attributes, the striking, bluish, gray-green color of the blades, combined with the matching blue flowers that make this an eye-catching plant. It must be given space to roam because of the invasive tendencies. The aggressive top growth is the result of the continually moving and advancing root system. This trait makes the **blue lyme grass** an excellent choice for controlling erosion, while at the same time providing aesthetic benefits. Additionally, clumps can be planted in larger pots or containers, giving flexibility and adding another dimension to the container garden.

Tall phlox, *Phlox paniculata*—**Tall phlox** is an old time perennial that has welcomed many generations of gardeners to summer. A stout growing stem, almost unnoticed, reaches above the surrounding plant, ending finally with reversed cone clusters of flowers carrying a hint of fragrance. **Phlox** is a multiple textured plant if dissected, but when considered as a whole, it brings coarseness to a garden setting. Very much at home among other plantings, it's probably best not to crowd **phlox**. Give it room to stretch. Whether sited along a fence, at the backdoor, or in the furthermost reaches of the garden, it is simply impossible not to notice a **phlox** when they are in flower. **Phlox** is a "must have" plant in a new garden or a welcomed addition to an established one.

Head outside before the flowers are fully opened on the **obedient plants**, **blanket flowers**, **maiden grass**, and **Shasta daisies**. Collect flowers and leaves for centerpieces or to float in bowls of water.

If you are making vacation plans and will be gone longer than one week, arrange for someone to come by and check watering on the recently installed **hardy sage** and **lady's mantle** plants. Long-established plants may suffer if there is extreme humidity and high temperatures, but no long-term damage should occur.

Plan your work schedule around the heat of the day and do not work in the garden between the hours of 10 a.m. and 3 p.m.

PLANTING

Planting or transplanting should only be done on an emergency basis in this hot summer month. If you have to plant, water the plants and the garden area twenty-four hours ahead of time. If you are transplanting, dig up as much root as possible, lift and replant as soon as possible. Consider liquid root stimulator to help in the transition.

If a bare-root or containerized plant has shown no signs

of new growth, consider it dead. Make some notes as to the location, plant, planting period, and neighboring plants to determine the possible problem, and make adjustments in the planting and in next year's planning as needed.

CARE

Keep any declining and yellowing plants out of garden. They provide a safe harbor potential for insects and diseases.

If the mulch layer is less than one-half inch, then reapply. Use caution if you are taking the mulch from a large pile where there is a tremendous buildup of heat. If this hot mulch is placed next to stems of **peonies**, **daylily**, or the **barrenwort**, a burn could occur.

WATERING

Provide a minimum of 1 inch of water each week. If the weather is very humid and the ground appears damp, trowel down and check moisture under the soil surface. If it is wet, hold off on watering. Adjust your irrigation schedule at the timer to accommodate the raise in humidity.

HELPFUL HINTS

Lots of plants are in full bloom now. Take full advantage of the scenario and do some pressed flowers. Cut blooms early in the day, place flowers between a couple of sheets of folded newsprint, lay a book on top for about a month, and the end result is flowers preserved for gifts.

FERTILIZING

Top dress the perennial beds with one-half to one inch of compost.

Use an all-purpose fertilizer according to directions.

PRUNING

Remove any buds forming on fall blooming **mums** and on **windflowers** to insure later blooming.

Cut back **tickseed** by one-half to stimulate a new blooming cycle.

PESTS

Although this is probably the worst month for insects, strong and healthy plants can recover from almost any attack. For pest control, adopt this course of action:

1. Identify the pest. Examine the plant at various times during the day. Look at the undersides of the leaf.

2. Determine if the pest population warrants action.

3. Decide what level of control is needed to insure plant health.

4. Select a control method. Physically remove with fingers, use a stream of water, apply an insecticide, or release predatory insects.

5. Treat only those plants that have a pest problem.

The most problematic insects to watch for are spider mites and aphids in the sun garden, and slugs and snails in the shade.

Control weeds by hand digging; make sure you remove the entire root system. Make sure the weed is identified before the application of any herbicide.

NOTES

AUGUST

PERENNIALS & ORNAMENTAL GRASSES

PLANNING

Plan a new addition for part sun or part shade.

Lady's mantle, *Alchemilla mollis*—**Lady's mantle** is a semievergreen, low growing, and coarse textured plant that, when viewed at a distance, almost looks like a boulder covered with lichens and mosses. A close up inspection reveals a perfectly marvelous plant that has a subtle beauty that is hard to pinpoint. The unusual colored leaf emerges from a center point and the stems spray out parallel to the ground. Its round, saucer-shaped leaves have markings on the leaf edge that look and feel as if they were machine embossed. A bead of water sits in the center of the leaf after a rain, sparkling like a diamond floating on the leaf. **Lady's mantle** is truly a jewel when planted in any style of garden.

Plan a new addition in the full sun perennial garden.

Blanket flower, *Gaillardia* x *grandiflora*—**Blanket flower** has quite impressive credentials. It produces a great cutting flower for shorter vases, it thrives in a dry, well-drained soil, and propagation is successful from seed or divisions. The flower configuration is somewhat unique, not only in color, but also in the unusual notched petals that allow a large landing area in the center of the disc flowers. The extended bloom period occurs with no deadheading required. Use **blanket flower** as a specimen planting or in a mixed grouping of other sun perennials. Or place it along the front edge of a mixed community bed space, to unify and tie everything nicely together.

Though hot and humid weather is still here, the night temperatures begin dropping and the rate of growth decreases. It's a good time to evaluate the perennials, while at their maximum growth.

Decide now if another **maiden grass** is needed to fill in a bed, if the **blanket flower** on the slope needs help, or if the red **astilbe** could use a white variety as a backup.

PLANTING

Work the soil ahead of time if you are planting new beds. Plant and work in the garden during the cool morning hours or later in the day when evening temperatures drop.

Water any plants prior to planting and maintain soil moisture in the bed space prior to installation.

All spring blooming plants can be divided.

Check seed racks for **speedwell**, **balloon flower**, and **Shasta daisy**. Read seed packets for dispersal timing, and lightly rake the area just prior to spreading seed.

CARE

When moving in and out of bed spaces, the soil is getting compressed with each step. Lightly turn surface not to damage remaining plants.

WATERING

Before irrigating, take a shovel and dig down 6 or more inches. If the soil at this depth is moist, do not water. Or squeeze a handful of dirt into a ball, if the soil crumbles away from the ball when released, it's time to water.

Adjust the watering and irrigation schedule based upon sun intensity, wind factors, and exposure. Check plants early in the day for water stress. If they are perky in the morning, the soil is damp, and yet they wilt in the afternoon, there is no need to water them. Wilting is a built-in defense to reduce evaporation.

If spring mulch has disappeared, apply another 1 inch to give a crisp look to the planting and to save water.

If gaps have begun to crop up with fading perennials and expired annuals, pull up any dead plants and fill in the area with mulch.

FERTILIZING

This month is the final application of an all-purpose fertilizer on perennials.

Get a soil test every three years to determine any deficits. This is the time to work amendments into the ground, allowing for natural dispersal during the winter.

PRUNING

Continue to deadhead flowers.

Remove the foliage from plants that are going dormant. Leave some stem on the plants to indicate their location.

PESTS

Keep an eye on all your perennials. Check particularly on the undersides of leaves for insects.

Mildew and molds likely could be showing up on plants, mostly weather related. Take no action.

This month is the peak activity for weed growth. Hand dig, or apply herbicides, according to directions.

HELPFUL HINTS

If several stems of a particular plant seemed bruised, and wilting continues without signs of going dormant, it could be a virus, bacteria, or fungal problem. The best control is to dig the plant and remove it from the garden space. Discard diseased plants into the trash.

Increased bee activity, in response to cooler nights and shorter days, is forcing colonies to prepare for winter. This could mean the individual colony maintains its current size or it might split off a portion of the colony with a new queen, thereby increasing the potential number of bees next season.

NOTES

SEPTEMBER

PERENNIALS & ORNAMENTAL GRASSES

PLANNING

Add some new perennials and grasses to the full sun garden.

Maiden grass, *Miscanthus sinensis*—Since being introduced from the orient, **maiden grass** has risen in garden stature and is considered royalty in grass collections. Its popularity is reflected in the aesthetic qualities, the adaptability and versatility of the grass, and low care requirements. **Maiden grass** has a wide spectrum of landscape uses ranging from poolside or waters edge to foundation planting, next to a sidewalk, screening for a patio, and as a source for cut flowers. The design possibilities are endless, due to the fine textured foliage that is persistent from late May through January. Its vase shape offers protection from the midday sun for plants positioned at the base. Pinkish red summer inflorescence appears and rises above the foliage. Flowers and leaves slowly change to tones of tan as the days get shorter and temperatures turn cooler. This aging and maturing adds yet another dimension to the plant, and gives wonderful textural relief to the fall and winter landscape.

Hardy sage, *Salvia* x *superba*, has a spreading growth habit and flowers that arise on upright stems. Shades of breathtaking blue flowers emerge, during a time of the year when a cool blue can temper the heat of summer. The blanketing quality of the darker green leaves, in combination with vertical flowering stalks and two-fold texture, create quite a landscape impact. The crowning touch is the fresh and calming aspects of the flowers, from early to midsummer, when many plants have disappeared for the year. **Hardy sage** is very easy to grow and has extraordinary aesthetic attributes, making it an added plus to any garden, no matter the style.

If the collection of plastic flats, pots, and containers stacked or hidden away is ever increasing with each purchase of **astilbe**, **yarrow**, or **fountain grass**, find a recycling center or a local manufacturer of plastic wood made from recycled plastic products.

This month should bring the arrival of seed and plant catalogs. Take this opportunity to check out the newest varieties of **daylilies**, **mums**, or **Shasta daisies**.

It's time to plan garden strategy for next year. Take measurements; note any migratory plant movement, plant disappointments, and successes. Is the **obedient plant** moving via the root system? Are the **Shasta daisies** self-seeding? Is the **hosta** clump getting ever so wide? Did the **barrenwort** fail to put on any above ground growth during this first season? Now is the time to take notes, before you forget.

Collect seed from the garden from some of your favorites. Have small envelopes and a permanent-marking pen ready to label with the plant name and date collected. Allow wet (rain or irrigation) seed capsules to dry before gathering, to minimize disease problems.

If seeds will be grown indoors over the winter and into early spring, inventory and evaluate the plant cart, grow light fixtures, lightbulbs, bottom heat mats, seed-starter potting mix, and supplies.

The weather is perfect to work with the perennials. Gentle rains soak in, the ground temperature is warm to promote root growth, and timing is right to allow plants to acclimate before winter dormancy.

PLANTING

Blanket flowers, **live-forever,** and **blue lyme grass** growing in containers should be removed and planted into the garden. The option is simply to treat the perennials as annuals and discard. Plant survivability over the winter in containers is limited for perennials.

Do not spread seeds on the top of mulch. Rake the mulch back, make sure seeds have contact with ground, and cover with 1 inch of mulch or less. Any greater amount of mulch may inhibit germination and growth.

This month you can do divisions of **peonies**, **balloon flowers**, **daylily**, or **astilbe** to share with friends or to relocate in the landscape. Water the garden and the plants the day before to soften the ground. Then use a spade or shovel and cut a ring around each plant, pushing the digging tool deeply into the ground (root pruning at the same time). The circle should be approximately 6 inches outside of the stems. Pop the root mass out of the ground, divide, and relocate immediately. If you are giving bulbs as gifts, put the plants in a container or burlap bag, keep plants well watered, and place out of the sun and wind.

HELPFUL HINTS

Cool season vegetables, **lettuce**, **ornamental cabbage** and **kale** blended in with **pansies** and **toadflax** bring new life to the perennial gardens, through mid- to late December.

CARE

Continue care and maintenance of all **hardy sage**, **feather reed grass**, **rose mallow**, and **bleeding hearts.** Rewards will be realized with next year's growth.

Consider soil compaction as you move in and out of beds. Loosen your footprints as you work your way out of the bed.

Allow mulch layers to diminish during this month. The soil surface benefits from the added air circulation and direct sunlight to assist in control of disease spores.

WATERING

Check the rain gauges and compensate for a lack of moisture. Supply 1 inch of water every seven to ten days. If the days are cool and cloudy, allow for the expanded time frame between waterings. Do not allow plants to dry out as the microbes and soil structure could suffer.

FERTILIZING

No fertilizer is needed this month.

PRUNING

Keep all declining (going dormant) plant debris cut and removed to allow air circulation and direct sunlight.

PESTS

Insect damage season is over, but keep all plant debris picked up to eliminate over-wintering egg or adults.

Henbit, chickweed seeds, and other annual winter weeds will be germinating. Apply a pre-emergent (kills all seeds at time of germination—it will also kill seeds of **fall windflowers** or other desired plants) herbicide. Apply post-emergent (on weeds that are up and growing) herbicides carefully and directly to weed foliage, or dig the weed out, roots and all.

OCTOBER

PERENNIALS & ORNAMENTAL GRASSES

PLANNING

Plan some new additions for the full sun perennial border.

Live-forever, *Hylotelephium telephium,* is truly a four seasons perennial. During the winter, a low clump of miniature, pale gray-green foliage remains as a reminder of last year's garden joy and what is to come in the future. In the warmer days of spring, the cluster of leaves grows and appears to be wearing a helmet as it pushes up from the underground. For summer, the huge, broccoli-like rosette of flowers appears suddenly, perched atop the leaves. The stems lengthen, causing them to fall away from the center. Flowers open in an attractive pink hue that attracts late season butterflies and other pollen gatherers. While flowering, the center reveals next year's leaves already forming. This coarse textured plant, which makes no demands other than good drainage, is a plus in a new or well-established garden. It is particularly useful in children's gardens.

Yarrow, *Achillea millefolium,* possesses top-notch qualities that are hard to beat for the long blooming period and unique foliage and flower configuration. Add to this, the ease of care and maintenance, and it's just about the perfect plant. The fine textured, fern-like quality of the leaves spreads and moves through the planting space via an underground root system. Shooting up through these paler green leaves is the flower stalk that acts as a pedestal for a flat, plate-like disk of tiny, tightly clustered, yellow flowers. The new foliage growth begins at ground level, while still in flower, indicating that all is well for next year. The leaf is aromatic, and the flowers can be cut at various formation stages to insure a series of differing colors in floral arrangements. This plant is easy to grow, and is very attractive to many different pollinating insects. **Yarrow** is a perfect choice for a new gardener, a children's garden, or for just about anywhere in the landscape.

• **Rose mallow**, *Hibiscus moscheutos*—Standing straight up, with an almost shrub-like quality, **rose mallow** is mysterious, yet almost weedy to the unknowing. Its large green leaves, with pale undersides, are arranged to obscure the stem entirely. The mallow's coarseness provides a wonderful background for a perennial or annual garden setting, and is an asset to a mixed sunny shrub border. The heat of summer brings the beginning of the flowering season, when **rose mallow** becomes a center stage focal point. The purity of flower color is magnified by its shear physical presence. The perfectly circular-shaped flowers pop open and unfold to 10 inches across. Nothing is more attention demanding while in flower than this plant. The height and position of the flower makes it perfect for children to view.

If that carload of **hosta** or **yarrow** you purchased cannot be installed right away, place the plants in a protected location, and water to keep them moist until installation.

Spend time enjoying the **feather reed, maiden,** and **fountain grasses.** This is the peak season.

PLANTING

Divisions are best done earlier in this month, to allow plants to acclimate before winter.

CARE

Remove **peony** rings, **tall phlox** stakes, and any other unnecessary garden structure or equipment to prevent wintertime clutter.

Replace plant name labels as needed. Do it now so the beds are clearly marked, come spring.

Prevent falling leaves from collecting in large amounts on the top of perennial beds. The thicker layer will cause too much moisture retention, which can lead to diseases.

Depending on the location and exposure of plantings, frost or freeze kill will most likely occur first on plants with softer, fleshier stems.

Wait until the hard freeze to add a protective layer of mulch.

WATERING

Only supplement watering if there is not adequate rainfall to equal 1 inch of moisture every seven to ten days.

HELPFUL HINTS

If foliage and stems from **peonies** and **balloon flowers** are going to be composted, remember to layer debris with other materials to insure proper blending. A good compost pile will have noticeable steam rising during cooler temperatures, and little to no odor.

FERTILIZING

There is no need to fertilize, but if you are planting, use a root stimulator on new installations.

PRUNING

Remove all plant debris, as decaying plant materials harbor insects, eggs, and diseases over winter.

Allow the stems of late summer and fall blooming plants to remain. They offer some protection to the plants' crowns.

PESTS

Wildlife is sensing the impending cold. Chipmunks and voles are looking for nooks and crannies, under the patio or under the front stoop. Squirrels are everywhere—planting, digging, and gnawing (an essential activity that keeps lower teeth from getting too long). Deer are deep in the woods where there is plenty to eat—be grateful.

Controlling weeds with herbicides is becoming ineffective. The weed plant dormancy is a seasonal occurrence, and the translocation path (carries herbicide) from leaf to root is slowed. Hand weeding removes the entire root system.

NOVEMBER

PERENNIALS & ORNAMENTAL GRASSES

PLANNING

Plan a new addition to the shade garden.

Barrenwort, *Epimedium* x *versicolor*—Versatile and easy to grow, this woodland plant has marvelous attributes for the garden. As a ground cover, the somewhat evergreen qualities stabilize the ground, while providing greenery during the winter. In early spring, cut back the oval shaped leaves that are attached to wire-like stems. This helps rejuvenate the plant, while allowing for a better view of the flower and stem that is shorter than the foliage. New leaves emerge shortly thereafter. The unusual growing habit allows for use as a single specimen plant in the shady rock garden, or with a little work, **barrenwort** becomes the living edge along the winding pathways. Whether a single plant, edger, or ground cover, this plant should not be overlooked.

Add a new perennial to the sun border.

Tickseed, *Coreopsis verticillata* 'Moonbeam'—In the past twenty years, there has not been a plant more popular than this variety of **coreopsis**. The needle-like foliage, spaced evenly along the stem, appears as if it is not even there, whether viewing from a distance or up close. Positioned in the foreground of other sun loving plantings, **tickseed** visually breaks and softens the fall from taller plants in the background, while masking the bare lower sections of other perennials. When randomly dotted among other plants, or cloistered in larger groups, **tickseed** makes that section of the garden more vibrant. This airy characteristic is maximized with the addition of the artificial looking, perfect, yellow petal flowers, as they appear to float, unattached to any stem. From early June until late September, **coreopsis** brings a sense of amazement to the garden. The small stature of the plant makes it a perfect fit as a cut flower in a miniature vase.

The newest perennial varieties described in seed or plant catalogs may be available, but in limited quantities. If you are interested, place your order now.

Update the garden photo journal during the off-season. Use black-and-white film and color film to get a more critical look at the views from looking out the windows, and from various angles in the yard. Compare earlier shots of the **hardy sage**, **obedient plant**, and **speedwell** sites in relation to the fall blooming **mums** and the foliage

Feeders and bird baths will keep the winter color going. Experiment with new types that are squirrel proof.

PLANTING

During perennial bed installation, consider the proximity to downspout outflow and to building or tree overhangs.

Clean and sharpen all tools, and lightly apply oil to the clean piece to reduce rusting during the winter.

You can take divisions of perennials this month. Grow them under grow lights.

CARE

Rains have fallen and may have caused changes in ground surface drainage patterns. Keep close tabs on new beds as settling, shifting, or erosion could occur.

Soil compaction is a real problem (compacted soils prevent water absorption and root development), so always work backwards out of the beds, and work the soil wherever you left footprint depressions.

Stir the mulch around and check underneath for moisture. If the mulch seems overly wet, stir and toss it to aerate.

Full-grown **mums** (now finished flowering), either in the garden or purchased at garden centers for seasonal accents, should show small clusters of green foliage (next year's plant) at the base of existing stems.

WATERING

Have in-ground irrigation systems winterized and turn off (indoors) any faucets that are not frost proof.

Drain sprinklers, hoses, and watering cans, and store out of the weather to prevent freeze damage. Keep one hose available to use if winter drought occurs.

FERTILIZING

Inventory the types and amounts of fertilizers remaining. Store bags and bottles in a dry spot where there is no danger of moisture.

Consider the plant performance where a specific fertilizer was applied. Determine any changes for next year.

Clean fertilizer hose-end attachment. Cleaned nozzles are essential to insure correct calibration and application next year.

HELPFUL HINTS

The annuals, added for focal points in the perennial plantings, are showing signs of cold weather effects. The **pansies** may lie out flat as if dead. This reduces moisture loss and the **pansies** will recover and flower, as temperatures warm into mid-30s.

PRUNING

Do not cut back stems of any fall blooming **mums** or **windflowers**. Their structure catches blowing leaves that provide winter protection for the plant crowns.

PESTS

Proper storage of dry and liquid pesticides and herbicides minimizes losses due to carelessness. Take note of the shelf life (effective period) and properly discard any expired products. Contact Kansas Department of Health and Environment for disposal instructions. Additionally, storage is crucial for the other chemicals. The chemistry may be altered during the course of cold weather, if the product is frozen. Settling and hardening occur if the package is left open to humidity.

Hand weeding to remove the entire root system is the only control you have for weeds at this time of year. Cooler weather makes herbicides ineffective.

NOTES

DECEMBER

PERENNIALS & ORNAMENTAL GRASSES

PLANNING

Plan for a new addition to the perennial shade garden.

Astilbe, *Astilbe* x *arendsii*—Fulfilling the same role for the shade garden as the **daylilies** do for the sunny areas, the **astilbe** add color to the shade that is unequaled by any other plant. A fine textured, heavily segmented, collection of leaves grows into a soft mound. As the heat of late spring begins to build, the spikes of many feathery plume flowers push above the foliage. The earlier bloomers bring the shade garden alive, as the spring plantings fade or go dormant. A carefully planned bed of **astilbe** produces a series of color that continues to highlight shady areas.

In your planning process, add something new to the sun border.

Balloon flower, *Platycodon grandiflorum*—A little patience from two perspectives is needed in growing the **balloon flower**. First, the new growth may be the last to emerge from winter's dormancy. Secondly, the stems may be weak and creep along the ground. This may occur during the first two years after installation. The wait is worth it. The glossy, medium-green foliage rises up, and adds a vertical relief in any sunny garden setting. As the small round flower buds move towards maturity, a balloon-like swelling occurs. Upon reaching almost an inch in diameter, the balloon pops, and the star-shaped petals peel backwards. The **balloon flower** is a real delight for children and adults alike.

PLANTING

You should not be planting or transplanting outdoors unless there are some home construction projects going on that require tree removal or bed disruption.

CARE

Make a final sweep through the garden; remove anything that looks out of place: debris, stakes, ties, and supports.

Keep mulch depth at 1 to 2 inches and allow only a minimal amount over the crowns of plants. Too thick of a layer of mulch may lead to moisture buildup.

Take stock of anything plant related and take care of any maintenance or winterizing. Check the compost pile to make sure it is steaming. Change the oil in the rototiller. Clean the birdbaths.

WATERING

You should only have to provide supplemental water if there is not enough moisture falling naturally to supply the perennial beds with a minimum of 1 inch of water every seven to ten days.

FERTILIZING

No fertilizers need to be applied during this month.

PRUNING

Just a final cleanup is all that is necessary. Allow the stems of late summer, fall bloomers to remain, as they offer protection to the plant crown.

PESTS

Check potted divisions under the grow lights for gnats and tiny whiteflies. Hang yellow sticky tape for some control and to monitor numbers. If you see tiny spider webs between the stem and leaf, this is mites. Wash plants with soap and water.

Mole activity is slowing. Keep an eye for new tunnels and place traps as needed.

On warmer days, get out with a weeder and hand dig weeds out, roots and all.

HELPFUL HINTS

"Learning Botanical Names"

Name	Botanical Name	General Meaning of Species
Balloon flower	*Platycodon grandiflorus*	large flowered
Barrenwort	*Epimedium x rubrum*	red
Bleeding heart	*Dicentra spectabilis*	remarkably showy
Blue lyme grass	*Leymus arenarius*	of sandy places
Fountain grass	*Pennisetum setaceum*	bristle-like
Hosta	*Hosta fortunei*	person's last name
Ice plant	*Hylotelephium spectabile*	remarkably showy
Lady's mantle	*Alchemilla mollis*	soft, hairy
Maiden grass	*Miscanthus sinensis*	of China
Obedient plant	*Physostegia virginiana*	from Virginia
Peony	*Paeonia lactiflora*	white milk flowers
Rose mallow	*Hibiscus moscheutos*	musky
Speedwell	*Veronica spicata*	with spikes
Tall phlox	*Phlox paniculata*	compound flower structure
Tickseed	*Coreopsis verticillata*	in circles around stem

Buying Tip: The national catalog companies offer complete shade or sun perennial gardens that can be delivered to your door next spring. Inquire as to the location of the grower, when and how the plants are shipped, if the plants are bare-root or containers, and the size of the plants. Research the plant list and cultural survivability in Kansas gardens before you invest.

NOTES

CHAPTER SIX

ROSES

Roses are supreme, creating insatiable excitement—a feeling that began over 200 years ago as the first wild rose was hybridized for cultivation. Now 20,000 fascinating varieties later the electricity continues. There can be as many as 100 newly developed varieties released for test growing in some years. A national rose test garden is located at the Missouri Botanical Garden, where roses of all types are grown, evaluated, and graded. Rose varieties which pass a set of rigorous standards are given the ARS (American Rose Society) stamp of approval. The hybridizer will then accelerate production of these newest varieties for public viewing and purchase. Another 20 million roses are grown in greenhouses for bouquets and arrangements. Forty million plants are purchased and planted yearly. Thought, preparation, and commitment are keys to growing and enjoying the rose experience. Modern products (season long fertilizer, systemic pest and disease controls), newer varieties, and sharing information (at rose society and garden club meetings) are a few reasons why growing roses continues to be extremely popular. Rose versatility is shown with roses growing in containers, over arbors, mixed with shrubs and perennials, and always filling the view with magic. Whether it is 1 or 100 rose bushes, no one can help but take time to "stop and smell the roses."

INFORMATION, REQUIREMENTS AND TIPS

Types

• Include climbers, carpets, trees, miniatures, grandiflora, floribundas, cabbages, teas, pillars, ramblers, multi-floras, polyanthas and others, each with unique aesthetic characteristics.

Grafted

• Two separate plant parts are conjoined (knot between canes and roots is an indicator) for stronger top growth and better root support system. Non-grafted rose have canes and roots that are continuous. They are tough, durable, and equally spectacular.

Grading System

• #1: largest and healthiest—3 canes—larger than index finger pointing in different directions.

• #1.5: less than 3 and or undersized canes—can require close attention.

• #2: 1 cane under-developed—can require several years of close attention.

Purchasing Plants

• Buy in late February thru early September.

Availability

• Bare-root and dormant plants in late winter, container grown. Some larger shrub types are balled and burlapped.

FROM SITE EVALUATION TO PLANTING

Location

• Full sun (minimum 6 hours daily) in urban high rise balconies, rural split rail fences, and open yards.

Bed Preparation

• Build highly organic well-drained planting bed. Fill with pH 6.5 acidic soil. Ideally soil work is

CHAPTER SIX

HELPFUL HINTS

Newer or Re-Releases

- Canadian Explorer Series—'William Baffin', 'David Thompson'
- Carefree Series—'Carefree Beauty', 'Carefree Wonder'
- Dream Series—'Dream Red', 'Dream Yellow'
- David Austin English Series—'The Herbalist', 'Winchester Cathedral'
- Historic Shrub Series—'Madam Hardy', 'Reine Victoria'

done 1 year in advance to allow for amendments and soil to blend.

- Shovel or rototill to mix 6 inches of organic matter (compost, peat moss, 1 year or older rotted manure, or sphagnum peat moss) with existing soil, and add supplements indicated by a soil test. Also add 1/2 pound super phosphate per 100 sq. ft., and rake to level the surface.

Containers and Pots

- It's essential to have bottom drainage holes.
- Pot Mixture: 1/3 soil-less potting mix, 1/3 potting soil, and 1/3 traction sand or pea gravel.
- Optional: super absorbent inorganic polymer, season long fertilizer pellets.

Pre-Planting

- Bare-root: unpack and soak overnight in water/root stimulator mix.
- Boxed/Plantable Container: if waxed gently break coating at planting.
- Potted-actively growing: full size dark green unspotted leaves.

PLANTING

- Planting varies according to plant type purchase—remove all flowers.
- Plantable box: read instructions carefully.
- Bare-root or Potted: use prepared soil and dig hole 2 feet x 2 feet x 1 foot and make mound on bottom center of hole.
- Prune: damaged or crossing stems/canes
- Check depth: depth of stems/crown/graft should be 1/2 to 1 inch below surface.
- Spread roots over 6-inch mound of soil formed in bottom.
- Back fill: replacing dirt around roots and firm soil.
- Water: water and back fill any sunken areas.
- Mulch: add mulch to 1 inch deep over roots; keep mulch away from canes/stems.

AN OUTLINE FOR CARE AND MAINTENANCE

Note: Any use of water (from irrigation, stream, or as part of chemical mixture) is best practiced in the morning, which allows foliage to dry, reduces the chance of nighttime fungus, and prevents sunlight in droplets from becoming a magnifying glass and causing damage.

Mulch

The practice of mulching roses is type dependent:

- Grafted: mulch 1 inch during growing season. After hard frost when roses are dormant, cover crown 6 inches with loose organic bark, and 4 inches of dense compost. A covering of small branches holds mulch erosion.
- Non-grafted: maintain 1 to 2 inches over root system year round.

Weeds

- Remove as soon as possible, since these compete for water and nutrients, and harbor pests or diseases. Hand-dig or use an herbicide.

Fertilizing

• Soil testing every 3 years provides a basis for making adjustments as needed. Fertilizing with a combination of inorganic (faster reacting man-made), and organic (compost, aged manures, blood meal, fish emulsions) is the favored option but not essential.

Watering

• Preventing drought is crucial to maintain flowering cycle and plant vigor.

Pruning

• Allow a maximum leaf count for overall health. Immediately remove any dead, diseased, dying, damaged, or unusual growth, and deadhead flowers. Cut stems at a 45 degree angle at the first or second group of 5 leaflets below the rose being removed. Stop removal of flowers in mid September allowing rose hips to form. This is a beneficial step towards triggering winter dormancy.

• Hybrid teas, grandiflora, floribundas: prune in early spring. Cut to 18 inches, remove winter kill (blackened stems); in mid April cut to 8 inches above emerging growth. During the growing season keep center open (remove crossing canes) to improve air circulation.

• Shrubs, climbers, pillars, trees, miniatures: remove unruly dead or damaged growth.

Diseases

• We have a natural problem related to Kansas's humidity, rainfall, and dew. Any reduction in green leaf surface or total leaf count can interfere with photosynthesis and weaken roses' overall resistance.

• Black Spot: airborne or physically transmitted spores, looks like small black spots with yellow edges that spread across leaf surface causing defoliation.

• Mildew: leaf covered with gray film, more common in older varieties, deforms leaf.

• Brown Stem Canker: small purplish white spots that enlarge to a small bruise. Infected canes appear weak, wilted and die. Control by removing infected stems; cut several inches below spotting or bruise. Clean pruners with 1 part bleach and 9 part water solution after each cut, reducing the chance of a spreading problem.

• Rust: orange spotting is less destructive unless in combination with other problems.

• Crown Gall: appears as woody plant part-bloating. Destroy this plant immediately.

• Rose Rosette/Witches' Broom: wild maroon heavily thorned canes suddenly appear. Destroy the plant.

• Pests: aphids, Japanese beetles and mites (spider family) are the most troublesome, though cane borers, thrips, and leaf hoppers are among the multitudes of others. Despite this, rose popularity does not falter.

• Control starts at planning stage. Allow several feet between plants (do not overplant designated space); select and grow varieties with noted resistance; keep areas surrounding roses debris free.

HELPFUL HINTS

Historic Rose Trivia

French type—dominant rose type from 1200-1900s, petals maintained aroma when dried powered
Damask—discovered during Crusades, used in Eastern Europe for making attar of rose
Bourbon—natural occurring hybrid found on island in Indian Ocean
Sweetbrier—noted for fragrant foliage
Alba—seen in many Italian Renaissance paintings
Cabbage—multiple petaled prominently depicted in Renaissance paintings

• Options: synthetic products, Neem (extract of tropical plant), or a mixture of baking soda (2 tablespoons per gallon of water). Begin spraying before problem is visible. Liquid sprays have proven more effective than powders. Mix in spreader sticker (increases adherence to leaf), spray upper and lower leaf surface.

Insects

• Found in overwintering fallen leaf debris, wind blown, introduced from any plants. Insects require separate controls for 6 legged insects and 8 legged mites. Constant monitoring works best; visual damage varies, impact on plant is related to health and the attacking insect population.

• Aphids: multiple colors, some winged, soft bodied, on newest growth. They suck sap and leave sticky residue that can promote some bacteria growth.

• Japanese beetles: adults are shiny green metallic. They eat foliage (leaving veins) and flower petals.

• Control by hand picking and removal, release predatory insects, and use pheromone traps, insecticidal soaps, or organic or synthetic insecticides (chemicals).

• Spider Mites: these are tiny, reddish, true web producing spiders that suck the underside of foliage causing yellowing and browning. They are problematic in drier spells or seasons, and transmit several devastating diseases such as rose rosette (reddish very thorny stems).

• Control with a stream of water to wash the upper and lower leaf surface, or use chemical miticides.

• Wildlife: these problems come in all sizes from small mice that gnaw bark, damaging canes, to medium size rabbits that gnaw and eat canes, to large deer that eat canes regardless of thorns.

• Control with traps, repellents (predator urine and pepper sprays), hanging spinning mirrors, and reflective tapes.

ROSE BASICS

Reading the Rose Clock

• This guideline can be used whether growing a single rose, a freestanding rose bed, or roses are integrated into other plant communities. When growing roses, consider Kansas's weather, changing daylight length, and the location of the roses. All of these factors have a great deal of influence on the overall health and performance of your roses.

• The timing of usual maintenance tasks is the cornerstone of growing roses. The time of year affects mulching (application or removal), fertilizing (type), diagnosing pest and disease problems (taking appropriate action), and pruning (when and how). The timing, placement, and soil preparation, along with a dash of common sense, allow the rose to become a longstanding member of any landscape.

Watch Out!

• Early in the growing season, an unexpected bright red or purple shoot suddenly erupts; the foliage is crinkled; the stems are covered with massive numbers of thorns. This is a deadly disease called "Rose Rosette" or "Witches' Broom." The disease was first identified on **multiflora** roses (large **shrub rose**), but quickly spread to most rose types. It is transmitted by a microscopic, wingless spider mite that travels on wind currents. This disease is fatal. Do not attempt to cut it down, apply a miticide, or wash the foliage. Dig up the infected rose (stems, roots, and all), and wrap it in a plastic bag. Call the County Extension Service to determine the method of disposal. Do not put the diseased bush in the compost pile. Then keep your fingers crossed that carrier mites have not moved onto other nearby roses.

Deadheading Roses

• Historically, the advice has been to make a 45-degree cut, just above the first five leaflets that emerge below the spent flower. This technique guaranteed that the resulting stem would be smaller in size. If you moved further down the stem, you would have a longer stem rose, but pruning that far down could significantly reduce the quantity of leaves and side branching.

• A current trend for deadheading roses is to simply cut just below the rose sepal, leaving a noticeable "spike" sticking up. This allows for a larger number of leaves to remain, making for an overall healthier plant. This will not work if you are cutting roses for traditional, long-stemmed display, but it is great for floating blooms in a shallow bowl with water.

Foliage Diseases and Spots

• The seriousness of this problem changes from year to year, depending on Midwestern weather patterns. There are many ways to deal with this problem, such as applications of manufactured fungicides, and applying home remedies of water and baking soda. Either method should be applied before you see any problems. Also, pick up the fallen rose bush leaves lying on the ground. Once they pile up, essential air circulation is minimized, and spores can form and erupt.

Roses

AESTHETIC ATTRIBUTES:

Flexibility for trellis, arbors, fencing:	'New Dawn', 'Improved Blaze', 'Handel', 'Doubloons'
Floriferous (multiple bloom periods):	'Sun Flare', 'Iceberg', 'Simplicity', 'Betty Prior', 'Linda Campbell'
Sturdy upright canes:	'Gold Medal', 'Carousel', 'Queen Elizabeth', 'Shreveport'
Fragrant:	'Sun Bright', 'Mister Lincoln', 'Tropicana', 'Peace', 'Crimson Glory', 'Tiffany', 'Sutter's Gold', 'Granada', 'Fragrant Cloud', 'Sunsprite', 'Double Delight', 'Fragrant Hour'
Less than 2 feet for pots/containers:	'Starina', 'Rise N' Shine', 'Rainbow's End', 'Pacesetter'
Multi-stemmed bushes:	'Topaz Jewel', 'China Doll', 'Blanc Double de Coubert'
Huge plants:	'Paul's Himalayan Musk', 'Rambler', 'Paprika'
Large bloom size:	'Bibi Maizoon'
Changing petal color:	'Joseph's Coat', 'Spectra'
Attractive to butterflies and bees:	'Dainty Bess', Rosa chinensis 'Mutabilis'
Part shade tolerant:	'Gruss an Aachen'

NOTES:

Some varieties listed above are not detailed below, but care is similar. Botanical names are not provided with roses; all roses have the genus *Rosa*. Remember the best growth and healthiest plants will occur in full sun all day.

Variety, Name and Classification, Type:	Universally noted, basic group
Growth Habit, Height:	Silhouette, average at mature
Fragrance:	Scented
Color, Flower Type:	Hue, petal number/configuration
Landscape Use:	Beyond rose garden

Variety/Name–Classification:	'Altissimo', pillar
Growth Habit, Height:	Upright stiff vase-like, 10 feet or more
Fragrant:	Yes
Color, Flower Type:	Dark red, single
Landscape Use:	Background in mixed plantings

Variety/Name–Classification:	'Baby Grand', miniature
Growth Habit-Height:	Mounded, 1-2 feet
Fragrant:	Yes
Color, Flower Type:	Pink, double
Landscape Use:	Container

Variety/Name–Classification:	'Brandy', hybrid tea
Growth Habit, Height:	Upright, 3 feet
Fragrant:	Yes
Color, Flower Type:	Blended pink, double
Landscape Use:	Cut flower

Variety/Name–Classification: 'Child's Play', miniature
Growth Habit, Height: Conical, 1 to 2 feet
Fragrant: No
Color, Flower Type: Pink or white underside, double
Landscape Use: Bed edger

Variety/Name–Classification: 'Europeana', floribunda
Growth Habit-Height: Upright-narrow 4 feet
Fragrant: No
Color-Flower Type: Deep red-double
Landscape Use: Hedging highlighter

Variety/Name–Classification: 'Evelyn', shrub
Growth Habit-Height: Mounded-5 feet
Fragrant: Yes
Color-Flower Type: Yellow-double
Landscape Use: Mixed in shrub bed

Variety/Name–Classification: 'Francois Rebalais', floribunda
Growth Habit-Height: Mounded-3 feet
Fragrant: Lightly
Color-Flower Type: Deep red-double
Landscape Use: Focal point

Variety/Name–Classification: 'Frau Dagmar Hastrup', tree
Growth Habit-Height: Mounded-3 feet or more
Fragrant: Yes
Color-Flower Type: Pink-single
Landscape Use: On walkway

Variety/Name–Classification: 'Katherine Moberly', shrub
Growth Habit-Height: Upright rounded-8 feet
Fragrant: Yes
Color-Flower Type: Pink-double
Landscape Use: Screening

Variety/Name–Classification: 'Leonidas', hybrid tea
Growth Habit-Height: Upright-5 feet
Fragrant: Lightly
Color-Flower Type: Orangish yellow-double
Landscape Use: Cluster at property corners

Variety/Name–Classification: 'Love's Promise, grandiflora
Growth Habit-Height: Upright narrow, 3 feet or more
Fragrant: Yes
Color-Flower Type: Red-double crinkled
Landscape Use: Narrow spaces foundation planting

Variety/Name–Classification: 'Pascali', tree
Growth Habit-Height: Rounded-2 feet
Fragrant: Yes
Color-Flower Type: White-double
Landscape Use: Container

Variety/Name–Classification: 'Scarlet Meidiland', shrub
Growth Habit-Height: Spreading-3 feet
Fragrant: No
Color-Flower Type: Red-double
Landscape Use: Slope-hillside

Variety/Name–Classification: 'Sharifa Asma', tree
Growth Habit-Height: Upright, 3 feet or more
Fragrant: Yes
Color-Flower Type: Pink-double
Landscape Use: Front entry

Variety/Name–Classification: 'Sonia', grandiflora
Growth Habit-Height: Upright long cane, 5 feet or more
Fragrant: Lightly
Color-Flower Type: Pink-double
Landscape Use: Close in easy access for cut flower

Variety/Name–Classification: 'The Fairy', floribunda, polyantha
Growth Habit-Height: Cascading, 2 feet or more
Fragrant: Lightly
Color-Flower Type: Pink-double
Landscape Use: Cascade over wall, off deck edge

Variety/Name–Classification: 'Zephrine Droughin', climbing
Growth Habit-Height: Open willowy, 15 feet or more
Fragrant: Yes
Color-Flower Type: Pink-semi double
Landscape Use: Gate, arbors

JANUARY

ROSES

PLANNING

Call the local utility companies to locate any underground lines before you make any major additions to the landscape.

Check subdivision, neighborhood, city, or county bylaws and easements prior to planning new designs.

Perform a site analysis of surrounding buildings, tree size and heights, casting shadows, slopes, access to water, and ease of moving tools through the area.

Have a soil analysis done and add your own observations when planning the site. Note any existing vegetation, turf areas, evergreen shrubs, and conifers. Observe the soil drainage for the area. Will the area need barriers from wildlife?

Gather all the necessities for planting and growing roses so you are ready when the season begins. Inventory your supply of potting mixes, cleaned pots, and chemicals (fertilizers, pesticides, fungicides).

Comb through all your notes related to rose performance in previous years.

Plan some new rose ventures. Plan for a 'Don Juan' **climbing rose** on the new trellis, or 'Red Fairy' **tree rose** for the patio. Plan a new rose bed that is comprised of only historic **shrub roses** such as 'Ispahan', 'Louise Odier', and 'Madame Hardy'.

PLANTING

During warmer days, spread 1 to 2 inches of compost on rose plantings. Work it into the soil, and use this time to inspect the canes.

If changes are indicated in the soil test results, purchase the recommended amendments, and read the label to minimize any confusion later when you are making the application.

During this colder month, do some early preparation indoors. Prepare the window boxes, pots, and containers for rose planting. Check the garden center greenhouse for their **miniature rose** selections.

CARE

Prune only severely storm damaged stems and canes on 'Evelyn' rose. Make the cut at a 45-degree angle. Do not cut back any darkened branches from winterkill.

Check **climbing rose** 'Zephirine Drouhin' after each ice or windstorm to make sure ties are in place.

Check styrofoam cones to see if they are still properly anchored.

WATERING

During dry periods, if you don't have an all-weather hose outside, use buckets to carry supplemental water to the roses. Use cold water out of the faucet to soak the area around the canes.

Investigate the use of leaky hose or soaker hoses for roses. These hoses provide water in a slow, constant discharge, eliminating the use of overhead watering on the roses.

FERTILIZING

Check the fertilizer storage area to determine if any freezing has occurred. Safely discard any suspect product that may have been affected. Make a note to find a more suitable site to store the fertilizers.

PRUNING

Gather all tools (shovels, trowels, pruners, loppers, hedge trimmers, sprayers) for maintenance. Sharpen (or change blades), clean, and apply oils. Evaluate tool performance level. Consider having a separate set of pruners for the roses, and dipping them in bleach and water (1 to 10 ratio) between cuts while moving from plant to plant. This practice reduces the chance of spreading disease to another plant.

PESTS

If you notice field mice living in the mulch pile, set baited traps. If deer are eating stems or canes, consider hanging mirrors nearby, placing predatory animal urine vials, or stringing fishing line horizontally between posts surrounding the planting.

Check any potted roses growing indoors for spider mite webbing between the leaves. Wash the tops and undersides of the foliage, and isolate the plant. Check the plant again before moving next to other plants.

HELPFUL HINTS

Polyantha roses are a smaller version of the floribunda. They are more adaptable and versatile for the general landscape. They do fine if they are mass planted, mingled with sunny perennials and shrubs, or dotted in the yard for emphasis.

Check the date of purchase (marked with waterproof pen when purchased) on chemical products, and safely dispose of expired products. If you are unsure of the expiration date, call the manufacturer.

NOTES

FEBRUARY

ROSES

PLANNING

Garden centers, the Extension Service, and city parks may offer classes on using roses in the landscape. The local rose society or garden clubs are great places to pick up tips from experienced rose growers.

For more information:

American Rose Society
P.O. Box 30000
Shreveport, LA. 71130
www.ars.org
Email-ars@ars-hq.org

When purchasing plants by mail order, ask about the grade of the roses. Insist on Number 1 grade and a shipping date from early March through May. Ask if the plants are shipped bare root or in containers. Also determine if the company has a plant guarantee.

PLANTING

Weather permitting, begin the process of working the soil in the new rose beds to prepare for the recently ordered 'Brandy' and 'Altissimo' roses.

Prepare bare-root plants prior to installation by soaking the roots for 12 to 24 hours in a solution of water and rooting stimulant (follow label). Prepare containerized roses by watering with a root stimulator and water solution prior to planting.

To plant an individual bare-root rose, dig a 2 feet wide x 1 foot deep hole. Form an inverted cone in the center of hole for the roots. Make sure that the crown is 1/2 to 1 inch below the soil surface.

Carefully remove container roses from the container. Prune any damaged or crossing stems, uniformly spread the roots over the mound, back fill, and firm the soil after each shovelfull. Make sure rose crown is 1/2 to 1 inch below the soil surface, and water thoroughly. Add 2 inches of mulch (not needed in a container). Avoid placing the mulch directly against stems.

After installation, apply a root stimulator to the soil at the recommended label rate.

CARE

Winter broadleaf and perennial weeds are starting to grow. They are easiest to control at this time of year by digging to remove or by herbicide application.

Check the **climbing roses** after each ice or windstorm to make sure the ties are in place.

Check the mulch layer to make sure the depth is correct and the hard rains haven't caused movement.

WATERING

Keep roses installed during the previous two years well watered. Their root systems are not completely established.

FERTILIZING

The longer days stimulate growth on 'Baby Grand' **miniature rose** that is grown indoors. Apply water-soluble rose food at one-half the label rate. Apply once each month, starting at the end of this month.

PRUNING

Prune only severely storm damaged stems and canes. Make pruning cuts at a 45-degree angle.

HELPFUL HINTS

The rose series 'Carefree' are roses with extreme disease resistance. The 'Carefree Beauty', 'Carefree Delight', and 'Carefree Wonder' all share the resistance. The wonderful, dark green foliage acts as a backdrop for flowers in various shades of pink. 'Carefree Beauty' has large, fragrant, semidouble flowers; 'Carefree Delight' has a single flower, and 'Carefree Wonder' is only the second **shrub rose** to win the All American Rose Selection.

PESTS

Several leaf-chewing, flying insects are weather dependent, and they could be emerging from winter hibernation. Although rose growth has not begun, still keep an eye out for the pests. Note the date and time of sightings to build a calendar of events for the roses, and to remember the natural sequence of pests.

Control wildlife rooting through the mulch and munching on the leaves of roses.

Apply horticultural (dormant oil) spray to stems and canes of roses to control overwintering pests and eggs.

Disease and pest control may require the use of a hose-end sprayer. Determining the calibration (the rate at which the chemical is discharged), and mixing the chemical at the recommended ratio is essential. Inaccurate amounts (too much pesticide or too little) negate the time, effort, and money expended. There could be phytotoxic reactions from the plants. Purchase separate sprayers for insecticides, fungicides, and herbicides. Read the supplemental information regarding calibration, safe use instructions, and mixing ratios.

NOTES

MARCH

ROSES

PLANNING

Plan to install a rose hedge. Consider using **shrub rose** 'Bonica' that produces large numbers of pale pink flowers all summer long. Hand pruners and loppers are always the best way to prune roses, but you can prune this rose with a power hedge trimmer if you're short on time. 'Bonica' rose has a quick recovery (three to four weeks) period after the "make over," and then it goes right back into the bloom cycle.

PLANTING

Perform bed preparation for the roses by first removing undesired plants, either by digging or by using a herbicide. Prepare a soil sample, and send it out for testing. The soil pH should be between 5.5 and 6.5 (acidic) for the best growth. The soil test may recommend limestone to adjust the pH.

The best soil structure for roses is similar to that of a fertile vegetable garden. Rototill or spade the area; add 2 inches of organic matter. Aged (minimum of one year old) manure is one of the best amendments. Peat moss, leaf mold, or composted material works also. Mix the organic matter thoroughly with existing soil. Repeat the layers of organic additions until you have added a total of 6 inches of soil amendments. Incorporate after spreading each 2-inch amendment layer. This process creates a raised bed space. Rake to level the planting surface. Add approximately one-half pound of super-phosphate to the surface of the soil. It will work its way down to the roots.

To plant a rose in a container, fill the container to within 1 to 2 inches of the rim. Mix two-thirds soilless potting mix with one-third potting soil. Add a super-absorbent polymer to help reduce watering frequency; follow package directions for rate. If you are planting large containers with a rose and companion plants, make sure all the plants have similar cultivation needs.

CARE

Check the ties on the **climbing roses** and replace as needed.

Monitor the mulch layer, especially after a hard downpour; the force of water can cause shifting.

WATERING

Do not allow the roses to drought stress. Maintain 1 inch of water per week.

If you don't have a weather-proof hose bib outdoors, carry buckets of water to the 'Love's Promise' rose, and pour the water slowly and gently around the root crown to allow the water to seep into ground.

FERTILIZING

Do some organic fertilizing this month on the 'Francois Rebalais' rose and others. Spread a 1-inch layer of compost on the soil surface and water in. Mulch over the top of the compost.

PRUNING

Prune only severely storm damaged stems and canes. Make the cut at a 45-degree angle.

Do not cut back darkened winterkill areas on branches yet.

PESTS

Pests are weather and location dependent. Check the garden journal to help you know what to expect—and when.

Wildlife is giving birth to young, and activity is increasing. You will find field mice living and tunneling in the mulch. Set baited traps. The deer eat the rose stems and canes. Hang mirrors nearby, place predatory animal urine vials, or string fishing line horizontally between posts surrounding the roses.

HELPFUL HINTS

Marie-Josephe-Rose de Tascher started the tradition of opening a formal rose garden for public viewing. Madame Tascher collected over 250 roses, and had them planted out in a formal (angular) pattern. She opened the beautiful display for viewing, also hybridized her roses, and painted and sketched her favorite plant—the rose.

NOTES

APRIL

ROSES

PLANNING

If you have not previously taken an inventory of rose care products, do so now, and replenish low supplies to prepare for the growing season. Plan for any changes in the care regime now.

Plan to add a new series of roses to your rose garden. The 'Dream' rose series are sold individually as Dream 'Pink', 'Yellow', 'Red' or 'Orange'. They are similar to the traditional **hybrid tea** or **floribunda** roses in growth habit and bloom, but they require much less time for the care and maintenance. They require less disease control, and are not so picky about deadheading and cutting the blooms. Furthermore, they are versatile in use, and are beautiful when planted alone, in masses, or in containers.

PLANTING

For planting instructions and tips, see February and March calendars in the Planting sections.

CARE

Look for plant tags and labels naming 'Europeana' rose and other specific cultivars. Replace any missing or faded tags, and log the cultivar name in your garden journal.

Keep the soil area around the rose plants loose and not compacted. Compacted soil interferes with water penetration. Each time you are walking around the plants, work the soil up to break up the compacted soil surface, before moving on to another area.

Each week, during the month of April, remove 25 percent of the winter mulch protection covering the root crowns of the roses. If the weather remains at freezing or below, delay the mulch removal until temperatures start to steadily rise. Use the mulch to make a bowl shaped basin around the rose dripline to hold water.

WATERING

Continue to monitor the indoor **miniature** 'Pacesetter' rose, and water deeply as soon as the soil shrinks from the sides of the pot.

Check the rain gauge to monitor the rainfall in your area. Don't rely too heavily on weather information. Rainfall amounts could be completely different from one microclimate to another. Make sure that your roses are getting a minimum of 1 inch of water per week. Supplement if necessary.

FERTILIZING

To prepare **miniature rose**, 'Rainbow's End', to move outdoors, apply a water-soluble fertilizer at the full label rate.

Apply an organic fertilizer to all planted roses. Spread a 1-inch layer of compost on the soil surface in the entire rose-planted area.

PRUNING

This month, you can remove sections of stems and canes that are blackened from frosts and freezes. Cut back to new green growth.

Cut back healthy stems and canes of **floribunda**, **grandiflora**, and **hybrid tea** roses to 18 inches.

Prune **shrub roses** and **climbers** to shape and to control size and direction of growth.

PESTS

For weed control near the 'Scarlet Meidiland' rose, consider using a wick applicator or painting the herbicide solution directly onto the weed leaves. Digging the weed out (roots and all) certainly works well. Water the area the night before to make for easier pulling.

Do not attempt to dig out nutgrass or yellow nutsedge. The physical removal causes a single plant to release "nuts" (seeds) that are attached to the end of each major root. The seeds germinate and grow, forming large colonies of the invasive weed. Use a systemic herbicide formulated for nutgrasses. Follow directions carefully.

Watch for the eastern tent caterpillars (dropping from webs located in overhanging trees) that could damage any newly emerging leaves on the roses.

Aphids can make an appearance this month on any new plant growth of the 'Iceberg' rose or other roses.

Control increased wildlife activity. Watch for field mice and deer.

HELPFUL HINTS

Lavender colored **hybrid tea** or **floribunda** roses, including 'Angel Face' and 'Paradise', are among the most difficult roses to successfully grow, due to the hybridizing process. Next in the "degree of difficulty" list by cultivar are white roses such as 'Caroline de Monaco', followed by yellow bloomers like 'Gold Badge', orange blooming 'Brandy', and pink flowered 'Electron'. The most durable and easy to grow are the red roses, such as 'Granada'. However, achieving successful results is possible for any color, with consistent care and common sense.

NOTES

May

ROSES

PLANNING

Plan to add a **rugosa shrub** rose to your rose collection. **Rugosa** roses even look tougher with their very glossy, crinkled leaves and thorny stems. They are known for their immunity to diseases and resistance to pests. They have winter hardiness, and the ability to grow well in poorer soil conditions. Varieties include 'Hansa', 'Henry Hudson', 'Therese Bugnet', and 'Sarah Van Fleet'. Although **rugosa** roses may not be considered sophisticated by rose connoisseurs, these larger growing bushes will amaze and delight you from the first sign of growth in the spring, until the last rose hip dries up in late winter.

PLANTING

If possible, install 'Charisma' or 'Red Fountain' roses on overcast days to reduce transplant stress.

This is a good month to plant roses of all types. See soil preparation and planting tips in February and March calendars.

If you have purchased a rose in a plantable container, follow the label instructions for planting procedures.

CARE

If some existing roses are not showing signs of growth, remove them and replace with another type.

Check for plant tags and labels of your rose cultivars. Replace them if they are faded, and log the types and locations in your journal as well.

Remove the final 25 percent of winter protecting mulch from the crown of 'Yankee Doodle' rose, and use it to make a bowl shaped basin for holding water around the rose.

Keep the mulch back from the base of the canes. Check this frequently and correct piling of mulch caused by animals or foot traffic.

WATERING

Check the rain gauge to monitor the rainfall. Supplement any deficit, making sure that the roses receive at least 1 inch of water per week during the growing season.

Keep the soil area around rose plants loose and airy. Compacted soil interferes with water penetration. After working in the rose garden, work the soil up around the plants, breaking up the surface, before moving on to another task.

FERTILIZING

Roses are hungry this month. Use a fertilizer combination of inorganic (bagged, special formulation, faster acting) and organic fertilizers. Use rose food, formulated specifically for roses in a ratio 1-1-.5 with iron added, in combination with compost, aged manure, bloodmeal, or fish emulsion.

Containers of 'Red Fairy' and 'The Fairy' **tree roses** need fertilizing twice monthly because the nutrients are flushed out through the drainage holes with frequent watering.

A time-saver is the use of fertilizers that contain fungicides and insecticides. Read the label thoroughly before using, follow instructions to the letter, and provide close monitoring of the roses for any signs of chemical burn.

PRUNING

Make all pruning cuts at a 45-degree angle to expose more of the natural healing components of rose stems and canes.

As the flowers finish (petals drop or sag), cut off the faded blooms. Make a 45-degree angle cut on the stem, cutting no more than 6 inches below the faded blooms.

Remove erratic growth on **climbing** and **shrub roses**. Cut out blackened stems, cutting back to healthy green growth. If canes are blackened, cut out the entire cane.

Remove any fast growing shoots emerging from below the graft on 'Mister Lincoln' and 'Medallion'roses.

If you didn't get around to it in April, cut back healthy stems and canes of **floribunda**, **grandiflora**, and **hybrid tea** roses to 18 inches.

Prune **shrub roses** and **climbers** to shape and control size.

PESTS

Control weeds among the 'Shreveport', 'Queen Elizabeth', and 'Sundowner' roses. Use a wick applicator, paint the solution directly onto the weed leaves, or dig the weeds out, roots and all. Avoid digging out nutgrass or yellow nutsedge. The physical removal explodes the "nuts" (seeds) underground. They germinate, and grow into weed colonies.

This month is the ideal rose weather. Enjoy the perfect clear and clean foliage; with the knowledge that disease control was initiated before any problems are observed. See February and April Calendars for control information. If you are using chemical controls for fungus problems, follow the prescribed application program and continue the applications per package directions. Spores of black spot, powdery mildew, and others are air borne and continue to cause problems during the growing season.

Aphids, thrips, mites, and midges are expanding and moving through landscapes. Control as soon as they are observed.

HELPFUL HINTS

Well-drained soil is essential for good rose growth. If this is not possible for the projected planting area, consider building a raised bed. A raised bed is made from wood, timbers, manufactured composite material, stones, bricks, or blocks. Build the sides 1 to 2 feet tall. The size of the raised bed depends upon the number of roses the types of roses that are going in the space. **Hybrid tea roses** 'Antigua' and 'Leonidas', or **grandiflora roses** 'Love's Promise' and 'Pink Parfait', should have a 2-foot soil buffer from the exposed wall sides to the plant. Also calculate the space necessary between rose bushes to allow for adequate air circulation and bloom development.

NOTES

ROSES

PLANNING

Enjoy a stroll though the garden centers. This month could be rose heaven with 'Cherish', 'New Dawn', and 'Impatient' roses in bloom.

Plan to add some workhorse roses to the landscape. Many **shrub roses** survive and are robust in less than great conditions. The best performance occurs when they are provided with a good growing site. **Shrub roses** 'Evelyn' and 'Katherine Moberly' give back what is given them by controlling erosion or serving as a living fence, and they do so with the additional bonus of having salt spray tolerance.

When shopping for roses, look for Number 1 Grade roses with three sturdy canes showing active growth.

PLANTING

This is a good month for planting roses. For soil preparation and planting instructions, see February and March calendars in the Planting Sections.

If possible do plant installation on days which are overcast, to reduce stress on plants

'Mona Cheri' rose is sold in a plantable cardboard box. Follow the special planting instructions exactly.

CARE

If you enjoy sharing your roses with friends and guests, be sure to update any faded or missing plant labels on a regular basis. Log the information in your journal as well. That way, when guests ask you what the beautiful rose is, you can tell them.

Mulch serves to buffer all sorts of weather conditions. In the winter, it serves as a root insulator against frost and freezes. In the summer, it serves as a water basin to hold water and to protect the roots from drying out. Check the mulch around the roses to make sure the basins are in place, and that the mulch is not piled up against the canes of the 'Electron' rose.

Compacted soil interferes with water penetration and leads to a host of other problems. Work up the soil in rose beds as you finish your tasks.

WATERING

Temperatures are heating up. Check the rain gauge to monitor the rainfall, and make sure the roses receive 1 inch of water each week.

FERTILIZING

Combine a specially formulated rose food (1-1-.5 with iron added) with organic nutrients such as compost, aged manure, bloodmeal, or fish emulsion.

Fertilize container roses twice each month.

For nutrient needs and to control the aphid population on 'Cayenne' rose, look for a fertilizer that contains an insecticide that controls this pest. Follow label instructions.

PRUNING

Make all pruning cuts at a 45-degree angle to expose more of the natural healing components of stems and canes. Do not allow pruners to come into contact with diseased leaves and stems. If you have to prune out diseased wood, dipping the pruners in a solution of bleach (1 part) mixed in water (10 parts) offers some protection from spreading the disease.

This month, prune to deadhead the roses, and to remove erratic growth on **climbers**, **shrub rose**, 'Reine des Violettes', and other roses in your garden. Cut out brown and blackened leaves and twigs. If canes are blackened, remove the entire cane. Remove any unusual looking fast growing shoots emerging from below the graft.

PESTS

Control weeds around the roses by using chemical controls (pre-emergent, post-emergent), using a wick applicator, a sprayer, or even paint the solution on the leaves for those weeds growing too close to the canes. Digging the weed out, roots and all, certainly continues to work well, and if the problem is demanding considerable attention, water the area the night before for easier pulling. There are special chemicals developed for control of nutgrass and nutsedge. If you try to dig them out, you end up spreading the seed underground.

Each different species of weed requires a different chemical for control. If you are unsure what is moving in, take a sample to the University Extension Service or to a knowledgeable garden center technician for identification to determine the control.

This month is a transition time as we move from the ideal rose weather to daytime and night-time heat, combined with very high humidity levels. This is ideal weather for disease explosions. Do not be caught unaware, as diseases suddenly spread from leaflet to leaflet during pop-up thunderstorms or gentle rains; even wind or your clothes offer easy transportation for spores.

You should be in the middle of routine fungicide drenches or applications. Keep up with the schedule. The spores of black spot, powdery mildew and others are airborne, and could still cause your roses trouble.

Japanese beetles, aphids, thrips, mites, midges are at highest population level and the most damaging this month. Control is a must.

HELPFUL HINTS

On a 15-foot **climbing rose** bush such as 'New Dawn' or 'Constance Spry', it takes over 6000 leaves (covering twenty square yards if they were spread out) serving as photosynthesis factories to keep a rose bush healthy and happy.

NOTES

JULY

ROSES

PLANNING

Take this opportunity to visit public gardens or attend garden tours. Take a note pad along to jot down performance levels of unknown varieties, as well as your garden favorites, such as 'French Lace' and 'Little Darling'.

Evaluate the performance of your rose collection. Eliminate the underachievers, freeing energy and time for those plants that are producing envisioned results.

PLANTING

This is not a good month to transplant or install roses unless unusual circumstances (home remodeling construction projects, moving) force the planting. The best approach is to dig the rose bushes up, and pot them up in containers until the weather cools and you can plant them in their final destination. Keep the pots watered well, and place them in a semi-shady area to keep them cool during the heat of July.

CARE

Keep soil area around 'Sarabande' rose plants loose and not compacted. Compacted soil interferes with water penetration. When you walk through the rose garden and work around the plants, be sure to work up the soil as you finish to keep the airflow and water flow working.

Top dress the area over the rose root systems with 1 inch of mulch, offering some insulation from sunlight.

WATERING

It is difficult to use the weather service to determine exactly how much rain your area received. Use the rain gauges in your own garden to determine if you need to provide supplemental water to the roses. Provide a minimum of 1 inch of water each week.

FERTILIZING

Use a combination of organic fertilizer (subtle, slow release), such as compost or leaf mold, spread onto the planting area surface, with a chemical granular, or water-soluble fertilizer applied through a hose-end sprayer. Apply the combination monthly during the growing season.

Use a chemical fertilizer specifically formulated for roses on 'Walko' rose to insure that it receives all the required nutrients, and in the proper amounts.

PRUNING

Remove rose blooms as they sag or drop their petals. There are two schools of thought on making the cut. Either make the cut closely below the faded bloom (maximum of 6 inches), or cut down to the next stem having five leaflets.

You should only prune to remove erratic growth on the roses this month. Also prune out any browned or blackened twigs. If a cane is blackened, remove the entire cane.

Remove any fast growing stems or canes emerging from below the soil surface and below the graft.

PESTS

This is a stressful month for the roses with the increase in daytime and nighttime temperatures, combined with very high humidity levels. What may have seemed like an insignificant spot, now suddenly spreads from leaflet to leaflet during pop-up thunderstorms or gentle rains. Even the wind or your clothes offer easy transportation for spores. At first sighting, apply fungicides. You will have to follow the directions and keep up with regular applications in order to prevent the spread of the disease.

There could be Japanese beetles on the 'Nearly Wild' rose. Aphids, thrips, mites, midges are at their highest population level this month, causing the most damage. Control is a must. Make a proper identification and use the proper control. Read the label for safe application instructions and rates.

Control weed invasions by getting rid of the weeds as soon as you see them. Use chemical and physical controls.

HELPFUL HINTS

You probably have seen roses described in catalogs as:

1. **single floribunda rose** 'Betty Prior'. This type of rose has fewer petals with an open center.

2. **semi-double climbing rose** 'Paprika'. This type of rose has more petals and a less observable center.

3. **David Austin shrub rose** 'Sweet Juliet'. This double-flowering rose has a maximum petal count, with no obvious signs of the center.

This labeling system refers to the flower parts that nature developed to entice insects to pollinate them, allowing for the formation of seed, that leads to the ultimate goal of species survival. The most noticeable flower components include the petals (color) and sepals (green petal holder). Constituting the center portion of the flower are the stamens (male pollen production) and stigma (female pollen receptacle). Rose hybridizers work to rid the rose of all sexual parts; stigmas and stamens were traded for more flower petals. Plant reproduction for roses is now done by grafting or cuttings.

NOTES

AUGUST

ROSES

PLANNING

Fertilizing and watering consistency is important when growing roses. Plan ahead for those times you are away from home. Either consider installing an automatic irrigation system, or ask a favor from a gardening friend to help. Don't forget the containerized roses.

Keep up the performance notes on **tree rose** 'Frau Dagmar Hastrup'. At the end of the growing season, make decisions on whether to increase the number of roses or to try another cultivar. These decisions are much easier if you have notes you can refer back to.

PLANTING

Prepare the soil for planting the new rose addition, 'Tropicana'. Remove weeds either by digging or by using a herbicide. Systemic herbicides are transmitted from the leaf, through the entire plant via the vascular system, so they are very thorough. Some may take as much as two to three weeks to do their job, so plan accordingly. Read the label before applying.

For planting tips, see February calendar, under Planting.

It is so warm this time of year, it is best not to transplant or install new roses until the weather cools down. If you have an "emergency" planting, then pot the rose up using potting soil, firm the soil around the roots, and keep plant moist until you can plant.

CARE

Maintain a mulch basin around 'Mary Rose', 'English Garden', and 'Abraham Darby' roses. Move any mulch away from stems and canes if it rains. Check placement of the mulch often in case it has moved from foot traffic. Roses will still be sold at the garden centers until the first part of September. Since it is too hot to plant this month, give extra care to the container roses until it cools off enough to plant.

WATERING

Check rain gauge to monitor rainfall (do not relay upon weather information as rainfall amounts could be completely different from what is falling in specific sites) and make sure 1 inch total per week is provided for all plants (potted and in-ground).

FERTILIZING

This month marks the final application of rose food. Move the mulch to the side, apply granular fertilizer at the recommended label rate, and then replace mulch. Water-soluble fertilizer may be applied over the mulch, but make sure you water it in so it gets to the root crown.

PRUNING

Single flush (basically bloom once a year) **roses** 'Madame Hardy' or 'Gloire de Dijon', are stimulated to flower as the weather cools. Give them a light pruning this month. Cut back stems by just ten percent.

This month will be the final pruning on **hybrid tea** 'Portrait', **floribunda** 'Iceberg', **grandiflora** 'Love', **miniature** 'Rise N, Shine', and **tree rose** 'Gypsy'. Prune all repeat bloomers.

Remove erratic growth on **climbing** and **shrub roses**, and remove any fast growing shoots emerging from below the graft.

PESTS

Continue to control weeds. If you pull them out by hand, get the entire plant, roots and all. If the weeds are close to the rose, consider using a wick applicator or painting the herbicide directly onto the weed. Nutgrass and yellow nutsedge must be eradicated through the use of specially formulated herbicides. Follow directions for their use.

This is the most stressful month for pests and disease. The daytime heat may be waning somewhat, however we also have lower (very humid) nighttime environments—still the perfect scenario for disease establishment. If you have a history of disease, use fungicides on a schedule to prevent disease.

Japanese beetles, thrips, mites, and midges are at the highest population level and are the most damaging this month. Control is a must (see chapter introduction for specifics).

Knowing the type of insects you have and how they attack plants will help you find the most effective control. Insects feed on plants differently. Piercing and sucking insects like aphids, spittlebugs, white fly, spider mites, and lacebugs are controlled by an insecticide that is absorbed by the plant (systemic), then as the pest feeds, it ingests a good dose and is killed. The chewing and rasping types, such as fungus gnats, thrips, and rose chafer, are controlled using a surface-coating insecticide (contact), as their feeding may barely skim the plant surface.

HELPFUL HINTS

• Pop-up lightning and thunderstorms bring much needed moisture to the landscape, but resist the temptation to stay outdoors and finish that one last job. Though lightning strikes at humans are not a common occurrence, people every year are killed by strikes. Lightning carries approximately 100,000 amperes (a lot of electricity), and can be 30,000 degrees in temperature, which is hotter than the sun's surface. The most dangerous time to be out in a storm is if less than ten seconds lapse between the flash and thunder.

• Did you ever wonder how much weight you are moving around when preparing a new bed space? For one cubic foot of compacted clay soil, you could be lifting up to 100 pounds. If that soil is saturated, the weight is well over 100 pounds. If you are lucky enough to have previously worked the soil and it is dry, you may be lifting only 80 to 90 pounds per cubic foot of material. If you are removing concrete to make way for a new rose bed, one cubic foot of concrete weighs at least 140 pounds. Be prepared with either well-maintained equipment or muscle power.

NOTES

SEPTEMBER

ROSES

PLANNING

Plan a new rose for the arbor using **climbing rose** 'Joseph's Coat'. Add a new hedge of 'Martin Frobisher' along a fence, or enhance the fragrance garden using 'Armada', 'Nymphenberg' and 'China Doll' roses. While planning for all these new additions to the rose collection, just be sure to give your roses a minimum of six hours of direct sun each day, a well-drained soil with a pH of 5.5 to 6.5, and adequate space for access and air circulation.

PLANTING

This may be the last month to check at garden centers for **shrub roses** 'Madam Isaac Pereire', 'Henry Kelsey', or 'Graham Thomas'. Planting them this month is somewhat chancy, but if the plants look good and the bed space (or cold frame) is ready, it is worth a try.

CARE

If some of the roses are to be kept indoors for the winter, move them in and out of the house every few days to acclimate them before you move them in for the long winter. Do the acclimation prior to the furnace being used to help reduce stress.

Winter is approaching, and **hybrid tea rose** 'Just Joey', **grandiflora rose** 'Lasting Peace', and other roses in these categories require winter protections. Apply a dense layer of mulch over the crown of the plant, then use a styrofoam rose cone for added protection. Use the cones that have a removable cap to release heat buildup during warmer stretches in winter. Anchor the cone in place to prevent it from blowing over during windstorms.

WATERING

Monitor the rainfall and make sure 1 inch of water per week is provided for all roses, potted and in the ground.

FERTILIZING

Prior to Labor Day, give potted roses one last seasonal fertilizer application. Use one-half the recommended label rate.

This month, apply one-half inch of compost topdressing around the landscape roses. Work the compost into soil surface by raking lightly with a leaf rake.

If you purchase your mulch in bulk, turn the pile before using to reduce the naturally occurring heat buildup.

PRUNING

Minimal pruning is done this month on roses. If any pruning is done to eliminate browned or weak stems, make cuts at a 45-degree angle. Examine roses closely for splits and cracks where the cane emerges from the graft. Most **hybrid tea roses** ('Peace'), **grandifloras** ('Camelot'), and **tree roses** ('Pascali') are prone to this damage because they are grafted. Keep ample distance between plants so you can do your work without damaging the stems.

Do not deadhead blooms after mid-September. Allow rose hips to form to prepare the rose for dormancy.

PESTS

Watch any plants indoors for mildew on the leaves and spider mites. Keep your roses away from infected plants, and give them their own space.

Make regular maintenance sweeps around the roses to cleanup all fallen rose leaves. Dormant fungus and bacteria spores and insect eggs live and prosper on the leaves.

ROSES

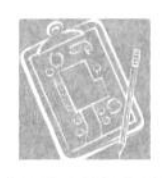

PLANNING

Plan on adding plants to the rose garden. Try 'Cottage Rose', 'Fair Bianca', and 'The Dark Lady' to give the space more year-round appeal. Consider green mountain **boxwood** as a backdrop, and add Asiatic 'true' **lilies** or a row of **baby's breath** to provide texture and color. All can be planted this time of year. When you sketch out the plan, remember that roses need good air circulation help deter leaf fungus problems.

Prepare garden areas for future development in anticipation of next season's planting.

PLANTING

This is a good time to "un-plant." Appraise the rose performance levels, either with photographs, notes, or your memory. Get rid of any underachiever, bad performer, or any roses that are prone to disease and constantly host pests.

CARE

Do not allow fallen leaf debris to remain against the roses. The debris has the potential to mat around the canes, either reducing water penetration or holding too much moisture, the perfect setting for fungus and bacteria trouble.

WATERING

Monitor the rainfall and make sure 1 inch of water per week is provided for all roses, including 'Dainty Bess' and 'Gypsy Carnival'.

FERTILIZING

Apply a final light fertilizing to the roses you brought indoors. Use one-half the label rate.

PRUNING

Perform minimal pruning this month. Prune only to remove dead or declining parts.

Do not remove rose hips. The hips keep out of season growth surges to a minimum.

PESTS

This is a great time to make a final spraying of systemic pesticides and fungicides. This can greatly reduce next season's problems.

Weed control with herbicides is limited, as the plants are going dormant. Remove weeds by digging out the entire root system. Do not dig nutgrass or nutsedge. The "nuts" underground release seed when moved. Use a special formulated herbicide for these weeds.

Watch for mildew on leaves and spider mites on plants indoors. If possible, keep the roses away from other plants because of these problems.

Earlier in the year, you may have noted in your journal that the rose buds of 'Desert Peace' or 'McCarthy' roses were undersized, black, and crooked. This damage could have been caused by a rose midge (tiny flying insect) that lays eggs on the growing points (flower buds in particular, but foliage also) of roses. When larva hatch, they feed on the rose for a few days, then drop to ground to continue their life cycle. In the future, if midges are suspected of causing similar damage, cut open a bud and if you see (use a magnifying glass) small whitish worms, then you have midges. Cut the rose plant way back, and discard the rose parts. Do not compost the parts of the plant. The midges can survive for many seasons. Next year check those infected roses as often as possible, and have your pruners ready for action.

NOVEMBER

ROSES

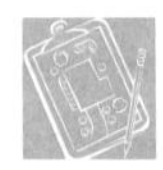

PLANNING

Cold frames are set below the surface, and have removable opaque or clear coverings. They are a great place to drop containerized roses into for overwintering. Rather than digging new holes in the garden each year, a cold frame would also work for winterizing **tree roses**.

If you have a successful **climbing rose** 'Rhonda', alternated with 'Colette', and 'Blaze Improved' show signs of decline, and the amount of sunlight and care has not changed significantly, then take a look around for a nearby tree. The tree roots may be encroaching and undermining the roses. Roses do not compete with the roots of any trees or larger growing shrubs. You will have to root prune the tree roots, or relocate the rose. Use this knowledge when you plan spaces for your roses.

PLANTING

Unless a disaster has struck, or moving to a new home is eminent, do not move your roses from their current location. If you have to dig them, plant them in containers, and protect from the harsh winter elements.

CARE

Light or moderate frosts (temperatures above 30 degrees) should have little impact on healthy roses. If any flowers or buds are still present, they will probably end this month with the frosts, and there will be no more formed this year.

If you have some roses that are grown in black plastic nursery pots, and then placed in decorative pots for display on the deck or balcony, these should be winterized as well. Pull the nursery pots out of their decorative containers, and sink the plant, pot and all, into a protected spot in the garden. Make sure there is good drainage. Dig the hole 6 inches deeper than the pot and fill the bottom of the hole with traction sand (just to be drainage safe). Drop the pot in the hole, making sure there is 1 inch of pot rim above the surrounding soil level. Water well, and mulch the same as your other roses.

After a hard frost (mid-to upper 20s), all grafted roses should have the crown covered for winter protection. Apply a 2-inch layer of a lightweight material, such as oak leaves or styrofoam peanuts. These materials permit ample air circulation. Next, add an 8- to 10-inch layer of well-draining mulch, formed in the shape of an inverted cone, with the peak located directly over the graft. Lay a few tree branches on top of the mound to deflect hard rains and pile shifting. There are also several manufactured products that assist with winterizing roses. Styrofoam cones are effective. Be sure to leave the cap open to release building heat on sunny days. Wire cages set over the rose bush, and then filled with mulch, eliminate most of the shifting.

Shrub and **climbing roses** require a 3- to 4-inch layer of mulch over the root system for winter protection.

Container grown roses require a protected spot, away from any wind or chill. Do not allow the soil to dry out. Container roses are difficult to winter over, and if they do survive, their overall performance generally does not match previous years.

WATERING

Monitor the rainfall and make sure that the roses get 1 inch of water per week.

FERTILIZING

If a 1-inch topdressing of compost is not visible around the **climbing roses** 'Joseph's Coat' and 'Handel', add it now. It will break down over the next four to five weeks, adding to the soil structure and richness.

When purchasing fertilizers, buy a smaller quantity of a few different types. Each offers a slightly different combination of ingredients. By rotating through several different product lines, there is a greater opportunity to create a soil environment that contains more of the essentials.

PRUNING

This is probably the last month for any chance of cutting roses. Allow all roses to remain as is. Stopping the pruning and allowing rose hip formation are crucial to lead roses into total dormancy.

Keep pruners handy, but only for removal of dead, damaged, or diseased parts.

PESTS

Diseases and insects have been forced into dormancy due to colder temperatures and shorter days. Take a close look at 'Mr. Lincoln' and other roses if there has been an extended warm spell that would hint at powdery mildew.

HELPFUL HINTS

Allow rose hips (small apple-like fruits on ends of branches) to remain over the wintertime. This gives a stronger signal to the rose to remain dormant until removed. The hips can be pruned off after February when the harshest weather has past.

NOTES

ROSES

PLANNING

Do not forget **miniature tree roses** may be available at the garden center, making a unique centerpiece when white 'Pacesetter' and red 'Starina' are placed together. The care is exactly the same for these as other **miniature roses** grown indoors.

Next year's ideas start with a look out the window or a stroll through the garden. Take some winter pictures and check your notes. Look in the newly arrived catalogs, and see if a 'Tropicana' or 'Eutin' rose is available. Also check for supplies on next year's wish list.

PLANTING

In these winter months, evaluate the amount of time and effort put into the planting area and the end-performance of the rose bush. Get out the photos to recall the roses in bloom, and consider making adjustments if needed for next year.

CARE

There are a couple of options for overwintering **tree roses**. You can bring the rose into a protected location, where temperatures will not drop below the upper 20s. You can also remove the rose from its container, plant it in a large black plastic nursery pot and water it well. Pack the soil down to eliminate air pockets, and wrap it in burlap. Dig a trench large enough to lay the **tree rose** on its side. Cover the root crown the same as if you are mulching any other rose. The third option is to simply discard the **tree rose** and buy another one next May.

Work the soil up around the roses after they have been mulched and winterized to allow the ground beneath the mulch to soak in moisture and to reduce runoff. The added moisture works as further insulation around the roots.

Maintain meticulous weed control in areas that are not mulched.

Check **climbing roses** to make sure the ties are holding the canes to the support structures. If new ones are needed, use either specific rose tie products or flexible tapes. Tie in a "figure 8" technique, and keep ties loose enough to allow movement in the wind, but not so loose to allow stems to bang against the structure.

'Frau Dagmar Hastrup' grown as a **tree rose** loses some of its hardy qualities when not allowed to grow in its natural form. Normally, this rose is an extremely hardy variety when planted directly into the ground. The care noted above for all **tree roses** must be adhered to or there is little chance for winter survival of this rose.

WATERING

Continue insuring 1 inch of water weekly, and soak plants just prior to applying mulch.

FERTILIZING

Seal bags of dry and granular fertilizers to minimize moisture gathering during the freeze/thaw cycles.

PRUNING

Remove only stems and canes that are prone to wind or ice storm damage. Cut only necessary sections of the **climbers** that may be obstructing access.

HELPFUL HINTS

Winter hardiness is certainly related to the mulching and protection that you provide after a hard freeze (temperatures in mid-20s) this month. However, the continuous good care you give the roses through the entire growing season insures that the 'Oklahoma', 'LeAnn Rimes' and 'Jar dins de Bagatelle' will all come out next spring healthier and better performers.

PESTS

Perform a final inspection of all plant parts and the surrounding ground for any foliage or unhealthy stems. Remove all.

If you historically have invasions of small mammals (mice, voles) causing trouble, place a circular piece of durable screening around the plant. The screening also keeps mulch from shifting.

Each week, spray off the **miniature rose** plants growing indoors, with a strong spray of water. Don't forget the undersides of the leaves.

Chemicals (dry and liquid) are best stored in an area that does not freeze.

NOTES

CHAPTER SEVEN

SHRUBS

Shrubs offer brilliant colors with the leaves of purpleleaf sand cherry, red barberry, and the huge ball shaped pure white flowers of the snowball bush. Wanting to create more formality? Think boxwood. Want to solve a landscape problem in a lower wet area? Deciduous winterberry holly or pussy willow will work and in a relatively short period of time. Many shrubs have the ability to do either, with a little forethought and preparation. Planning a change to a more natural appearing transition from a group of trees? Lantanaphyllum viburnum and spring witchhazel are perfect. Globe arborvitae's rounded shape easily sweeps a view from front to the sideyard; summer's flights of fancy from butterflies, bees, and moths look to abelia and Saint Johnswort to provide just this and embrace a patio at the same time.

To alter a view in sun think lilac or shade summersweet. A bonus of each is fragrance and bloom in different seasons. Mockingbirds singing a favorite tune will be attracted by the berries of the firethorn. Try making scented candles—crushing fruits of bayberry is one way to start. In sprawling country properties, suburban subdivisions, urban courtyards, and larger pots or containers—shrubs start working as soon as planted. This diversity is truly unique but the best aspect of such a wide category to choose from is that each plant can fill a very specific niche without disrupting other plans or existing plants. Deciduous shrubs can offer wonderful ever-changing qualities such as flowers, fruits, fall color, and/or winter branching habits. Coniferous and broadleaf evergreens really bring a sense of stability to the landscape with permanence and consistency. There are considerable differences overall making the final decision great fun.

DEPENDABLE SHRUBS

Shrubs are truly reliable, 24-7, 52 weeks, year in and out. To illustrate the diversity of selection, here are more good examples for highlighting and interest in all 4 seasons:

Winter—a pfitzers bluish needles and berries or branches of red twig dogwood

Spring—white flowers of bridal wreath spirea or needles of yellow false cypress

Summer—sweet spire for fragrance or upright yew backing annual flowers

Fall—holly berries or red foliage burning bush. Newer or recently discovered varieties offer a chance each year for a landscape to have a modest or complete makeover.

Versatility, strength, and toughness do not mean all common sense can be pushed aside and simply a hole dug and plant dropped. Success is not without thought, planning and preparation. Site evaluation, soil preparation, healthy plants, correct installation, and care and maintenance are all important. The rewards received are unparalleled, and the number of shrub contenders is astounding. Enjoy the world according to shrubs. And if your interests change over time, a single shrub, a hedge, or a collection can be replaced without tearing up the entire yard or landscape.

CHAPTER SEVEN

BASIC GUIDELINES

Inspect the shrub at the time of purchase. A healthy plant is essential for successful planting. Look for:

- A consistent color of green in the leaves.
- Some flexibility in stems and twigs in woody shrubs.
- Be sure the pot is not too large for the shrub. If the shrub has been potted recently, the root system may be stressed.
- Make sure the pot is not undersized. The plant may be top heavy or overly rootbound and may not recover from transplanting.
- Check the container drainage holes, on the bottom and sides, for moisture and soil dampness. If the top of the soil is wet and the bottom is dry, then watering could have been sporadic or insufficient to develop a strong root system. Select a different plant.
- Look for insects, spider mites (webbing between leaves), thrips (mosaic green coloration on leaf), and spittle bugs (wad of spit) on tops and bottoms of the leaves, and along the stems and trunk.
- Daring gardeners give the soil a sniff. If there is a sour or foul odor, there may be root rot. Move on to another plant.

For the adventuresome gardener, grow azalea and rhododendron shrubs. Kansas's weather makes growing azalea and rhododendron a challenging experience, but successful growing of this plant group provides an unforgettable springtime experience. The following varieties are some of the more successful types for Kansas. 'PJM' rhododendron signals the beginning of the rhododendron and azalea blooming and planting season. The blooming sequence depends on the exposure.

- White: 'Cunningham's White' 'Rose Greeley'
- Red: 'Hino Crimson', 'Nova Zembla'
- Subtle Pink: Rene Girard 'Pink Delight'
- Purple: 'Poukhanense', 'Purple Splendor'

Additional varieties of azalea: 'Rosebud', 'Boudoir', 'Herbert', 'Girard's Hot Shot', 'Karen', 'Snow'

Additional varieties of rhododendron: 'Chionoides', 'Purpureum Elegans', 'Roseum Pink', 'The General', 'President Lincoln'

REQUIREMENTS AND TIPS

Ground work for new bed preparation or renovation: Outline space (hose or landscape paint) and/ or remove undesirable plants by digging or using herbicide, rototilling, or digging with a spade to a depth of 6 to 8 inches. Use caution under existing trees to avoid possible root damage. To amend soil add 6 inches of organic matter (compost, leaf mold, etc.) and work into ground. Rake until level; don't allow soil to buildup against existing trees. Otherwise you could have a bark rotting problem.

Container Growing: Use a blend of 1/3 potting soil, 1/3 potting mix, and 1/3 pea gravel. Fill, leaving 1 to 2 inches from soil surface to pot rim.

Plants: Size (variety dependent): Buy bare-root (no soil), or containers from 1 quart to 5+ gallons, or balled and burlaped (generally sold by height). When purchasing check root volume (tip upside down and let gently slide), root volume, and size. Larger sizes cost more but plants should have a better root system and have greater initial impact. Check for the presence of fertilizer granules; inspect for broken twigs or branches, damage scrapes, scars, breaks, or insects. Look at foliage color and size and whether the plant display has good light and air circulation. Ask about a guarantee. If mail ordering ask about the packing and shipping date.

Where to Plant: Check amount of sun, ground slope (run-off), proximity of underground irrigation, buried power lines, and proximity to larger trees or existing shrubs (their roots compete for moisture and nutrients). A canopy structure or overhang (umbrella) can influence effects of wind and rain. Shrubs planted closely (in a bed or container) must have similar fertilizer and water needs.

Installation:

1. Prior to installation place plants in a sheltered location
2. Water to prevent drought stress
3. Plant into prepared soil
4. Dig hole 3 times the width of the root system
5. Remove and gently shake off the excess growing medium/soil
6. Check roots and loosen if pot bound
7. Place root ball in hole slightly higher than surrounding ground
8. Back fill firm soil around roots
9. Water thoroughly—soak surrounding ground
10. Mulch 3 to 4 inches maximum; minimize direct contact with bark of twigs and stems
11. Decorative container or pot. Start with one that is a diameter of 2 inches or larger than plant root ball (in height and width)

AFTER PLANTING CARE

Weeds: New or renovated beds can have a possible problem for five years; prevent by hand digging, or use pre- or post-emergent herbicides. Read label carefully before using any chemical control.

Watering: Established planting needs 1 inch every 7 to 10 days. New installations should not be allowed to have drought stress. Wilting at sunset or morning indicates dry soil.

Fertilizing: Fertilize new plantings monthly in the growing season. Use balanced (1-1-1 ratio) formula for 3 years to establish plants. Apply at the label rate—if unnatural growth or flower petal burn occurs, cut the rate.

Mulch: The depth of mulch should never exceed 3 to 4 inches. Watch for the presence of mildew, mold, or fungus growth. These may occur on the mulch surface. The impact on healthy plants is minimal. Gently stir the area. It may return or pop up elsewhere.

Pruning: You need tools such as a long handled loper, hand pruner, pruning saw, or hedge shear. Keep them oiled and sharp to reduce frayed endings. The best time to prune spring flowering shrubs is after bloom (flower on old previous year growth). On summer and fall flowering shrubs, prune prior to new growth mid spring (you won't want to prune flowers on the new growth).

STYLES AND PURPOSE

Heading back: Removing ends to healthy bud (swollen lump) on twig. The impact on shortened twig is a sprouting at the new end.

Thinning: Allows light penetration and increases air circulation. On multiple-stemmed shrubs and single-trunked multi-branched shrubs, select specific twigs and remove completely at the main intersection. With no stubs the twigs receive more nutrients and/or stimulate more and healthier suckering from the root system.

HELPFUL HINTS

Unusual Occurrences

If your spring-blooming shrubs are flowering or showing weak foliage coloration in late summer or fall, this indicates plant stress. The causes could be excessive or inadequate watering during the summer, a poor growing location, a lack of soil nutrients, or inadequate soil preparation.

Fight the Summer Doldrums

Plant late bloomers such as pee gee hydrangea (*Hydrangea paniculata* 'Grandiflora' var. Pee Gee), crapemyrtle (*Lagerstroemia*), and blue mist (*Caryopteria*).

Maintenance: As soon as observed, remove damaged, diseased, or insect infested sections.

Pest and Disease Control: Healthy plants can recover from problems. Follow label rates if applying chemicals, organic or synthetic. Predatory insects are effective. In sunny locations plants have more insect and pest problems. Fungicides are effective if applied prior to visible symptoms (possible from plant history being noted from previous years).

Shrubs

AESTHETIC ATTRIBUTES:

For Flighted Wildlife: Birds, Bees, Butterflies, Moths:	glossy abelia, Saint Johnswort, firethorn, lantanaphyllum viburnum, summersweet
For Multi-Season Appeal:	pfitzer, sweet spire, spring witch hazel
For Texture and Forms:	bridal wreath spirea, globe arborvitae, boxwood, snowball bush, upright yew
For Versatility:	burning bush, lilac, purpleleaf sand cherry, pussy willow, red barberry

KEY:

Common Name:	Location (city or town) specific
Botanical Name:	Universally recognized name
Category:	Evergreen / deciduous
Related Varieties:	Different characteristics-same care and maintenance
Height-Width-Silhouette:	Size-growth habit
Exposure for Best Growth:	Sun-shade
Landscape Use:	Getting the most

Common Name: Abelia
Botanical Name: *Abelia* 'Edward Goucher'
Category: Deciduous
Related Varieties: *Abelia* x *grandiflora*
Height-Width-Silhouette: 5 feet x 5 feet upright spreading
Exposure for Best Growth: Sun-part shade
Landscape Use: Focal point

Common Name: Boxwood
Botanical Name: *Buxus microphylla* 'Winter Gem'
Category: Evergreen
Related Varieties: *Buxus microphylla* var. *koreana* 'Green Mountain'
Height-Width-Silhouette: 2 feet x 3 feet
Exposure for Best Growth: Sun-part shade
Landscape Use: Mix in various gardens

Common Name: Bridal wreath
Botanical Name: *Spirea* x Vanhouttei
Category: Deciduous
Related Varieties: *Spirea* x *bumalda* 'Anthony Waterer' or 'Limemound'
Height-Width-Silhouette: 5 feet x 5 feet weeping
Exposure for Best Growth: Sun
Landscape Use: Background-mix in various gardens

Common Name: Burning bush
Botanical Name: *Euonymus alata* or *alatus*
Category: Deciduous
Related Varieties: *Euonymus alatus* 'Compactus'
Height-Width-Silhouette: 10 feet x 10 feet mounded
Exposure for Best Growth: Sun-part sun
Landscape Use: Screening

Common Name: Deciduous winterberry holly
Botanical Name: *Ilex verticillata* 'Winter Red'
Category: Deciduous
Related Varieties: *Ilex verticillata* 'Fairfax' or 'Bonfire'
Height-Width-Silhouette: 9 feet x 9 feet – upright spreading
Exposure for Best Growth: Sun-part shade
Landscape Use: Wetter areas or backdrop

Shrubs (continued)

Common Name: Firethorn
Botanical Name: *Pyracantha coccinea* 'Teton'
Category: Deciduous
Related Varieties: *Pyracantha coccinea* 'Red Elf' or 'Shawnee'
Height-Width-Silhouette: 8 feet x 8 feet – upright
Exposure for Best Growth: Sun-part sun
Landscape Use: Mix in various gardens

Common Name: Globe arborvitae
Botanical Name: *Thuja occidentalis* 'Woodwardii'
Category: Evergreen
Related Varieties: *Thuja occidentalis* 'Little Gem' or 'Rheingold'
Height-Width-Silhouette: 5 feet x 5 feet – rounded
Exposure for Best Growth: Sun-part sun
Landscape Use: Foundation planting or backdrop

Common Name: Lantanaphyllum viburnum
Botanical Name: *Viburnum* x *rhytidophylloides*
Category: Deciduous
Related Varieties: *Viburnum* x *rhytidophylloides* 'Alleghany' or 'Willowwood
Height-Width-Silhouette: 10 x 8 feet upright spreading
Exposure for Best Growth: Sun-part shade
Landscape Use: Screening

Common Name: Lilac
Botanical Name: *Syringa vulgaris*
Category: Deciduous
Related Varieties: *Syringa vulgaris* 'Edith Cavell' or 'Night'
Height-Width-Silhouette: 10 feet x 10 feet upright
Exposure for Best Growth: Sun
Landscape Use: Mix shrub planting – backdrop

Common Name: Pfitzer
Botanical Name: *Juniperus chinensis* 'Pfitzeriana'
Category: Evergreen
Related Varieties: *Juniperus chinensis* 'Blue Vase' or 'Gold Coast'
Height-Width-Silhouette: 8 feet x 8 feet – spreading
Exposure for Best Growth: Sun-part sun
Landscape Use: Screening – backdrop

Common Name: Purpleleaf sand cherry
Botanical Name: *Prunus* x *Cistena*
Category: Deciduous
Related Varieties:
Height-Width-Silhouette: 6 feet x 6 feet upright
Exposure for Best Growth: Sun
Landscape Use: Focal point-mix in various gardens

Common Name: Pussy or goat willow
Botanical Name: *Salix caprea*
Category: Deciduous
Related Varieties: Salix caprea 'Pendula'
Height-Width-Silhouette: 10 feet x 10 feet or more-upright
Exposure for Best Growth: Sun-part sun
Landscape Use: Background – tolerates wet soil

Common Name: Red barberry
Botanical Name: *Berberis thunbergii* var. *atropurpurea*
Category: Deciduous
Related Varieties: *Berberis thunbergii* 'Crimson Pygmy' or 'Aurea'
Height-Width-Silhouette: 6 feet x 6 feet – mounded
Exposure for Best Growth: Sun
Landscape Use: Focal point – hedging – foundation planting

Common Name: Red twig dogwood
Botanical Name: *Cornus sericea* 'Kelseyi'
Category: Deciduous
Related Varieties: *Cornus sericea* 'Isanti' or 'Cardinal'
Height-Width-Silhouette: 5 feet x 5 feet – upright
Exposure for Best Growth: Sun-part shade
Landscape Use: Background – tolerates wet soil

Common Name: Saint Johnswort
Botanical Name: *Hypericum* 'Hidcote'
Category: Deciduous
Related Varieties: *Hypericum frondosum* 'Sunburst'
Height-Width-Silhouette: 4 feet x 4 feet – upright
Exposure for Best Growth: Sun
Landscape Use: Hedge-mixed in various gardens

Common Name:	Snowball bush
Botanical Name:	*Hydrangea arborescens* 'Annabelle'
Category:	Deciduous
Related Varieties:	*Hydrangea quercifolia*
Height-Width-Silhouette:	4 x 4 feet – mounded
Exposure for Best Growth:	Part sun – part shade
Landscape Use:	Focal point – mix in various gardens

Common Name:	Spring or vernal witch hazel
Botanical Name:	*Hamamelis vernalis*
Category:	Deciduous
Related Varieties:	*Hamamelis virginiana*
Height-Width-Silhouette:	8 feet or more x 8 feet-upright
Exposure for Best Growth:	Sun-part shade
Landscape Use:	Background

Common Name:	Summersweet
Botanical Name:	*Clethra alnifolia*
Category:	Deciduous
Related Varieties:	*Clethra alnifolia* 'Paniculata' or 'Rosea'
Height-Width-Silhouette:	10 feet x 6 feet – upright
Exposure for Best Growth:	Sun-part shade
Landscape Use:	Background – tolerates wet soil

Common Name:	Sweet spire
Botanical Name:	*Itea virginica* 'Henry's Garnet'
Category:	Deciduous
Related Varieties:	
Height-Width-Silhouette:	4 feet x 4 feet – mounded
Exposure for Best Growth:	Sun – part shade
Landscape Use:	Hedging – mix in various gardens

Common Name:	Upright yew
Botanical Name:	*Taxus* x *media* 'Hicksii'
Category:	Evergreen
Related Varieties:	*Taxus* x *media* 'Hatfieldii', 'Tautonii' or 'Nigra'
Height-Width-Silhouette:	8 feet or more x 4 feet – upright
Exposure for Best Growth:	Sun-shade
Landscape Use:	Screening – hedging – background

Addendum: For the *experimental* at heart, there are wonderful success stories and numerous disappointments.

Below is a partial listing of spring blooming broadleaf evergreens—proven most weather tolerant. All azaleas are rhododendrons. The breakout is generally based upon foliage, overall mature size, and flowering habit.

Azalea: 'Hot Shot', 'Kathy', 'Christmas Cheer', 'Hershey's Red', Hino Crimson, 'Herbet', Poukanense, 'Rose Greeley', 'Karen', 'Rosebud', and 'Purple Splendor'.

Blue holly: 'Blue Princess', 'Blue Prince', 'China Boy', 'China Girl'

Rhododendron: English Roseum, 'Lee's Dark Purple', Roseum Elegans, Nova Zembla, and 'PJM'

Yellow false cypress: 'Filifera Aurea', 'Boulevard', 'Squarrosa'

PLANNING

Plan for a new shrub addition that grows in full sun, part sun, or part shade.

Holly, *Ilex* x *meserveae* is broad leaf evergreen with year-round appeal that makes it an instant hit in many yards. **Holly** has glossy, dark blue-green leaves highlighted by dark red fruits. **Holly** is used as a single plant in perennial gardens, as a background planting during the bloom season, and as a focal point during the winter. It works well as a transition plant, grouped at the base of deciduous or evergreen plantings. **Holly** is easily pruned or sheared to a specific height or width. This allows for use in smaller urban yards, medium sized suburban landscapes, and if not pruned at all, makes a considerable showing in more open spaces.

Review and evaluate the previous year's plantings of evergreen and deciduous shrubs in relationship to their original purpose. Look at the specific locations, but also consider the entire landscape. Was the **Saint Johnswort** providing enough highlight to companion plantings, while at the same time providing the perceived backdrop in the perennial garden? Did the **holly** grow as much as anticipated to fill the front foundation planting? Was the combination of round **globe arborvitae** and roundish **burning bush** too much of the same shape?

Look at the big picture and make adjustments if need be. Take notes and plan your actions now so you can make preparations during these winter months. Has the **red twig dogwood** in pots provided privacy for the patio? Now that the surface is changed from concrete to brick, would an **upright yew** fill the space better? Is the colonizing (suckering) of the healthy **spring witch hazel** starting to encroach and squeeze the **hosta** and **ferns** out? Has the removal of a large tree now exposed the **snowball bush** to full sun? Is the bird feeding area too close to the **bridal wreath**?

Look for winter color, texture, shape, and form that each planting provides. The bright red branches of the **red twig dogwood** and the subtle brown of the **witch hazel** bark offer character to the yard. The fine textured foliage of the **pfitzer**, viewed close-up, suddenly becomes an impressive, coarse-textured mass when stepping away. Open-layered, spreading **firethorn** contrasts nicely with the vase silhouette of the **lilac**. Consider the changing qualities of the landscape through the seasons.

Good planning includes a series of steps. The initial purchase determines the size of the plants to be installed. Establish the time frame you have available to install the plants. Avoid buying so many plants that they are subjected to stress from environmental exposure while waiting to be installed. Give careful thought to the required care and maintenance during the establishment period, as well as continued care for the matured specimen.

Take some classes offered by local garden centers, Kansas State University, the county Extension Service, botanical gardens, or park departments. Attend garden club meetings for additional information.

PLANTING

If you are growing cuttings under lights, use only clean or new containers. Wash used containers thoroughly to eliminate last year's residues, and soak overnight in a solution of ten parts water to one part bleach. Scrub with a stiff bristled brush and rinse. Discard any cracked (harbor site for bacteria spores) pots.

Cuttings need full spectrum lighting. It may be necessary to have both incandescent and fluorescent bulbs. Maintain a 2- to

3-inch space from top of the plants to the lightbulbs. Avoid burning the upper leaves. Adjust placement of light fixtures accordingly.

Plant root divisions in a soilless potting mix that contains slow-release fertilizer.

CARE

To prevent stress fractures on evergreens, gently sweep away any accumulation of snow that is bending **upright yew** branches excessively. There is not much you can do to prevent ice buildup on the **holly**.

Check for weeds during warmer days. There may be some newly germinated weeds or some previously missed. Hand dig to remove the entire root system.

Spread shredded bark as an insulator, 3 to 4 inches thick, over the entire root system or bed space. Minimize the amount piled against stems.

When the wind chill factor is below zero, evergreen shrubs show windburn on the north or northwest side of the plant. Healthy plants recover with the spring growth surge. A monthly application of an antidesiccant reduces this problem.

HELPFUL HINTS

Almost overnight the **winterberry holly** red fruits have disappeared. The local birds discovered a food source and are now taking advantage. Also, many smaller birds will seek nighttime protection in the evergreen branches of the **pfitzer**.

WATERING

A moist soil is essential for rooting cuttings under grow lights.

Monitor the rainfall during the month. If it is less than normal, pull the hoses out, and water evergreens. Evaporation continues even during the colder months.

Check the rain gauges. Be prepared to compensate for less than 1 inch of rainfall every seven to ten days. Watering frequency depends upon the amount of bright sunlight and wind.

Monitor new installations that have been acclimating less than one growing season. Water if the plants are wilted in the morning hours.

Keep all plants watered prior to installation.

FERTILIZING

It is not necessary to feed cuttings under grow lights; they receive nutrients contained in the soil mix.

If the winter is mild, top dress **red barberry**, **witch hazel**, and all shrubs with one-half inch of compost placed around the stems. Place the compost under the mulch.

PRUNING

Only remove storm damaged branches.

PESTS

Monitor all cuttings closely for any unnatural brown or discolored growth on the stem at the soil surface. Treat the soil with a fungicide drench. If the problem is not eradicated within five days, discard the cuttings.

Watch for small mammal (voles, chipmunks) activity burrowing into mulch around shrubs. The bark is a source of food. Set trap, pull the mulch away from the trunk, and wrap the plant base with wire screening.

SHRUBS

PLANNING

Plan for a new shrub addition for the full sun garden.

The **yellow false cypress,** *Chamaecyparis nootkatensis* 'Aurea' has unusual needles and coloration that make this shrub an eye-catcher wherever it is planted. The **yellow false cypress** has long thin branches showing very little woodiness during the first years in the garden. The weeping and cascading habit offers a softer texture to the landscape. The juvenile, nondescript shape evolves into a mature pronounced mound. The **yellow false cypress** is at home in a dwarf conifer collection, but is also well received in any setting with a day of full sun. Position it near other plantings with bluish or darker green foliage for an eye-popping contrast. The yellow color is toned down somewhat if the **yellow false cypress** is placed near natural brown sandstone boulders.

Plan for a new addition of spring or vernal **witch haze**l, *Hamamelis vernalis,* for the full or part sun garden.

The **witch hazel** is a rugged, rustic, multistemmed shrub that works best mingled among other plants, as opposed to being used for a focal point. The **witch hazel** is undemanding and bounces into prominence as an aesthetic harbinger of spring. Yellow-red flowers pop out, when most of nature is still in winter hibernation. The flowers, though small, command attention by a truly unique fragrance, not duplicated by any other plant. The summer foliage is dark green, with almost square individual leaves, set around gray branches. The **witch hazel** is not finished offering beauty; mid- to late fall brings bright yellow leaves filling the canopy. The late turn of color brings increased time for enjoyment. At that time of year, a heat wave is less likely to occur, bringing quicker defoliation. Give **witch hazel** room to grow and spread.

Investigate and take notes regarding possible reasons for any growth, decline or changes among the shrubs. Has the water flow pattern changed due to construction, increasing foot traffic and soil compaction near the **globe arborvitae**? Check your garden records for a late season use of herbicides, fungicides, and fertilizers. Has **Saint Johns-wort** and **red barberry** become a tangled mass? Is the red berry production of the female **holly** less than previous years? This month is a good month to make decisions based upon observations. Should the soil be worked up adjacent the **arborvitae**? There were no late season chemical applications made last season, so slow growth is not due to that reason. Decide what tangled plant should stay, and what plant should be removed. Keep the graph paper and sketchpad handy to jot down thoughts to help with decisions.

Most evergreens do best in acidic soils. Test the soil early in the season to determine the soil pH and any nutrient deficiencies. Dig up approximately a quart of clean soil (no mulch, dead stems, or leaves), and have it tested by the local Extension Service or soil testing lab. You may have to mail the sample to the nearest lab. The earlier the sample is sent, the quicker the results will return. Then if changes are needed, you have plenty of time to plan. If the results are confusing, contact the lab and ask for help.

PLANTING

Check the soil to determine if the time is right to prepare a new bed for **firethorn**. If the ground is overly wet, working the soil creates air pockets that serve as collection sites for harmful cold air and rains. Do a soil probe test. Push a shovel or trowel into the ground, if you hear a sucking sound, or if the tool has soil stuck to it after removing, then it is too early to plant.

If you want to add a **lilac** to serve as a buffer from the street, you can divide (if temperature is above 40 degrees) an existing large shrub and move it to the new location. Use a root stimulator for faster establishment. Be careful of any spring flowering bulbs planted in the proposed new site. Use a waterproof pen and a plastic tag to note the date of the shrub division and movement. Hang it on an out of view branch. Make a note in your journal for future reference.

Divide overgrown shrubs now. Lift the entire plant, cut the roots into pieces, being conscious of the crown, and replant the root divisions into the same area or into another bed space.

Remove any struggling cuttings growing under grow lights. Keep only the healthiest, and immediately discard any with signs of rot or fungus. Increase the "On" cycle of the grow lights to maintain upright growth, and to acclimate cuttings to longer daylight hours.

Stroll through the garden to check for early signs of bud break—signs of early spring enliven the day.

Keep up with weeds now. Check your garden journal for any self-seeding perennials, annuals, or vines that may be germinating, so you know what plants not to remove.

A 3- to 4-inch layer of shredded bark, compost, or leaf mold, spread over the entire root system of shrubs, offers frost protection to the roots. Minimize the amount piled against stems.

Neutralize the damage to sidewalks and streets where de-icers were spread. Apply a light layer of gypsum. It may require several applications to be effective.

WATERING

Keep soil moist on potted cuttings.

Keep an eye on rain gauges, and note amounts of snow melt (take gauge into a warm location, allow snow to melt, and note quantity). As soon as possible, compensate for any below-normal amounts. Supply at least 1 inch of water every seven to ten days. Place several rain gauges throughout landscape, and have a few spares to replace any broken gauges.

FERTILIZING

Apply a very light rate of water-soluble fertilizer to healthy seedlings and plants being grown indoors.

PRUNING

Prune no more than twenty-five percent of the plant per year. Severe pruning and leaving stubs is discouraged. Recovery takes several years, and sometimes the shrub never recovers.

Do not prune spring flowering shrubs. Pruning now eliminates buds along the stems that provide flowers in spring.

Prune summer or fall blooming shrubs this month.

PESTS

Inspect the soil surface of plants growing under grow lights. Look for gray mold on the soil surface. Stir the soil very lightly and add a fan for air circulation.

Control flying insects with yellow sticky traps. Wash off the leaves if you see webbing from spider mites. Use a soap and water solution to remove any dust (spider mite breeding area).

Use physical barriers for animal pest control. Predatory animal urine or pepper sprays may be immediately effective, but they are temporary solutions. Place traps for underground tunneling, either over the tunnel or at entrance. Again, a constant vigil is needed.

Keep plants healthy with regular watering and feeding. Healthy plants provide the best resistance from pests.

PLANNING

Plan a new addition that thrives in all exposures in the garden. The **upright yew**, *Taxus* x *media* 'Hicksii', has become the standard by which all of the evergreen shrubs are measured. The rate of growth is fairly consistent on plantings that are sitting in full sun or shade, so a hedge, foundation planting, or freestanding **yew** planted at the same time should be a similar size as time passes. Foliage color is in the darker shades of green, with some varieties turning a paler green in the winter. Red berries (cones) are on female plants, and when flowering males are shaken, the yellow pollen floats into the air. The **Hicks yew** is a darker needled variety that needs pruning only to control its height. This upright growth allows for usage in very narrow planting spaces, as a backdrop for a rose, annual or perennial garden, or as a symbolic gateway to the woodland or shade garden.

If you are looking for a new addition for full sun, plan for a **bridal wreath,** *Spiraea prunifolia.* A fountain of growth erupts from the ground and shoots high into the air, and gently cascades back to earth. **Spiraea** is a living bouquet when in flower, and entices one to come closer for inspection. The sheer number of double-white flowers that bounce with the slightest spring breeze is undeniably breathtaking. The very thin, fine textured stems persist into maturity, resulting in a shrub that maintains its vigor and original role in the garden for many years. Small, darker green leaves cover almost the entire length of the stem, and foliage colors to pale orange in the fall. This disposition and posture places the **bridal wreath** anywhere. It makes an excellent backdrop for plants that bloom in the summer or fall, and can be sited in a smaller yard, as well as in an open space.

PLANTING

As soon as the ground is dry enough to dig, shrubs can be planted this month.

• Prior to planting, keep the rootball moist. Water all containerized shrubs with a root stimulator.

• Dig the planting hole three times the diameter of rootball, and deep enough to allow 10 to 15 percent of the rootball to sit above soil surface. This allows for a bit of settling due to the plant's weight.

• For shrubs that are container grown and overly potbound, use a strong bladed knife to make four to six vertical slices in the container, and peel the plastic sections down, fully exposing the roots. If the roots are a solid mass, cut four to six vertical slices, about 1 inch deep, into the roots to stimulate growth and reduce root girdling (self-choking).

• For shrubs that are balled and burlapped, dig the same sized planting hole as for container plants, remove the nails from the burlap, roll the burlap down, and lower the plant into the hole.

• Adjust the shrub depth to insure that the top section of the rootball sits above the soil surface.

• Check the vertical standing of the shrub to make sure it is straight.

• Back fill the planting hole, firming and packing the soil as you go.

• Water the shrub thoroughly. If soil settling occurs, add backfill.

• Cover the rootball with mulch, allowing no direct contact with the trunk. This can lead to trapped moisture and rot.

• Prune only to remove flowers or flower buds. Do not prune branches.

• Water thoroughly.

• Work backwards out of the bed and loosen any compacted soil. This reduces the amount of soil compaction near the shrub.

CARE

When purchasing **yellow false cypress,** ask the garden center how to acclimate the Oregon grown shrub to insure that damage from a cold snap will not be fatal. Find out how long the shrub has been at the nursery and what measures they take to minimize damage. Shrubs are tough, but blackened frozen leaves or needle tips are not very appealing, particularly when the shrub was just installed.

Apply a 3- to 4-inch circular layer of mulch, placed one-half the distance from the stems to the longest extension of the branching. Make a bowl-like shape and leave minimal amounts of mulch adjacent to the stem bark.

WATERING

Check the rain gauges, and prepare to compensate for less than 1 inch of rainfall every seven to ten days. The amount of bright sunlight and wind dries soils at a quicker rate, so you may need to water more during these times.

Monitor new installations that have been acclimating less than one growing season. Water if the plants are wilted in the morning hours.

HELPFUL HINTS

The leaves or needles of any evergreen shrub occasionally drop from the interior of plant. It is a natural defoliation. Some leaves persist for two years and longer; but eventually older foliage will fall off, with newer foliage taking its place. This occurs at different times in plants even among the same variety.

FERTILIZING

Prior to mulching around the spring planting areas, sprinkle a light application of granular, all-purpose (5-5-5) fertilizer onto the ground and work it into the soil. The added fertilizer compensates for the nutrients tied up by the mulch as it decomposes.

PRUNING

Prune out any snow or ice storm damaged branches.

Prune no more than 25 percent of a plant per year. Severe pruning and leaving stubs is not recommended. The shrub may take several years to recover, if at all.

Do not prune spring flowering varieties. Prune summer or fall blooming varieties.

PESTS

Check new purchases for any weeds growing in pots.

Keep up with the weeds early on by using herbicides (follow label rate).

Be sure to enter information into your garden journal regarding nights where a hard freeze has occurred. This information assists in the diagnosis of blackened twigs on the **holly**, **firethorn,** or **lantanaphyllum viburnum**. The appearance is similar to fungus or rot. Noting the recent cold may eliminate the unnecessary application of fungicides.

Wildlife is multiplying, so there is the potential for damage to the **witch hazel** or **upright yew**. These plants are tough, but the damage from the increases in population harm in the long run. Use all deterrents available. Try wire screening wrapped around the stems or entire plant for a physical barrier; apply hot pepper sprays or wildlife predator urine drops.

SHRUBS

PLANNING

Plan a new shrub addition to the part sun, part shade, and full shade garden.

Plan for a **summersweet,** *Clethra alnifolia*, that ladens the hotter months of summer with its surprising aroma. **Summersweet** can be used in almost any garden setting from full sun to shade. Though a moist soil maximizes all its attributes, in drier areas, the rate of growth and mature size are the only obvious signs. The densely leaved branching suckers from the base, making **summersweet** an excellent hedge or screening plant. Spikes of white flowers at the ends of the branches appear to float above the plant. Note of caution: the fragrance is very attractive to bees. Site in the landscape accordingly.

Plan a new full sun shrub addition to the garden.

The **purpleleaf sand cherry,** *Prunus* x *cistena*, has deep reddish purple leaves and a willowy upright habit that allows it to serve many purposes in today's landscape. It works best in multiple plantings, as a single plant appears lost and out of place in the landscape. As a plant grouping, **purpleleaf sand cherry** is truly an eye catcher. Moving away from being used as a traditional foundation plant allows for a newer appreciation. The foliage color, in combination with the darker colored bark and branching habit, offers a wonderful framework for catching the snow. The structural framework is perfect for birds to nest.

Make plans this month regarding any changes in the shrub plantings. Doing it this month reduces the pressure of having to decide, prepare the ground, purchase, and install the plants in rapid succession. Remember that you are working outdoors for fun and enjoyment.

Consider color, texture, growth habit, and mature size when determining if the dwarf or regular **red barberry** would work best. Or would the smaller, denser **snowball bush** work better for your formal garden than the larger, open branching **summersweet**? Different areas of the garden can have qualities of both the formal and informal styles, but it usually works best if one idea is the dominant message.

Now with new ideas and plans, move outdoors to review previously established bedding spaces and possible new locations. Outline the space (flags, ribbon, or marking paint), measure the area to determine how much soil amendments are needed. (Figure approximately 1 cubic yard per 100 square feet of space.)

Take note of a shrub that may be overgrowing its site. If it requires consistent pruning to maintain the stature and size to fit the location, consider another shrub or plant for the location. Do some research prior to purchasing, and select a shrub that will fit the space without routine pruning. This enables more time for gratification, less labor, and an overall healthier plant.

PLANTING

There is still time remaining to rework new or established beds. Check for soil wetness before any major undertaking. Working in overly wet soil causes compaction, in addition to the creation of large air pockets that allow the root systems to dry.

Rewrite faded nametags and hang on out-of-the-way branches.

Push a shovel deep down around a shrub and cut a pie wedge piece for root cuttings. Lift the root mass out of the soil, cut out a section of root, stem, and leaf, and move to new locale. Replant the mother plant, and back fill the hole.

CARE

Keep a close eye on any newly installed plant for two weeks and eliminate any observed problems, such as water sitting around plant, pet digging, etc.

Maintain a 4-inch layer of mulch around shrubs. Do not dump mulch to cover plants. Depending upon the plant type, it may not have the ability to push healthy growth through the mulch.

WATERING

Check the rain gauges and compensate for less than 1 inch of rainfall every seven to ten days. You may have to water more if there has been a lot of bright sunlight and wind.

Monitor new installations acclimating less than one growing season closely. Water if the plants are wilted in the morning hours. This is the best time of day to ascertain a lack of water, as during the heat of day, shrub leaves will often fold or wilt to minimize moisture loss.

Keep plants watered until they are installed in the ground.

HELPFUL HINTS

Put the date of purchase on package or bottle of any chemical fertilizer, pesticide, herbicide, or amendment. Do not write over the application instructions. Store liquids to prevent freezing. If any chemical is suspect, safely and properly discard. Purchase quantities that can be consumed during one season.

FERTILIZING

Feed shrubs monthly during their establishment period (minimum of one growing season). Use a balanced analysis fertilizer.

Apply fertilizer or amendments, according to soil test results, to mature shrubs.

Follow the label or use less than the recommended rate of granular or liquid type fertilizers. Less is best; more could cause unnatural floppy growth or fertilizer burn.

PRUNING

Cut no more than 25 percent of a plant's canopy per year. Severe pruning and leaving stubs is discouraged, as the shrub may take several years to recover, if at all.

Do not prune spring flowering varieties. This eliminates buds along stems that are next season's flowers.

Prune summer or fall blooming shrubs this month.

Male deer rubbing on the shrub causes major limb damage higher up in a mature **burning bush** or **viburnum**. Use loppers, pruning saw, or a hand pruner to make clean, sharp angular (45-degree) cuts to remove any jagged or frayed bark edges.

PESTS

Continue to carry a weeding tool and remove any weeds by hand digging. If you have a sudden large outbreak of weeds, consider herbicide use (read and follow label).

Insect hatching is rampant; therefore sucking, eating, and disease transmittal occurs as well. Double and triple check for pests. Take action at the first signs. Use physical removal, insecticidal soap, or similar product.

SHRUBS

PLANNING

Plan for a new shrub addition for the full sun garden. Plan for a **pyracantha,** *Pyracantha coccinea*. The **pyracantha** is not on the top of the well-known shrub list, however it needs to be, if the area planned for requires a larger growing plant. **Pyracantha** cannot only survive, but is robust in poor, sterile, rugged, and thin soils of a hilltop, as well as in heavy compacted clay soils. Toughness is important, but the **pyracantha** has a sophisticated demeanor in most settings. An upright, somewhat open twiggy habit is softly mounded at the top with fragrant leaves, giving an umbrella-like form. The broad canopy offers annuals, perennials, and ground covers plenty of light, but still provides protection from the intense midday sun. **Pyracanthas** offer many solutions for landscape situations, ranging from streetside plantings, screening situations, and as a freestanding specimen in the far corner of the backyard.

Take the time to observe the planned position of new bed spaces from all angles. Prior to installation, use flags, marking ribbon, or landscape friendly paint to delineate or designate a new planting space.

Be aware of your own physical capabilities and the influence of the weather when planning a new planting task. Purchase plants early and have them tagged as "SOLD" at the nursery. Schedule the deliveries in stages. This allows the professionals at the nursery to care for your purchased plants until installation time.

PLANTING

Prepare for the most immediate task and have necessary tools and goods readily available. This saves time and steps.

If several **holly**, **sweet spire**, or **yellow false cypress**es are to be planted, store the plants in a shaded, protected area, and bring out into full sun just prior to installation. Stop and water each newly planted shrub before moving to the next. The best days to plant are cloudy, with little or no breeze.

Grow **yews**, **globe arborvitae,** or **red twig dogwood** in containers. Select pots that are a minimum of twice the rootball width. They will add nicely to the deck or patio.

Take divisions of multistemmed **bridal wreath** and **sweet spire**. Use a spade or shovel to cut a round section out of the mother plant. Make the cut at least 6 inches from the main stem of the shrub. Pry up the circular piece, relocate or pot immediately. To store for later use, put the division in a container or burlap bag. Place out of sun and wind, and keep plants watered until you are ready to use. If the divisions are being held past mid-December, mulch around the grouping and between the individual plants (not over the tops).

CARE

The natural process of mulch breaking down ties up several nutrients in the soil. Before replenishing (a 3- to 4-inch layer of mulch is maximum) mulch around plants, sprinkle some low analysis (5-5-5 or less), granular fertilizer to compensate for the loss.

WATERING

Moisten (no flooding) prepared beds and potting mixes prior to plant installation. This is essential to minimize root damage. Water again as each plant is put into the ground, or after every few plants. Water thoroughly, and look back to see if the soil has sunk or if the roots are exposed. Add backfill, and water again. If the day is bright, sunny, and windy, several light waterings may be required.

Although it is spring, check the watering tools (hoses, sprinklers, nozzles, etc.), and replace any worn or damaged pieces with similar parts. Ask at the garden center for new equipment that is on the market that may save time, produce a more efficient water discharge, and is more cost effective.

FERTILIZING

Plants that grow in the shade may require less water and less fertilizer than those in full sun require. Adjust the fertilizer rates and application frequency accordingly.

PRUNING

Remove damaged stems, twigs, branches, and dead leaves. Make the cut as close as possible to the nearest healthy portion.

Cut no more than 25 percent of the entire plant per year. Avoid leaving stubs.

Do not prune summer or fall flowering shrubs this time of year. This eliminates the buds that produce the flowers.

Prune spring blooming varieties this month after they are done flowering.

PESTS

Weeds could be trouble for up to five years in a new garden. Exercise caution to be on the safe side when using any post-emergent herbicides. Read the label to determine whether the chemical is labeled for a wide plant group like grasses (goose grass) or broadleaf (dandelion) weeds. If you are using a pre-emergent herbicide, read the label prior to making the purchase and again before applying. Pay particular attention to any impact on the garden soil and new plant installations. The safe alternative is hand digging.

The use of geo-textile weed barriers slows weed establishment.

If you are considering the use of predatory ladybugs, praying mantis, or lace- wings, there must be a food source (pests) present in large enough numbers, or the predators will move on to seek food elsewhere.

Insect (pest) adults emerge or the eggs hatch depending upon the air temperature. Begin monitoring the plantings as daytime highs reach into the 50s. The aphids and tent caterpillars are most problematic early in the season. Use a stream of water or simply smash between your fingers. If insecticidal soap or other contact insecticide is used, they must be applied directly on the pests to be effective.

This is not the case regarding the use of fungicides. These should be applied in anticipation of problems as a preventative measure. Apply fungicides if a problematic history exists.

NOTES

JUNE

SHRUBS

PLANNING

Plan for a new shrub addition for the full sun garden. Plan for a **Saint Johnswort**, *Hypericum prolificum* 'Hidcote'. **Saint Johnswort** has an open habit allowing for surrounding plants to thrive. Step out into the backyard from late May through June, and watch with amazement at the buzz of activity by the butterflies, moths, bees, and a host of other pollen gatherers that are drawn to this shrub. The fine textured structural properties make it stand out from other sun loving shrubs. Branches support greenish gray leaves, where unusually shaped flowers erupt from tight conical buds. The **Saint Johnswort** benefits if sited in a full sun location, with protection from the worst winter wind chills.

Plan on a **sweet spire**, *Itea virginica*, for a full shade garden.

Sweet spire has exceptional ornamental qualities, and the versatility to live and prosper in moist to wet soils, as well as in drier soils (slower growth rate and less flowers). The ability to grow in full sun and in full shade is the capping glory of this relatively new to the market plant. This shrub offers a different quality in each season. The spring brings out dark green foliage on an open branching habit, allowing for a good view of all surrounding plants. During the summer, the air is filled with a light fragrance, produced by dense clusters of white flowers. The fall season is highlighted by a striking display of red foliage that appears to radiate from the twigs.

All the birds, gold and purple finches, hummingbirds, and chickadees will be making visits into the landscape. They will be taking advantage of **witch hazel** or **lilac** branches for a rest stop, and for a safe sleep protected by the needles and density of the **upright yew**. Dot the thistle feeders and annual **sunflower** plants (many varieties great in pots) throughout the garden. Hummingbird feeders allow the ruby throated types to stay a bit longer during the migration north, and they may possibly stop by on their way south in later August.

Have there been any changes to the area designated for a water garden that was to be backdropped with **red twig dogwood**, **summersweet**, and **winterberry holly**? Consider neighboring yards also, as the impact of their landscape activity relates to existing and new plantings in your garden. A previously shaded area becomes sunny as a tree was removed. The emergence of a tree's surface roots impacts the shrubs growing in your landscape.

PLANTING

Finalize and complete all proposed plantings before midmonth to reduce summer heat and humidity trauma to plants.

Soil compaction is the enemy of every shrub root system, so when working in the garden, loosen and remove your footprints before moving on.

CARE

Check for all name tags on shrubs, and replace any faded, lost, or destroyed tags.

Maintain 4 inches (or less) of mulch around shrubs. Do not cover the plants with the mulch, just their roots need mulch. Change natural mulches occasionally to offer varied nutrients from the breakdown process.

Consider using living mulch in the form of a ground cover. Underplant the **upright yews** growing in the shade with **dead nettle** (see ground cover vine chapter). The umbrella canopy created by the **bayberry** would be a perfect spot for the evergreen **myrtle.** The deep green color of the **globe arborvitae** would be accented with the **stone crop dragon's blood.**

WATERING

This is generally a month with adequate rainfall, but continue to check the rain gauges and provide supplemental water to insure 1 inch of water every ten days on existing shrubs.

Watch shrubs installed this previous spring for signs of wilt. Check in the morning hours, and if there is wilting on **bridal wreath**, **snowball**, or **red barberry**, water the shrubs.

Wilting in the heat of the day is sometimes a protection mechanism of the shrub to reduce leaf surface evaporation. Check the soil for dampness before you water. Wilting is not always a sign of drought.

Water early in the day to reduce potential bacteria and fungus problems.

FERTILIZING

Apply a balanced fertilizer monthly to plants still in their establishment period (minimum of one growing season). Beyond this time frame, add fertilizer or amendments according to soil test results.

HELPFUL HINTS

Do not consider an overly large plant (a 3-foot **pfitzer** in a 1-gallon pot) in a small pot, a bargain. The shrub could be overly potbound and might not recover transplant shock, allowing it to acclimate into the landscape. Gently pull the plant from pot. If the roots are a solid mass, pass on the plant, and select a different plant with the crown and root system in balance.

Follow the label recommendations, or use less than the recommended rate. Less is best; more could cause unnatural floppy growth or fertilizer burn.

PRUNING

Cut no more than 25 percent of the plant per year. Severe pruning and leaving stubs is discouraged.

Do not prune summer and fall flowering shrubs this month. Pruning now eliminates the buds that lead to blooms. Prune spring blooming varieties after they are done flowering.

PESTS

Weeding is an unpleasant job, but keep the area clear around new plantings by hand digging or by cautious use of herbicides. Newly installed bushes have the majority of new roots near the soil surface. The aggressive nature of weeds slows shrub development by absorbing the water and nutrients.

Check for damaging insects during the early morning and evening hours. Insect activity is highest during those times. Examine stems, tops and bottoms of leaves, and on the ground for trails (slugs and snails). Contact pesticides must be directly applied to the pest.

Mole tunnels are showing up everywhere with the young moles large enough to tunnel in beds. Cultivated beds are easy to dig in the soft soil, and generally have a higher earthworm population—the moles favorite food. Set traps and move daily.

JULY
SHRUBS

PLANNING

Plan a **snowball bush,** *Hydrangea arborescens* 'Annabelle' for the shade garden.

In contrast to the summer heat and humidity, the white flowering **snowball bushes** brighten up the landscape. The storybook blooms make this shrub an instant hit with children and adults alike. Placement in a partly shaded setting makes the flowers appear as though they provide elevated landscape lighting. Use **snowball bush** as a specimen plant, in a grouping aligning the house, or clustered in mass among the woodland perennials. **Snowball bush** presents a course texture in the landscape, as the stubby stems shoot almost straight up from the ground, bearing large dark green leaves. Huge, heavy, round flowers cause a slight bending to the branches, exposing the open interior. The inflorescence will fade to brown and persist into the winter.

Compare shrubs growing in different locations. Visit local parks, botanical gardens, or commercial developments. Check out **burning bush** and **Saint Johnswort** used as companion plantings. Look for all the different **viburnum** varieties that are now setting fruit. Take notes and photos. Always take time out for enjoyment and appreciation of the outdoors.

The family out-of-town vacation was planned long before the April planting of **winterberry holly** and **yellow false cypress**. If your time away is longer than fourteen days, make sure the watering will be done, either with an irrigation system or by a gardening friend.

Schedule the work in the sunny garden areas before 10 a.m. and after 3:00 p.m. to prevent any heat related problems. The shaded areas provide a perfect oasis during the hottest times of the day.

PLANTING

Best not do any shrub installations, unless it is a planting emergency—the great deal at the garden center, or a special shrub division from a friend. Just make sure the plants are watered thoroughly. Water around the individual plant and the surrounding bed space. Apply liquid root stimulator to help in the transition.

CARE

If unknown weeds are showing up in the shrub planting, take a sample to the garden center for identification. Check the label of any herbicide planned for use, as many have a temperature range recommended for the most control, and a temperature limit where application can damage surrounding plants. Read and follow label directions.

Do not add mulch this month. The heat buildup can cause damage to new stem growth on the **red twig dogwood** and other shrubs.

If the leaf edges of the **viburnum** appear sun scorched or burnt, this is exactly what has occurred. This is due to the inability of the shrub to absorb enough water. This is not a culturally damaging symptom. If the shrub's overall health is good, there is no need to take any action.

If you have noticed little or no growth during the first two years after planting a **snowball bush** or **pfitzer**, it may be due to the plants using their energy for root system establishment. If the foliage and stems appear healthy, then all is well.

WATERING

If the weather is very humid, and the ground appears damp, trowel down and check the soil below the surface. If you find the soil moist, hold off on watering. Monitor the irrigation systems on automatic timers.

FERTILIZING

Feed shrubs in the establishment period (minimum of one growing season) during the growing season. Use a balanced fertilizer and apply monthly.

Beyond the initial establishment period, add fertilizer or amendments according to soil test results.

PRUNING

Prune out no more than 25 percent of the plant per year. Severe pruning and leaving stubs may cause a slow recovery period—sometimes death of the shrub.

Do not prune summer or fall flowering varieties this month to maintain the buds that lead to the blooms.

Prune spring blooming varieties this month after they are finished blooming.

PESTS

This is the worst month for insect pests. Strong and healthy plants can recover. Identify (look at various times during the day and check the undersides of the leaf) the pest. Determine if pest populations warrant the use of insecticides or the release of predatory insects. Many times pests can be removed physically by running your fingers along the stem or by a direct stream of water. Watch for spider mites and aphids in the sun garden and slugs and snails in the shade.

HELPFUL HINTS

Watch for an unusual amount of bee (ground hornet, yellow jacket) activity in the hedge planting of the **upright yew**. The hornets burrow a hole into the ground to establish a nest in the protection of the yew. These insects can sting and bite. Use a professional exterminating service to eradicate the problem.

NOTES

AUGUST

SHRUBS

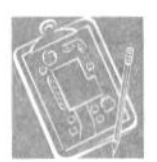

PLANNING

Plan for a new shrub that grows in full sun, part sun, and part shade.

Plan for a deciduous **winterberry holly,** *Ilex verticillata* 'Winter Red'. Wetness or dryness does not stop the **winterberry holly** from thriving. Many times the tougher locations provoke a grander performance from the **winterberry holly**. The versatility is demonstrated by its success in the full sun or in part shade. The structure is very twiggy, creating a fine texture enhanced by the near black coloration. New growth appears as suckers rising from the ground, and will colonize an area forming an impenetrable thicket, if allowed to do so. This rough and twisting demeanor suggests that the 'Winter Red' should be part of a natural setting to take full advantage of the heritage. In mid-fall, the dark green leaves turn yellow, and fully expose the scarlet red berries that persist until discovered by the local bird population. Female plants produce the fruits, with the male plants needed for pollination. Though tolerant of wet conditions, it is not necessary to have such conditions to enjoy the 'Winter Red' deciduous **holly** year-round.

Plan a new addition for the full sun garden. Plan for a **burning bush**, *Euonymus atropurpureus* **Burning bush** is a head-turning bright red in the fall, leaping to the garden forefront as summer fades into cooler nights and shorter days. This shrub makes screening, hedging, or embracing a garden area as bookends look so easy. The overall form is built upon a series of impenetrable horizontal twigs and stems that have an extra corky flap running their entire length. The textured stems offer winter highlight, whether covered in snow or in bare silhouette. The branching arrangement is ideal for birds nesting or seeking a protected place to land. The circular ball-like form is a tremendous foil when sited among plantings with vertical or upright presence. Although not known for the flowers, which are yellow-green appearing in mid-May through early June, the blooms add another unusual aspect to take pleasure from during the casual stroll in the garden.

PLANTING

Working the soil ahead of time, on existing garden areas that are scheduled for expansion and on newly created spaces, allows for blending of amendments and for soil settling to take place. This approach removes a considerable amount of work pressure in the fall.

Although it is still hot, the days are shorter and nights are beginning to cool. This change in the weather, in conjunction with new plant materials arriving at the garden centers, creates a great opportunity to add more **yellow false cypress** to the landscape. The best time to work in the landscape is in the morning or later in the day, when there is less chance for plant stress.

Take stem cuttings from where the old (brown) twig transitions to new (green) growth. Cut a 6-inch section; remove the foliage and needles from the bottom 3 inches. Dip the cut end into rooting hormone, and place into growing mix formulated for starting seeds or cuttings. Place the pot under grow lights or sink into the ground or in a cold frame. Protect the cutting from direct sun or wind. Water to keep soil damp, but not wet. Allow a minimum of four to six weeks before checking on root development. Gently tilt the pot so the cutting and potting mix slides out. If one-half of the container is filled with roots, the cutting is ready for planting out. If the root mass is not adequate, return the cutting to the pot, and water with a root stimulator. Check every 3 weeks for roots.

CARE

The soil compacts with each trip in and out of a bed space. At the end of the work schedule, look around, and churn up the compressed soil. This prevents water pooling and allows for proper air circulation in and out of the ground.

When spreading mulch, avoid broadcasting the mulch, allowing it to pile up against any branches or stems.

WATERING

Change the watering schedule based on sun intensity, wind factor, and exposure. Check the soil moisture prior to irrigating. Do not depend on automatic timers. Overwatering encourages rot or fungus problems for **upright yew**, **holly,** and **Saint Johnswort**. Take a shovel and dig down 6 or more inches. If the soil is moist, do not water. Or try a hand test. Squeeze a handful of dirt into a ball, if the shape remains, don't water, if it breaks down, apply water.

HELPFUL HINTS

Take divisions from the **winterberry holly** or **summersweet** early in the day; place section in nursery pot or transplant directly to new location. Blend together the existing soil with some seed-starter soilless potting soil and water.

Morning is the best time to check for any wilting. Plants that are drooping should be watered, unless the ground is overly wet.

FERTILIZING

Make final fertilizer applications of the year. If a granular fertilizer is used, water after application to move the fertilizer through the mulch.

Have a soil test done every three years. Should the analysis indicate a nutrient problem, amend the soil as recommended, and water area thoroughly after application.

PRUNING

Any pruning this month can expose previously shadowed needles and leaves to full sun, causing sunburn and leaf scorch.

Cut off spent flowers to improve overall aesthetics.

PESTS

To temporarily control wildlife, use physical barriers, predatory animal urine, or pepper sprays.

To discourage underground tunneling, place traps (depending on pest) either over the tunnel or at the entrances. A constant vigil is needed.

Keeping plants healthy, by consistent watering and regular feeding, provides the best resistance and resilience to attacks by insects.

Summer weeds are at their peak level of growth, so herbicides will be extremely effective. Use caution, and do not allow herbicide to drift and come in contact with **red barberry** or **globe arborvitae** foliage.

When hand digging weeds, dig up the entire root system.

SEPTEMBER

SHRUBS

PLANNING

Plan a new shrub addition for full sun, part sun, or part shade.

Plan for a **globe arborvitae**, *Thuja occidentalis* 'Woodwardii'. No pruning is needed to keep this perfect globular-shaped, smaller growing, evergreen shrub within bounds. The **globe arborvitae** performs many different tasks in a wide mélange of yards. The mature size needs much contemplation of purpose and intent when considering its use in the landscape. Formal qualities are enhanced when planted as a traditional foundation hedge planting, or when spotted at pre-determined intervals. A grouping can highlight windows or other architectural features, or make a smooth transition from front to side to backyard. Moved away from the house, and placed at the corner of a vegetable or herb garden, or dotted among sun or shade perennials, brings out the informal attributes. Another clever use is placing this evergreen at the edge of the lawn to smooth movement into the tree line. The uses are limited by the imagination for this shrub.

The plastic container collection continues to grow with each purchase of a potted **snowball** or **red barberry**. Check in the phone book for a recycling center or for a local manufacturer that recycles. Combine efforts with garden clubs, garden writers, and garden centers.

The summer surge of growth is over, so it is time to take note of what has happened with the shrub collection. Did any birds nest in the **viburnum**, and how far above the ground was the nest? How much did the new division of **lilac** grow in height? Has the **red twig dogwood** started to lose its reddish hue on the oldest stems? Take stock of everything that has happened since the last information gathering. The time spent now allows for better evaluations for the future. Are changes needed this fall or is the status quo quite good?

Fall brings gentle rains (soak in). The ground temperature is the warmest of the year (promotes root growth), and time is generally less intense than the spring rush. This allows any changes made in the landscape plenty of time to acclimate before going dormant for the winter.

PLANTING

Plant pots with upright yews and sit them at the front door or back door, creating living greenery to welcome you home. Female yews will have red berries.

Keep rootballs moist on shrubs prior to planting. For planting steps, see the March Calendar.

You can still do divisions of multistemmed **bridal wreath** and **sweet spire.** Use a spade or shovel to cut a ring 6 inches from the stem and gently pry the section up. Relocate or pot up immediately. If you are saving the divisions for gifts or for planting later, put the cutting in a container or burlap bag, and place out of sun and wind. Keep the divisions watered. If they are being held beyond mid-December, mulch around the grouping and between the individual plants (not over the tops).

Plant herbaceous plants, such as **pansies, ornamental cabbage** and **kale,** and **red leaf lettuce** from seed for color, texture, and shape in front of the shrubs. This will pay unexpected rewards for several months, as nature prepares for a less colorful season.

CARE

Fall cleanup begins as the summer and fall blooming shrubs finish flowering, and the foliage of deciduous plants fall to the ground. As stems are exposed, examine them for anything out of the ordinary, lumps on the stems, unusual twisted growth, and a less than rigid stem structure. Determine if the problem is excessive (affecting more than 50 percent of plant). Remove and discard damaged or diseased sections. Next year's growth will show positive signs from the extra effort.

Work up the soil in planting beds of **yellow false cypress** and **globe arborvitae,** or around single planted **witch hazel** to reduce soil compaction. Fall rains will penetrate ground easier and fill the below-surface air pockets, reducing root system damage from cold air.

Do not re-apply mulch this month, allowing the depth to diminish. The soil surface benefits from air circulation and the direct sunlight assists in control of disease spores.

HELPFUL HINTS

Combine **globe arborvitae** and **daffodils, summersweet** plus **grape hyacinth,** and **surprise lilies** with **snowball bushes**. These bulbs are available now at the garden centers. The combination plantings with bulbs will make wintertime quickly forgotten when spring blooms arrive.

WATERING

Provide 1 inch of water every ten to fourteen days, either through rainfall or irrigation. If a period of cool and overcast skies occurs, then extend the time frame for another seven days. However, do not allow drought to occur, as the microbes (living elements in soil) and soil structure suffers, impacting plant growth

FERTILIZING

Apply root stimulators to transplants.

PRUNING

Cut no more than 25 percent of the plant per year. Severe pruning to points showing no active growth, and allowing stubs to remain, is discouraged.

Do not prune spring flowering varieties as this eliminates the buds along stems that produce the flowers.

Prune summer or fall blooming varieties after they are done flowering.

Hand prune or shear plants to control the shape and size, and in preparation for the winter season. Do not allow cuttings to remain on top of plants (could harbor bacteria and disease spores through the winter), clean-up debris.

PESTS

Insect damage season is over, but keep all plant debris picked up to eliminate overwintering egg or adult sites.

Henbit, chickweed seeds, and other annual winter weeds will be germinating. Apply a pre-emergent (kills all seeds at time of germination) herbicide to discourage weed seed germination. It will not be effective on weeds actively growing. Hand digging with a weeding tool always works if the root system is removed.

OCTOBER

SHRUBS

PLANNING

Plan for a versatile shrub addition that thrives in part sun, part shade, or full shade.

The **lantanaphyllum viburnum,** *Viburnum* x *rhytidophylloides* has superb foliage. It is larger growing for a deciduous shade shrub, and has astounding fruit production. Though the shade is not necessary for the shrub, the aesthetic qualities are enhanced with placement in part shade or full shade conditions. The large, pointed-spear leaves are two-toned, with the upper surface a pure darker green, and the lower, a contrasting, paler green. When the wind blows, this viburnum gives a fan dance show. Additionally, the leaves persist well into the fall, offering one last glimpse of the past growing season. The coarse texture of this viburnum, under the shadows of large trees and surrounded by fine-textured plants, produces a style that is out of the ordinary. The **lantanaphyllum viburnum** gives a lot of bang for the buck.

Plan for a new addition for the full sun or part sun. Plan for a **firethorn**, *Pyracantha coccinea.* A most unusual quality of the **firethorn** is its preference for a poorer soil in order to achieve maximum aesthetics. An overly organic or fertilized site makes for spindly growth and increased propensity to disease problems. The clusters of white flowers in the spring make a bright showing, whether the shrub is a single specimen, a clustered group, an espalier on a trellis, climbing a fence, or planted as a hedgerow. The flowers become brilliant orange fruit that is unmatched in the landscape. These berries are attractive to many birds, in particular to the mockingbird. The thorns and semi-evergreen leaves offer protection for many types of birds to build nests.

Take late season, color photos focusing on the shrubs with fruits. Take distant and close-up photos to determine if the fruits are prominent enough to showoff the fall tints and hues. Note the brilliant red and blue of the **winterberry holly**, the vivid orange **firethorn**, and the **pfitzer** cones in small clumps of blue. Watch how the fruits disappear or shrivel on the plants as the season progresses. Take photos and observe the garden from all angles looking out and looking in.

PLANTING

Finish any shrub planting projects before mid-October. After this date, the winterkill potential is greater.

- Prepare the site for planting.
- Outline the planting space, remove undesirable plants by digging or using a herbicide.
- Rototill or spade to depth of 6 to 8 inches.
- Blend a total of 6 inches of organic matter into the existing soil, and rake smooth, creating a raised bed.
- Use biodegradable (paper weave) erosion netting, if necessary, during establishment.
- Dig a hole twice the width of root system.
- Remove plant carefully from the pot. Loosen the roots if potbound.
- Place in the hole slightly higher than surrounding ground.
- Back fill, firm soil, and water thoroughly.
- Remove existing flowers.
- Apply mulch to a depth of 1 inch.

CARE

As the **red twig dogwood** or **bridal wreath** foliage falls, examine the nearby fence section or bench that was partially covered during the growing season. Repair or replace any damaged artwork, pergola, or trellis.

Check for plant name labels, reset or replace as needed. Pay particular attention to plants slated for transplanting.

Do not allow large accumulations of fallen leaves to pile up on shrub stems and branches. Rake leaves into the open, and mow over them, creating leaf mold, and scatter in light amounts through the garden.

Maintain a maximum of 4 inches of mulch around shrub plantings. Do not dump and spread the mulch to cover the plants.

WATERING

Established shrubs, in the landscape for more than one growing season, should receive 1 inch of water every seven to ten days.

Monitor new installations, acclimating less than one growing season, for water needs. Water if the plants are wilted in the morning.

HELPFUL HINTS

Remember to layer plant debris with other materials (topsoil) to insure proper blending. A good compost pile has noticeable steam rising during cooler temperatures.

Keep all shrubs watered in the pots while they are waiting to be planted in the garden.

FERTILIZING

Fertilize transplants if you did not in September (see September).

PRUNING

Remove all plant debris after pruning. The clippings harbor insect pests and their eggs during winter.

When cutting out damaged branches, cut all the way back to the healthy growth. Do not leave a stub.

Do not prune spring flowering varieties as this will eliminate the buds that will be spring blooms

Prune summer or fall blooming varieties this month.

PESTS

Wildlife is sensing the impending cold. Chipmunks and voles are looking for nooks and crannies under the patio or front stoop. Squirrels are planting, digging, and gnawing (essential for the squirrel too keep lower teeth from getting too long). Deer are deep in the woods where there is plenty to eat—be grateful.

Weed control with herbicides is becoming ineffective with weed growth slowing down, thereby slowing movement through the translocation path (carries herbicide) from leave to root. Hand weeding is the best control now. Remove the entire root system.

NOTES

NOVEMBER

SHRUBS

PLANNING

Plan a new shrub addition for full sun, part sun, or part shade.

The **red twig dogwood**, *Cornus stoloniferia*, is subtle in the summer when it is fully leafed out, and demands to be a focal point in the winter when the bright red twigs are exposed. The open habit allows for placement in the foreground or among other shrubs, perennials, and groundcovers. Performing well in the sun or shade, in either wet or not overly dry soil, the **red twig dogwood** does many things with very little care. Small clusters of white flowers pop out in mid- to late spring, giving way to white fruits in late summer to early fall. When foliage begins to fall and the twigs are exposed, the season comes to close in the **red twig dogwood's** final glory.

Plan for a **pfitzer**, *Juniperus* x *media* 'Pfitzeriana', in the full sun landscape.

Pfitzers are tough, durable, and really fit into many of today's landscape scenarios. They are evergreen, require minimal care, and have a lovely, graceful, spreading habit. Perhaps overused as an "under the picture window" shrub for most all suburban landscapes during the 1950s, the **pfitzer** may have been forgotten or overlooked in the current landscape trend. When properly placed, the **pfitzer's** shorter green needles stretch and fill many voids. The wider-than-tall growth habit equates to needing fewer plants for the evergreen screen or large hedge. The pale bluish fruits add to the big picture, when the slightest breeze brings animation to this durable long-lived shrub. The very nature and habit make the **pfitzers** an incredible bird-attracting plant. Allow it room to grow, and the **pfitzer** pays dividends for many years.

Almost yearly, new varieties of **holly**, **lilac**, **cypress** and many others are previewed in the plant catalogs. If you want to try something new, place your order early, as new introductions may be available in limited quantities.

Take black and white photos. This eliminates possible distractions and clarifies design lines, functions, and purpose of the shrub bed outline in relationship to structures, and to the view as a whole.

Birds will only add to the outdoor environment, so make sure feeders and birdbaths are kept full.

Stay flexible. If **burning bush** and **purpleleaf sand cherry** are purchased for installation, and the weather or your time available does not cooperate, place the pots in a protected location, and water to keep moist until installation.

PLANTING

All tools should be cleaned and sharpened. A light application of oil reduces rusting during winter.

CARE

Colder falling rains not only cause the final deciduous leaves to drop, but allow for a check of drainage patterns. Raise the soil level to prevent puddles. Check any new beds or plantings for settling, shifting, or erosion. Clean out gutters that are full of leaves so they can do their job.

Maintain a 4-inch layer of mulch (or less) around shrub plantings. Do not dump and spread mulch to cover the plants. Lay the mulch over the soil, avoid covering the leaves or plant crown.

WATERING

Winterize the in-ground irrigation system this month.

Drain the sprinklers, hoses, and watering cans, and store out of the weather to prevent freeze damage. Keep one hose available to use if a winter drought occurs

FERTILIZING

No fertilization is necessary this month.

Inventory the fertilizers and amounts remaining from the season. Store properly so that no moisture will come into contact with the bag.

Consider plant performance where a specific fertilizer was applied. Determine if there are any changes you want to make in next year's fertilizer regime.

Clean the fertilizer hose-end attachments to insure correct calibration and application next year.

PRUNING

Unless pruning is essential, minimize pruning and cutting back shrubs this month. The existing branch tips are the toughest (due to season-long exposure) and will protect the interior growth from frost.

HELPFUL HINTS

Hand pruners are one of the most important tools used for growing shrubs in the landscape. Pruners with scissor action are best. They make a cleaner cut, allowing for speedier wound healing. If your pruning hand is stressed after working a short time, the pruner may be too large for your hand. Spread your hand out, open the pruner, and lay it on your opened hand. The handles should not have a wider spread than the space from your finger to the thumb tip. You may need a smaller pruner.

Wintercreeper, English ivy, or **Boston ivy** may become intertwined in the stems and suckers of the **lilac**, **summersweet** or **purpleleaf sand cherry**. This presents no problem, unless the ground cover growth climbs into the shrubs and begins to shade out branches and buds. Prune out this dense growth as necessary.

PESTS

Proper storage of dry and liquid products minimizes losses. Note the shelf life of chemicals and properly discard expired products. Contact the Kansas Department of Health and Environment for disposal instructions.

Proper storage is crucial for pesticides and fertilizers. The chemistry may be altered during the course of cold weather. Settling and hardening can occur if packages are open to humidity.

Hand weed this time of the year. Be sure to pull the weed out of the ground, including the entire root system.

NOTES

DECEMBER

SHRUBS

PLANNING

Plan on some new shrub additions for the full sun garden.

Red barberry, *Berberis thunbergii,* brings a long list of adjectives—bright red, yellow, deep reddish purple, zig-zag, thorns, dense, heat tolerant, long lived, and eye-catching. Each of these descriptive words focuses on some of the high points of this exceptional landscape shrub. Yellow flowers in April give way to bright red fruits in June, hidden by the thick mass of thorny twigs that lend to its appeal. In October, the brilliant colored fruits become more pronounced as the leaves fall. Use **barberry** as a focal point, hedging, or mass planting. Do not place the thorny **red barberry** near walks, entrances, or seating areas.

The **lilac,** *Syringa vulgaris,* has historical significance for almost everyone. Just about everyone had one in their own yard, in their grandmother's yard, or in the neighbors yard, and the neighborhood would be full of **lilac** fragrance in the spring. The scent would move through the air according to the direction of the winds. A thicket of limbs, persistent suckering, and salt tolerance make this a superior shrub for reducing the unwanted aspects of a street or lane. Pruning out the older larger branches at ground level keeps the **lilac** healthy and performing for many years.

PLANTING

Do not plant this month.

CARE

Find plant labels and replace as needed.

Take a shrub inventory for the end of the season, and compare it to the inventory last spring. Anyone missing?

Make a final sweep through the garden removing anything that looks out of place, debris, stakes, ties, and supports.

A 4-inch layer of mulch around shrubs will hold in moisture and protect the roots from frost.

WATERING

Monitor new installations acclimating less than one growing season for water needs. Check for wilting in the morning hours. Some shrubs wilt in the afternoon as a way to minimize moisture loss, so an early morning check should tell you the best story.

Water established plants, in location for minimum of one growing season, so that they receive 1 inch of water every seven to ten days.

FERTILIZING

Apply no fertilizers this month.

PRUNING

Make a final pruning sweep to prepare for winter. Just cut dangling or broken branches.

When taking cuttings for indoor arrangements from **holly**, **viburnum**, or **firethorn,** take care not to cut off so much that you damage the overall structure or form of the shrub. Pruning too deeply (near main trunk) exposes previously protected bark and buds, and may lead to winter wind damage.

PESTS

Hand dig weeds during the winter months.

The mole activity is slowing, but keep an eye out for new tunnels and place traps. Victor spear or choker loop types have proven most effective.

HELPFUL HINTS

Why not use these winter months to learn the botanical Latin name of shrubs. Common plant names will vary from nursery to nursery and from state to state. Learning the botanical name will help you when shopping via catalogs or in nurseries, and when visiting botanical gardens and parks. Many times, the species name (the second name in a botanical name) is descriptive (see *Month by Month in Kansas* Introduction for more complete explanation). This can help you remember the botanical name of a plant.

Common Name	*Botanical Name*	General Meaning of Species
Firethorn	*Pyracantha coccinea*	scarlet
Globe Arborvitae	*Thuja occidentalis*	western, New World
Lilac	*Syringa vulgaris*	common
Pfitzer	*Juniperus chinensis*	of China
Saint Johnswort	*Hypericum prolificum*	prolific
Sawara	*Chamaecyparis pisifera*	pea bearing
Snowball Bush	*Hydrangea arborescens*	woody
Spring Witch hazel	*Hamamelis vernalis*	of spring
Summersweet	*Clethra alnifolia*	alder leafed
Sweet spire	*Itea virginica*	from Virginia
Winged Spindle	*Euonymus alatus*	winged
Winterberry Holly	*Ilex verticillata*	circles around stem

Buying Tip: Consider **choke cherry** (*Aronia*), **spice bush** (*Calycanthus*), and **fothergilla** (*Fothergilla*). They are deciduous shrubs with multi-season qualities.

Landscape fabric is available at garden centers. Spread the fabric across a planting space to act as a weed barrier. The fabric prevents perennial weeds from penetrating from below, and retards annual weed seed germination from above. After placement, cut cross-sections, fold back flaps, and install plants. Lay a 3- to 4-inch layer of mulch over the fabric. Bear in mind that nothing is going to work 100 percent, so keep an eye out for weeds, to be on the safe side. Never use black plastic in the landscape. It suffocates the ground, leading to major bacteria and rot problems.

NOTES

CHAPTER EIGHT

TREES

Trees and their aura can be the basic building blocks of a landscape. Creating favored views, signaling what changes may be needed in a yard—theirs is a legacy in the making of pure fascination in size and splendor.

Neighborhood, town or city qualities can be dictated by the mere presence of trees. Starting from something as small as a crabapple seed or acorn the fascination grows from germination. Each new leaf or inch of height always adds to the anticipation. No matter the yard size—smaller urban, mid-sized suburban, or acres—trees will play many roles. Trees can be used for shading a walk, deck or patio, framing a structure, or unifying architecture with horticulture. With seasonal color of leaf, flower or needle, branches offer protection for birds, flower nectar for butterflies, or a living umbrella for shelter during a rain. Whipping in the wind, holding morning dew, ice, or snow crystals—a white pine, littleleaf linden or Washington hawthorn will offer a new view with each minute of every day. Maidenhair and Norway spruce native to distant lands can fill a gap and make native dogwoods and redbuds more striking in spring, summer, fall, and yes even winter. Red sunset maple, keteleeri juniper, Rosehill ash, or Donald Wyman crabapple are examples of hybrids making great trees into unbelievable ones, with great fall color, disease resistance, or consistent growth.

Flowering fringetree, aristocrat flowering pear, fruits of the serviceberry, or the improved dogwood, are some of the great ones. An added bonus with some trees is fall leaf color—making for multi-season appeal. Shade producers are black gum, red oak, and river birch, with completely different leaf densities and sunlight penetration. Between the red leaf Japanese or amur maples—redbuds can be found growing. Looking for distinctive characteristics? Try unusual bald cypress for fall needle color and drop, river birch for peeling bark, and Chinese dogwood for its number of flowers will work nicely. Evergreen white pine or keteleeri junipers are the saviors of not only winter (as perfect backdrops or screens), but also offer ornamentation with different cones/seeds hanging from limbs. As the evergreen Norway spruce ages, the branches will sweep down from the trunk and upwards at midpoint.

Do not be detoured by the fact that it may take several years before a tree begins to fulfill the landscape goal. Watching the changes is rewarding. Give time and consideration to picking the best tree for the location. Correct planting and care will make any tree part of today's landscape with only greater things to come.

INSIGHT, CULTURAL REQUIREMENTS, AND TIPS

Planting

Guidelines to consider for selection and different sizing:

1. overall height of the trees from ground to the top of the branching
2. caliper—diameter of the trunk approximately 1 foot above ground level.
3. containers (plastic or biodegradable cardboard-like) sized 1 gallon (6 inches in diameter) and up

Note: If you have balled and burlapped (field dug-root system wrapped to hold soil), or bare root (packed with no soil), check closely for amount of roots, consistent needle or leaf size, and color. Larger sizes (10 feet or more) can take longer to acclimate to a new location. Root ball should be proportional with height—approximately 3 inches of root ball diameter for every foot of height.

Timing: Availability and ground conditions that are neither frozen nor saturated are two main criteria. Deciduous (lose leaves during winter) red sunset maple, or coniferous evergreen Norway spruce will benefit from installation during dormant periods of the year (October through early March). Give time for the planting hole soil to settle around roots, and allow them to become adapted to site before temperatures and weather induce a surge of growth.

Location

1. **Exposure:** Amount of sun, surroundings—buildings, mature trees, fences, underground and overhead utilities, property line, proximity to walks, drives, patios, decks, existing garden features
2. **Soil profile:** Rocky, sandy, heavy clay, understand drainage
3. **Soil chemistry:** A soil test will indicate all is good or indicate potential problems

Installation:

1. Keep all trees (balled burlap or container) well watered in a sheltered location out of wind and direct sun to reduce stress. If holding for several days keep root balls moist. The night prior to planting, water area, soak bare root trees in water with root stimulator mix 12 hours before installing.
2. Whether a single planting or being planted among others, dig a hole for the tree that is 3 times the diameter of root ball. Depth should allow for 10-20 percent of root ball top to be above surrounding ground. Allow for settling. Rooting stimulator is optional. Prune only damaged or broken limbs (hormone at tips help trigger new root growth).
3. In new garden space remove undesirable plants by digging or using herbicide, rototiller or spade to work soil to depth of 6 to 8 feet. Blend 6 inches of organic matter (compost, leaf mold, etc.) to the existing soil and rake smooth. This will create a raised (higher than original elevation) bed.
4. If tree is from a container, remove the tree and shake off any potting soil (it loses structure and disappears outdoors), loosen roots if pot bound, place in hole, check depth of planting and adjust if needed. Back fill, firm soil, water thoroughly, mulch 3 to 4 inches directly over the root ball, preventing direct contact with bark to reduce moisture and fungus problems.
5. If tree is balled and burlapped, place in hole, water, unpin (removing nails) and fold into bottom burlap (failure can allow a wicking action, pulling moisture away from root system up to surface), back fill, firm soil, and water thoroughly. Mulch 3 to 4 inches directly over root ball to prevent direct contact with bark and reduce moisture/fungus problems.
6. If using plantable pots (high tech cardboard), after placing in hole cut or tear away the top 1/3 of pot and follow container instructions.

AFTER PLANTING CARE

Weeds: If controlling with pre- or post-emergent herbicides exercise caution, and read and follow label. Hand digging requires removal of the entire root system.

Watering: Do not allow any prolonged drought to occur as the microbes (living elements in soil) and soil structure suffers. Place hose on top at root ball and run at trickle for 2 to 3 hours, allowing moisture to penetrate deeply. Established trees need 1 inch of water every 7 to 14 days (check rain gauge). New installation should be monitored closely to prevent wilting. If wilting occurs soak entire area completely.

Fertilizing: Established trees need fertilizer to keep healthy and vigorous and resist disease or insect problems. Use deep root feeding: soak area under tree(s) the day prior, use earth auger (drill bit size 1 to 2 inches and length 1 to 2 feet), begin drilling 1/3 of the distance from trunk to the furthermost extension of the branches, make auger holes 1 foot deep and 2 feet apart in circle pattern around tree. Fill each hole with 1/2 cup of compost or low analysis (less than 5s) fertilizer at 1 pound per 1 foot of trunk diameter. Continue to beyond dripline. It's not necessary to backfill holes. Smaller or newly installed trees can be fed during the growing season beginning after the first growing season, using a technique similar to shrubs.

Mulching: The depth of mulch should never be more than 3 to 4 inches. Keep away from trunk. Adding mulch in late fall to early winter and late spring to early summer is most beneficial to the tree.

Pruning: Immediately remove damaged, diseased, or insect infested sections. Always use caution with your long handled lopper, hand pruner, pruning saw, or chain saw (extreme caution). Keep tools oiled and sharp for best cuts and to reduce fraying ends. Thin branches to allow greater light penetration through the tree and onto the ground below. The best time for pruning is during dormant periods late fall through winter while insect and disease activity is minimal (exceptions are birches, maples, and beeches, which have extreme amounts of winter sap flow, making summer pruning preferred). Winter pruning does not harm trees. There's no need to worry about sap oozing from the cuts. Consider seeking professional help from an insured and licensed arborist to either answer questions or work on any tree.

Propagation: Propogate twig or branch cuttings in late October or during winter dormancy. Select a healthy branch, make cut 6 inches from tip, angle at 45 degrees. For evergreens, strip 1/2 of needles, dip cutting into rooting hormone, and place into soilless potting mix specifically formulated for cuttings. Bury pots outdoors with top 1 inch of pot above ground surface. Water well, mulch over lightly. Cuttings left to remain in pots for 2 growing seasons allow root development for transplanting. The potential does exist for growing trees from the seeds of a white pine cone, acorn, or maple tree. See Annuals chapter regarding growing plants from seed.

Pest and Disease Control: The best approach is to first select the best tree for the location. Proper planting and maintenance of healthy trees helps them recover with minimal long term damage.

1. Positively identify source of problem, determine if currently present before taking action.
2. Practice integrated pest management (IPM).
3. When using chemicals or any fungicide, insecticide, or herbicide, read, understand and strictly follow all instructions on the label.

HELPFUL HINTS

Bark Sun Scald

Younger or smmoth-bark trees are prone to splitting of bark. The vertical splits usually occur on the south or southeast exposure. If this happens, wrap the wounded bark with tree wrap for one growing season to allow healing. Then remove the wrap and cut away any loose bark.

CHAPTER EIGHT

Trees

AESTHETIC ATTRIBUTES:

For Flighted Wildlife such as Birds, Bees, Butterfly and Moths:	Donald Wyman crabapple, fringetree, littleleaf linden, Washington hawthorn, keteleeri juniper
For Multi-Season Appeal:	Serviceberry, white pine, improved and Chinese dogwood, redbud
For Texture and Forms:	River birch, rosehill ash, red oak, Norway spruce, red sunset maple
For Versatility:	Amur maple, bald cypress, black gum, red leaf Japanese maple, maidenhair tree, aristocrat flowering pear

ADDITIONAL TREES TO CONSIDER:

Common Name	*Botanical Name*	Highlight
Alder	*Alnus glutinosa*	produces small cones
American holly	*Ilex opaca*	broadleaf evergreen
Dwarf Colorado blue spruce	*Picea pungens* 'Fat Albert'	
Franklin tree	*Franklinia alatamaha*	sporadic blooming thru summer
Golden raintree	*Koelreuteria paniculata*	yellow flowering-early summer
Hornbeam	*Carpinus betulus*	tough durable
Japanese pagodatree	*Sophora japonica*	mid-late summer blooming
Sweet bay magnolia	*Magnolia virginiana*	fragrant flowers
Silverbells	*Halesia carolina*	unique flowering
Whitespire birch	*Betula plataphylla* 'Whitespire'	bark color

KEY:

Common Name:	Location (city or town) specific
Botanical Name:	Universally recognized name
Good or Related Varieties:	Different characteristics-same care and maintenance
Height-Width:	Mature size
Height in 10 Years:	Average growth rate
Bloom Time/Color:	Season/flower color
Type:	Evergreen or foliage drop in fall
Light Requirements:	Sun-shade-for healthy growth

Common Name:	Amur maple
Botanical Name:	*Acer ginnala*
Good Variety(s):	'Compactum', 'Durand Dwarf'
Height and Width:	20 feet x 20 feet
Height in 10 Years:	10 feet
Bloom Time/Color:	-
Type:	Deciduous
Light Requirements:	Full Sun – Light Shade

Common Name:	Aristocrat flowering pear
Botanical Name:	*Pyrus calleryana* 'Aristocrat'
Good Variety(s):	'Redspire', 'Whitehouse'
Height and Width:	40 feet or more x 20 feet or more
Height in 10 Years:	20 feet
Bloom Time/Color:	Mid Spring/White
Type:	Deciduous
Light Requirements:	Full Sun

Common Name:	Bald cypress
Botanical Name:	*Taxodium distichum*
Good Variety(s):	'Shawnee Brave', 'Monarch of Illinois'
Height and Width:	50 feet x 30 feet
Height in 10 Years:	25 feet
Bloom Time/Color:	-
Type:	Deciduous Conifer
Light Requirements:	Full Sun

Common Name:	Black gum
Botanical Name:	*Nyssa sylvatica*
Good Variety(s):	-
Height and Width:	40 feet x 30 feet
Height in 10 Years:	15 feet
Bloom Time/Color:	-
Type:	Deciduous
Light Requirements:	Full Sun – Light Shade

Trees (continued)

Common Name: Chinese dogwood
Botanical Name: *Cornus kousa*
Good Variety(s): 'Milky Way', 'Moonbeam'
Height and Width: 20 feet or more x 15 feet
Height in 10 years: 15 feet
Bloom Time/Color: Late Spring/White
Type: Deciduous
Light Requirements: Full Sun – Part Shade

Common Name: Donald Wyman crabapple
Botanical Name: *Malus* 'Donald Wyman'
Good Variety(s): 'Autumn Glory', 'Beauty', 'Coral Cascade', 'Tina'
Height and Width: 20 feet x 25 feet
Height in 10 years: 15 feet
Bloom Time/Color: Spring/White
Type: Deciduous
Light Requirements: Full Sun

Common Name: Flowering dogwood
Botanical Name: *Cornus florida* 'Cherokee Princess'
Good Variety(s): 'Cherokee Chief', 'Pendula'
Height and Width: 20 feet or more x 15 feet or more
Height in 10 Years: 15 feet
Bloom Time/Color: Mid Spring/White
Type: Deciduous
Light Requirements: Part Sun – Shade

Common Name: Fringetree
Botanical Name: *Chionanthus virginicus*
Good Variety(s): -
Height and Width: 15 feet x 10 feet
Height in 10 Years: 10 feet
Bloom Time/Color: Late Spring/White
Type: Deciduous
Light Requirements: Full Sun – Part Shade

Common Name: Keteleeri juniper
Botanical Name: *Juniperus chinensis* 'Keteleeri'
Good Variety(s): -
Height and Width: 25 feet x 15 feet
Height in 10 Years: 15 feet or more
Bloom Time/Color: -
Type: Evergreen
Light Requirements: Full Sun

Common Name: Littleleaf linden
Botanical Name: *Tilia cordata*
Good Variety(s): 'Pendula Nana', 'Swedish Upright'
Height and Width: 40 feet x 30 feet
Height in 10 Years: 15 feet
Bloom Time/Color: -
Type: Deciduous
Light Requirements: Full Sun

Common Name: Maidenhair tree
Botanical Name: *Ginkgo biloba*
Good Variety(s): 'Fastigata', 'Pendula'
Height and Width: 50 feet x 40 feet
Height in 10 Years: 20 feet
Bloom Time/Color: -
Type: Deciduous
Light Requirements: Full Sun

Common Name: Norway spruce
Botanical Name: *Picea abies*
Good Variety(s): 'Pumila' or 'Repens'
Height and Width: 30 feet or more x 25 feet
Height in 10 Years: 15 feet
Bloom Time/Color: -
Type: Evergreen
Light Requirement: Full Sun

Common Name: Redbud
Botanical Name: *Cercis canadensis*
Good Variety(s): var. *alba*, 'Forest Pansy'
Height and Width: 20 feet or more x 20 feet or more
Height in 10 Years: 15 or more
Bloom Time/Color: Mid Spring/Pale Purple
Type: Deciduous
Light Requirements: Full Sun – Light Shade

Common Name: Red oak
Botanical Name: *Quercus rubra*
Good Variety(s): -
Mature and Width: 60 feet x 40 feet
Height in 10 Years: up to 15 feet
Bloom Time/Color: -
Type: Deciduous
Light Requirements: Full Sun

Common Name: Red leaf Japanese maple
Botanical Name: *Acer palmatum* 'Bloodgood'
Good Variety(s): var. 'Dissectum' 'Ever Red', 'Waterfall'
Height and Width: 20 feet x 20 feet
Height in 10 Years: 15 feet
Bloom Time/Color: -
Type: Deciduous
Light Requirements: Sun – Part Shade

Common Name: Red Sunset maple
Botanical Name: *Acer rubrum* 'Red Sunset'
Good Variety(s): 'Columnare', 'Globosum'
Height and Width: 50 feet or more x 40 feet
Height in 10 Years: 20 feet
Bloom Time/Color: -
Type: Deciduous
Light Requirements: Full Sun

Common Name: River birch
Botanical Name: *Betula nigra*
Good Variety(s): 'Heritage'
Height and Width: 50 feet or more x 40 feet
Height in 10 Years: 25 feet
Bloom Time/Color: -
Type: Deciduous
Light Requirements: Full Sun – Part Shade

Common Name: Rosehill white ash
Botanical Name: *Fraxinus americana* 'Rosehill'
Good Variety(s): 'Autumn Purple', 'Greenspire'
Height and Width: 50 feet or more x 30 feet
Height in 10 Years: 20 feet
Bloom Time/Color: -
Type: Deciduous
Light Requirements: Full Sun

Common Name: Serviceberry
Botanical Name: *Amelanchier arborea*
Good Variety(s): 'Autumn Sunset'
Height and Width: 20 feet or more x 10 feet or more
Height in 10 Years: 15 feet
Bloom Time/Color: Late Spring/White
Type: Deciduous
Light Requirements: Full Sun – Part Shade

Common Name: Washington hawthorn
Botanical Name: *Crataegus phaenopyrum*
Good Variety(s): -
Height and Width: 20 feet or m ore x 20 feet or more
Height in 10 Years: 15 feet
Bloom Time/Color: Late Spring/White
Type: Deciduous
Light Requirements: Full Sun

Common Name: White pine
Botanical Name: *Pinus strobus*
Good Variety(s): 'Pumila', 'Fastigata'
Height and Width: 40 feet x 25 feet
Height in 10 Years: 20 feet or more
Bloom Time/Color: -
Type: Evergreen
Light Requirements: Full Sun

JANUARY
TREES

PLANNING

Plan for a new tree addition that grows in full sun or part sun.

The **white pine,** *Pinus strobus,* is a majestic and graceful tree that has a pyramidal shape and animated form. Add adaptability, serviceability, and branches that are pleasing to the touch and the entire picture is painted. The **white pine** grows from a young, dense-pyramid shape to an open branched umbrella form. This evergreen grows relatively fast so its purpose and function in the landscape are realized quickly. A darker gray bark covers the trunk and bluish green needles soften parallel branches. Large pinecones form on branch tips, giving the tree a classical look. **White pines** can be pruned and sheared to control the height and spread. This ability to recover after pruning opens the possibilities for use as large screening shrubs or hedges. If a more natural look is preferred, select a specimen that is park grade or has not been sheared.

Examine and evaluate previous years' landscape photos. Consider the original purpose of the planting.

Is the **Washington hawthorn** working as a sheared hedge behind the sun perennial garden?

- Did the **Norway spruce** grow as much as anticipated in the front yard?
- Did the combination of the dense growing **amur maple** in front of the open **river birch** provide contrast to the back property line?
- Has the performance of the **kousa dogwood** in an open lawn area allowed for an understory planting of **hosta?**
- Has the privacy provided by the low branching **littleleaf linden** been great, but the bee activity a concern?
- Have the fallen needles of the **white pine** prevented any shrubs, perennials, or annuals from growing to their full potential?
- Is the bird nesting in the 'Donald Wyman' **crabapple** the highlight of spring, but the bird's seeds dropping underneath are creating a weed patch in the plantings below?

These are examples of looking at the big picture and making necessary adjustments. Take notes and plan spring actions now so you can use the winter months to prepare.

Look for winter colors, textures, shapes and forms of each of your trees and their relationships to the surroundings. The **upright keteleeri juniper** cones are uniquely blue gray. The buds along the branches of the **maidenhair tree** are a great color contrast to the bark. The fine textured, open habit of the **serviceberry** is noticeable closeup or across the yard, as opposed to the coarseness of the **Norway spruce**, that is enjoyed from a distance. **River birch** is willowy and vase shaped, as the **red oak** brings a giant balloon-like form to the landscape. Qualities change through the seasons as trees leaf out, grow, drop their needles and leaves, and conform to nature and the weather.

Attend classes offered by local garden centers, universities, or the Kansas Extension Service. Visit botanical gardens and park departments for ideas and design concepts. Attend garden club meetings for additional information.

Information is the key to good planning involving a series of steps: The initial purchase determines the size of the plants to be installed. Consider the time frame available after the purchase. Do not overbuy and allow the plants to suffer stress through exposure to environmental conditions before they are planted in the ground. Finally, plan for after planting and establishment care, and routine care and maintenance while the tree reaches its mature size.

PLANTING

Prepare bare-root trees prior to planting. Soak the rootstock in a solution of rooting hormone and water for one hour or until any dry appearing roots have begun to swell and show signs of absorption. If there are some roots that have questionable viability after soaking, notify the source of the deficit. Upon recommendations of the grower, pot up the bare-root tree, grow it on, and transplant into the garden when healthy.

CARE

To prevent stress fractures on evergreens, use a broom to gently remove any accumulation of snow that is excessively bending the **Norway spruce**. Nothing can be done about the ice buildup on the **keteleeri juniper**, so keep your fingers crossed.

Maintain 3 to 4 inches of mulch around the base of trees to buffer the fluctuating ground temperatures.

Winter windburn occurs (unexpected browning found on the north or northwest side of the plant) when the wind chill factor is below zero. Healthy plants will recover with spring growth surge.

HELPFUL HINTS

Have you seen red fruits of the **Washington hawthorn** disappearing? Local birds discovered this food source and are now taking advantage. Birds will seek nighttime protection in the evergreen branches of the **Norway spruce.**

WATERING

Monitor the rain and snowfall melt (6 to 8 inches of melted snow equals approximately 1 inch of water) during the month. If it is less than normal, pull the hoses out and water the trees. Pay special attention to evergreen trees, as evaporation and transpiration continues even during the colder months.

FERTILIZING

If the winter is mild, the areas surrounding the **fringetree** and **rosehill ash**, can be top-dressed with one-half inch of compost.

PRUNING

Remove storm damaged limbs carefully. For larger limbs or those adjacent to buildings or power lines, use the services of a professional arborist.

PESTS

Watch for small mammal (voles, chipmunks) activity showing burrowing into mulch around trees and shrubs. The bark is a source of food. Trap the pests, or pull the mulch back and wrap the base of the plant with wire screening.

During warmer days, check around newer plantings and hand dig weeds, making sure to remove entire root system.

NOTES

FEBRUARY

TREES

PLANNING

Plan for a **littleleaf linden**, *Tilia cordata,* as a new addition in a full sun location. Toughness, aesthetics, and congeniality are the traits of the **littleleaf linden**. It is a superb tree to plant and grow in larger landscapes. **Littleleaf linden** makes a good shade tree, and is exceptional as a street tree, aligning long, wide walkways, in the center meridian of parkways, or in large planters. Some situations require removal of the lower branches for access; but the **linden** takes pruning easily, which makes it useful for hedges as well. The round buds open and heart shaped, dark green leaves unroll. In early summer, white, fragrant flowers fill the air and provide nectar for the bees. The yellow fall coloration may not be considered spectacular, but still **linden** offers a rare hue later in the fall season. As the tree matures, a smooth trunk supports a dense canopy that provides ample shade. **Littleleaf linden** is one of the best large trees to plant.

During these winter months, there is time now to investigate reasons for unusual growth, plant decline, or drastic changes among trees. Decide on plans to implement changes based upon your observations. Keep graph paper handy and jot down thoughts now to help with decisions later.

PLANTING

Do not perform new bed preparation for mixed plantings of **serviceberry,** native wildflowers, and flowering shrubs. If the ground is worked when it is overly wet, air pockets form that harbor cold air and excess water. Do a probing test using a shovel, spade or trowel. Push the tool into the ground, if you hear a sucking sound, or the tool turns up a soil that sticks to the blade, it is still too wet to prepare the soil.

If the temperature is above 40 degrees, use a root stimulator to speed establishment of **Norway spruce.** Evergreen trees do best in acidic soils, so get a soil test done early in the season. The earlier the sample is sent, the quicker the results return. If you have changes to be made, you will have plenty of time before the spring planting season.

CARE

Check for early signs of bud break on trees. Take a few cuttings and bring indoors for flower or leaf forcing. Place the cutting in a vase filled with water, and set it in a warm sunny location. Depending upon the specific tree, the branch buds could open within three weeks.

Maintain up to a 3- to 4-inch layer of mulch around trees. Do not dump, spread, or pile the mulch directly adjacent to the tree trunk.

WATERING

Make sure established **black gum** or **amur maple** trees receive 1 inch of water every fourteen days. Have several rain gauges placed throughout the landscape and a few spares to replace any broken gauges.

FERTILIZING

Deciduous and evergreen trees that have been in the ground one year or longer require deep root feeding every three to four years. This practice encourages better health and vigor, enabling the trees to resist problems. The tree doesn't necessarily grow any faster, but it will be a much healthier and stronger tree.

Fertilize before the new growth emerges. Soak the area under the tree the day before the fertilizer application. Use an earth auger (with a drill bit 1 to 2 inches x 12 to 24 inches). Drill a circle of holes starting about one-third of the distance from the trunk, extending out to the end of the branches. Drill the holes 12 to 18 inches deep, and fill with one-quarter to one-half cup of organic material. The next row of circles is 2 feet further away from trunk. Use a total of 1 to 1¼ pounds of compost for every inch of tree trunk diameter. It is not necessary to back fill holes.

PRUNING

Clear out crossing, storm damaged, and pest or disease weakened branches if necessary. Never remove more than twenty-five percent of a tree's canopy. Stubbing causes weak whip-like growth that is prone to wind damage. Cut damaged or diseased branches back to healthy wood.

PESTS

Keep a weeding tool handy to enable you to dig deeply to get all the weed roots out.

HELPFUL HINTS

Use gypsum in areas that de-icer may wash into. Tree roots can be damaged by the chemical action of many de-icing products. Gypsum will neutralize and tie up the de-icers chemically to minimize root damage. The best approach is to lightly spread gypsum around the **Norway spruce** and **red oak** trees several times during the winter.

If cuttings or tree seedlings are being grown indoors under grow lights, inspect the soil surface for gray mold on the soil surface. Stir the soil very lightly and add a fan for air circulation.

Control flying insects with yellow sticky traps. If you spot webbing from spider mites, wash the individual leaves with a soap and water solution.

Pathways or small tunnels into the mulch surrounding the **redbud** could be voles or chipmunks. They may be gnawing on the tree bark (see January). In warmer weather, set out larger mousetraps with peanut butter or soft cheese to trap animals.

Give trees an application of a dormant oil spray. Dormant oil is an environmentally safe product that suffocates overwintering adult pests and the eggs.

NOTES

TREES

PLANNING

Plan for new tree additions to the landscape. Plan on using a **fringetree,** *Chionanthus virginicus,* for full sun, part sun, or part shade. **Fringetree** has multiple characteristics that include fragrance, an unusual flowering habit, and varying textures that change from fine, to medium, and to coarse during the year. Add to the list its adaptability to numerous growing conditions, and a mature size that works in all landscapes from small to large. The gray bark, in combination with the floppy, medium-green leaves spaced widely apart, create a structure that allows the cloud-like flowering habit to seemingly float among the tree branches. The openness between leaves also permits a good deal of sunlight to penetrate through and strike the plantings underneath. During fall, the green leaf coloration is replaced with a distinctive golden yellow hue. When selecting a **fringetree,** choose one with pliable limbs and numerous robust buds up and down the stems. The growth habit ranges from multi to single trunk.

The **Chinese** or **kousa dogwood,** *Cornus kousa* is the Oriental cousin of the **dogwood** found in the eastern half of the United States. A young tree can look top-heavy and out of proportion, but with age the trunk and perpendicular branches create a tree unique to individual settings. The peeling bark is earth toned and the far-reaching limbs are densely covered with dark green leaves in the spring. Unlike the native variety, the **kousa dogwood** flowering occurs after the leaves fully develop, usually in late May to early June. In late summer, berry-like fruits take the place of the flowers. Rounding out a top-notch year is the show of fall foliage that fills a vista with variations of deep reddish maroon foliage that persists for several weeks before the last leaf falls.

PLANTING

When your bare-root river birch and 'Donald Wyman' **crabapples** arrive, soak the root stock in a solution of rooting hormone and water for one hour or until any dry roots have begun to swell and show signs of absorption. Notify the vendor if there are any roots with questionable viability. You may need to pot up the sapling and grow it on to healthy size before transplanting it into the garden.

Use a root stimulator solution on trees after installation to speed up the establishment period.

Recent rains or not (stay out of wet beds), always work backwards out of a bed and loosen any compacted soil. This reduces the amount of soil compaction damage to the **serviceberry** and **redbud** roots.

CARE

Ask questions about your new trees at the garden center. Was the **dogwood** tree grown in another climatic zone? If so did the nursery take extra measures (cover plants with burlap) to minimize damage during our cold nights? Should you do the same?

Have you seen the interior needles of a **white pine** or **upright juniper** turn brown and then drop? It is a natural defoliation. The term "evergreen" does not mean leaves stay on the tree forever. On some evergreens, the leaves persist for two years or more, but they eventually shed and produce new leaves. It is a natural occurrence and happens at different times for different trees.

Apply 3 to 4 inches of mulch to newly installed and established trees. Place the mulch circling the tree at half the distance from the stems to the longest extension of the branching. Use minimal amounts adjacent to the bark.

If you are using a landscape fabric, lay it down prior to spreading mulch. If you want to install the fabric in areas previously mulched, rake the area to clear first. Do not place fabric over mulch.

HELPFUL HINTS

Have you seen major damage on the lower branches of a **crabapple** or **maidenhair tree**, as if something had scraped and frayed the bark, while mangling and breaking limbs? This is a rubbing from a male deer to mark its territory during the mating ritual. Use loppers, a pruning saw, or hand pruners and make clean, sharp, angular (45-degree angle) cuts to remove any jagged portions. Cleaning up the wounds expedites the healing process.

WATERING

Check new tree installations daily for soil moisture. If it has been windy for two weeks, you may need to water. Insure that the soil is damp to the touch and that no puddles or pools form around the tree's root crown.

Check established trees regularly and year-round for correct soil dampness.

Walking around in a wet bed compacts the soil and could have an adverse impact on drainage.

FERTILIZING

Check with garden center at time of your tree purchase to determine what their fertilizer regime has been.

PRUNING

Prune out crossing, storm damaged, and pest or disease weakened branches. Avoid stubbing of tree branches. Prune back to healthy wood.

PESTS

Check new purchases for any weeds growing on rootball. Pull before planting.

Keep up with the weeds, use herbicides (follow label rate) as needed. Apply nonselective herbicides directly onto the weed. Avoid spraying other plants.

A hard freeze (temperatures below 30) can cause newly sprouted buds of the **bald cypress** to turn brown (tree will recover) or kill the entire flower bud of the **flowering pear** tree (only aesthetic damage). The appearance is similar to fungus or rotting damage. Note the recent cold snap in your journal; this may save you from unnecessary fungicide applications next year.

Wildlife is giving birth to their young, so there is the potential of bark being torn from the base of the **red leaf Japanese maple** or **rosehill ash.** These plants are tough, but the damage from the increased population can do harm in the long run. Use all the deterrents available, wire screening wrapped around the stems or plants to act as a physical barrier, application of hot pepper sprays, and wildlife predator urine drops dotted through the area.

NOTES

APRIL

TREES

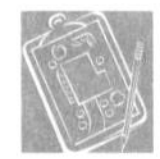

PLANNING

Plan for some new trees that thrive in full sun.

Norway spruce, *Picea abies*, is a graceful, symmetrical, pyramidal tree at maturity. For the first ten years of its life, it appears stiff and rigid with chopped qualities, but with age, the dark-green needled branches begin to turn upward on the ends, giving it an unusual form and shape. Pinecones, 4 to 6 inches long, occupy the tips. In the winter, the snow-covered tree presents a classic winter wonderland silhouette. Versatility in the world of evergreens is the byword; the **Norway spruce** serves as a specimen tree or grouped in a mass planting, provides a screening and weather barrier, and its strong scaffolding provides a bird habitat and a climbing tree for children. The growth rate is fastest in its youth if the **Norway spruce** is given the room to grow and a little care. Select a tree that has a dark green color, with flexible branches covering a straight trunk. The best acclimation and growth occurs when trees are planted when they are 3 feet to 12 feet tall.

The **red oak,** *Quercus rubra*, has all the exemplary qualities associated with the **oak** family. The **red oak** is one of the faster growing varieties. A strong and rugged trunk, covered with a bark of darker shades of brown and gray, lend timelessness to this majestic tree. The perpendicular branching pattern provides a symmetrical form. The reddish foliage unfurls in the spring, followed by the maturing, pointed, shiny, deep green leaves. In fall, the foliage turns a rich brownish red, with acorns and their caps adding another dimension. Pick a tree, 4 feet to 15 feet tall, with a strong central leader with numerous flexible branches that are fully budded. If fall leaf color is important, select the tree at that time of year.

With new ideas and plans determined, move outdoors and check previously established bedding spaces and new areas. Outline the sites using flags, ribbon, or marking paint where the **littleleaf linden** is to be planted. Then view the selected site from all angles and directions to be sure of your design decision. Pulling an established tree out of its home is not easy or fun—for you or the tree.

PLANTING

Soil compaction and an overly wet location are the worst enemies of all new plantings. Though plenty of time remains for construction of new beds or for the reworking of established beds, check the soil for wetness before any major undertaking.

Locate existing tree name tags if they have become lost during the winter or have faded. Replace the tags and hang on out-of-the-way branches. This tagging makes record keeping easier as you monitor the growth of the **amur maple** and **Washington hawthorn**.

CARE

Note the date of purchase and planting of the **redbud** and **black gum** in your journal.

Keep a close eye on any newly installed trees for their first month. Eliminate problems early. Look for insect infestations, water pooling around the tree, family pet digging, soil settling, and anything out of the ordinary.

Maintain a 3- to 4-inch layer of mulch around trees. Do not dump, spread, or pile the mulch directly adjacent to the trunk.

WATERING

Check the rain gauges, and prepare the hoses and the irrigation system to compensate for less than 1 inch of rainfall every ten days. The temperatures are warming now, so the moisture level needs to be replenished sooner.

Check new installations daily. If it has been windy, soil dries out quicker. Water to insure that soil is damp to the touch.

Walking wet garden beds causes soil to compact. This could have an adverse impact on drainage.

FERTILIZING

If trees have been in the ground less than five years, apply a root stimulator solution.

Check with the garden center when you purchase trees, regarding any previous applications of fertilizers. Ask for recommendations of what to use to fertilize the young trees.

HELPFUL HINTS

Have you seen trees planted in an area that requires continuous maintenance to make the tree conform to that site? Planting a **white pine** that has a potential of growing to 25 feet wide in a spot that is 10 feet away from a house foundation would be a poor planning choice. A **keteleeri juniper** in the same spot would be a better plan. Make your tree selections carefully. Do research prior to installation. Save on maintenance and grow a healthier tree. This allows for more fun time in the yard.

PRUNING

Prune out crossing, storm damaged, and pest or disease weakened branches. Never remove more than twenty-five percent of the tree canopy. Prune back to healthy wood. Avoid stubbing branches as it causes weak whip-like growth that is prone to wind damage and entry wounds that are prone to insect and disease infestation.

PESTS

Carry a weeding tool to remove weeds by the roots. If perennial weeds become more prominent, choose a herbicide. Read and follow label directions.

Before using any pre-emergent herbicide adjacent to a new tree installation, read the label for information regarding use around new plantings.

Insect hatching is rampant this month, bringing with it sucking, eating, and disease transmittal as well. Double and triple check for signs of pests. Take action at the first signs using physical removal or insecticidal soap or similar product.

Wildlife, adults and newborn, is everywhere. Consider diversions with a motion detector using light or irrigation devices, or physical barriers.

Control pests with integrated pest management.

Some insecticides are contact killers. Contact insecticides must be applied directly on the insects.

Put the purchase date on chemical fertilizers, pesticides, herbicides, or amendments. Do not write over application instructions. Store any liquids to prevent freezing. Safely discard any suspect chemicals and purchase quantities that can be consumed during one season.

MAY

TREES

PLANNING

Plan a new addition for the full sun exposure. **Red sunset maple,** *Acer rubrum* 'Red Sunset', is a hybrid of the native **red maple** and is considered a four-season tree. Spring brings showy, small red flowers, followed by red tinted helicopter-like seeds that twirl from the highest branch until they drift on the wind and gently land. The foliage is clear green on the top with pale undersides, and is attached to the twig with a reddish stem. The slightest wind causes leaves to shiver. The cool dense shade provided by the canopy is certainly an oasis during summer. As the temperatures drop, autumn comes alive with brilliant red leaves. 'Red Sunset' is one of the first trees to announce the harvest season. As the leaves fall to the ground, the smooth gray bark is enhanced, bringing attention to the **red sunset maple** during the winter months. This hard maple is extremely resistant to any type of storm damage, making it a tree destined for a long life.

Take a water garden class during the winter to stimulate the idea of incorporating one in your backyard. Even if you have no trees in the area, several large, mature **rosehill ash**, **red oak,** and **Norway spruce** are growing in the neighbor's yard. Before you locate a pond or any hardscape feature in your landscape, dig test holes to determine the number of roots from your neighbor's trees that may be crossing the area. The trees may or may not be affected, and the roots may impact the pool liner and cause leaking.

The above caution applies to any new garden space, whether establishing a new butterfly garden or expanding upon an existing one. Always sink a few test holes to see what is happening below the surface. This will benefit the existing **fringetree** and 'Donald Wyman' **crabapple,** as well as the new plantings.

PLANTING

Save time and wasted steps. Prepare for your scheduled work and have all the necessary tools and supplies readily available.

If several trees are to be planted, be sure to water thoroughly the night before, and water the area completely during and after installation. Place the tree into the hole at the proper depth, back fill a portion of the soil and tamp the soil around the roots. Water and allow soil to settle around the rootball. Repeat this process until the hole is filled. Thoroughly soak the rootball of the tree before moving onto the next tree. Check back on the planted trees to determine if the soil has settled and the roots exposed. Add more backfill to bring the level over the root crown. If the trees are in leaf or flower and the day is sunny or windy, cover the branching with a sheet or tarp to reduce the potential for sun scorch, and keep tree roots damp until you can plant. The best day to plant is a cloudy one with minimal wind that might reduce soil and plant moisture.

CARE

The natural process of mulch breaking down ties up several nutrients, so before replenishing with a 3 to 4 inch layer, sprinkle some low analysis (5-5-5 or less) granular fertilizer on the soil surface.

WATERING

Continue to check rain gauges, as explained in April.

FERTILIZING

Apply root stimulator to trees that have been in the ground five years or less.

PRUNING

All damaged stems, twigs, and branches should be removed. Position the cut, staying clear of the branch collar and branch bark ridge, and leave no more than 1/2 inch of the branch. Do not leave longer stubs or cut into the branch collar; both of these activities interfere with the tree's natural healing process.

PESTS

If you are considering using predatory ladybugs, praying mantis, or lacewings, there must be ample food source (pests) present or the predators will move on to other areas seeking food.

Insect (pest) adults emerge or eggs hatch depending upon the air temperature. Begin monitoring plantings as the daytime highs reach into the 50s. Some of the early arrivers are aphids and tent caterpillars. Use a stream of water or simply smash between your fingers. If insecticidal soap or a contact insecticide is used, apply the spray directly on the pests for control, and repeat applications. Contact sprays have very little residual (lasting effect).

Keep a pest identification book on hand to make correct diagnosis of the bug before you apply chemicals. Use caution when applying chemicals to young plantings. Some cause leaf scorch if the weather is sunny and warm.

Apply fungicides as a preventative measure, but only if a problematic history exists.

Use herbicides with caution. Do not apply any spray during a windy day; herbicide drift can cause burn on newly emerged foliage and can drift to nearby plants.

HELPFUL HINTS

Check all of the watering tools (hoses, sprinklers, nozzles) before they are needed, and replace any worn or damaged pieces with similar products. Ask at the garden center if there is any new equipment on the market that may save time, provide more efficient water discharge, and be more cost effective.

NOTES

PLANNING

Plan for a new addition for the full sun garden. Plan for a *Malus* 'Donald Wyman' **crabapple.** 'Donald Wyman' **crabapple** is an improved variety of **crabapple** that has springtime flower buds that begin to swell with a pale pinkish red color. Then they suddenly burst open into a pure white flower that invites pollinators. This begins the formation of the crabapple fruits. The 'Donald Wyman' vibrant red fruits grow to a mature size of less than $^{1}/_{2}$ inch, and persist through much of the winter, unless the birds discover them. A bumpy and scarred gray bark covers the trunk, with ascending branches holding onto the shimmering dark green leaves. 'Donald Wyman' **crabapple** is one best varieties with all of the aesthetic rewards, and with resistance to fungus problems. Select a tree with the spread greater than height.

Plan a new tree addition for full sun, part sun, or part shade. The **red leaf Japanese maple,** *Acer palmatum* 'Bloodgood' has few rivals that match its eye-catching appeal. Because of its smaller (up to 20 feet) size, this **maple** tree can fit anywhere in the landscape from larger pots to rural settings. The natural grace and presence is felt whether viewed in the distance or up close. Nothing diminishes the magnetism and focal point qualities. The darker color bark of the trunk and branches are virtually invisible when the tree is in leaf. However, during the winter, the large number of small twigs calls out for attention. This twiggyness adds to the overall picture when the tree is in full leaf, when the willowy branches bounce and sway softy during the slightest breeze. The beauty does not stop there. In the fall, the deep red leaf drop is mesmerizing. Some years, the foliage is held through winter and pushed off by new spring growth. The 'Bloodgood' **maple** is available in several different trunk configurations.

Plan a new tree addition for the full sun or part sun garden. The **black gum**, *Nyssa sylvatica,* is a tree that is virtually unknown to most people. Some of the unfamiliarity is because the tree silhouette of the **black gum** tree changes many times throughout its life. Sizes and shapes vary from oval and flattop, to almost pendulous and rounded. When in leaf, the foliage is darker green, elliptical shaped, and has a polished appearance. Even the casual observer will stop and wonder what the tree is. The summer foliage turns into a varied range of fall colors, from yellow to scarlet red. The fall coloration is different from tree to tree, so if you are looking for a specific color, purchase **black gum** during the fall. A consistent trait among the varied trees is the zigzag pattern of the branches as they grow out from dark tree trunk. This combination creates a striking view against a clear blue winter or early spring sky, and an even more pronounced silhouette, when the **black gum** is covered with snow. Small fruits (not sweet gum balls) appeal to birds and wildlife.

This month is the perfect time to update your garden photo journal, as the spring blooming **pear** trees and **crabapples** are forming fruits (still green), the **red leaf Japanese maple** becomes dominant, and the **white pine** and **Norway spruce** take a backseat for the next five months or so.

PLANTING

Complete all proposed plantings before midmonth to reduce summer heat and humidity trauma.

CARE

Check for all name tags on your trees. Replace faded, lost, or destroyed labels as needed.

The upcoming scorching summer heat will dry soil and influence the overall root health of trees. Mulch the trees, but allow for no more than 3 to 4 inches of mulch.

HELPFUL HINTS

To reduce expense and save time in the future, consider growing living mulch under your trees. Underplant the **bald cypress**, **red oak** or **upright keteleeri junipers** with **dead nettle** (see Ground Cover and Vine chapter) or evergreen **myrtle.**

WATERING

Generally we have summer months with adequate rainfall, but check the rain gauges and make up the difference to insure 1 inch of water every ten days for the trees. Watch trees installed this previous spring for signs of wilt. Check in the morning hours for foliage wilting on the **redbud**, **dogwood** or **serviceberry**. Wilting in the heat of the day can simply be a protection mechanism to reduce leaf surface evaporation; it is not necessarily a sign of drought. Wait and see if the tree is still wilted in the morning before supplying supplemental water. It is also best to water trees early in the day to reduce bacteria and fungus problems, and there is less evaporation.

FERTILIZING

No need to fertilize in June.

PRUNING

This is the best time of year to prune **red maples**, **beech,** and **river birch** trees.

Clear crossing, storm damaged, and pest or disease weakened branches. Do not leave stubs that can cause weak 'whip-like' growth, leaving the tree prone to wind damage. Cut back to green, healthy growth.

PESTS

Weeding must be done on newly installed **black gum**, **redbud** and **upright juniper.** Newly planted trees have the majority of new roots near surface. Keep the area clear with hand digging or cautious use of herbicides.

Check for damaging insects during early morning and evening hours, as insect activity is highest during those times. Examine the stems, tops and bottoms of leaves, and on the ground for trails (slugs and snails). Contact pesticides must be directly applied to the pest.

Mole tunnels are showing up everywhere. Set traps and move daily.

NOTES

TREES

PLANNING

Plan a new addition of the improved **dogwood,** *Cornus florida* 'Cherokee Princess' to the part sun or part shade landscape. There are several vari-eties of the **dogwood** that have been hybridized to flower at a younger age. Flowering **dogwood**s are one of the most recognized trees in the woods, parks, and landscapes. The improved variety 'Cherokee Princess' has all the temperament and structural aspects of the native **dogwood,** but shows these traits at a much younger age. This means that those wonderful, rustic and knurled trunks will be thicker and fuller much sooner, and the limbs will start setting buds for those unforgettable pure white flowers as well. Following the flower show is the medium-green summer foliage held on an open branching habit that allows filtered light to pass through. Fall coloration is varied, but is usually in tones of red. The fall leaf drop further reveals red fruits. Select a tree 4 feet to 10 feet in height, with no open wounds. Branching can start at ground level and continue to the top of the tree, or it may start anywhere along the trunk. The leaf buds have a very pointed shape.

Plan for some new full sun trees. Plan for a **maidenhair tree,** *Ginkgo biloba.* All aspects of the **ginkgo** tree with the deep bark furrows, branching habit, bud shape, and the smooth textured leaves make this an excellent choice for larger landscapes. The **maidenhair tree** has a history that is traced back to fossil and pre-historic times, which shows the durability of this great tree. Leaves pop from dark colored buds on stems growing from a light tan bark, giving an unusual contrast. The leaf has a pale gray-green color in the summer, followed by a vibrant yellow hue in the fall. A truly a unique quality occurs during the fall when the majority of the leaves drop from the tree within a one to two day period, creating a golden yellow carpet that is quick and easy to clean up.

The improved **flowering pear,** *Pyrus calleryana* 'Aristocrat' is an improvement to a very popular group of ornamental trees. It has a wider angle between the trunk and branches that reduces the chances of storm damage. The textured, dark brown bark is a perfect background for the white flowers. The foliage that emerges after flowering is shiny and dark green, and becomes very animated with the slightest breeze. The foliage changes in the fall to an unmatched maroon color, fading to a soft brown tone, sometimes persisting late into the season. Select a tree 12 feet or less in height, with a straight trunk and numerous ascending branches. The limbs should be very flexible and covered with a large number of closely positioned buds.

If a vacation takes the family out of town, the Chinese and improved **dogwood** installed in April may need supplemental watering. If your time away is longer than fourteen days, make sure the watering will be done, either with an irrigation system or by a gardening friend.

Working around trees gives relief from the intense summer sun, so schedule work in the shade of the **red oak** and **rosehill ash** between 10 a.m. to 3 p.m.

PLANTING

Unless absolutely necessary, do not plant trees in this month.

CARE

Use caution when spreading mulch this month. It can cause a heat buildup and damage the tree bark and young surface roots.

WATERING

Very humid weather reduces the amount of evaporation of water from the ground, but check the ground to determine if you need to water. Check the soil moisture by pushing a shovel down (not directly adjacent to trunk) around the tree to check if the soil is moist. If it is moist under the surface, do not water.

PESTS

Use caution when eradicating poison ivy. Check the label of any herbicide planned for use, as many will have a temperature range when they are effective, as well as a range that may lead to damage of surrounding plants.

Knowing what the weeds are will help you determine the controls to use.

Broadleaf weeds with fat multibranched veins are annual (live one year and drop seeds for future plants) or perennial (returns from the root system after a period of dormancy). Perennial weeds colonize by underground offshoots of the mother plant, and they also reproduce and colonize other areas by dispersing seeds. Examples of broadleaf weeds are dandelions, violets, chickweed, and spurge.

Grass weeds have skinny narrow leaves with the veins running parallel to the leaf margin. Grasses are annual or perennial, and colonize by underground modified roots (tillers) or seeds. Examples include crabgrass, wild onions and garlic, and goose grass.

Sedges are weeds resembling narrow bladed grass plants, but they have a triangular stem that emerges from the ground. Sedges have similar qualities of broadleaf and grass plants. A perennial sedge spreads seeds both under and above ground, and also has a root system that will tiller to colonize other spaces. Nutgrass or nutsedge is the most common example.

Identify any pests and determine if the population warrants the use of insecticides or the release of predatory insects. Watch for spider mites and aphids.

HELPFUL HINTS

Established **red leaf Japanese maple**, **littleleaf linden**, and **dogwood** all have foliage edges that appear as if sunburnt, the leaves are brown with crispy margins. This summer occurrence is simply due to the inability of the tree to uptake enough water to offset the heat of the sun. If trees appear healthy, do nothing.

NOTES

TREES

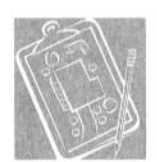

PLANNING

Plan some new tree additions for full sun and part sun gardens.

The **river birch,** *Betula nigra,* lives in habitats ranging from river bottoms and low lying flood plains to dry rocky bluffs. This wide range indicates how versatile this tree is, but it is best known for its wet soil tolerance. Add to the durability the notable feature of pale brown bark that peals from the trunk on any branch larger than 2 inches in diameter. The **river birch** has much more to offer larger landscape settings with its bold architectural and structural features. Most often it is sold as a multitrunk tree. The river birch has open and fine textured branching with spacing between the leaves allowing for filtered light to strike the ground adjacent to the trunk. This sunlight is adequate enough to support numerous types of plants, making it user friendly. In the spring, the male catkins hang and bounce in the slightest breeze. Look for good spacing between the trunks, a lot of twigs, and heavily budded or leafed.

The **bald cypress,** *Taxodium distichum,* is native to the lowlands and is truly a swamp dweller. But this is only one use, as a drier landscape scenario works just fine too. The tall straight trunk is supported in wetter areas by an unusual root growth called "knees". Fine textured needles, yellow-green in color during the growing season, appear to almost rust on the tree just prior to dropping in the fall. As the needles fall, the parallel branching and cinnamon colored bark comes into view. Powdery blue cones hang from the branches in the winter, providing a nice visual surprise over and over again. The **bald cypress** really needs a larger landscape area to fully mature.

PLANTING

Select cooler days to work in the garden areas that are scheduled for expansion, for newly created beds, or for additional bedding spaces. All areas would benefit from working the soil ahead of time. This allows for any amendments to blend and much of the soil settling to take place. Do this prep work now, and remove a considerable amount of work pressure in the fall.

Though still hot, the days are shorter and nights are beginning to cool. This fact, in conjunction with new plant materials arriving at the garden centers, make for a great chance to add a few **black gum**s to the tree line.

Take 6-inch stem cuttings where the old (brown) twig transitions to new (green) growth. Remove any foliage or needles from the bottom 3 inches. Dip cut end into rooting hormone, and place into a growing mix formulated for starting seeds or cuttings. Place the pot under grow lights or sink it into the ground or cold frame, protected from direct sun or wind. Water to keep cutting soil damp, but not wet. Allow a minimum of four to six months to pass before checking on the quantity of root hairs. To check, gently tilt the pot so that the cutting and potting mix sides out, if one-half of the pot is filled with roots, it is ready for planting out. If the root mass is not adequate, return it to the pot, water, and apply root stimulator. Check every three months for development.

CARE

Watch compaction in areas when you work around the **amur maple** and **white pine** if they have been planted within the previous five years. Churn up any soils in areas where you have worked.

Maintain a 3 to 4 inch layer of mulch. Do not dump, spread, and pile mulch adjacent to the tree trunk causing extra moisture retention and potential bark rot.

WATERING

Check the soil moisture prior to irrigating. Do not use automatic timers at this time of year. Overwatering could result in rot or fungus problems for the **Norway spruce** or **redbud**. Take a shovel and dig down 6 inches or more to check for moisture. If the soil is moist, do not water. Or squeeze a handful of dirt into a ball, and if the ball breaks down or crumbles, then water.

Morning is the best time to check for any wilting. If the leaves of the improved **dogwood** or 'Donald Wyman' **crabapple** are droopy, this likely indicates dry soil. However, if water is standing, there has been root damage, and the tree wilts as a result. To check soil wetness, follow the above procedure.

PESTS

Growth activity of summer weeds is at peak level, so herbicides will be extremely effective. Use caution and do not allow any herbicide to drift and come in contact with leaves on the lower branches of the **littleleaf linden** and **upright juniper**.

HELPFUL HINTS

If you see unusual amounts of odd looking mushrooms, fungus, or similar growth popping up in the mulch in various locations, this growth is caused by the decomposition of the mulch and will continue until the source of food for the fungal growth is exhausted. No action is recommended. Simply allow nature to take its course.

NOTES

SEPTEMBER

TREES

PLANNING

Plan for a **redbud,** *Cercis canadensis,* addition to the full sun, part sun, or part shade landscape.

The redbud has an extremely open habit and a very dark gray trunk with cinnamon red-orange fissures. A twisting and turning growth habit makes the branches and trunk look older than they are. In spring, another unexpected quality greets us with crimson blossoms with a color that is unequaled in nature. Leaf buds open in a pale purple hue until the heart-shaped leaf unfurls in a moderate shade of green. Though the fall color is nothing to rave about, the dark brown pea pods dangle in spots previously occupied by the flowers. The **redbud** is a single or multi-trunked tree that has a sparse and open branching habit with zigzag patterning. Put this all together and the **redbud** makes a very strong and uncommon landscape statement.

The spring and summer surge of growth is over; it is time to take note of what has happened with the collection of trees during the past months. Did any birds nest in the **Washington hawthorn** and how far above the ground was the nest? How much did the new **Norway spruce** grow in height? Have any of the famous "knees" of the **bald cypress** made a showing at ground surface? Are changes needed this fall or is the status quo quite good? This time spent evaluating the trees allows for better planning for the future.

Fall brings gentle rains that soak in. The ground temperature is the warmest of the year to promote new root growth, and your gardening time is generally less intense as opposed to the spring rush. This will allow your trees to acclimate before going dormant for the winter.

PLANTING

Have planting locations ready before the arrival of new trees. Pre-digging enables an almost straight-into-the-hole scenario.

Take 6-inch stem cuttings where the old (brown) twig transitions to new (green) growth. Remove any foliage from the bottom 3 inches and dip cut end into rooting hormone before placing into growing mix. Place the pot under grow lights, or sink into the ground or cold frame out of direct sun or wind. Keep damp and check for root development at 4 to 6 months.

Add to the fall color by planting **pansies, ornamental cabbage** and **kale**, or **red leaf lettuce** from seed in pots and place for accent under **maidenhair** and **red oak** trees. Plants in pots are easier for cleaning away fallen leaves, they are mobile, and will be more prominent in the fall landscape.

CARE

Triggered by the shorter days and cool nights, the perennials, annuals and shrubs shift into the slower pace mode. Fall cleanup begins as the foliage of deciduous **rosehill ash**, **fringe tree,** and **river birch** begins to fall in large amounts. Now the long forgotten twigs and branches are exposed for enjoyment. Examine the deciduous trees carefully for anything out of the ordinary, lumps on the stems, unusual twisted growth, and less than rigid stem structure. Determine if any problem needs attention, removal of a **red oak** lower branch that is overshadowed and losing vigor or maybe the same thing is happening to a **white pine**.

Work up the soil in woodland planting beds near the **Japanese maple** and **Chinese dogwood** in anticipation of adding spring flowering bulbs or simply to reduce soil compaction. Fall rains will penetrate the ground easier and fill below surface air pockets, reducing root system damage from cold air.

Do not re-apply mulch, allowing the depth to diminish. The soil surface benefits from the added air circulation and direct sunlight.

WATERING

During periods of cooler and overcast skies, an additional seven days can be added to the time frame reference. However, do not allow the soil to dry out, as the microbes (living elements in soil) and soil structure suffers and this impacts plant growth.

Check new installations daily if it is windy for two weeks. Water to insure that the soil is damp to the touch and do not allow puddles to form.

Walking around in beds compacts the soil and could have an adverse impact on drainage.

FERTILIZING

Check with the garden center at the time of purchase for any previous applications of any fertilizers. Ask for information on when to apply fertilizers and what to apply.

HELPFUL HINTS

Daffodils, grape hyacinth, and **crocus** bulbs are available at the garden centers. So while out looking for the best **serviceberry** and **redbud** trees to add in the front landscape, why not pick up some bulbs? The ground is going to be dug for planting the trees; and an additional few minutes of soil preparation adds magic to the spring.

PRUNING

Do not prune spring flowering varieties. This eliminates buds along stems that are next year's flowers.

PESTS

Annual winter weed seeds (henbit, chickweed) are germinating; and others seem to suddenly appear. Apply a pre-emergent (kills all seeds at time of germination) herbicide. Herbicide application to weeds actively growing is partially effective this time of year, as the plant metabolism is slowing in preparation for winter. Hand digging with a weeding tool always works, as long as the entire root system is removed.

Insect damage season is mostly over, but keep all plant debris picked up to eliminate overwintering egg or adult sites.

NOTES

OCTOBER

TREES

PLANNING

Plan a new tree for the full or part sun landscape. Plan for a **Washington hawthorn,** *Crataegus phaenopyrum* 'Washington'. The **Washington hawthorn** has broken out of the pack and should be considered for use in many landscape scenarios. Before the leaves appear in the spring, these single or multitrunk trees appear somewhat scary with their 1 to 2 inch thorns standing out among the leaf and flower buds. Then the arrival of spring brings leaf buds popping open and a rugged softness becomes the dominant feature. Several months later, in early June, white flower clusters appear with bees as constant visitors. These pollinators turn the flowers into bunches of red-colored fruits that become a prominent feature by mid- to late September. Fall foliage ranges from yellow-orange to red, with each year's tone determined by the fall weather. Nothing compares to a **hawthorn** during a snow with its dark pitted bark against the white vista. Uses include a free-standing specimen plant, grove or colony, or as a screen or barrier. **Hawthorns** will take a considerable amount of pruning.

Plan a new tree addition for full sun. The **upright keteleeri juniper,** *Juniperus chinensis* 'Keteleeri' is a member of a huge grouping of plants with close relatives found throughout the world. There are almost limitless names and types of growth habits, ranging from very flat, to tall and vertical, as the **keteleeri** is. The varieties native to China are the best plants to incorporate into today's landscape as they have disease resistance. The **keteleeri** strikes a commanding pose with its teardrop shape and branches flowing to the ground. This habit makes this **juniper** an excellent year-round candidate for a larger hedging and screening situation, or as a stand-alone evergreen. The dense, short, shiny spike-like green needles conceal the trunk and interior structure entirely. Small brown male and bluish female cones are produced each year. Select a plant with no dead patches and an obvious pointed top. Check that there are no bagworm sacks on the tree.

Colorful fruits are equal to the seasonal change of the leaves. Take photos from a distance and closeup; use these pictures to determine that the fruits are prominent enough to be considered an aesthetic plus or winter food for the birds. **Chinese dogwood** will have shiny red fruits; a red-orange fruit appears on the **Washington hawthorn**; and the **upright juniper** female cones are small clumps of blue. Note if fruits disappear or shrivel on the plants as the season progresses.

PLANTING

Purchase of a **red oak** or **littleleaf linden** can be made, but have an idea in mind for a course of action if the planting is to be more than one day after the tree's arrival. Protect the trees from sun and wind damage, and keep watered during any storage period. To water, place hose on top of rootball, and trickle the water until rootball is soaked. If the trees are going to be stored in their containers for an extended period of time (seven days or more), place some mulch around the trees for better protection.

Balled-and-burlapped trees remaining above ground for more than one to two days before planting benefit from being clustered in close proximity (allow light and air circulation), and covered with a layer of mulch to protect rootballs from drying out.

CARE

Autumn brings **amur maple** and **river birch** leaf drop. It is a good reminder to check out the other aspects of the landscape. Fence sections or a bench that was partially covered during the growing season, artwork, pergola, or the trellis could require repairs or replacement.

Rake or mow over fallen leaves on a regular basis. Large accumulations of fallen leaves under the trees will be difficult to move.

Maintain a 3- to 4-inch layer of mulch. Do not dump, spread, and pile mulch next to tree trunks. This leads to moisture retention around the trunk and potential bark rot.

WATERING

Monitor new installations closely while they are acclimating (less than one growing season). Water if the plants are wilted in the morning.

Established trees in a location for a minimum of one growing season should receive 1 inch of water every seven to ten days.

HELPFUL HINTS

The **black gum** or **serviceberry** leaves that are raked and piled up are a perfect component in the compost pile. **Red oak** leaves or the needles of the **white pine** are acidic and very slow to decompose, so their use is limited. When composting, remember to layer plant debris with other materials to insure proper blending. A good compost pile will have noticeable steam rising during cooler temperatures.

FERTILIZING

Apply no fertilizers this month.

PRUNING

Do not allow previously cut branches to remain on the ground surrounding the tree. Cut branches may contain or harbor insects, eggs, and diseases over the winter, only to cause problems the following spring.

Do not prune spring flowering trees; this eliminates the buds along stems that produce next year's blooms.

Prune out crossing branches, storm-damaged branches, and pest or disease weakened limbs. Do not leave stubs that cause whiplike growth prone to wind damage. Cut back limbs to healthy green growth.

PESTS

Controlling weeds with herbicides is becoming ineffective as the weed plants slow down and into winter dormancy. Hand weeding is the best defense. Remove the entire root system.

Shorter days and cooler temperatures cause wildlife to sense the impending cold. Chipmunks and voles are looking for nooks and crannies. Squirrels are planting, digging, and gnawing (an essential function to keep their lower teeth from getting too long). Deer are more than likely deep in the woods, where there is plenty to eat—be grateful.

Landscape fabric (plastic, woven, or burlap) is available at garden centers for weed control. After installing a tree, cut a circular piece (1 foot wider than tree planting hole); slit the material halfway through to install around the tree. Cover the fabric with 3 to 4 inches of mulch.

NOVEMBER

TREES

PLANNING

Plan for a **serviceberry**, *Amelanchier arborea*, addition to the part sun, part shade, and full shade garden.

Many times **serviceberry** is mistaken for the **dogwood**, although the **serviceberry** blooms a month earlier than its better-known woodland neighbor. Found in many valleys and along tree lines of the Midwest, the **serviceberry** bends and conforms to larger areas and to small niches among more substantial shade trees. **Serviceberry** white flowers dot a landscape when very little else is occurring among the woody plants, and the flowers chime the end of winter in the landscape. The subsequent red rose-hip-like fruits are edible by humans and, of course, the birds make quick work of them. Fall brings an array of leaf colors, ranging from yellow to red. Pointed flower buds are found along somewhat frail looking limbs.

Take black-and-white photos for design orientated information for *your journal*. Black-and-white photos eliminate distractions from the spectacular fall color of the **black gum** or **Chinese dogwood,** and clearly illustrate the function and purpose of a single or group planting.

Birds add to the outdoors, so make sure the feeders and birdbaths are kept full.

PLANTING

All tools should be cleaned and sharpened. Add a light application of oil to reduce rusting during winter.

Before purchasing trees, inspect the plants for consistent leaf color and size; check the amount of roots, the stem flexibility, and the number of buds on dormant trees.

For steps to follow for tree installation, see Basic Guidelines at the beginning of this chapter.

CARE

Trees in the ground for less than two years suffer problems from soil compaction that prevents water absorption and root development. If you are working around young trees, try to stay outside of the branch (drip line) area.

Rain this month causes the final **dogwood** leaves or needles of the **bald cypress** to drop. This is a reminder to check the drainage patterns. Is there a change from the previous year or from what is expected? Have gutters become full of **red sunset maple** leaves or are the **flowering pear tree** leaves causing water to cascade over the top?

Examine any new beds or plantings for settling, shifting, or erosion.

WATERING

White pine, **upright keteleeri juniper**, and **Norway spruce** are evergreens and will suffer damage during a winter drought, so keep a hose or bucket available to supplement water.

Winterize the in-ground irrigation system, and if outside faucets are not frost proof, turn them off indoors.

Drain sprinklers and hoses, and store out of the weather to prevent freeze damage.

Check soil moisture daily on new tree installations. If there has been wind during the past two weeks, check the soil often. Maintain a damp soil, but do not allow water to puddle.

FERTILIZING

It is too early to begin deep root feeding. Inventory fertilizers and make sure that they are stored correctly so that no moisture will come in contact with the bags. Evaluate last year's fertilizer program, and determine if any changes will need to be made to fertilizer applications this year.

Prepare the hose-end attachment for applying water-soluble fertilizers. It must be cleaned thoroughly to insure correct calibration and application next year.

PRUNING

Do no pruning this month.

Newly installed trees, whether **fringetree** or **maidenhair** tree, require spring pruning to control growth and to shape a strong structural framework. The hand pruner is the most important tool; one with scissors-cutting action is best. This type makes a cleaner cut and allows for quicker wound healing. If your hand is stressed after working just a short time, the pruner may be too large. Spread your hand out, open the pruner and lay it on your hand. The handles should not have a wider spread than the space from your finger to thumb tip. If this is the case, consider purchasing a smaller size.

PESTS

Hand weed this month. Be sure to pull the entire weed, including the root system. The cooler weather makes herbicides ineffective.

Proper storage of dry and liquid products minimizes losses. Note the shelf life (effective period), and properly discard any expired materials. Contact the Kansas Department of Health and Environment for disposal instructions. Additionally, storage of chemicals is crucial as the chemistry may be altered during the course of cold weather. Settling and hardening can occur if the package is open to humidity.

HELPFUL HINTS

Ground covers, such as **wintercreeper, English ivy,** and **Boston ivy** growing on the trunks of the 'Donald Wyman' **crabapple**, **red oak,** or **bald cypress** doesn't present problems, unless the ground cover growth climbs into the trees and begins to shade out branching and budding areas. This relationship of trees and ground cover adds texture and an unexpected quality to any landscape.

NOTES

DECEMBER

TREES

PLANNING

Add a tree that will grow in the full sun, part sun, and part shade.

The **amur maple**, *Acer tataricum,* is a smaller tree with a dynamic growth habit and visual qualities. The framework is naturally round, with shiny small leaves that are trident in shape, unlike most **maples**. Equally unusual is the springtime fragrant flowers, followed by smaller winged fruits. In the fall, the color ranges the full spectrum, from golden yellow to a pure clear red. The individual tree can have single or multiple trunks. The **amur maple** is a tree for everywhere, from a single plant in the front lawn, to working equally as well planted as a small grove. If a particular fall color is important, choose the **amur maple** when in full fall show.

Plan a new addition for the full sun landscape. Plan for a **rosehill white ash**, *Fraxinus americana* 'Rosehill'. A few years after installation, the **rosehill white ash** makes its presence felt. The faster growing habit does not indicate that it will mature into a soft wooded tree. **Rosehill ash** is an improved variety of the **white ash,** with a unique bark that has a diamond patterning in varied shades of gray. Darker green foliage, with more vibrancy during the summer, is truly a plus. Cooler fall temperatures turns green into a reddish gold; and this variety will not produce the seeds associated with **ash** trees. A smaller stature allows for use in the residual landscape. Add a tolerance for poorer alkaline soils, and you have a tree that allows for its use in many tough locations.

PLANTING

Tree installation tips are available at the beginning of this chapter in Basic Guidelines.

Pine (cones) seed, and **oak** (acorns) seed should be allowed to darken and start to split before collecting for storage, for sowing in a prepared bed space in the landscape, or to grow indoors under grow lights. The growing medium should be formulated specifically for plant propagation. Place potted seeds under grow lights or in a protected (out of direct sun and wind) locale. Keep mix damp until germination.

CARE

Replace and rewrite plant labels.

Have the birds been spending the night in the **upright keteleeri juniper**? Add a birdfeeder and bath nearby.

Walk through the entire landscape and remove debris, stakes, ties, and supports.

Multitrunk **flowering pear,** low-branched **littleleaf linden,** and large, older **rosehill ash** that have a narrow angle between each major section of the trunk system may need cabled. The practice actually ties branches together with metal roping (cables) to minimize movement or structural stress to individual parts during windstorms. This sort of specialized work should be done by a licensed arborist.

Maintain a maximum of 3 to 4 inches of mulch around trees. Do not dump, spread, and pile the mulch adjacent to trunks. This leads to added moisture retention and potential bark rot.

WATERING

All container trees must be kept watered and out of direct sun and wind until they are planted. Balled-and-burlapped trees above ground for more than 1 to 2 days benefit from being clustered in close proximity (allow light and air circulation), and mulched to protect the rootball from drying.

Closely monitor new tree installations that have been acclimating less than one growing season. Water if the trees are wilted in the morning hours.

Established trees, in a location for no more than one growing season, should receive 1 inch of water every seven to ten days.

HELPFUL HINTS

Use these winter months to learn botanical names of trees. The second part of the botanical name (official) is the species. Many times this word is descriptive. (See *Month by Month in Kansas* Introduction for a more complete explanation.) Knowing the botanical names assists you with plant identification and signage in catalogs, nurseries, parks, and botanical gardens.

Common Name	*Botanical Name*	General Meaning of Species
Bald cypress	*Taxodium distichum*	vertical positions
Black gum	*Nyssa sylvatica*	forest dwelling
Fringe Tree	*Chionanthus virginicus*	from Virginia
Improved dogwood	*Cornus florida*	flowering freely
Littleleaf linden	*Tilia cordata*	heart shaped
Redbud	*Cercis canadensis*	from Canada
Red leaf Japanese maple	*Acer palmatum*	lobed leaves
Red oak	*Quercus rubra*	red
Red Sunset maple	*Acer rubrum*	red
River birch	*Betula nigra*	black
Serviceberry	*Amelanchier arborea*	tree-like
Upright keteleeri juniper	*Juniperus chinensis*	from China
White ash	*Fraxinus americana*	from America
White pine	*Pinus strobus*	coneflowers

FERTILIZING

Deep root feeding for all trees is best done after the deciduous trees drop their leaves. For trees that have been planted one year or more, deep root fertilize every three to four years to encourage better health, vigor, and stronger resistance to disease. Soak the area under the trees the day prior to application. Using an earth auger (bit size—2 inches x 12 to 24 inches), drill holes in a circular pattern, starting about one-third of the distance from the trunk to ends of the branches. Drill holes 12 to 18 inches deep, and fill with one-quarter to one-half cup of organic material. Drill the next row 2 feet further away from trunk. Use a very low analysis fertilizer at 1 to 1.25 pounds per inch of trunk diameter. It is not necessary to back fill holes.

PRUNING

No pruning should be done on **birch**, **beech**, or **maple** trees during the winter. Pruning causes excessive sap flow and could weaken trees. Prune these trees during the summer months. On other trees, prune crossing, storm damaged, and pest or disease weakened branches. Do not leave a stub, and make cuts back to healthy green growth.

PESTS

Many small mammals such as voles, chipmunks, and field mice use mole tunnels during the winter. Root damage by any animal causes increased plant stress. Although mole activity is slowing, keep an eye out for new tunnels and place traps (Victor Spear or choker loop types) as needed.

Hand dig weeds when the ground is not frozen.

CHAPTER NINE

WATER GARDENS

"Unique" and "rewarding" are not enough words to describe the feeling achieved when working to create and maintain a successful water garden. Potential combinations are nothing short of phenomenal.

Create a guaranteed focal point in the landscape. If it's your first time, start small. Adding on is easier than you think. If you make your water gardening too big and it's not well cared for, it can become a mess.

The Kansas natural environment provides great insight into the broad band of possibilities—whether you're a casual observer or a knowledgeable well seasoned water garden lover. Mother Nature has put together water and gardens and plants with just about everything covered. Start with cold clear bubbling springs erupting from rock hillsides splashing below into dark pools, then consider ancient sink holes abundant with rare or endangered plants and wildlife. Think of slow moving rivers where vegetation holds the banks in place despite the sudden gush of storm water out of a normally calm creek. Rainfall or melted snow miles uphill roars across jagged rocks turning them into smooth skipping stones. Water gardens provide cascading springs and quiet pools, formal or informal qualities for sitting at night or looking into during the day.

Layers of stone can be laid so all the grain (just like wood) flows parallel to build a small waterfall that spills into a pool surrounded by cardinal flowers and midget cattails. On the far side where the water barely ripples, a pot of hardy dwarf waterlilies blooms and blooms. A troublesome lower area in the landscape suddenly becomes a focal point where the weedy lawn was covered with pea gravel. The next step can be edging with Japanese iris, and then each summer tropical elephant ears, bog/spider lilies and red stemmed cannas that were wintered over in the basement can be planted, giving the appearance of an exotic faraway sand bar. Sparkling, shimmering, water gardens offer a respite for thirsty butterflies, moths, and birds, allowing for a really close-up look. Water gardens, regardless of the style or location, are places of contemplation, and build character into every yard. Getting started in the right direction will eliminate many frustrations and problems.

Consequently, it is recommended this entire chapter be reviewed and any addition, subtraction, location, and relocation to or from any existing or new water garden. Kansas's climate and outdoor change is a constant. Remember many crucial and critical chores overlap, and until a rhythm is established you should review, review, and oh yes, review. The end result will be a happy water garden and a happier water gardener.

UNDERSTANDING AQUATIC PLANTS

The common element of water connects this varied group together, however their heritage, habitats and subsequent cultural requirements can be as extremely different as their terrestrial counterparts. In other words, hybridized midget cattail cannot survive among a stand of a taller growing, more aggressive corkscrew rush, though each grows along the water's edge or in a bog area. Remember, you might not be able to enjoy waterlilies if

CHAPTER NINE

HELPFUL HINTS

Basic Water Garden Guidelines

Designing a water garden into a landscape is complicated, and with any project of this size, the ideas tend to outgrow the spaces. Installing a water garden into a home landscape creates a beautiful naturalistic scene, but it is in a somewhat less than sympathetic scenario. As any idea comes to fruition, it is under the initial stress of the continually changing weather. Influences of adults, children, and pets add further challenges. Into the mix, add the predatory visits by creatures from subterranean (moles, voles, chipmunks, grubs) depths, and the airborne visitors (aphids, weed seeds, birds, including acrobatic squirrels). The demands are great, but the rewards are tremendous. Eventually, those well-planned ideas fit quite nicely into garden spaces.

What inspires you? The first step is to recognize the catalyst point. What was it that spurred the decision to build a water garden? Was it a picture in a magazine, a visit to the botanical garden, watching a home and garden television show, spotting a water garden on a garden tour, or just looking over the fence into your neighbor's yard? Evaluate the water garden that caught your eye. Take note of the style, the purpose it served in the garden, and the water garden's relationship to other landscape and structural components. All of these elements are crucial to reach the desired end product—the enjoyment of your own water garden. Use the observations from the water garden that inspired you, and develop your own space by borrowing and perfecting those ideas. The goal is to create intensity, drama, and tranquility—and to avoid anxiety, mistakes, and chaos.

they are too close. They could release hydrogen sulfide with natural foliage breakdown, which does not smell nice. The water chemistry can spill beyond the actual pool and into the surroundings. Taro should have an alkaline pH, but marsh fern prefers more acidic soil. The nutrient level of the water, resulting from an individual plant fertilizing or simply the breakdown of debris, can make the aquatic mint invasive, while in a similar rich environment the cardinal flower will limp along. Basic considerations are needed for compiling a wish list. Does the plant match the home? Is the garden in sun or shade? Is the water still or moving? Any information collected will make the final choice a better one.

FOUR MAJOR AQUATIC PLANT CATEGORIES

Free floating water lettuce drifts around, pushed by water movement (wind, fountain, falls) and tends to collect in one location. The less movement the better. If you're purchasing water lettuce, 2 to 3 inches diameter is the minimum. Smaller plants will begin to shrink and disappear immediately. Ideal circumstances could still require several purchases each summer. Both marsh fern and water aloe free floaters will add to water surface excitement.

Watch and remove free-floating duckweed, a miniature 3-leaf cluster (clover-like configuration) with small white roots dangling below. It can be a nuisance; its self-propagation is unbelievable.

With surface floating foliage, anchored in shallow water, the royalty of all water gardens is water lilies, hardy and tropical, whose root/tuber needs to be planted in a very heavy clay/potting soil mixture (not soilless mix). Placement of the tuber is very similar to that of the iris (flags). The eyes (growth points) are comparable to those of a potato. Water hyacinth foliage is upright, making it a good complement.

Note: water hyacinth will flower infrequently unless sitting in approximately 1 inch of water, with its roots in contact with a nutrient rich soil. Both have stringent requirements (see informational plant listing) for reaching your desired goals.

Oxygenators are an essential part of any garden with fish; they exchange gases, create shade/temperature and set the underwater environmental tempo. Some are hardy like the coontail and pondweed (flowers stick above water surface) while others like anacharis/water thyme is not. Effectiveness requires approximately $^1/_3$ of fish pool volume to be filled.

Margin/bog/emergent plants are fundamental to smooth transitions to and from an informal water garden setting. Versatile dwarf or other lotus, and red stemmed water canna need direct constant moisture (on water's edge). The carnivorous pitcher plant can be placed in a low, detached, bog-like space. Across the yard can sit elephant ear, with variegated sweet flag as its under planting.

PLANNING YOUR WATER GARDEN

Formal water gardens will be symmetrical or give that impression, created by using pronounced and severe outlines, with a minimal variety of materials anywhere in, out, and near its surroundings.

Informal water gardens will be have a more free-flowing, easy outline, and an almost unlimited number and variety of plants and materials that are somewhat open to personal tastes. Remember, the garden can lose its impact when you try to do everything you've ever dreamed of all at once. You will be rewarded by practicing some restraint.

Patience will be needed as there may be possible disillusionment or disappointment during the establishment period or the first few seasons. Water gardens bring together plants, fish, and water, for an animated combination creating a distinctive microclimate of enjoyment. Formulated pre-packaged gardens, or those developed over time will need time to acclimate. Adjustments may be needed from your original concepts, and will be continuous.

GENERAL REQUIREMENTS AND TIPS

Keeping all plants labeled is extremely beneficial in making needed evaluations. (It may require a label stuck in the ground).

Think of neighbors when siting a water garden. Make sure it's 100% properly constructed and maintained, or it can have an impact real or imagined that is not to their liking (such as having an odor, or attracting mosquitoes, frogs, flies, wasps, etc.).

Soil preparation can vary for each of the four major plant categories. Use organic soil for tropical or non-hardy plants (rooted in pots or containers), fertilizing monthly through the growing season. Native or naturalized plants feed once a year (late spring).

Growing water plants from seed is a considerable task, whether indoors under lights or outdoors sown directly into the garden. Professionally grown plants are available at garden centers, and via the internet.

Equipment needed includes pumps, a filtration system, a liner, plumbing, electrical equipment, a skimmer net, lighting, etc. from local garden centers or mail order. Prior to making any purchase have specifics or a roughed out idea of what your plans are. Will electricity be needed for pumps, fountains, or waterfalls? Consider the water volume for a proper filter and liner size. Time spent in preparation on can pay back 10 fold in minimizing hassles, headaches, and returns.

If you want fish, you'll need 5 to 6 gallons of water per roughly 1 inch of fish length (a 6-inch koi needs 30 gallons). Ten 1-inch fantail goldfish fit a half whiskey barrel tub garden. Feed with fish pellets in measured amounts. The quantity given per feeding should be eaten within a minute or two.

Uneaten pellets sink to the bottom, decompose, and stimulate algae blooms that green the water.

SITING AND INSTALLATION

Surface tree roots or overhanging branches near a water garden will cause grief, puncturing the liner, or dropping debris.

Cut sod and/or remove all surface vegetation and rooting systems.

When removing soil, keep in mind to initially take less soil than you think you should, then fine tune as needed. More soil can be removed, but replacement (backfilling) at the same compaction level and contour it had before is difficult.

When you reach your approximate planting depth, start checking the sides and bottom of the hole for anything out of place. Be aware of utility lines, buried construction debris, rocks, and broken glass.

Enjoy! Updated ideas and reasonable prices have made it so that anyone with an interest can have a water garden.

Water Gardens

AESTHETIC ATTRIBUTES:

For Bright Flowers with Extended Bloom Periods and/or Unique Seed Heads:	cardinal flower, dwarf lotus, water canna, dwarf hardy waterlilies
For Foliage Color or Unusual Leaf Shape/Growth:	arrowhead, bulrush (umbrella palm), corkscrew rush, horsetail, parrot's feather, pickerel rush, pitcher plant, water poppy
For Texture and Forms:	bog lily, coontail, elephant ear, lizard tail, marsh fern, midget cattail, water hyacinth, water lettuce, anacharis
For Fragrances: (Leaf or Flower)	aquatic mint, Japanese iris, variegated sweet flag

Note: For winter storage non-hardy varieties, see amaryllis in bulb chapter

KEY:

Common Name:	Location (city or town) specific
Botanical Name:	Universally recognized name
Additional Variety:	Different characteristics-same care and maintenance
Height:	Mature size
Habit:	Silhouette – growth
Color:	Flower or foliage
Hardy:	Withstand winter outdoors
Light Requirements:	Sun – shade – for healthy growth
When to Plant Outdoors:	Best Season
Where to Plant:	Exact location
Highlight:	Distinctive characteristic

Common Name:	Anacharis, water thyme
Botanical Name:	*Elodea densa*
Habit:	Sprawling, at and under water surface
Flower Color:	Pale green
Hardy:	No
Light Requirements:	Full sun – part shade
When to Plant Outdoors:	Early summer
Where to Plant:	Non-specific, drop into water
Highlight:	Usually used In aquariums, serves as an oxygenator

Common Name:	Aquatic mint
Botanical Name:	*Mentha aquatica*
Height:	Up to 3 feet
Habit:	Mounded
Flower Color:	Purple
Hardy:	Yes
Light Requirements:	Full sun – part shade
When to Plant Outdoors:	Late spring thru mid summer
Where to Plant:	Bog – lower wet area, not in water, in pot to control invasiveness
Highlight:	Foliage strongly fragrant

Water Gardens (continued)

Common Name: Arrowhead
Botanical Name: *Saggitaria* sp.
Additional Variety: *ruminoides* (red Stem)
Height: 3 feet or more
Habit: Upright
Flower Color: Green / White
Hardy: Yes
Light Requirements: Sun – part shade
When to Plant Outdoors: Spring
Where to Plant: Margin, water depth to 1 inch
Highlight: Very tropical looking, appearance philodendron-like (houseplant)

Common Name: Bog lily, spider lily
Botanical Name: *Crinum bulbisperium* var. Album
Additional Variety: Roseum
Height: Up to 3 feet
Habit: Upright – vase
Flower Color: White
Hardy: No
Light Requirements: Bright, no direct sun-11:00 – 3:00
When to Plant Outdoors: Potted plant, move outdoors in late spring
Where to Plant: Margin with water depth to 6 inches
Highlight: Focal point – strap-shaped leaf with extraordinary petal

Common Name: Bulrush, paper reed, umbrella palm
Botanical Name: *Cyperus alternafolius*
Additional Variety(s) *isocladus* (dwarf) – papyrus
Height: Up to 5 feet
Habit: Upright
Flower Color: Brownish
Hardy: No
Light Requirements: Full sun – light shade
When to Plant Outdoors: Potted houseplant, move outdoors in late spring
Where to Plant: Margin with water depth to 6 inches
Highlight: Visually unusual

Common Name: Cardinal flower
Botanical Name: *Lobelia cardinalis*
Additional Variety: *siphilitica* (different species)
Height: Up to 3 feet
Habit: Upright
Flower Color: Red
Hardy: Yes, native
Light Requirements: Full sun – part shade
When to Plant Outdoors: Spring or fall
Where to Plant: Water's edge
Highlight: Striking late summer bloomer, attracts hummingbirds

Common Name: Coontail, hornwort
Botanical Name: *Ceratophyllum demersum*
Habit: Sprawling, at and under water surface
Hardy: Yes
Light Requirements: Full sun – part shade
When to Plant Outdoors: Late spring
Where to Plant: Non-specific, drop into water
Highlight: Very animated with water movement, used In aquariums

Common Name: Corkscrew rush
Botanical Name: *Juncus effusus* var. Spiralis
Additional Variety: *Zebrinus*
Height: Up to 6 feet
Habit: Upright
Flower Color: Yellowish green
Hardy: Yes
Light Requirements: Full sun
When to Plant Outdoors: Late spring thru mid summer
Where to Plant: Margin with water depth to 6 inches
Highlight: Unusual twisting leaf

Common Name: Dwarf lotus
Botanical Name: *Nelumbo lutea* var. Skirokunshi
Additional Variety(s): 'Baby Doll', 'Charles Thomas'
Height: Up to 2 feet
Habit: Weeping, upright
Flower Color: White
Hardy: Yes
Light Requirements: Full sun – light shade
When to Plant Outdoors: Spring
Where to Plant: Margin, water depth to 6 inches, can be potted
Highlight: Very unusual flower shape and seed pods

Common Name: Elephant's ear, taro
Botanical Name: *Colocasia esculenta*
Additional Variety: Fontanesia (purple veined)
Height: 3 feet or more
Habit: Arching
Hardy: No
Light Requirements: Full sun– shade

When to Plant Outdoors: Late spring to early summer
Where to Plant: Margin, not in water, 2 to 3 inches below soil surface
Highlight: Phenomenal leaf size and growth each year

Common Name: Horsetail
Botanical Name: *Equisetum hyemale*
Height: Up to 3 feet
Habit: Upright
Hardy: Yes
Light Requirements: Part shade – shade
When to Plant Outdoors: Spring or fall
Where to Plant: Bog, woodland setting
Highlight: Very primitive plant, is fern ally-producing spores

Common Name: Japanese iris
Botanical Name: *Iris ensata* var. Innocence
Additional Variety: Variegata (striped leaf)
Height: 3 feet or more
Habit: Upright
Flower Color: White
Hardy: Yes
Light Requirements: Full sun – part shade
When to Plant Outdoors: Spring or fall
Where to Plant: Margin, water depth to 6 inches
Highlight: Tremendous showing, foliages/flower, many varieties available

Common Name: Lizard's tail
Botanical Name: *Saururus cernuus*
Height: Up to 3 feet
Habit: Upright – branching
Flower Color: White
Hardy: Yes
Light Requirements: Full sun – light shade
When to Plant Outdoors: Late spring to early summer
Where to Plant: Margin, water depth to 6 inches
Highlight: Fragrant flowers

Common Name: Marsh fern
Botanical Name: *Thelypteris palustris*
Height: 1 to 2 feet
Habit: Mounded
Hardy: Yes
Light Requirements: Part shade – shade
When to Plant Outdoors: Spring
Where to Plant: Margin – moist, no long periods of standing water
Highlight: Creeping rhizomes, allows for naturalizing

Common Name: Midget cattail
Botanical Name: *Typha minima*
Additional Variety: *angustifolia* (narrow leaf)
Height: 2 feet
Habit: Upright
Flower Color: Brownish
Hardy: Yes
Light Requirements: Full sun
When to Plant Outdoors: Spring or fall
Where to Plant: Margin, water depth to 6 inches, can be potted
Highlight: True dwarf, less invasive due to hybridizing

Common Name: Parrot's feather
Botanical Name: *Myriophyllum aquatica*
Habit: Sprawling, below water surface
Hardy: No
Light Requirements: Full sun – part shade
When to Plant Outdoors: Late spring to early summer
Where to Plant: Non-specific, drop into water
Highlight: Submerged oxygenators, foliage 4 inches above surface, good texture

Common Name: Pickerel rush
Botanical Name: *Pontederia cordata*
Additional Variety: *azurea* (blue-flowered sp.)
Height: Up to 4 feet
Habit: Upright
Flower Color: Purple
Hardy: Yes
Light Requirements: Full sun – light shade
When to Plant Outdoors: Late spring to early summer
Where to Plant: Margin, water depth 6 inches
Highlight: Showy spikes of multiple flowers attract butterflies

Common Name: Pitcher plant
Botanical Name: *Sarracenea purpurea*
Additional Variety: *flava* (this species not hardy)
Height: 3 inches or more
Habit: Basal
Flower Color: Greenish / white
Hardy: Yes with protection
Light Requirements: Protection from direct sun 11:00 – 2:00
When to Plant Outdoors: Early summer
Where to Plant: Margin, not In water, keep potted, move to protection in fall
Highlight: Carnivorous plant, conversation piece, kids love them

Water Gardens (continued)

Common Name: Red-stemmed water canna
Botanical Name: *Thalia geniculata*
Height: 5 feet
Habit: Upright
Flower Color: Purple
Hardy: No
Light Requirements: Full Sun
When to Plant Outdoors: Late Spring to Early Summer
Where to Plant: Margin, up to 1 inch water
Highlight: Large bracts with reddish purple undersides

Common Name: Variegated sweet flag
Botanical Name: *Acorus calamus* var. Variegata
Additional Variety: *gramineus* var. Variegatus (white striped leaf)
Height: 2 to 3 feet
Habit: Upright, spreading
Flower Color: Greenish
Hardy: Yes
Light Requirements: Part sun – part shade
When to Plant Outdoors: Spring or fall
Where to Plant: Margin, no standing water
Highlight: Yellow-striped foliage and fragrant unusual shaped flower

Common Name: Water hyacinth
Botanical Name: *Eichorinia crassipes*
Additional Variety: var. Major (rosy lilac flower color)
Height: 6 inches
Habit: Floating on surface
Flower Color: Blue
Hardy: No
Light Requirements: Full sun
When to Plant Outdoors: Early summer
Where to Plant: Margin, water depth less than 1 foot
Highlight: Distinctive appearance, drifts according to water movement

Common Name: Water lettuce
Botanical Name: *Pistia statiotes*
Height: 3 to 4 inches
Habit: Floating on surface
Hardy: No
Light Requirements: Full sun – light shade
When to Plant Outdoors: Early summer
Where to Plant: Margin, where root system is in contact with soil
Highlight: cup and saucer-like appearance

Common Name: Water lily
Botanical Name: *Nymphea odorata*
Additional Variety(s): Numerous, tropical, night blooming, red-striped foliage, dwarf
Habit: Foliage floats on surface
Flower Color: White
Hardy: Yes and no
Light Requirements: Full sun
When to Plant Outdoors: Late spring to early summer
Where to Plant: Water depth to 1 inch, with root system in soil
Highlight: True champions, regardless of specific variety or type

Common Name: Water poppy
Botanical Name: *Hydrocleys nymphoides*
Habit: Surface, floating leaf
Flowers Color: Yellow
Hardy: No
Light Requirements: Full sun
When to Plant Outdoors: Late spring to early summer
Where to Plant: Margin, root system must be in contact with soil
Highlight: Ease of cultivation, cluster of flowers followed by seed capsule

HELPFUL HINTS

C.O.N.N.E.C.T.O.R.S.

C Concepts: perceived reasons and observations create the interest that leads to defining the purpose of having a water garden in your home.

O Orchestration: a blending of the water garden with the architecture of the setting has a ripple effect on existing plants and buildings.

N Necessities: the requirements to complete the picture are determined by the environmental exposure and the demands for privacy.

N Notability: the location must have appeal from daytime to nighttime, and from season to season, and it must be attractive from all viewpoints, inside and out.

E Elements: components needed and the percentage they play in the whole, and their relationship to each other, determines the construction materials (rocks, concrete, wood deck, trellis, fencing).

C Configuration: the site evaluation of hills, slopes, wet or dry locations, sun, shade and seasonal changes, and the relationship to the topography for the area to be developed and to those remaining status quo.

T Tightness: refers to the budget allowance that will establish priorities, and employ a simple process to implement the plan as funds allow.

O Ornamentation: allows for changes and for including other interests (container gardens, birds and butterflies, landscape lighting).

R Re-evaluations: occur frequently as plans are updated and stages are completed. Re-visit and review anticipated perceptions and the status of progress towards the goals, time and materials already invested, and projected ongoing maintenance for the garden.

S Safety: a realistic analysis of garden visitor comings and goings, security of rocks, boulders, waterfalls, and surfaces, and the effects of plant growth rate on the features.

NOTES

JANUARY
WATER GARDENS

PLANNING

Check for websites, classes, and meetings of the local water gardening society. Any combination of these can only make understanding, appreciation, and success a bit easier to reach. If you are heading out of Kansas for a respite to a warmer climate, make some pre-departure phone calls and do some research related to botanical gardens, public parks with aquatic displays, retail nurseries, and even shopping malls with water features. In this competitive world, there are horticultural experiences everywhere.

Organize photos and information gathered from previous years.

Mail order catalogs and gardening magazines offer information on specific plant varieties and give comparative advantages of one variety over another. Information is available relating to cultural tips, spacing, care of the dwarf or full size **lotus** and their design impact, and reasons why **water lettuce** seems to get smaller everyday.

Purchase a new tabletop fountain to add subtle tranquility to the indoors during the winter months. The small indoor water feature is an orientation into the joys of water gardening.

Take a walk around the landscape, and let your imagination go. Consider turning the low wet area in the landscape into a bog garden. Research the types and aesthetics of plants that will survive in such a place. Take what nature has given you, and enhance the enjoyment.

If you are lucky enough to live near a retail nursery with a year-round specialty section of tropical aquatics, stop by for an imaginary trip south of the equator.

Water gardening suppliers are a huge source of information, not only for the beginner, but also for all levels of gardeners. Visit a supplier to see new pumps, planters for **water lilies**, pipes, valves, and innovative lighting techniques that are constantly being developed.

PLANTING

Take cuttings or divisions from tropical plants (if aquarium space is available) this month.

Pull out and divide the dormant **bog lilies**, cut off and propagate the **taro** side shoots, and split the **bulrush**, discarding the dead reeds.

A high organic content is essential for growing aquatic plants in pots or containers, and there must be drainage holes to allow for passage of water and oxygen to the root systems. This is crucial for success.

CARE

Harmful gases can build under a sheet of ice in the water garden outdoors. Check it routinely, and keep a hole open for ventilation. Never break the ice with heavy blows that may send harmful shock waves to the fish. Prevent an ice sheet from forming or reoccurring, and place a floating object in water, or use a pool heater.

Inspect the netting (placed over the pond surface in the fall) to minimize the amount of leaf, twig, and stem remains from falling into water; if a large mass sits on top, it may cause the net to sag into the water, negating the purpose. Pull the net, and empty it before the buildup occurs.

Check on any equipment left outdoors for winter damage from freeze/thaw cycle; take action if needed to prevent any further damage. Perform any routine maintenance now to reduce the spring rush.

Inspect all tubers, bulbs, roots, and rhizomes for signs of bruises or soft spots. Discard any severely damaged bulbs. Cut out small damaged areas and separate them from other bulbs. Bulbs are recovered if they show signs of callus.

Plants under grow lights should be receiving at least eight hours of light per day.

WATERING

Do not allow the soil to dry out entirely. Maintain a water depth to allow the **water hyacinth** to float with the root system just touching the soil.

FERTILIZING

If overwintered **anacharis** look undernourished and abnormally pale, a very light application of water-soluble fertilizer could help, however the fertilizer may trigger an algae bloom.

PRUNING

Cut back and remove all remaining leaves on the **Japanese iris**.

HELPFUL HINTS

When planning or designing a water garden, use a dark material for the bottom and sides to maximize the mirror-like quality the shimmering surface provides, and the dark coloration gives a much greater sense of depth. Lighter colors are reflective, giving the water a transparent and unnatural appearance.

PESTS

Various wildlife could cause problems in the outdoor water garden. In mild winter temperatures, the fish may stay active, and are prime candidates for roving raccoons.

Algae growing on the surface of overwintering plants are not harmful, except aesthetically.

Check the entire foliage surfaces for any signs of insects or the eggs. If you are unsure of what something is, isolate the plant, and keep an eye on it. Take a sample to the garden nursery for a diagnosis and treatment. If it is a severe problem that may affect other plants, don't hesitate to get rid of the plant.

If you see deer or other animal tracks heading to the pool and emerging on the opposite side, check the pond liner for water level drop. The hooves could have punctured the liner; repairs require pumping out the water and patching the holes.

NOTES

WATER GARDENS

PLANNING

When planning the outdoor water garden, simpler is better. Avoid trying to duplicate the public garden waterfall or nursery ponds. They are configured to maximize all features in a single space.

Beware of specially priced, overstocked deals where you end up with combinations of ten hardy and tropical **water lilies** ('Pink Star' to violet purple 'Director Moore', ending with 'Red Flare'), plus twenty submerged plants that you don't have room for in the already full water garden. If you really must have the plants, you have the option of planning and digging a second pond.

If you are designing a pool for the first time, or making some changes to an existing one, consider adding 3 to 6 inches to the depth, allowing for a rock or gravel bottom. This type of lining provides an entirely different impact, and works with either formal or informal designs.

Subsurface design is extremely important. The use of contours in depth, and ledges for seating potted **paper reed,** smooth transitions from one depth to the next, allows for the added opportunity to incorporate **pickerel weed**, fish, snails, and the necessary equipment (pumps, lighting) without the pond looking cluttered.

If you are planning on having fish in the pond, they require a depth of two or more feet for winter survival, as well as an opening if the water freezes over.

Plants only have a real impact for six months (dispersed **midget cattail** seedheads or frozen **horsetail** stems leave a bit to be desired.) out of the year. Therefore, other structural considerations (shape, location, stone and rock embellishments) are crucial.

Smaller pools, with a depth of less than 15 inches, have potentially more problems with algae blooms. The same problems arise in ponds that are deeper than 3 feet. Algae blooms are related to water temperature fluctuations.

In-ground ponds with an overhang of stone make for a smooth transition into the surroundings. During the growing season, bog or margin plants do this.

Fountains (formal multi-tiered or informal spray head) have a difficult time blending with plant material. Several varieties of plants, such as surface floating **water celery** and its variegated hybrid, are beaten and battered by too much water activity (including waterfalls).

The number and diversity of aquatic plants that can be grown indoors is impressive. Convert the under-utilized workbench in the basement or an area in the solarium into a tropical oasis. Lighting is crucial. Use both incandescent and florescent lights to insure a maximum light band. Another option is using a multi-tiered mobile flora cart, available on websites or in catalogs. The ultimate dream is an attached greenhouse, offering a respite from winter doldrums. Contact a local franchised dealer or contractor with experience in construction of greenhouses for an evaluation of plumbing, electrical, and other essentials.

PLANTING

Winter stored, bare-root **bog lily** and **taro** can be potted this month. Empty potted plants onto a table and have a look at the roots. If everything appears okay, then place the plant back into the same container using fresh potting mixture, including sand, to insure a well-drained growing medium. If there are any signs of fungus, rotting, or bruising, cut out the bad section, dust with sulfur, let it air heal, or discard the plant if it is too far gone.

Check notes and photos from previous years to determine if the hardy 'White Sultan' or 'Pink Sunrise' **water lily**, and the dwarf, double pink 'Momo Botan' **lotus** appear to have smaller leaves than last year. If so, it is time to dig up the tuber, inspect, and divide. Plan to dig, inspect, and divide every three to five years.

CARE

If an extended period of cold is predicted, and prior to major freezing temperatures, decrease the pond water level by 1 to 2 inches, either by siphoning or by baling out the water. The air bubbles offer an expansion joint of sorts that can prevent damage caused by an expanding ice sheet to a PVC or fiberglass lining.

Increase the grow light time by one hour.

WATERING

Don't allow bog plantings of **arrowhead** or **horsetail** to suffer during dry periods in the winter. Also, the roots of plants in the ground for less than two years may be adversely impacted. On warmer days, soak the ground thoroughly. Have no qualms about hooking up a hose, and allowing the water to trickle out for an hour or two.

Watch all containers indoors for evaporation, and refill.

HELPFUL HINTS

Consider adding **marsh marigold** (*Caltha palustis*), **meadow sweet** (*Filipendula ulmaria*) or **cardinal flowers** (*Lobelia cardinalis*), to the garden area, as these plants are not liked by grazing deer.

FERTILIZING

Continue to fertilize plants growing indoors, including the **parrot's feather**, **red stemmed water canna,** and even the cuttings of the **aquatic mint** taken last October. Use a very light application, at one-fourth the label rate.

PRUNING

Remove any browning foliage on aquatics grown indoors. Dead tissue could set off bacteria, virus, or fungal outbreaks.

PESTS

If wildlife are problematic eating plants, going after the fish, or disturbing bed spaces, consider installing a motion detector/ sprinkler device (movement triggers the sprinkler and startles the pest). The device should not be used if temperatures are below freezing. Give some thought in determining the best configuration.

Watch for mole activity. Normally their time is spent in a lower tunnel system, but with the arrival of warmer weather, the area near a water garden can be easy digging, so take action with traps. Mole tunnels could channel storm water directly at the pool, causing undermining that leads to liner stress or collapse.

NOTES

MARCH

WATER GARDENS

PLANNING

Before digging anywhere, have the local utility company come out and locate any underground lines you should be aware of.

The addition of any water related landscape feature changes the entire perspective and visual priorities of the area; it becomes the focal point up to 90 percent of the time.

Never locate any pool or water feature at the lowest point of the yard. This placement allows the possibility of undermining and lifting the liner, preformed pond, or the concrete basin. A rainy spring or fall season can cause overflow. If you must place the pond in this location, design a swale, or build a drainage system to move the water away from the feature.

Water movement (fountains, waterfalls, bubblers) keeps temperatures balanced, and disperses oxygen and nutrients through the water environment.

A bog garden makes a great transitional from a water feature to the rest of the landscape. It can serve as a problem solver for those always-too-wet areas, and a bog garden makes a beautiful focal point. To build a bog garden:

- Dig the basin according to the type of plantings selected. The depth should be 1 to 2 feet. If the bog garden is positioned next to a pond, make sure that the bog components will not leak or seep into the water feature.
- To determine the quantity of underlining material, calculate the entire square footage, and double that measurement. Fold the lining in half, and make any necessary adjustments to cover the entire area. If the bog is associated with the water feature, be sure the folded edge is adjacent to the water feature. This creates a stronger barrier to prevent mingling of garden components. Then puncture drainage holes in the liner bottom.
- Backfill with a rich, organic mixture composed of compost, peat moss, leaf mold, and good topsoil.
- Irrigate until soil blend is uniformly wet.
- Install plantings. Water the plants in, and correct any plant shifting or leaning.

Select bog plants from the following list.

- Hardy perennials: **turtlehead** (*Chelone lyonii*), **snakeroot** (*Cimicifuga racemosa*), **meadow sweet** (*Filipendula ulmaria*), **forget-me-not** (*Myosotis scorpiodes*), **butterbur** (*Petasites hybridus*)
- Nonhardy tropicals: ***coleus** (*Plectranthus*), **calla lily** (*Zantedeschia aethiopica*)
- Shrubs: **cinquefoil** (*Potentilla fruticosa*), **snowball** (*Hydrangea macrophylla*) and **golden elderberry** (*Sambucus canadensis* 'Aurea')

PLANTING

Keep sand damp on tropical **water lilies,** yellow 'Aviator Pring' (day bloomer) or white 'Missouri' (night bloomer) stored in traction sand in jars for winter. There should be no standing water in the bottom of the jar. Dump a portion of the sand out, and look for growth. The "eyes" should be obvious and indicate active growth. They are ready for potting outdoors later. To hold them indoors, place the pot in a tub filled with water to half the height of the pot.

Plant hardy **water lilies**; apricot colored 'Clyde Ikins', 'Red Dwarf', or full sized orange 'Ozark Queen'. You will need a **water lily** basket, or a container with adequate drainage holes, ten or more quarts of good heavy clay garden soil (do not use commercial soilless potting mixes), two **water lily** fertilizer tablets, and pea gravel. Fill one-third of the container bottom with pea gravel, place fertilizer tablets, and add clay soil to fill one-half of the pot. Position the tuber so that two-thirds of the tuber is below the soil surface. Gently back fill and pack the soil; checking to make sure the eyes (growing point) are not below the soil level. Thoroughly water to settle any air pockets, allow to sit and settle further. Leave 1 inch of space between the top of the tuber and the pot rim. Fill this gap with pea gravel.

Placement in a pool depends upon the size and type of the plant. Larger growing varieties sit 12 to 18 inches below the water surface; position dwarf varieties 6 to 12 inches below the surface.

If you are planting the tropical night-blooming red 'H.C. Haarstick' **lily** or a white 'Juno' **lily**, the procedure is basically the same. The difference is that the tropical **lily** is more of a traditional bulb, and it sits on top of the soil surrounded by pea gravel, with the roots down into the clay soil.

CARE

You may find fish visible on warm days, do not feed them yet. You may start to see some new growth on the margin or bog plants.

Log the water temperature in your journal. Use this information to establish a correlation between the water temperature and **water lily** growth.

HELPFUL HINTS

The **horsetail** stems can be used for polishing metals; **arrowhead** and **elephant's ear** (poi) roots can be eaten and are cultivated in the Orient; **bulrush** is used to make paper by soaking the pith from the stalks in water and then pressing them together.

Increase run time by one hour on the grow lights.

You may notice the hardy margin/bog plants appear to be dead in the middle. This is no cause for alarm. It is the natural clump growth that allows plants to continue moving into less nutrient depleted soils for survivability.

WATERING

Plants growing under lights indoors should be showing good bud formation. It is important these plants do not experience any totally dry period. Such a circumstance could set the plant back after months of nurturing.

FERTILIZING

Apply a very light application of water-soluble fertilizer to all plants under grow lights.

PRUNING

Prune out any weak leaves and stems that materialize. Cut off and throw out, whether indoors or out.

Remove any new growth that is frost damaged, the decaying plant material could harbor problems.

PESTS

Check for gnats and aphids.

The spread of bacteria, fungus, and diseases can suddenly show up with no previous signs. Keep an eye open and examine plants frequently.

Winter is ending and the food sources are depleted. Wildlife could be checking out the garden for any fresh vegetation, new foliage on the **Japanese iris**, **aquatic mint**, **water lily**, and **lotus**.

WATER GARDENS

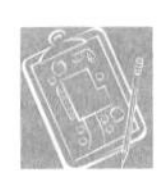

PLANNING

Plan a cobble fountain as an underground source of audio enjoyment.

• Select a nonporous tub, large enough to hold a submersible pump.

• Dig a hole and line it with sand. Place the tub, and backfill around the edges.

• Position the pump, hook in to an electric source, and add a spray head, long enough to remain above the projected surface.

• Use a piece of liner to seal the tub and to keep any eroding soil from getting into the tub.

• Place strong wire hardware mesh over the tub.

• Add your favorite rocks or stones to cover the wire.

• Turn on the water. As it shoots up, it splashes back onto the rocks, spilling into the tub below, where it is recycled back through the system.

PLANTING

Before starting a planting project, have all essential tools and supplies within reach. You will need new or cleaned pots, a sharp knife to make divisions, a shovel and trowel, potting soil (see March) for containers, or inground bed space.

Whether just beginning a new venue or working in an established garden, do not pull out plants from beds, unpack from shipping boxes, or remove **bulrush** or **pickerel rush** from pots, unless the task can be completed. Disruption of plants is stress enough, regardless of the season, but if projected transplanting is suspended, the damage to the plant is magnified.

Plants that get hefty and outgrow the container or location can be lifted and divided.

CARE

A total water garden renovation takes three or more years, involves the removal of all fish and aquatic plant materials, draining the water, and making necessary repairs to the containment materials.

To clean a pool or pond:

• The air temperature should be between 45 and 70 degrees.

• Assemble a holding tank, aquarium, or clean plastic trash can for the fish, a stiff brush, a pump with tubing or hose, bucket, fish net, and additional netting to cover the holding tank.

• Set the holding tank in a shaded area. Place a small pump in the bottom to circulate air, and fill the tank with water from the pond.

• Remove any animal life from the pond, put into holding tank, and cover the tank.

• Pump or bale out the water. Discharge water in your landscape, do not discharge water into the neighbor's yard.

• Remove the plants, but leave them in the pots. Cover with wet burlap or newspaper.

• Scrub the bottom of the pond with a brush, and flush with clean water. Do not scrub the sides; the beneficial algae should remain. Rinse, and bale out excess water.

• If the pool uses a pump and filter system, clean it, or replace worn out pump.

• Fill the pool, and either allow it to sit for 24 hours, or add chemicals to reduce the chlorine content.

• Prepare the fish being reintroduced by placing in a plastic bag filled with old pond water; seal with an air bubble. Place the bag into the new pool, allowing it to float for one hour to acclimate fish to the temperature and prevent shock.

• Repot plants if needed, and reposition.

Warmer days offer the chance to start the acclimation of overwintered plants to the outside. Place plants out of direct sun, in tubs or containers filled halfway with water, at a similar temperature to that in the indoor growing space. Do not place plants in cold water that can shock plants.

Increase grow lights by one hour.

FERTILIZING

Apply a very light application of water-soluble fertilizer to all plants under grow lights.

PRUNING

There is no need to prune this month. Prune out unhealthy growth only.

PESTS

If the water does not have movement (falls, fountain), no fish are present, and the weather is warm, midges, gnats, and mosquito wigglers more than likely are showing up. Drop a safe, naturally occurring bacteria into the water for control. The garden center should carry this product.

HELPFUL HINTS

Crystal clear water is desirable in a formal reflecting garden. If fish are to be introduced, they will not survive, as the chemistry and water profile are out of balance.

Algae bloom may occur. The less action taken, the better. Allowing it to cycle, die, and settle to the bottom is the course of least resistance. Other techniques for control include application of algaecides (generally copper based) or the use of a mechanical filter, either a modular type (sits in water) or drum (sits out of the water) type.

There are two types of mechanical filters. In a modular type, the water is drawn into inlets, and passes through a series of pads that are embedded with cleaning bacteria. The pads are flushed or discarded and replaced regularly. The pool water volume determines the pump size and filtration capacity.

In a drum filter, the water is pumped from the bottom of the pool, and is pushed to the top lid. The water trickles down through the pads (gravity fed), and through granulated material that contains beneficial microbes for cleaning. The pads and granulate are removed and replaced as needed. A drum filter size and filtration capacity is also determined by the volume of pond water.

There is an increase in population of pests that may require physical barriers and motion detector/lighting or irrigation mechanisms to reduce damage.

NOTES

MAY

WATER GARDENS

PLANNING

Plan the construction of a water garden using a poly liner or a similar product.

• Purchase materials manufactured for water gardens at the garden center.

• This sort of liner pond fits within informal and formal design styles, but almost always takes on the informal look.

• Mark the shape of the pond on the site with marking paint, rope, or hose. Avoid any abrupt curves or narrow inlets. Consider the arcs and lines of the pond, in terms of digging, building, and structural integrity.

• Site and check the basin perimeter, making sure it is level at all points.

• Measure the pool bottom length and width for total square footage. Add one-third to one-half more to compensate for sides, ledges, and necessary folding to shape the liner. Do not undersize the liner. The additional cost may be substantial, but it is important to have one solid piece. Gluing two pieces of liner together can be done, but there is more chance of leaks.

• Use peat moss, sand, multiple layers of wet newspaper, or carpet padding to line the hole before liner is placed.

• Spread stretchable liner across the hole and pull taut, anchor the liner all the way around on the top edge, using small weights such as bricks or 1-pound bags of sand. You may need to get into the hole to physically push and pull the liner over and around contours.

• Place the hose in the center of the liner, and turn water on at a slow flow. As the liner begins to sag because of the water weight, it conforms to the hole.

• Stay at the site throughout the entire filling process. As the pond fills, gently pull on liner to reduce wrinkling. It may be necessary to fold sections on top of one another.

• Fill pond to within a few inches of the top rim.

• Allow the pond to settle for one week. During this time, add neutralizing chemicals.

• After settling is complete, trim excess liner from the rim edge. Leave approximately 8 inches of overlap to serve as an anchor, and to reduce surface undermining.

• The remaining flap is either buried under soil, or used as an underlining for stone coping.

Visit a nearby park, retail garden nursery, or flower show to look at different types of aquatic oriented displays.

PLANTING

Water and soil temperatures are warming this month, stimulating surges of growth in plants and algae.

Slim down the **aquatic mint**, **midget cattail**, and **lizard's tail** if they are overgrowing their spaces. Share the divisions with members of the local water garden club or friends.

Tropical **bog lily**, **paper reed**, and **red stemmed water canna** are ready to plant this month. Prepare a location for in-ground installation or prepare containers.

Divide hardy margin/bog plants every two to three years. Discard older parts in the plant center and retain younger vigorous segments on the plant perimeter. Divide tropicals every one to two years, just prior to bringing outdoors in late May.

CARE

Maintain moisture on plants being moved from the indoors out, and on recent purchases. Do not allow plants to sit in the direct sun without adequate soil moisture.

Minimize any action in the pond while repositioning or moving plants. Avoid stirring up the water and creating extended cloudiness.

If an algaecide was applied to the pool when the water was dirty and murky, (either due to improper planting, erosion, or an excess of decaying organic materials) and nothing happens, the algaecide is bound up. Wait for the water to clear and settle before applying the algaecide.

FERTILIZING

No fertilizing needed this month.

PRUNING

Remove troubled leaves, seedheads, or pods that have formed on the **dwarf lotus.** Use in arrangements. Stems and leaves of horsetail and corkscrew rush highlight seasonal centerpieces.

Oxygenating **coontail** can occupy up to one-half of the water volume, but one-third coverage is preferred. Lift out and prune errant growth, or snap off sections to control size.

HELPFUL HINTS

If fish are part of the water garden, their nutrient and vitamin needs change from spring to autumn, with summer being their most active season. Purchase food accordingly.

PESTS

Watch for traditional gnats, midges, and mosquitoes that are always associated with water. Also watch for other typical plant trouble makers, such as aphids, leafminers, leafhoppers, and spider mites. Always turn the leaves over to check for pests.

Marsh fern and **pitcher plant** leaves are burned due to leaf scorch. If the discoloration smears when rubbed, it could leave smut, caused by fungus and bacteria. It is best to discard the plant for the benefit of the remaining water garden.

Cardinal flower, **midget cattail**, and **Japanese iris** suddenly have holes punched in leaves. Place a piece of wood near the plants, and check the underside in the morning. Count the numbers of slugs and snails attached in reference to the amount of damage. Use this information to determine the control measures to use, from baits and traps to physical removal.

NOTES

WATER GARDENS

PLANNING

Tubs and containers make lovely small water gardens. Made of wood or plastic, this style lends itself best to an informal design style. Small water gardens allow flexibilty, as they can be moved from the deck, to a patio or terrace. Small ponds move easily on a cart. Water gardens such as these are a great garden for a beginner. The container should hold a minimum of ten gallons of water. A large pot or whiskey barrel works well. Line or coat the inside of the container if it is porous or not watertight. Site the water garden in a location with no direct sun between the hours of 10 a.m. and 3:30 p.m. The water temperature can become overly warm in a small container, a detriment to fish and plants.

PLANTING

Drop some **anacharis**, **parrot's feather**, or other oxygenators into the water feature. Push down sections allowing for a more natural appearance and healthy growth.

Water lettuce and **water hyacinth** need to be situated so that the root systems are in direct or close contact with the soil. If this is not possible, plan to purchase these plants every month or so.

Try the unusual tropical **water poppy**, floating on the surface in combination with the **glamour water lily**.

If **horsetail** stems grow well beyond the intended location, control by digging and removing the underground root system. Gather stems for bunching or for arrangements.

CARE

This month begins preparation of the water garden for the stressful summer. Heat, humidity, and intense sun can play its toll on water plants not monitored regularly.

WATERING

Check the water level on the water garden every month. Water losses occur because of evaporation and lack of rainfall. If the pond water level drops, a whole host of problems can occur, from material degradation caused by exposure to the sun, to harming the plants and fish.

FERTILIZING

Depending upon the pool design and the placement of plants, it may be necessary to get into the pool to apply fertilizers. Use extreme caution for your safety as the sides and bottom are covered with algae. Use only fertilizers specially formulated for aquatic plants. Push tablets deeply into the soil, but not directly adjacent to the roots, and backfill the hole if needed. Be patient and work slowly. Try not to stir up the water too much, and make sure you correctly apply the fertilizer.

Apply a granular fertilizer with 1-2-2 ratio (5-10-10), monthly to hardy bog plants, **pickerel rush** or **variegated sweet flag**. For tropicals, use a water-soluble fertilizer poured directly in the pot. Applying fertilizer monthly will not cause growth explosions, but it is enough to maintain vigor and health, enabling plants to survive any problems. Curtail overfertilization to control weeds and slime molds.

PRUNING

Prune out aggressive growth that is out of place, declining leaves (cut as soon as any discoloration occurs), and seed pods.

How about cutting a white **night blooming lily,** 'Sir Galahad', for floating in a bowl during dinner?

PESTS

Mosquitoes may be driving people indoors. If fish are present, bacteria were added last month, and no quarter-inch-long water wigglers are present, then the problem is somewhere else.

Aphids cluster on the softest, newest growth. The new growth is the easiest area for them to insert the proboscis to feed. Look for them there.

Marsh fern and **pitcher plant** may show leaf burn. If there is rust, and it rubs off with your fingers, discard any affected leaves or parts.

Check the **dwarf fragrant water lily** and **arrowhead** for snail and slug damage. Check into the center of the **water lily**, and look at the undersides of the leaves. Aquatic snail damage to plants is minimal, and their presence is beneficial to the balance of the water feature.

HELPFUL HINTS

Algae are not harmful to plants or animals; the impact is primarily aesthetic. Established pools have an algae bloom every spring (timing is weather dependent). Each time more than 10 to 15 percent of the water is exchanged out, either for scheduled maintenance or because of a heavy downpour, another algae bloom will be right around the corner.

Dragonflies and damselflies, bees, wasps, moths and butterflies rotate in and around the water. The aerial show sometimes puts the plant material into a supporting role.

Weed the water garden every week or so. Recently germinated seed can have a taproot 6 inches long with stabilizers, requiring a digging tool or fork and a sharp tug.

NOTES

WATER GARDENS

PLANNING

Plan a concrete pond that fits with both formal and informal design strategies. It is the most expensive pond, but is the longest lasting, and requires minimal maintenance. Additional considerations need to be given to acquiring building permits, and construction parameters related to wall and bottom width and the freeze line (generally 36 inches). It may be best to hire professional cement, plumbing, and electrical contractors. After the concrete is dried and sealed, some further preparation is required for plants and fish.

Use the excavated soil that includes 4 to 6 inches of topsoil, for planting around the water feature or in other sites in the landscape. The heavy subsurface clay soil has uses as a growing medium for container plantings that need the weight to sit below the water surface. The remaining soil can be used to create a berm, mound, or slope.

Take photos of the water feature monthly. This is especially important during the first two to three years. The information gathered during the early years assists in making good choices and decisions in future years.

PLANTING

If you are contemplating an addition to an existing bog or water garden, small changes should not require a lot of aftercare if the garden is healthy and all aspects seem to be in harmony. Make sure the water and soil temperature is proper for promoting root establishment. The nutrient level can be adjusted in each individual pot.

Do not attempt to install plants in a space previously unplanted, or if diseased or dying plants were removed. Live with the open space until fall, when you can work the soil and temperatures are cooler.

Wide-open gaps can be plugged with houseplants available at your favorite garden center. Many are adaptable to many types of circumstances; ask garden center staff questions before you buy.

Acclimate any transplanting projects by covering the area with a piece of burlap or shade cloth for a few weeks.

CARE

If **water lettuce** or **water hyacinth** have shrunk, or have not appreciably increased in size since placement, remove and replace with big healthy specimens.

WATERING

Evaporation in the pond, or severe drying of the soil in a bog garden space, occurs quickly. The temperatures are the highest of the year this month and the rainfall could be down from the seasonal norms. Keep a close eye on the water levels in water features.

Think about setting out an oscillating sprinkler in the morning, and turning it off by 10 a.m. Overhead watering washes dust from the foliage, waters the entire setting surrounding the water feature, and cools everything down.

FERTILIZING

If you didn't fertilize container plantings in the water feature last month, do so this month. For more information, see June Calendar, Fertilizing section.

Provide a monthly fertilizer application to hardy bog plantings, using a granular type fertilizer with a 1-2-2 ratio (5-10-10). Use a water-soluble fertilizer for tropicals. Carefully pour into the pot. Follow directions for the rate; do not overfertilize.

PRUNING

Remove any spent flowers before the seedheads form. This timely deadheading conserves a great deal of plant strength.

Remove discolored or dying foliage as soon as possible. If allowed to decompose on the plant, the added nutrients provide the environment for algae to bloom.

The emergent foliage on **elephant's ear** is probably yellow due to overshadow by more recent and larger leaves. Prune the growth off, rather than trying to rip it off. Ripping can cause open wounds in the stem.

Reach down into the water and pull up the **anacharis.** Cut it back by one-third to increase vitality.

Remove the ball-like seeds ripening in the pods of the dwarf reblooming 'Pink Angel' **lotus**.

PESTS

Use a skimming net to remove duckweed if it has made an appearance.

Suspend most chemical applications (insecticide, herbicide, or fungicide) to any plant this month. The damage incurred from applying in the heat of summer could be greater than the problem.

HELPFUL HINTS

Evaporation is going to be greater if any type of water motion is operating. Keep an eye on the feature, and refill it frequently. If you let the water diminish to a point where you are adding more than 10 percent of the water volume to replenish, you run the risk of inducing algae bloom.

If there is a troubled plant, remove it, and isolate it from the pond. Try to maintain a similar environment to encourage progression of the problem, so you can get a diagnosis. Once you know what is causing the problem, consider courses of action. It may grow out of the difficulty, or it might warrant a burial in the compost pile.

There is an algae that grows on the bottom of ponds that resembles the coontail plant. You can make a positive identification by touching it; it is very coarse, and gives off a skunk-like scent. It is a filamentous algae; control it by removing or use an algaecide. The other common algae are planktonic, plant forms that have massive numbers of single, detached, primitive plants. Either algae in bloom is a problem. As they die, they decompose, and rob the water of oxygen and other nutrients in this process—a thievery that affects all other life in the pond.

NOTES

AUGUST

WATER GARDENS

PLANNING

Plan a preformed fiberglass or high impact plastic water pond. This sort of a pond fits in well with both formal and informal design styles. The curvilinear ponds are better for informal styles; the rectilinear forms are best with formal designs. There are numerous sizes, shapes, depths, and widths available, with a wide arrangement of attachments or inserts available, such as waterfalls, ledges, out-of-sight places for pumps, wiring, lighting, and others. Delivery depends upon your transportation situation and the size pool that you buy. Professional installation may not be required if you have the ability to handle the physical labor, and have the time. Relatively flat bottomed, preformed pools can actually be set right on top of the ground, with padding to cushion it. Soil is brought in to mound around the sides, and then the mound is tapered into the landscape. If you choose to set the pond into the ground, careful siting is required to accommodate the rigid qualities of the pond. The topography must be perfect, and the pool must sit in the spot with no soil undulations or mounds that can crack the pool. If the proposed area cannot be easily dug and hand graded, then select another spot. Minor flaws can be smoothed with an underlining of peat moss, sand, multiple layers of wet newspaper, or carpet padding. After lining the hole, place the pool, and check all points with a level to insure that everything is plumb. It may take a few times of removing the pond, adding or removing soil, and regrading to set the pond correctly. Ultimately the pool edge should be about 2 to 3 inches above the surrounding ground to allow for backfilling, that is then graded to provide positive drainage away from the feature. No water should sit adjacent to the pool; even bog areas should be com-pletely separated, reducing back-flow problems.

There are end-of-the-season sales offering hardy **zebra rush**, **purple pickerel rush**, **pepperwort,** or **tropical umbrella palm**, large and small **water snowflakes.** If you have the facilities indoors for some new water garden additions, take advantage of the sale.

PLANTING

The temperatures start to cool by the end of this month, triggering the start of dividing and transplanting season. Divide and transplant to increase a species in the landscape, and to reduce size. Divide **Japanese iris** and any hardy plants that bloomed more than eight weeks ago.

Start thinking about preparing all indoor aquariums, tanks, grow lights, and growing spaces for the winter months. Determine which tropicals are good candidates for overwintering. Cut and isolate sections of **anacharis** and **parrot's feather.**

Pull up (pots or plants) **paper reed** and **bog lily.** Repot them carefully. Check for slugs, snails, and other pests to prepare them for their stay indoors. Duplicate the pond water as close as possible, but place the storage tank in a reduced sunlight setting to minimize the harshness of grow lights.

CARE

The daylight length is decreasing, and all plants will reflect this in their growth rate.

Reduce the amount of fish food being offered. Just as with the plants, the fish are sensing seasonal changes and eat less. Any leftover food sinks, biodegrades, and offers up nutrients for future algae blooms.

WATERING

Monitor rainfall to prevent drastic drops in water levels or drought stress.

FERTILIZING

Maintain the fertilizer regime for pond plants, using a fertilizer in tablet form that has been specially formulated for pond plants.

Continue monthly fertilizer applications to hardy bog plants. Use a granular fertilizer with a 1-2-2 ratio (5-10-10). To fertilizer tropicals, use a water-soluble fertilizer applied carefully into the pot.

HELPFUL HINTS

If the lawn runs right up to the coping, edging, or very close to the pool, blow clippings away from the pond when mowing. They might become food for algae blooms and seeds for weeds.

PRUNING

Cut any spent flowers off before seedheads form. Removal discolored or dying foliage as soon as possible. Add all clippings to the compost pile, but do not make a thick layer of aquatic plant, as it will deter the breakdown process in the compost pile.

PESTS

The biggest concern this month is to keep declining stems, leaves, and flowers out of the water as much as possible. Maintain the balance in the pond, and you have less pest and disease problems.

NOTES

WATER GARDENS

PLANNING

Plan to add lights to the fountain or waterfall. It is best if the electrical lines are underground and run through PVC pipe sleeves, for safety reasons. Make sure all the electricity is off before connecting the lights.

Plan some algae controls for the pond. The natural method is to use one bunch of oxygenating plants for each 1 to 2 square feet of water surface. These plants absorb carbon dioxide and mineral salts that are algae bloom promoters. Also add frogs, tadpoles, and aquatic snails that eat the algae. The alternate control is adding a mechanical filtration system. As with any equipment, the system requires regular operation checks and routine maintenance. Change the pad or filter element as needed.

If you are planning a water garden that includes plants, site it in a location that gets a minimum of five hours of direct sunlight each day. When planning the quantities of plants to buy, no more than 50 percent of the surface should be covered with plant material.

Structural additions to the water garden lend more presence and pizzazz. Plan for a small bridge spanning across a corner. To avoid visual confusion, any features should be added in one-third or two-third increments (rather than siting a bridge spanning the pond at the halfway point). Adding the bridge allows greater visual contact, and may even make routine maintenance easier, since you will have better access to the plants—less wading in to fertilize.

PLANTING

This is the ideal time of year to spend time in the bog garden dividing all overgrown hardy aquatic plants. The soil and water temperatures are warm enough to promote root growth, the shortened day length limits the amount of top growth, rains are gentle and soaking, and the dormancy of winter is approaching.

Consider purchasing and installing a few marsh loving **hollies** such as the dwarf **inkberry,** *Ilex glabra* 'Nordic', or try the broadleaf evergreen cultivar, 'Shamrock'. Consider the vibrant red or orange fruited, deciduous **winterberry**, *Ilex verticillata* hybrids. Plant separately, in plant combinations as a backdrop, or intermingle them with existing plants.

CARE

Keep any debris (leaf, mulch, pots tipping over) from getting into the water. Biodegradation creates a gas that is particularly harmful to fish. After the final cleaning sweep through the water gardens, and you have removed all nonhardy tropicals, and cut everything back, consider a netting system lying over the water to keep as much fall and winter debris out of the water garden as possible.

The nonhardy plants floating on the subsurface and floating begin to shrink and disappear as the days get shorter. If you are planning to overwinter them, they should be gathered, potted, and moved indoors well before this process begins, usually around mid-August.

After you have removed all the plants you are overwintering, do a partial change-out of the pond. Siphon off 20 to 25 percent of the water, and refill to proper level. This process refreshes and reinvigorates the water chemistry, and there is minimal chance of algae bloom this time of year.

WATERING

Migrating butterflies will always welcome a respite for a stopover drink. Keep pond water level up.

FERTILIZING

There should be no application of any fertilizers to any plantings, even if the **bog lily** is looking weak, the **red stemmed water canna** stopped flowering, or the **midget cattail** is shrinking.

PRUNING

Complete any major cutting back of water plants at this time. Start on one side of the garden and simply work back and forth until the foliage is pretty much gone. The only exception would be to leave foliage on any plants still showing signs of active growth and no signs of seasonal decline. You will want to finish the final pruning as soon as possible, to allow time to get the catch net over the pond to collect any fall foliage drop from trees and plants.

HELPFUL HINTS

If the pool has a dramatic change in water depth, there may be a crack in the liner or pool. The options are to continue maintaining the water level by adding water as frequently as necessary. Depending on the severity of the leak, this could be daily. Eventually, living plants and fish could suffer major damage with the constant addition of water and the upset in the chemical balance. As soon as possible, it is best to pull everything out, drain (siphon) the water, find the problem, and repair the pond. You will have to start all over with adding neutralizer and re-introducing plants and fish. If the pool is a natural or clay bottomed, buy powdered bentonite (volcanic) clay and follow directions on the bag to make repairs.

PESTS

Bees, wasps, and others are intense during this month. The workers are trying to build up the pollen supply for the overwintering queen. This activity level creates thirst, and skimming the water, or landing at various pond locations for a drink is a constant occurrence. If personal allergies are a problem, move the seating. Avoid swinging or swatting a bee; many times this makes passive into aggressive. A hornet killed releases an odor calling all other hornets to action in retaliation.

NOTES

OCTOBER

WATER GARDENS

PLANNING

Take photographs, both color and black-and-white, and add detailed journal entries for what is really the end of the gardening year for water gardens. Make an appraisal of "How Did the Garden Do?" The who, what, where, when, and why is documented now for use later.

If you are planning on adding a water garden for the first time, or making changes to the existing garden, consider an all inclusive pond kit. A full kit includes written instructions and a detailed video, and all the supplies you need, such as pond liner, underlying material, pump, pump discharge, check valve assembly, complete filter system, skimmer net, glue, sealant, flexible PVC piping, and more. It is probably best to not buy a kit that includes plants or fish as part of the package. Take one thing at a time, and add those later.

Have you seen rows of pumps of all sizes and types at the garden center? To determine which pump is best for your situation, consider the height the water is going to be pumped (from the pool to the top of waterfall), the waterfall width, the water surface and volume, the availability of proper electricity, and the budget.

New plant material is always being introduced that enhances the water garden. Consider a variegated leaf **red twig dogwood**, *Cornus stolonifera* 'Isanti', for bright, scarlet-red vertical relief. A black **chokecherry**, *Aronia melanocarpa.* offers berries for the cardinals, now taking up residence next to the pond. Remember the **pussy willow**, *Salix caprea*, that were just sticks being pushed into the wet ground last March? Now they are fully budded, and waiting for the dead of winter to be cut and brought indoors.

The newly arrived catalog has a pure white **Japanese iris**, *Iris ensata* 'Innocence'. The hardy **hibiscus**, *Hibiscus moscheutos* 'Lady Baltimore' and 'Lord Baltimore' actually prefer a wet environment, so maybe their huge pink and red flowers can brighten up the pond in late summer.

PLANTING

For information on building a bog garden, see March Calendar in the Planning section.

See Helpful Hints for more on planting.

CARE

Prepare the tub gardens for winter. Remove the plants and siphon the water. Turn tub on its side, or store in a protected spot for the winter. The fish and plants of this wonderful patio experience will not be able to survive the winter, due to the volume and depth of the water (does not offer enough insulation). If the tub was placed on a wheeled cart, push it to a protected location, which may enable some plant materials to live through a mild winter.

After a frost kills the foliage of hardy **water lilies,** cut back to 1 inch above the tuber, remove them from the growing ledge, and place on the pool bottom (if the pond is 2 or more feet deep and will remain filled). If the pool is to be drained, treat the **water lily** as a tropical nonhardy type, and either place it under grow lights in a water-filled container, or store over the winter in a glass jar containing damp (no obvious water sitting on bottom) sand.

If any remaining tropical plants have not been brought indoors, and either placed in aquariums or in containers under grow lights, this is the last opportunity to do so. Your overwinter inventory may include the **parrot's feather** floating in water, the **bog lily** pots placed in a dark out-of-the-way spot, or the **red stemmed water canna** tuber that has been propagated by planting its pups. If the **anacharis** is still outdoors, it is too late in the season to move it inside; just throw it out.

WATERING

Keep the water level up to insure any plantings under grow lights do not suffer from drying or exposed root systems.

FERTILIZING

Apply no fertilizers this month.

Using compost as mulch, cover over the bog/margin plantings. Compost is a very low analysis fertilizer and is more beneficial than shredded bark or wood products.

PRUNING

Remove all debris on hardy plants such as **corkscrew rush**, **cardinal flower** (cut stems to 6 inches), **arrowheads**, and **pickerel rush lizard's tail** (cut it shorter).

At the first sign of foliage browning, resulting from frost or freezing, cut back bog plants by one-third. Do not cut below the water line. The stubs remain through winter for insulation as a self-mulching cover.

Removal and cleanup continues; everything should be cut and cleared by the end of the month.

PESTS

Carefully inspect any plants being moved indoors. Provide thorough washing or dunking into a bucket of mild soapy water, allow it to drain, and wipe off foliage.

HELPFUL HINTS

The soil preparation for planting should be as follows:

S – **Scope:** Evaluate the entire scope of the site, everything natural and manmade, and the impact on the entire site

O – **Order:** organize the sequence of events, putting them in order of priority.
Delineate area, take a soil sample, control existing plantings as needed, prepare the site, purchase, install, and stabilize plants.

I – **Intermingle:** the blending and building up of the earth includes shoveling and rototilling the area four separate times. Add and incorporate amendments, both organic (leaf mold, compost, peat moss, topsoil) and inorganic (sand, gravel). Add approximately 2 cubic yards per 100 square feet of planting space. The grade will change with the additional volume, elevating the area as much as 6 inches. Finish grading the area, providing positive drainage.

L – **Liveliness:** determined by the health of the plants. Check leaves, stem consistency, size of pot, moisture level, insects, and smell. Use proper installation techniques; dig the hole, shake off potting soil, check the roots, and plant at the same depth it was before, and backfill.

S – **Safeguard:** protect the new plantings by helping them through the transition. Water plants immediately and check daily. Apply 1 to 2 inches of mulch. Deadhead to remove flowers or damaged foliage.

Safety Tip: If the pond is in an area with free access, consider installing a low impact fence for the safety of smaller, unsupervised children. Add a floating swimming pool alarm as a precautionary measure.

NOVEMBER

WATER GARDENS

PLANNING

Planning a water bog garden using only native or naturalized plantings could include **watercress** (*Nasturtium officinale*) with white flowers from April through October. **Broad waterleaf** (*Hydrophyllum canadense*) has pinkish flowers from May through July. Showy **orchid** (*Orchis spectabilis*) has a white or pinkish bloom in May to June. **Swamp milkweed** (*Asclepias incarnata*) is pink blooming during summer. **Spatterdock water lily** (*Nuphar letea*) has fragrant yellow flowers in summer.

If you are planning an irrigation system to the lawn and traditional shrub and perennial borders, consider adding a separate line with pop-up heads to water the pond or bog garden plantings. This could free up some time during the dry season for more exotic things, like adding the new **marsh fern clump**, potting up the **paper reed**, or setting a **water lettuce** plant free onto the pond.

If nighttime enjoyment of the pool is difficult due to lack of lighting and algae problems, consider installing a small floating lighted fountain. This device takes care of both quandaries.

PLANTING

Planting baskets (similar to miniature laundry baskets) of various shapes and sizes are available for water plants. Design the basket for specific plant types from **elephant's ear** to **dwarf cattails.**

There should be no planting outdoors of any hardy plantings. If tropicals were brought in, empty the pots, clean off soil, and store plants for the winter.

Clean and rinse all containers for the water garden, and inspect for breakage or damage. Do an inventory of needs for next year.

CARE

If the pool contains fish that will winter over, check the water heater, or make sure a couple of 4-inch or larger logs are available. Use both sources to insure that the surface does not entirely freeze over, causing harm to the dormant fish.

Reduce grow lights by one hour. This helps replicate what is occurring in nature. Also, check the brightness of the system. If plants are leaning, add lights.

WATERING

Hoses, sprinklers, Y-valves, and washers should be brought in out of the weather to prolong longevity. Keep one hose handy in case of an extra dry winter or early spring. Keep all plants watered and water basins filled to the proper depth.

Tropicals can go through somewhat of a winter drought to mimic nature, but do not allow the soil to become so dry that it shrinks from the side of the pot.

FERTILIZING

The maximum shelf life of fertilizer is extended with good storage practices and habits. Avoid temperatures below 32 degrees and above 95 degrees. High humidity and light intensity degrade products as well; keep tops on liquids tightly closed, and granular products bagged in plastic and off the floor. If a product is more than two years old, it should be considered for discarding. Check with the local Missouri Extension Service, the Department of Natural Resources, or a local waste management company regarding proper disposal.

Macronutrients (the larger series of three numbers on the container of fertilizer) are nitrogen, phosphorus, and potassium, and are the main sources for good plant health. Check the label for additional micronutrients included in the formula. Boron, iron, manganese, and sulfur, are a few examples. These supporting role players make the difference between a plant simply surviving and fulfilling a prescribed niche and a plant that exceeds expectations and performance.

PRUNING

Many of the tools used to maintain water gardens rust, or wetness impacts the handles and grips. Evaluate the amount of use of each water garden tool, and your level of satisfaction (Did it take several nips at a small section of **corkscrew rush** to cut it off?) with the tool. If it is reasonable to take it apart, clean all parts separately, sharpen, and oil. Reassemble, and hang in an out of the way location, ready for use next year.

PESTS

Update your journal. It may be necessary, depending upon the level of entries, to have several.

HELPFUL HINTS

Lotus (*Nelumbo* sp.) grows wild in various locations throughout Southeast Missouri. This native bog plant was an important food source for the Native Americans of the region. The tubers were dug and eaten as vegetables, and the ripened green seeds were hulled and roasted for consumption. The seeds taste a bit like chestnuts, and are also favored by waterfowl.

Keep good records of any chemical activity of fertilizers, insecticides, herbicides, and fungicides. Log in specifics such as the type, rate, and time of day. Check treated plants the next day for any hints of related damage, any harm will begin to show up within 24 hours.

Thoroughly clean (140-degree water and soap) all pesticide and chemical application equipment. Use a separate washtub. Dry and store properly, making sure any plastic or rubber components have not become worn. If any parts show wear, this is the time of year to get replacement parts, or an entirely new mode of application.

When purchasing a new product (chemical in nature), take the time to write the date of purchase (with a water-resistant pen) on the outside of the package. This reference information could prevent a damaging application in the future. Always read and follow label instructions.

NOTES

DECEMBER

WATER GARDENS

PLANNING

Use these cold winter months to learn the botanical Latin names for bog and water plants. Common names vary from region to region; botanical names are a universal language. The second part of a botanical name is the species. Many times, the species name describes a feature of the plant. Not only do you learn more about the plant by learning the botanical name, you also can converse about a particular plant with anyone, anywhere, and they will know what plant you are talking about. Learning the botanical names also helps you when searching through catalogs, attending classes, and visiting botanical gardens and parks. See Helpful Hints for a guide to learning some names of water plants.

Planning garden activities for the water garden is dependent upon reading nature's clock and trying to take advantage of the windows of opportunities. Our weather is very unpredictable from hour to hour, day to day and month to month. Additionally, a northern exposure is entirely different from a southern one in any individual garden. This impacts the temperature, moisture, and wind speed, creating varied microclimates throughout the landscape. The combination of the seasonal weather and the microclimates relate to timing of water garden chores. The removal of mulch and adding pool netting, moving tropicals outdoors, transplanting or installing plants, fertilizer applications, and pesticide use are all dictated by proper timing. A miscalculation can harm various plant parts, ranging from stems, buds, and leaves, to damaging the entire plant. The best guide is to look out the window, or to go for a walk in the garden. Write down information as you receive it, whether from your own observations, or through study. Try to understand how the diverse elements are brought together to create a sensation. A dash of common sense, and the realization that not everything in a garden is going to be as envisioned, keeps gardening fun and exciting. Thank goodness the science of landscaping and gardening has not been related to a virtual landscape on the computer screen, and it will always remain the real stuff and great, unending fun.

PLANTING

No dirt on the trowel or under the fingernails this month. Allow everything to rest as is. There is plenty of time later for all the shifting and moving around of plants and soil.

Keep doing those jumping jacks and sit-ups in preparation for all the bending and squatting to be done in a couple of months—as the water garden awakens.

CARE

Remove any dead, diseased, or unhealthy stem, leaf, or the entire plant. Eliminating the problem prevents or curtails any movement of the source of the problem to other vegetation.

WATERING

When adding water to the holding tubs, use warmer water. This practice prevents cold shock to root systems. Fill buckets and jugs, and allow them to sit at room temperature. This time will allow the gases to escape and the temperature to moderate.

HELPFUL HINTS

Learn Botanical Names

Common Name	*Botanical Name*	General Meaning of Species
Anacharis/ water thyme	*Egeria densa*	dense growing
Aquatic mint	*Mentha aquatica*	water habitat
Bog/spider lily	*Crinum bulbispermum*	having bulbs
Paper reed/bulrush	*Cyperus alternifolius*	alternate leaves
Dwarf lotus	*Nelumbo lutea*	yellow
Elephant's ear/taro	*Colocasia esculenta*	edible
Horsetail	*Equisetum hyemale*	of winter
Marsh fern	*Thelypteris palustris*	growing in a marsh
Midget cattail	*Typha minima*	dwarf or smaller
Pickerel weed	*Pontederia cordata*	heart shape
Pitcher plant	*Sarracenea purpurea*	purple
Water hyacinth	*Eichoinia crassipes*	thick footed or stalked
Water lly	*Nymphea odorata*	fragrant
Water poppy	*Hydrocleys nymphoides*	floating heart

Growing tip: Check those notes taken during the growing season. The size and spread of water plants is dictated by the pond size, the water depth of the container or root, water temperature, the amount of sunlight, and fertilizer. Make necessary fine-tuning changes to your cultivation practices, in anticipation of next year.

Keep track of the rainfall in the landscape. If it is exceedingly dry, get the hose out and water. Water in the soil is an insulator for all plants, and is essential in the aquatic environments to survive through the winter dormancy.

FERTILIZING

Do not apply any fertilizer during this month.

Take an inventory of what you have in stock, and visit your favorite garden center for an end-of-the-year sale. While you are there, pick up a few houseplants, philodendrons, orchids, or bromeliads, and place them under the grow lights to make the overwintering water garden come alive and be more vibrant.

PRUNING

Make a final sweep outdoors through the bog, and remove anything that looks out of place.

Indoors, a heavy-duty pair of scissors is probably adequate for getting rid of plant parts that may die.

PESTS

Continue to keep a close eye under the leaves, on the stems, in the crowns, and in the holding tub water, for any pests.

GROWING LAWNS IN KANSAS

Lawns can unify neighborhoods, highlight landscape features, and provide great areas to view or play, but they do require a mix of common sense, science, and timing every month—with differences likely each year. Realize there are no pat approaches or answers to having a "nice" lawn regardless of where you live or what type of turf grass you've chosen.

CHOOSING THE RIGHT GRASS

Most areas in Kansas will support bluegrass, fescue, Bermuda, ryes, zoysia, and buffalo grass. Remember, your local conditions will have a great deal to do with success regardless of time and effort spent. While taking care of a lawn today, you must always be thinking about the future. Before choosing which grass to plant, make note of all potential factors which may influence your lawn: season, soil profile and chemical make-up, exposure, topography, existing plantings (especially trees and larger shrubs), proximity to structure or hardscape, and time available for maintenance. Getting things right from the start can save a great deal of real and mental money being spent unwisely, so don't rush.

Do not be afraid to seek help from professionals at garden centers, extension services, or a neighbor whose lawn is successful. Remember each season and year bring new equipment, chemicals (inorganic and organic), and techniques which could really help. Growing a great lawn in Kansas is a challenge, no doubt about it!

Two major types of lawn are cool season and warm season grass. Cool season types (bluegrass, fescue, rye) look best from September through May, while warm season (Bermuda, zoysia, buffalo) are vibrant from May through early October. Of course Mother Nature's weather sometimes changes this calendar. When out of season, grass goes dormant. It's alive but offers limited aesthetic qualities.

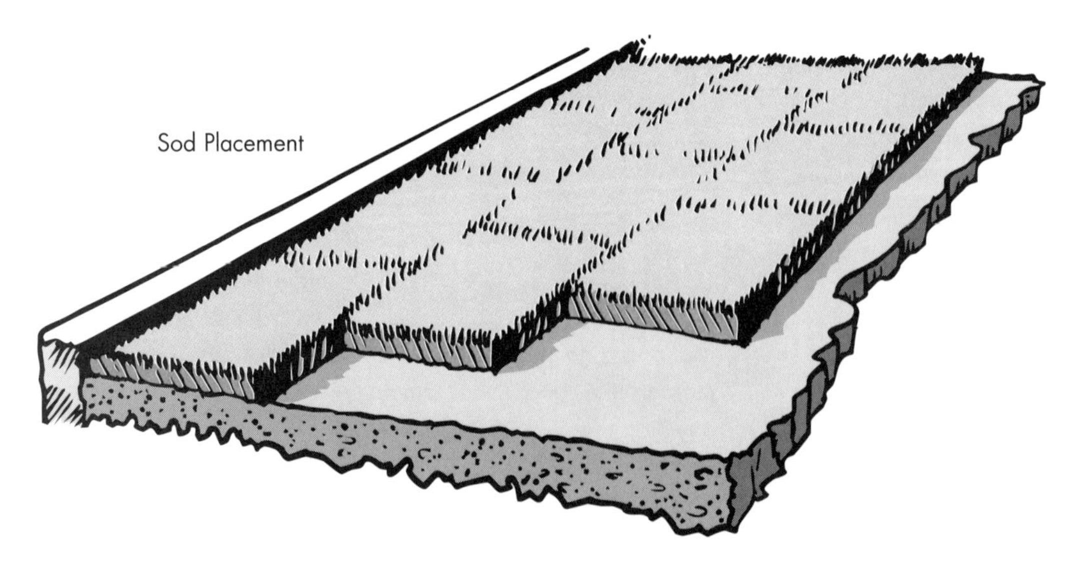

HELPFUL HINTS

Grass Seeding Reference Table

These hybrids are developed for regular mowing, foot traffic, and aesthetic qualities. To insure a constant rejuvenation of the turf areas, over-seed each year with fresh seed. Follow the label for application rates.

Grass Type	Season	Amount Seed/ Pounds per 1,000 square feet
Bluegrass	Spring	2-4
	Fall	2-3
Perennial Rye	Spring	9-11
	Fall	6-8
Fescue	Spring	9-11
	Fall	6-8

Other grass types are extremely difficult to grow from seed. I recommend the use of sprigs or sod. This will keep influx of younger vigorous plants, to fill gaps before occurrence.

Coloration can range from off-green to pale tan, depending upon type and depth of dormancy. Whether establishing a new lawn, renovating or patching, lawn work is a marathon. There are no quick sprints to the finish line.

Begin by measuring the size of area needing attention. The range can be from one square foot to thousands. Establishing or renovating larger spaces may require a great deal of work. Various methods include seeding, sprigging, plug-ging, patching and sodding. Certainly seeding will be most arduous, followed by sprigging, plugging and patching. Sodding is easiest, but may cost more.

Note: Bare spots in the lawn which are less than 6 inches in diameter will fill in through the natural growth of the grass plants, assuming the lawn is healthy and the square footage of bare areas when combined does not constitute more than 10% of the lawn area.

LAYING SOD

Sod is professionally grown and delivered from local sod farms or garden centers. Three types are generally available depending on the season: bluegrass, fescue, and zoysia. Bluegrass and fescue may be variety blends or may include a small percentage of an entirely different grass. Zoysia is usually a pure strain and would have limited availability due to cold weather dormancy. Sod pieces will cover 2 1/2 square feet each. Sod can be laid whole or cut into pieces to fit a specific space.

When selecting newly arrived pieces of sod, look for good coloration, no burnt spots, and white roots obvious on underside. Also, look for 1/2 inch of soil. Check closely if sod is staked on the shipping pallet. Look and smell at the center. This is where a tremendous amount of heat can build up and potentially kill this portion. If purchasing several pieces, lay them out in a shaded place and moisten. Make sure the ground is damp before laying sod into place.

The best weather for laying sod is cloudy with minimal wind. This prevents drying of blades or roots. Stop periodically and water all areas. Keep sod damp (not wet) until the root system begins to anchor into the ground. A slight upward tug will indicate if downward root growth is occurring.

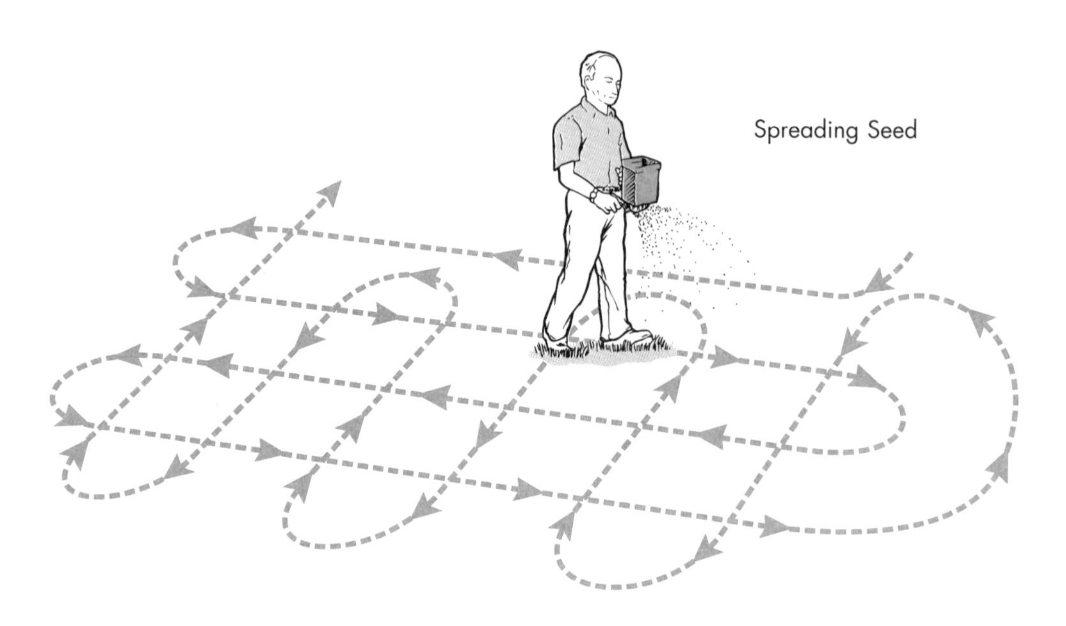

You can also plug bare spots with small pieces of sod or sprig with individual grass plants. When sprigging, simply divide a grass plant that grows with a spreading root system, such as zoysia and blue grass. This means taking the smallest division possible, one with an attached root and cluster of grass blades, then planting singly. In other words, a zoysia plug or piece of blue grass sod is a multitude of sprigs connected together. These methods have similar preparation requirements as laying sod. Note, smaller sections will take longer to become viable.

PLANTING SEED

Seed is professionally grown and harvested. A multitude of varieties are available, shade to full sun tolerant. It is sold in bulk or pre-packaged in boxes or bags. Seed is less expensive than sod, but requires considerable more time and effort (up to 5 years) before a classic thick lawn is achieved. Ground preparation is the same as for sod. Spread seed, followed by seed starter fertilizer. Then water and keep moist until germination (about two weeks). Then water less often but deeper, for longer periods of time.

You may want to spread straw over seed, but do not cover the ground entirely as fungus could kill your fragile newly germinated seed. Once established and actively growing, care and maintenance begins. Using correct tools and equipment will have a positive impact on your lawn health. (See the Lawn Seeding Reference Table on the previous page for suggested amounts of seed.)

WATER MOVEMENT

Besides shade and tree root competition, water movement will affect your lawn's development. Lawn grasses are not successful in poorly drained areas where water stands, so take time to establish proper water flow. Go out after a rain and check for puddling. Use landscape paint to mark areas that need to be re-contoured to prevent standing water. Depending upon severity of problem, it may take bobcat re-grading, rototiller, or simply mixing a small amount of new top soil with existing to fix 'ponding'. Keep positive drainage away from structures.

When rainfall is insufficient, you may need to water your lawn. Many irrigation systems are available. Rotary or impulse sprinklers have rotating heads that shoot water at a 45 degree angle in a full circle pattern. The jet flow is scattered by a pivoting arm. Many can be set to water partial circles. They are best used for larger open spaces. Stationary rings spray in an arcing pattern from a metal ring, and the flow evenly dispenses large volume quickly. They are best used for small open areas. The whirling head is basically the same except the water is dispensed outward rather than up. Oscillating-rotating metal bars spray water in an upward fan. The volume is adjustable, but most water is dispensed near the sprinkler. They are best used in rectangular areas, and they're great for kids to run through. Traveling small tractor-like vehicles with whirling sprinklers work best if the grade is basically level and the route is mostly straight. Soaker hoses are thin plastic hoses pierced with holes on one side to spray water directly onto the ground. They deliver slow, deep watering in narrow spaces.

LAWN TOOLS

A vigorous, actively growing lawn is much more likely to recover from insect and disease problems. It also minimizes weed invasiveness. You'll find powered and manual machines for almost every lawn maintenance task. However correct timing (season), equipment maintenance, settings and usage are essential.

When mowing, it's important to set the correct mower blade height. This protects grass plant crowns and prevents grass from matting down. Ground aeration using a core aerator or vertical slicer reduces soil surface compaction and improves water and air exchange. Lawn health also requires removing dead crowns, roots, and blades by raking or running a dethatcher.

A sharp blade will make a clean even cut to the grass top, which allows the plants to seal the opening quicker and easier, reducing the time available for disease, bacteria, or fungus to enter.

Take time to make sure all your tools are in optimal condition. Know your machine-turning radius. Set irrigation heads so your water hits grass, not your drive or walk. Please note: when working in your lawn, using the correct tools and wearing proper safety glasses, clothes, and gloves are a MUST.

Everyone likes to save money, but using a single apparatus to apply insecticide, herbicide, and fungicide may damage your valuable plants. Invest in multiple applicators. Rinse and clean all equipment periodically. Follow label directions for cleaner formula.

Drop spreader calibrations will vary for fertilizers, gypsum, lime, herbicide, and so on. Check your calibration (dropping rate) to ensure proper application. Be careful with hose end sprayers for liquids. All chemicals will leave a residue inside the bottle. Trigger sprayer for ready-to-use, premixed products should never be re-used. Read the label carefully for proper application. Hand pump sprayers for liquid or dry products produce an application rate related to the tank pressure and nozzle size. Keep the pressure consistent for proper coverage.

CHEMICALS

Lawn chemicals are available in a wide variety of formulations: wettable powder, dry powder, liquid, granular, and injector vials. Usage requires correct mixture and application technique, proper air temperature, no wind or other environmental restrictions, proper clothing, gloves, and foot wear. Shelf life varies product to product. Many dry products require "watering in" after application. Always read labels carefully.

Labels provide strict usage parameters and cautions. Follow them! Each product is intended for a specific purpose and improper use can have unexpected results. If you have questions, call the manufacturer or ask at your local garden center.

HELPFUL HINTS

Ten Most Common Lawn Weeds

Weed	Description	Category	-Control	Season
Henbit-mint family	upright square stem blue flower	Winter annual	Pre-emergent	Early Fall
Plantain	(2 narrow or wide rubbery leaves) lays flat vertical seed head	Perennial	Post-emergent	Year-round
Goosegrass	coarse blades, flat, center white, flowers 4 fingers	Summer annual	Pre-emergent	Spring
Yellow nutgrass (sedge)	triangular stem fast growing yellowish green flower brush-like	Perennial	Post-emergent	Year round
Spurge	grows flat, milky sap, tiny leaves	Summer annual	Pre-emergent	Spring
Chickweed	pale green vine tiny leaves	Winter annual	Pre-emergent	Early fall
Shepherds purse	leaf dandelion-like seed pod (small triangular) rises in center	Winter and summer annual	Pre-emergent	Spring/ early fall
Bindweed	creeping or climbing vine, spear-shaped leaf leaf white flowers	Perennial	Post-emergent	Year round
Ground ivy	round leaf on angular stem	Perennial	Post-emergent	Year round

Fertilizer is a catch-all term for supplemental nutrients, either organic or inorganic, applied to plants to establish and maintain health. A series of three numbers associated on fertilizer containers represent the percentage of macro-nutrients (nitrogen-N, phosphorus-P and potassium-K). Nitrogen (first number) can be formulated in two distinctively different forms: soluble and slow release. Soluble is quicker dissolving and works best when temperatures are below 50 degrees. It stimulates rapid growth and is depleted very fast. Slow-release nitrogen is just the opposite. Most lawn fertilizers will contain both, allowing for immediate and longer term availability.

Although liquid fertilizer applied with a hose end sprayer will green up your lawn quickly, this can cause problems. Lush growth needs mowing more often, and with lots of top growth, the root system is not able to provide necessary support. This could cause a decline if caution is not exercised. Granular types applied dry with a spreader provide more uniform, slow-release feeding. The advantage is slower, steadier growth with blades and roots in harmony, making stronger plants. This strength then allows for better resilience to bounce back from stress.

Fertilizers can be found in combination insecticides, herbicides and fungicides, but take note that many combination chemicals are dangerous to wildlife, beneficial insects, local streams and your neighborhood environment. Use them with caution.

WEEDS

Three major types of weeds may appear in your lawn. They are:

- Broadleaf—wide multi-branched veined leaf; can be annual or perennial; includes dandelions, violets, chickweed, henbit and spurge
- Grass—narrow blades with veins running parallel to margin, can be annual or perennial; includes crabgrass, wild onions, garlic, and goose grass
- Sedges—grass-like triangular stem at ground surface; nutgrass and nutsedge most common

CORE AERATION

A core aerator is a machine which physically removes small plugs of sod and soil from the ground. The aerator can appear like a barrel lying in its side with multiple hollow short pipe pieces sticking out around the entire circumference. The barrel turns when pulled, and each pipe pierces the ground, pulling up a plug and discarding it on the surface. This action reduces compaction so oxygen and moisture can freely move in and out of the ground. Smaller yards with limited access for larger mowers and aerators could use an aerating hand tool or an earth auger and electric drill to drill holes into the ground.

TOP DRESSING

Spreading a thin layer (1 inch approximately) of compost or other organic matter directly over the lawn is called top dressing. Microorganisms contained within this material help decompose thatch, the layer of dead root systems in your grass. Top dressing will also improve the soil's physical and chemical structure. After application, lightly rake or water to move materials through the blades and on to the ground surface. Otherwise, the drying sun and wind could reduce organism level. Fully composted materials of any sort can be used as well.

GRASS CLIPPINGS

When your lawnmower clippings are 2 inch or less, it is not necessary to bag or rake the clippings. This is true whether you use a mulching, reel or rotary blade mower. As grass absorbs nutrients, the excess collects at the tips of each blade. So when cut and left to decompose, the clippings are simply a dose of slow release fertil-

HELPFUL HINTS

Common Weeds and Reasons for Establishment

Weed (Common Name)	Reason for Establishment
Chickweed	thin lawn grass, excessive moisture
Annual bluegrass	low fertility, wet compacted soil, mower height to low
Clover	low nitrogen, dry and compacted soil
Crabgrass	thin lawn grass, low fertility, dry and compacted soil
Dandelion	thin lawn grass, low fertility and mowing, dry soil
Ground ivy	wet soil and shaded area
Moss	compacted soil, shaded area, mower height to low
Plantain	fertility and mower height low
Purslane	thin grass and excessive nutrient level
Wild Garlic	wet and heavy soil

izer, which greatly improves the lawn's health. If the clippings are over 2 inches long, you should mow more often to avoid disease and insect problems—and also to avoid raking the clippings!

REMOVING THATCH

If your lawn has developed a thick layer of thatch, schedule a lawn dethatching for late August or early September, getting ready for over-seeding with cool season lawn grass seed. Rental tools available include:

• Power rake—mower-like machine with rotating vertical tines which remove thatch and scratch surface for seeding (set height to insure surface preparation)

• Vertical mower—machine with blades that slice knife-like cuts into the surface for seeding

Note both power rake and vertical mower will loosen debris; be prepared to rake, bag or compost.

• Slit seeder—prepares soil with cutting discs attached to front, with actual seed distribution in rows at the same time; crisscrosses at several angles are needed for complete coverage.

SHADY AREAS

Never expect a shady lawn to equal in density, hardiness and aesthetic qualities an area that is in the sun. However, a few tips can help. Limb up and or thin trees to allow more sunlight to strike th ground. Do not over-fertilize shady areas. Use only 2 pounds per 1000 sq. feet applied in fall, when leaf fall begins. Keep leaves raked, and keep your mower blade at its highest recommended setting. Do not use herbicides; pull any weeds by hand. Keep shaded lawn areas on the dry side, and if possible, minimize foot traffic. Core aerate to reduce compaction.

UNDERGROUND PESTS

Moles are territorial and stronger ones will drive others from a particular lawn area. They tunnel towards distinctive sounds when looking for food. Basically the better and more healthy the lawn means the greater concentration of subterranean insects, such as centipedes, roly poly, spiders, grubs, and earthworms. These creatures make up the majority of the mole's diet, though they also consume plant roots in small amounts. (Voles, field mice, and chipmunks will use their abandoned tunnels to forage for plant roots.)

Moles live in and use a two tunnel system. The upper is to search for food, the lower sometimes 1 foot deeper acts as "highway" for returning to the nest or moving quickly from one place to another. Flattening tunnels by foot will not stop moles. If active feeding tunnels are flattened, they will be repaired within 24 hours. Though traps are hit-or-miss, multiple studies have proven that traps are the most effective, over moth balls, poison peanuts, juicy fruit chewing gum, gas bombs, or other means. This is not to say these other methods have no supporters.

Another underground pest is the yellowjacket or ground hornet. When you see a small hole in your lawn with bees flying in and out, be wary and stay clear if possible. Avoid wearing fragrance or brightly colored clothing when working near a nest. Check your soda can before taking a drink because one may be inside.

As days become shorter and cooler, simple vibrations from mowers or walking can cause a swarming attack. If confronted, stay calm and swish away the insects with slow deliberate movements. Fast swings can excite the yellowjacket. If you squash a yellowjacket, a chemical is released that calls others to attack. If you are stung, apply ice or meat tenderizer. If swelling continues past several minutes or if your throat or mouth swells, seek medical help at once.

Yellowjacket controls include scented traps and professional services. We do not advise attacking a nest with pesticides. There are usually secondary exits, and you may face a counterattack.

HELPFUL HINTS

Ten Most Common Lawn Disease Problems

Name	When—What to Look For—When—Additional Tips
Pink Snow Mold or **Fusarium Patch**	After melting snow—patches—whitish dead grass—reduce nitrogen
Dollar Spot	Late spring early fall—patches .5 to 1 feet, leaves look wet and then loose color—early morning webbing-like material—March—dethatch, Increase nitrogen
Helminthorsporium (multiple varieties)	Early spring and fall—thinning lawn with grass appearing brown or red with purple or reddish strips, may cause blades to become disconnected exposing discolored crown—dethatch, use balanced fertilizer
Summer Patch or **Frogs Eye**	Late spring thru summer—yellowish spots less than 6 inches which develop into 2- to 3-feet circles with green spot in center—dethatch, add calcium, avoid alternating over and under watering practices
Red Thread	Summer—large irregular yellowish and reddish spots with bright pink/red 'threads' hanging on tip of individual grass blades—increase calcium and nitrogen levels, avoid drought, and dethatch
Brown Patch	Late spring thru fall—areas ranging from 2 to 50 feet, first purplish green then wilts and browns, could have a purple ring bordering spots—core aerate, use more balanced fertilizer, mow frequently to reduce clipping length
Pythium Blight	Late spring thru early fall—1 to 6 inches spots initially appear water soak, then turn brown with early morning 'cobwebs' appearing—improve drainage (both surface and subsurface-total lawn renovation) use more balanced fertilizer, dethatch, if area shade consider alternative to lawn
Smut (Stripe)	Mid fall—grass plants turn pale green and then yellow, no noticeable growth, blades may curl and have blackened strip, and may appear as if shredded—dethatch, reduce frequency of watering while increasing time
Rust	Summer thru early fall—grass becomes reddish brown to yellow orange, individual blades will have red 'pimples' weaken plants prone to winter kill—reduce watering frequency but increase time of each watering
Zoysia Patch	Late spring thru summer—large areas edged with bright yellow orange blades, which fail to green up after winter, lawn appears thin, large weed count—dethatch, may be necessary to re-sod or add new plugs
Lime	It is NOT always necessary to spread lime on a regular basis to "sweeten" your soil. In Kansas, your lawn will perform best if the soil pH (relative acid-alkaline measure) is between 6.0-6.5, in other words slightly acidic. Application of lime should be based upon a true measurement provided by a soil test. Lime does have some 'micro-nutrients' like calcium and magnesium, but these can be added to soil (if needed) through other amendments available at your favorite garden center.

KANSAS BOTANICAL & DISPLAY GARDENS

Bartlett Arboretum (20 acres) historic, nonprofit arboretum located in Belle Plaine, privately owned, open only upon special request. Highlights: cypress, oaks, champion Japanese maples

Botanica Gardens in Wichita (9.5 acres) garden and park located at 701 North Amidon, Wichita, Kansas is city-owned and part of the Wichita City Park System. Highlights: aquatic collection; butterfly garden, tropical greenhouse, peony collection, rose garden and much more

Dyck Arboretum of the Plains (13 acre) botanical garden located at Hesston College in Hesston, Kansas. Highlights: 600 varieties of native and adaptable trees, shrubs, wildflowers, prairie grasses including a buffalo grass meadow

International Forest of Friendship an arboretum and memorial forest adjacent to Lake Warnock in Atchison, Kansas. Highlights: trees representing each of the 50 states and over 35 foreign countries, many with historic associations to America past

Kansas Landscape Arboretum (193 acres) nonprofit arboretum located in Wakefield, Kansas. Highlights: 1,000 species of native and exotic woody plants alone with four short trails, pond, prairie meadow and considerable area with native vegetation

Kansas State University Gardens (19 acres) developed and maintained by university Dept. of Horticulture, Forestry and Recreation Resources. Located on campus at intersection of Denison Ave. and Claflin Rd. in Manhattan. Highlights: daylilies, irises, roses, with cottage, native/adaptive plant gardens and insect zoo, addititional gardens planned for near future

Overland Park Arboretum and Botanical Gardens (300 acres) located a mile west of U.S. Highway 69 on 179th Street, Overland Park, Kansas. Operated by City of Overland Park. Highlights: mature trees, limestone bluffs, 5 miles of trails, two bridges across Wolf Creek with 80+% of the land maintained as natural ecosystems and Children's Discovery Garden

Parsons Arboretum (19 acres) is located at corner of 21st and Briggs Avenue in Glenwood Park, Parsons, Kansas. Highlights: daylily garden, wetland plantings, gazebo, wildflower bed

Reinisch Rose Garden and Doran Rock Garden is a garden located in Gage Park, at 4320 SW 10th Avenue, Topeka, Kansas. Highlights: 400 rose varieties (6,500 plants) one of 23 rose test gardens in United States. Adjacent to Logan Rose Test Garden is a reflecting pool and Doran Rock Garden

Sedgwick County Extension Arboretum is located in Sedgwick County, Kansas, USA at 7001 W. 21st North Wichita, Kansas. Highlights: 195 trees, representing 97 species adapted to south central Kansas

Ward-Meade Park Botanical Gardens (2.5) in Historic Ward-Meade Park at 124 NW Fillmore Street, Topeka, Kansas. Highlights: 500 varieties of flowers, shrubs, and trees, with footbridge, gazebo, and benches

COMMON GARDENING TERMS

Aeration: working ground and or opening holes to maximize air penetration.

Amendments: additives to water, ground, air, or directly to plant to promote, induce or stymie specific qualities.

Animals: broad term: including pets, wildlife: birds, deer, moles, etc.

Annual: non-hardy plant, full life-foliage, flower, seed-one growing season.

Balled and burlap: field grown, harvested with roots wrapped and bundled in cloth.

Bare-root: plants sold with root system naked (without a growing medium such as soil or potting mix).

Bark: outermost part of woody plant, essential for protecting veins and inner workings.

Bed preparation: using tools and amendments to change the soil profile and/or chemistry.

Biennial: full life cycle over two years, the first year producing foliage, the second flowering and setting seed.

Blade: pointed leaf, veins parallel to edge.

Branch: portion of plant growing from main stem, trunk or crown.

Breathing: essential function of a plant, mostly done by leaf and root, minimally by other plant parts.

Cabling: trunk, branch support system using guy wire, bolt system or Velcro straps.

Cambium: vein/layer just under bark that moves water amd nutrients, and heals physical wounds.

Composting: collecting and layering organic material, in a manner that encourages its breakdown. The final product is used for soil improvement, top dressing, mulching.

Conifer or coniferous: cone bearing tree or shrub usually with needles for leaves.

Container/pot: portable growing product made of various materials: cement, plastic, terra cotta, pressed styrofoam, woven natural fibers, etc.

Cool season lawn grass: blue, rye, and fescues, most actively growing in spring, fall, near dormancy in winter and summer, established using seed or sod.

Core aerating: mechanically removing small plugs of ground to reduce compaction.

Crown: active growing point that connects roots and above ground growth.

Deciduous: woody plants that have fall leaf drop. Leaves emerging from buds next growing season.

Deep root feeding: every 3 to 5 years, holes are augured within the drip line, and filled with low analysis fertilizer/compost. A side benefit: it allows for air/water penetration and exit.

Diseases: generally include bacteria, viruses, and fungus with new and or mutating varieties emerging constantly. They can be found indoor and outdoors, and their form is very diverse. Wounds on a plant such as from storm damage can make plants more vulnerable.

Division: separation of viable portion of plants (roots, stems, twigs, buds, eyes, etc.) for propagation or relocation.

Dormant: state of minimal or no active growth. Dormant timing is variable by plant.

Drip line: furthermost extension of a tree or shrub's branching, covering much of the root area.

Established plant: a plant that is acclimated, healthy and growing, and showing resilience to environmental, pest, or disease problems.

Evergreen: plant type with viable foliage held over a period of years before being dropped.

Fertilizer: supplemental nutrition, either organic or inorganic. Usage helps plant health by making nutritional requirements readily available.

COMMON GARDENING TERMS

Field adjustments: modifications in plans or ideas while a project is in progress.

Flats: shallow planting containers with multiple pockets used for starting seeds, or rooting cuttings.

Flower: aesthetic part whose purpose is pollination and seed production. There are 2 types: *monoecious* with both sexes found on a single flower, and *dioecious* with only a single sex on the flower.

Forbs: woody plants of various types.

Fruit: protective layer for seed resulting from flower pollination, i.e. apples or pine cones.

Fungicides: Products including chemicals or home made mixtures that are used to control, diminish, or eliminate a broad group of living organisms that threaten plant health.

Habit: growth tendencies of all plant parts, such as roots, colors, foliage, shape, flower types, etc.

Hardiness: a plant's ability to produce foliage, flower, stem, bud, etc. despite seasonal stresses.

Hardscapes: manmade surfaces such as drives, walkways, patios, and decks, that influence conditions in the landscape such as absorption and release of heat, channeling of water, leeching of compounds, etc.

Herbaceous: plants with soft stems/leaf parts.

Herbicides: improves absorption of nutrients to plant through stems, leaves or root systems.

Hose-end sprayer: plastic bottle/sprayer with dial to calibrate dispersal and attached to hose end. A chemical is placed in bottle, and physically mixed by running water dispersed thru the nozzle.

Hybrid: a plant created from several plants contributing various qualities.

Indoor forcing: encouraging flower/foliage growth indoors using artificial environmental conditions.

Inorganic materials: rock, gravel, or sand used as soil amendments or mulch.

Insecticides: organic and inorganic products used to reduce populations/concentrations of insects.

Pests: umbrella term for unwanted creatures—including cold-blooded, airborne, crawling, or tunneling—that are greatly effected and adapted to many environmental circumstances.

IPM (Integrated Pest Management): the process of correctly identifying pests by first assessing plant damage and determining what pest is responsible. Controls needed are determined to be physical (wiping leaves), mechanical (pruning off infested parts), cultural (keeping plant healthy), or biological (using a virus, bacteria, or predatory insects that are pest specific).

Product labeling: consists of crucial and critical product information resulting from extensive testing systems and possibly government regulations. The guidelines must be followed to get maximize results and benefits. Remember that failure to follow labeling information could result in a problem much worse than the original one.

Landscape design planning: using plant information to make decisions for outdoor use.

Landscape paint: non-toxic, used in marking planting locations and outlining beds.

Leaf/leaflet: vegetative plant part responsible for absorbing sunlight.

Mulch: organic/inorganic surface covering applied for landscape benefit and/or aesthetic uses.

Native or naturalized: plants historically found in a particular area, or introduced with an ability to survive without intervention.

Needle: slender pointed leaf/leaflet most common among conifers.

New wood: a woodies' structurally pliable and generally green current season's growth.

Old wood: 1 year or older, viable growth of woodies.

Organic dyes: additive to liquids that give coloring to an area as it's sprayed.

Organic matter: natural products such as compost, ground leaves, or well decayed manure that are mixed into soil or added as surface top dressing in lawn/garden spaces.

Peat moss: nature's compost, a brown fiber sphagnum used as soil amendment.

Perennial: herbaceous plant growing from crown or root system for 2 or more years.

COMMON GARDENING TERMS

Pest control: physical, mechanical, chemical, or organic means of minimizing the detrimental impact of insects or animals on plant material.

Photosynthesis: process of foliage (leaf/needle) to convert sunlight into energy.

Pinching: removal of herbaceous part to induce growth reaction.

Pollination: movement by insects, wind, animals, or man of male flower pollen to female flower receptacle, resulting in fruit/seed.

Potting up: placing plants, cuttings, or seed into container (with drainage holes) with a growing medium.

Potting mix and potting soil: blended growing medium for containers and pots.

Predatory insects: natural occurrence where one reduces the population and damage potential of another insect by consuming or disabling it.

Propagation: proliferation of plants from pollination, cuttings of root/stem, microscopic clones, or air layering.

Pruning: physical removal of any plant parts that controls shape, form, and/or growth habit.

Root: underground network responsible for absorption of nutrients, water, and physical support.

Seed: term representing reproductive stage resulting from flower pollination, or plant part containing genetic information and used for propagation/perpetuation of new plant.

Self seeding: natural propogation of seed.

Semi-evergreen: plant with partial foliage retention in winter. Weather, location, and plant health are major factors.

Sidedressing: fertilizing of seasonal plants such as annuals, bulbs, and edibles, to ensure continuous availability of nutrients.

Site evaluation: complete look at a growing location, taking note of environment prior to planting, sunlight, topography, rainfall, runoff, existing plant types and health, buildings, hardscapes, and overhead and underground utilities.

Soil chemistry: combination of compounds found in soil within a specific area that will impact growth/health of plants.

Soil preparation: modifications to existing soil using amendments, based upon either a soil test, observation, or diagnosis. This creates better soil structure and nutrient level.

Soil profile: physical factors (density, soil layer thickness, etc) that influence plant growth.

Soil test: laboratory analysis of soil nutrient level with recommendations targeted towards existing or projected usage. Each area (lawn, vegetable garden, etc.) must be tested separately.

Stem: above ground structure where leaves, needles and/or flowers emerge.

Subsoil: all ground below top soil that is penetrated by water, and deeper growing anchor roots.

Sucker: stem growth emerging from branch, root system, or trunk.

Top soil: upper 2 feet of ground where the majority of roots are concentrated.

Twig: newest and or smallest part of woody plants, emerging from buds.

Variety: a plant that has been defined by a refinement of specific attributes.

Variegated: distinctive color variance on single leaf (such as a mix of green, white, red, yellow, etc).

Veins: essential internal system that moves water/nutrients through a plant.

Warm season lawn: lawn that is active growing in summer with winter dormancy, often planted as sod, plugs, or occasionally seed.

Weed: unwanted plant, likely overly aggressive or invasive which inhibits or interferes with aesthetics or actual planned plant performance.

Woody: rigid year round structure consisting of branch, twig, and or trunk.

Zone: a growing area with a similar weather environment. Zone maps are commonly used to define areas of plant cold and heat tolerance.

BIBLIOGRAPHY

Kansas State University: Research and Extension–Plant Science Centers

Common-Sense Pest Control. Olkowski, Daar, Olkowski, Tauton Press, 1992.
Coincide-Orton System of Pest Management. Orton, Donald A. and Green Ph.D., Thomas L., Dennis W. Jamieson publisher Labor of Love Conservatory, 1989.
Hortus Third Cornell University-Staff of Liberty Hyde Bailey Hortorium., Macmillan Publishing Company, Inc., 1976
Manual of Woody Landscape Plants. Dirr, Michael A. Stipes Publishing Company, 1990.
New Pronouncing Dictionary of Plant Names. Florist Publishing Company, 1967.
Tree Pithy Points. Shigo Ph.D., Alex L. Shigo and Trees, Associates, 2000.

Other References

Plant Societies, Organizations, Publications and/or Newsletters

Sources of gardening facts, new hybrids, products, growing ideas:

American Orchid Society
Boxwood Society of the Midwest
HortIdeas, Patricia and Gregory Williams publishers
Mid America Regional Lily Society
National Council of State Garden Clubs / 4401 Magnolia Ave. / St. Louis, MO. 63110
North American Rock Society

Catalogs & Plant Listings

Nothing compares with a trip to a local garden center, nursery, but in the dead of winter I have found looking through various catalogs and plant listings is very enlightening and extremely informative. The following companies provide lists that I have enjoyed.

Arbor Village Farm
Ball Seed Co.
Beaver Creek
Camellia Forest Nursery
Colvos Creek
Dutch Gardens
Eastern Plant Specialties
Fairweather Gardens
Fedco Seeds
Garden Medicinal and Culinaries
Greer Gardens
Harris Seeds
Henry Field's Seed and Nursery
Johnny's Selected Seeds
Park Seed
Pinetree Garden Seeds
Roslyn
Seeds of Change
Seed Savers Exchange
Shepard's Garden Seeds
Southern Exposure Seed Exchange
Territorial Seed Co.
Thompson & Morgan
Totally Tomatoes
Vermont Bean Seed Co.
Walters Gardens Inc.
W. Atlee Burpee & Co.
Wayside Gardens
White Flower Farm
Windrose
Woodlanders, Inc.

INDEX

INDEX

INDEX

INDEX

INDEX

INDEX

INDEX

INDEX

INDEX

INDEX

MEET THE AUTHOR

Mike Miller

Mike Miller is a native St. Louisan who spent his early years living in the shadows of the Missouri Botanical Garden. His family moved out into the rural suburbs, where exploring and observing woods, meadows, hills, streams, and wildlife became a favorite pastime. After serving four years in the Air Force during the Vietnam War, he studied botany, horticulture, and landscape design at the University of California. In 1977, he was selected to join the Missouri Botanical Garden horticulture staff. During his five-year tenure Mike obtained the Missouri State Pesticide license for Ornamentals, Turf, and Aquatic Environments, and also began teaching in the Garden's ever-popular evening series and continues to do so today.

The author's professional career includes four years as General Manager of a retail garden center. He became a Missouri State Certified Nurseryman, was co-founder of a predatory insect store, and served seven years as a faculty member of the Horticultural Department at St. Louis Community College at Meramec. Mike has participated in programs sponsored by Powell Gardens of Kansas City, the Missouri State Department of Natural Resources, the Landscape and Nurseymen's Association of Greater St. Louis, and the University of Illinois Extension Service. His garden articles have been featured in local and regional newspapers and magazines. Mike's voice has been heard for ten years hosting the KMOX "Garden Hotline." In 1998 Mike Miller Designs, a landscape design and consulting firm, was established. Later that year Mike and Tracy Ann began hosting Holiday Vacations tour groups giving an opportunity to see and learn how gardeners design, care for, and maintain plants, many similar to those of Missouri's gardens.

Mike holds memberships on several citizen and advisory board panels, including St. Louis' Operation Brightside, a privately funded beautification organization. He also is the horticultural spokesperson for the AMEREN regional electric utility. As an epileptic, Mike also sits on the board of directors for the Epilepsy Foundation of Greater St. Louis.

Get Great Gardening Ideas Online

Learn2Grow – helping you become a more successful gardener!